MANUFACTURING SIMPLICITY

Manufacturing Simplicity
The Turnaround Playbook for Leaders Who Want to Eliminate Complexity and Build Systems That Last

Eduardo R. Pagani

Published by Game Changer Publishing

Paperback ISBN: 979-8-90158-219-0
Hardcover ISBN: 979-8-90158-184-1
Digital ISBN: 979-8-90158-185-8

www.GameChangerPublishing.com

Dedicated to the teams on the floor. You deserve systems that work for you, not against you.

This is for the hands that build the world.

Advance Praise

I've had the privilege of working with Eduardo for several years and getting to know him outside of work for the better part of a decade. This book is a testament to what true operational leadership looks like in practice. Eduardo doesn't just understand operations—he lives it. The lessons in these pages represent only a fraction of the insight, discipline, and hard-won experience he has applied consistently throughout his career. Anyone looking to build scalable, resilient, and high-performing operations will find this book both practical and invaluable.

—David Metrena, CEO/CCO

Lean is about simplicity, and that is exactly what this insightful and practical book delivers.

Eduardo Pagani distills more than 30 years of experience into a clear and actionable guide, bringing powerful Lean manufacturing concepts and tools into real-world application.

By following the path proposed in this book, organizations go far beyond simply implementing Lean. They build a strong and lasting Lean culture.

As the author puts it, "You don't do Lean, you *become* Lean."

A must-read for leaders and change agents committed to transforming their culture and achieving sustainable results.

—Denis Tarti, Operations Executive and Consultant

Manufacturing Simplicity breaks down Lean manufacturing in a way that feels practical, clear, and accessible, especially for a VP of Commercial Product Management like me without an engineering background. Rather than overwhelming me with jargon, Pagani helps build the mindset of seeing inefficiencies, understanding their business impact, and then identifying opportunities to make organizations, as he puts it, "unlock real, sustainable change." My only regret is that I didn't have this book at my previous job. It would have been so useful in helping connect operational improvement to how we worked with customer-driven product improvements. Waste not, want not!

—Mattias Isaksson, SVP of Marketing and Product Development

Complexity is the silent killer of profits and morale. In Manufacturing Simplicity, Eduardo Pagani gives you the surgical tools to strip away the waste and restore operational clarity. This isn't just another Lean book; it's a hands-on manual for building a resilient, high-performance organization. If you're tired of firefighting, this is your exit strategy.

—Cesar R. Pagani, Vice President

Read This First

Just to say thanks for buying and reading my book,
I would like to give you a special bonus!

Scan the QR Code here:

MANUFACTURING SIMPLICITY

THE TURNAROUND
PLAYBOOK FOR LEADERS
WHO WANT TO ELIMINATE
COMPLEXITY AND
BUILD SYSTEMS THAT LAST

EDUARDO R. PAGANI

Foreword

Lean is one of the most talked about and least understood concepts in modern operations. It has too often been reduced to tools, events, and terminology, disconnected from the philosophy that makes it effective. Many organizations believe they are practicing Lean, but in reality, very few are applying it in a way that fundamentally improves how their business performs. This book is different because Eduardo is different.

I hired Eduardo in 2005, and he worked for me for eight years. What became clear early on is that he does not approach improvement as an initiative or a program, but as a discipline—a way of thinking and a way of building organizations that perform better because they are intentionally structured to do so. While his experience within the Danaher system gave him a strong foundation, what stood out most was how completely he internalized Lean. He didn't just understand it, he lived it, believed in it, and consistently applied it in a way that produced real, lasting results.

Equally important, Eduardo is a person of strong character. He is trustworthy, grounded, and genuinely cares about people. That may sound secondary in a discussion about operations, but it is not. Real transformation requires trust, alignment, and a willingness from teams to engage, challenge old habits, and stay committed when the work becomes difficult. Without that foundation, even the best methodologies fall short. Eduardo brings that element to his leadership in a way that is both natural and effective.

I saw this firsthand early in his tenure, when we were facing serious challenges with a major customer—late deliveries, high scrap, and recurring quality issues. Eduardo approached the problem by going to the source, understanding root causes, and redesigning the process into a single-piece-flow line. The results were decisive: quality improved, delivery became reliable, and the customer relationship strengthened. That work led to multiple supplier awards and recognition across the customer's network. It wasn't an incremental improvement; it was a fundamental shift in how the operation performed, driven by clarity, discipline, and a willingness to eliminate complexity at its source.

That ability to cut through complexity and build something that works is the thread that runs throughout this book. Many organizations today are operating under constant pressure, where complexity has built up over time, and problems are managed rather than solved. Teams work harder, but performance does not improve proportionally, and over time, that becomes accepted as normal. It shouldn't be.

Manufacturing Simplicity challenges that assumption directly. Eduardo makes a clear and practical case that complexity is the real constraint, and that simplicity, when built with discipline, is a competitive advantage. He outlines how to see the current state clearly, align around what matters, and create systems that allow good people to succeed without unnecessary friction.

This perspective becomes even more critical as we enter the next phase of transformation driven by AI. There is a growing belief that AI will fix broken processes, automate inefficiency, and compensate for operational complexity. In reality, it will do the opposite. AI will amplify whatever system it is applied to. If the underlying process is fragmented or poorly designed, AI will scale those problems faster. If the foundation is simple, stable, and well-structured, AI becomes a powerful accelerator.

That is why Lean matters more now, not less.

The companies that benefit most from AI will not be the ones that adopt it first, but the ones that are operationally prepared for it. They will be the organizations that have already done the hard work of simplification, where processes are understood, problems are visible, and execution is disciplined. This book provides a practical path to building that foundation.

Eduardo writes from experience, not theory. He has operated under pressure, delivered results, and built systems that sustain performance. That credibility comes through in every chapter. If you are responsible for results and are looking for a more effective way to improve your operation and prepare it for what comes next, you will find this book both relevant and actionable.

I am pleased to introduce *Manufacturing Simplicity* and the thinking behind it.

Michael Tucci
CEO & President, Micro Technologies

Table of Contents

Preface

Running a business in today's world feels like navigating a minefield. Complexity is the enemy. Bloated processes, disengaged teams, and a disconnect from what your customers really want can slowly bleed the life out of even the most promising organizations. I've seen it happen countless times. That's why I wrote *Manufacturing Simplicity: The Turnaround Playbook for Leaders Who Want to Eliminate Complexity and Build Systems That Last.* This is your practical guide to your Lean transformation.

Before you go further, I want to share something personal. English is not my first language. I was born in Brazil to an Italian family, and although I've spent most of my adult life working in English, I still sometimes "translate" concepts in my head before I write them. That can lead to sentences that are more complicated than they need to be.

To make this book easier to read, I used AI tools such as ChatGPT, Gemini, and Grammarly to help me organize my thoughts, improve grammar, reduce repetition, and check the flow of ideas.

Every concept, story, and lesson in this book comes from me. From my experience. From the work I've done inside real businesses. The AI tools did not create the content. They helped me express it more clearly.

Over the course of my career, I've had the privilege of working with businesses across the globe, from South to North America, from Europe to Asia. I've been in the trenches, helping companies simplify their operations and drive rapid improvement, leading hundreds of kaizen (continuous improvement) activities. And I've discovered that true Lean principles aren't just buzzwords. When applied correctly, they're the key to unlocking real change that can help us save businesses, change cultures, and drive sustainable results. This book is the culmination of those experiences. It is a practical, no-nonsense guide for leaders and change agents like you.

Manufacturing Simplicity is not full of theoretical fluff. I want you to achieve real-world results. This is your hands-on playbook for building a culture of continuous improvement, where your team is energized, waste is relentlessly hunted down, and your customers feel truly valued.

Inside, you'll find a clear, step-by-step framework, packed with stories from the field and practical tools you can use immediately. We'll cover how to:

- Pinpoint the hidden inefficiencies that are holding you back.
- Implement Lean strategies to streamline your processes and maximize value.
- Inspire your team to embrace change and drive lasting results.
- Track your progress and make sure you're on the right track.

But here's the best part: at the end of every chapter, you'll find a "Reflection and Action" section. This is not meant to be a passive exercise; it's where you'll start building your turnaround plan. I'll ask you the tough questions, the ones that will force you to think critically about your organization. By the time you finish this book, you won't just have read about Lean transformation; you'll have a concrete, actionable plan ready to put into action.

Whether you're a CEO looking to revitalize your company, a COO tasked with driving operational excellence, or a change agent leading a specific project, this book will give you the tools and the confidence to make a real difference.

As you progress, you'll find us circling back to specific topics more than once. This is entirely by design. I've structured this journey so that each time we revisit a core concept, we're essentially **peeling the onion,** stripping away another layer to uncover more depth and insight than the last. By picking these subjects up multiple times, we ensure you aren't just scanning information but truly absorbing and mastering these principles for real-world application.

Although I encourage you to read the book sequentially the first time around, each chapter is designed to stand alone, so you can jump in wherever you need help most. You'll notice a pattern in most chapters. They usually begin with a story, not because I'm trying to entertain you, but because I want you to recognize the situation. I want you to feel the reality of what leaders face when performance is slipping and the organization is stuck.

After the story, we peel the onion. We start at the concept level; then we get more practical, and eventually, we go step by step. If you're not ready to implement that tool yet, feel free to skim the step-by-step section and move on. But don't skip the "Reflection and Action" section. That's where this book turns into your turnaround plan.

But trust me, transformation is a journey. *Manufacturing Simplicity* is here to be your trusted guide every step of the way. Keep in mind, some readers are new to the subject, others are looking for more knowledge, and others seek motivation and a guide. By first presenting the concepts and establishing the lingo, I intend to bring all readers to a similar level of understanding before peeling the onion further in subsequent chapters.

One more thing. This book is dense on purpose. I've packed years of lessons, mistakes, wins, and field-tested methods into a few hundred pages. If you feel overwhelmed at times, that's normal. Don't let that discourage you. You don't need to apply everything at once.

The goal is not to become a Lean expert overnight. The goal is to build momentum, create stability, and make your business simpler, faster, and more predictable, step by step.

Are you ready to roll up your sleeves and unlock the true potential of your organization? Let's dive in.

The Approach

In this section, I will briefly describe our approach when we go into a business that hires us to improve their operations. We strongly recommend that you read this brief section to gain a better understanding of how we do things. Then you can associate the specifics in each chapter with this overarching approach. Whether these businesses we help are in dire need of a turnaround, slowly sinking, or simply stagnant, we move to drive immediate improvement while forging a lasting, self-sustaining culture.

Although we are always eager to jump right in, especially when we see opportunities all around us, the wise approach is to assess the situation first. We find this step so important that we dedicated a whole chapter to the assessment phase: Chapter 3. This phase will allow you to understand what is actually happening in the business.

It is imperative that you get unfiltered input from as many perspectives as possible. Don't just ask what the executive team thinks. Of course, their input and points of view are significant, but walking around the business, talking to small groups and individuals at every level, in every department, and in every location, is the key to truly understanding the operation. Forge connections and build rapport. Look at the data. Ask questions and validate assumptions. Walk the process.

We find that people around the company typically have the solutions to many of the problems a business has. They just have never expressed their solutions to management. Sometimes, people don't bring things up because the company does not have a communication structure that promotes or even allows people to voice their opinions. In some cases, people voice their opinions and ideas, but they are ignored. In other cases, people are afraid to express themselves. And, unfortunately, many times, employees just don't care.

The effort to talk to people includes building rapport with them. This is hard to do the first time you see them, during the assessment phase, and it must continue throughout the process until it becomes part of the established culture. Chapter 4 will be helpful as you address cultural issues. Unless you have an involved, engaged team, your efforts are unlikely to be self-sustaining, and the team will need constant reminders and handholding.

As part of the assessment, look at the profit and loss statement and the balance sheet. What areas are dragging the business down? What are the main concerns? What are the causes? Look for the areas of focus. Now, talk to the salespeople. They are, or at least should be, facing the customers daily. Are they? Do your customers know them well? How is the company perceived: as a partner or as the lowest-cost supplier? Why do they buy from you? What are your customers' pain points?

Operationally, how is the company performing? Talk to the quality and regulatory team and their members individually. Learn about customer complaints, scrap rates, non-conformances, etc. Have a conversation with the folks in customer service and understand how the customers view the company. Ask for data, such as on-time delivery reports, customer feedback data, and scores.

When you speak with the production people, ask about schedule adherence and get downtime and other operational data. What is expected of them, and how are they performing? When you get to human resources, learn about employee feedback, request safety data, and review turnover and the reasons people leave. Basically, dig deep in every area, and you will end up with a ton of information that you will need to compile and prioritize.

Another essential tool to employ in your "discovery phase" is value stream mapping, or VSM. You will learn more about it in Chapter 5. This tool helps you map out the current state and envision the future state. The results of the initial assessment should give you clear indications of the problems and their possible solutions. When you map the current state, you will likely find many opportunities to improve as well. At this stage, you should be ready to develop a map of your future state, prioritizing the actions to close the gap between where the business is now and where it will be in the future.

I like to work with local management to develop a turnaround or improvement plan. Ideally, this plan should include a mix of long-term, high-return initiatives and immediate, lower-impact actions. Implementing a few easy things right away sends a clear signal that things are changing. This approach gives the team a sense of what winning feels like.

When we are called in to help a business, people often feel defeated and hopeless. As they see some of their ideas implemented and the business improve, they develop a sense of hope and become much more motivated. When these quick hits run in parallel with long-range plans, the team builds unstoppable momentum. This turnaround strategy must be communicated to everyone, and every single person in the business must understand the role they play in helping the company achieve its goals. Chapter 6 is all about strategy deployment and communication.

You see, the formula is not complicated. You must understand the business needs. Then you work with management to develop a strategy that will make it successful. While you do that, relentlessly implement initiatives that deliver immediate results, no matter how small the gains. The key is to take time to involve people as you implement change. Ask questions, listen, and make a genuine effort to understand people's points of view and implement their recommendations. When people realize you are listening and truly trying to make their work better, when they see you are implementing their recommendations, and when they understand that company success means their success, they will do what they can to make sure you succeed.

As you will see, I will frequently recommend Lean tools and techniques. I will also discuss culture, automation, and finances. But at the heart of it, I still believe Lean manufacturing is grossly misunderstood and underused. The key, as I mention a few times in the book, is not to implement Lean for the heck of it. Target the right technique at the right time based on business needs that should have surfaced in the assessment results.

You may apply different techniques concurrently in different areas if those areas have distinct problems and needs. Avoid falling into the "tools trap" and implementing Lean tools for the heck of it without the cultural depth. You don't want to "do Lean"; instead, you want to "be Lean." Again, Chapter 4 is dedicated to culture. Make sure you read it, since culture is the foundation on which you will build your Lean transformation, and the right culture will ensure its sustainment.

You will absolutely learn essential Lean tools in this book. But tools are not what make Lean succeed. The biggest difference between success and failure is not technical. It is behavioral. It is leadership. It is culture. It is sequencing. It is discipline. That is why this book spends as much time on the "how" of implementation as it does on the tools themselves. Most Lean failures happen not because the tool was wrong, but because the environment around the tool was not ready.

Imagine you are an operator who has, for years, been struggling to increase output. Your supervisor is under pressure and, as a result, constantly pressures you. But you have long changeover times, your equipment frequently breaks down, or your operation has many quality issues.

Then someone comes in, listens to what you have to say, and works with you to make your operation run smoothly, making your work more predictable and repeatable. You don't have to work as hard anymore. In fact, your job becomes easier and more rewarding, your results improve, and the pressure eases. Once you experience this, you will become a convert and a promoter of Lean.

Now, picture the opposite. You are under tremendous stress, as described in the paragraph above. People are breathing down your neck, pressuring you to increase output so the company can meet delivery commitments. Then a consultant arrives, saying that the company will "do Lean" and that the best place to start is to "do some 5S." The 5S methodology is great. It helps clean and organize an area, improving safety and working conditions, and eventually quality and productivity.

But right now, you are swamped, and there are many other tools and techniques that can address your issues immediately. You will probably be very frustrated that, although you would prefer things cleaner and more organized, the effort will not address the scheduling issues, long changeover times, or the machine breakdowns you are experiencing. Furthermore, every week-long 5S workshop will set the schedule back even further!

What ends up happening is that after months or even years of applying the wrong tool to each situation, people become opposed to Lean. Poor implementation gives Lean a bad name. They will associate any future Lean efforts with the time and resources spent on something that did not address the main issues they had.

Going back and trying to reignite the fire and reestablish engagement after a failed attempt is exponentially harder. I know. I'm the person they call to fix it.

CHAPTER 1

The Complexity Trap: *Why Simplicity Matters*

This may sound familiar. You arrive at work early in the morning. The parking lot is already filling up. Inside the building, machines are running, forklifts are buzzing by, and people are moving quickly between stations. On the surface, everything looks busy and productive.

Before you even reach your office, someone intercepts you in the hallway: "Third shift didn't finish the batch of the control product. The line stopped again."

You nod and keep walking, already adjusting your mental plan for the morning. A few steps later, another voice calls out: "QA just stopped another lot from shipping. They said something doesn't look right."

Now two problems are competing for your attention, and the day has barely started. By the time you reach your office, your assistant is waiting: "There's a customer on line one. They said it's urgent."

You put your bag down and pick up the phone, already sensing where the conversation is going.

This kind of morning does not happen once in a while. In many organizations, it happens almost every day. People are working hard, everyone seems busy, and yet the operation feels heavier than it should. Small issues cascade into larger ones. Decisions take longer. Fixing one problem reveals three more behind it.

Nothing about the situation suggests a lack of effort. The people around you are capable and committed. The equipment is modern. The demand is real. And yet something in the system is not working the way it should.

Over time, the pattern becomes clear. The organization has not become difficult because people stopped caring. It has become difficult because the work itself has become complicated. Layers of approvals, workarounds, reports, and exceptions have slowly built up until moving forward requires navigating obstacles that were never meant to exist.

This is how complexity takes hold.

By the time the first hour of the day is over, you have already dealt with production delays, quality issues, and a frustrated customer. None of them appeared out of nowhere. Each one is the result of something deeper in the system.

And if you pause for a moment, you may start to notice a pattern.

The problems are different, but the feeling is the same. Things that should be simple seem to take too long. Decisions require too many steps. People spend more time navigating the system than improving it.

Something in the organization has become heavier than it needs to be.

If you've been in business long enough, you've probably noticed something unsettling: What starts out nimble, clear, and exciting eventually becomes slow, bureaucratic, and frustrating. It doesn't matter if you make medical devices, run a family-owned bakery, or lead a software startup. The drift toward **complexity** is almost universal.

No one planned for the system to become complicated. It simply happened. You feel it in missed deadlines, bloated email threads, and frustrated customers asking why everything takes so long.

And it happens quietly. Complexity rarely arrives all at once. It builds quietly. A new approval here, an extra report there, a workaround added to solve a temporary problem. Over time, those layers accumulate until moving forward requires navigating obstacles that were never meant to exist.

What makes complexity dangerous is that it rarely announces itself directly. Instead, it shows up through symptoms that leaders try to solve one at a time.

The Reality Behind the Pain Points

Every business, regardless of size or industry, faces challenges. Some are external, driven by market forces, disruptive technologies, or unexpected global events. Others are self-inflicted, the result of internal inefficiencies, outdated systems, or a culture resistant to change. Most are a tangled mess of both.

These challenges, the ones that keep you up at night, are your pain points:

- High costs that never seem to come down
- Missed deadlines that frustrate customers and staff alike
- Increasing returns or warranty claims
- Disengaged employees doing the bare minimum
- Cash-flow crunches despite strong sales
- Quality issues you thought were already fixed

They're symptoms of a deeper problem: operational complexity. In Chapter 3, we'll look at how to identify these issues in detail using assessment tools that reveal what's really happening inside your operation.

Complexity in Disguise

Unnecessary processes accumulate. Layers of management multiply. The focus on the customer fades. What was once streamlined and agile becomes a lumbering giant, weighed down by its own structure.

Imagine you're a CEO. You're working sixty-hour weeks, but growth is stagnant. Competitors are gaining market share. Your best employees are leaving. Customer complaints are piling up. You're constantly putting out fires but never getting ahead. The problem, more often than not, is complexity, the hidden drag on performance, the silent killer of profits, and the destroyer of morale.

I've seen it take hold in companies that look successful from the outside. One client of mine was growing revenue every year, yet profits had flatlined. Every new sales push meant scrambling in production, more overtime, and more missed shipments. They didn't have a sales problem. They had a complexity problem. Later, in Chapter 5, we'll explore how mapping your value stream can make these bottlenecks impossible to ignore.

The uncomfortable truth is that most operations are not struggling because people lack effort or intelligence. They are struggling because the system itself has become too complicated to manage effectively.

The Subtle Symptoms of Complexity

Let's be clear: complexity doesn't always show up wearing a sign that says *"Problem."*

It hides in:

- **Duplicated effort:** Two departments solving the same problem in different ways.
- **Redundant approvals:** Four signatures for a purchase order worth less than the coffee budget.
- **Endless status meetings:** Talking about the work instead of doing it.
- **Unclear responsibilities:** "I thought she was handling that."
- **Slow decisions:** By the time you decide, the opportunity's gone.

Individually, these may seem harmless. Together, they create a drag on performance so strong that even the most talented teams can't outrun it. People stop suggesting improvements because "it'll never get approved." Managers play defense instead of offense. Opportunities slip through your fingers. This is why, in Chapter 4, we'll talk about building a culture where teams challenge waste and solve problems without waiting for layers of approval.

The True Cost of Complexity

Most leaders underestimate the cost of complexity. They might see wasted time and mild frustration, but they don't realize:

1. It's burning cash you can't see.

The "hidden factory" and its unnecessary meetings, rework, waiting, and systems quietly devours margins. I've seen companies bleed 20 to 30 percent of productivity without a single person realizing it until we put the numbers on paper.

Imagine the simple task of making a cup of coffee. Now imagine that process involves ten different people, each with their own set of instructions, forms to fill out, and approvals to obtain. The result? A cold cup of coffee, hours later, at an exorbitant cost.

This is the impact of complexity. It adds layers of bureaucracy, slows down decision making, and creates bottlenecks at every turn. Projects that should take weeks drag on for months, and opportunities are missed while the organization struggles to navigate its own internal maze.

That cold cup of coffee isn't just an inconvenience; it's a metaphor for lost opportunities. While your team is bogged down in bureaucratic red tape, your competitors are seizing market share. Those missed deadlines aren't just numbers on a spreadsheet; they're lost contracts, damaged reputations, and frustrated customers who may never come back.

2. It's driving your best people away.

Talented employees want to create value, not wrestle with internal nonsense. When bureaucracy wins over progress, they don't fight it; they leave. And when they go, they take their knowledge, skills, and experience with them.

Complexity breeds frustration. Employees spend more time navigating internal processes than they do serving customers or creating value. They feel like cogs in a machine, disconnected from the bigger picture. This leads to disengagement, decreased morale, and, ultimately, higher employee turnover. Talented people, tired of fighting the system, seek out organizations where they can make a real impact. The cost of replacing these employees, both in terms of recruitment and lost productivity, is significant.

Imagine being an employee who cares about their work but spends most of the day navigating internal processes instead of creating value. Over time, even highly motivated people begin to disengage. Eventually, many of them leave. In Chapter 4, you'll see how engaging employees early in your Lean journey prevents this kind of disengagement.

3. It's pushing customers into your competitors' arms.

Customers rarely care why *you're slow or inconsistent. They care that you* are. *In a world where alternatives are one click away, your inefficiency is someone else's growth strategy.*

In complex organizations, the customer often gets lost in the shuffle. Many processes are designed to meet internal needs, not customer expectations. Communication becomes fragmented, and customer feedback is ignored. The result is a decline in customer satisfaction, leading to lost sales and damaged reputation.

In complex organizations, the customer often becomes an afterthought. They're just a number, a transaction, a faceless entity. But customers are people, with needs, wants, and emotions. When they feel ignored or mistreated, they don't just go away quietly; they tell their friends, leave negative reviews online, and take their business elsewhere. In today's connected world, a bad customer experience can spread like wildfire, damaging your reputation and impacting your bottom line. In Chapter 6, we'll connect these customer pain points to strategy deployment so improvement efforts directly support what customers value most.

How Complexity Creeps In

Here's the trap: complexity often grows from good intentions.

- You add a new approval step to "ensure quality," and suddenly, a one-day process takes a week.
- You launch a new product line to meet demand and double your inventory-management headaches.
- You reorganize to "improve communication" and add three new layers between leadership and the customer.

Without discipline, every "improvement" becomes a new weight in your backpack. And before long, you're carrying more process than product. In Chapter 9, we'll see how these same patterns often plague administrative and office processes, not just the shop floor.

I once visited a plant where a simple engineering change required eleven approvals across five departments. No one believed that number when we first mapped it. Each approval had been added at some point to solve a problem. None of them felt unreasonable on their own. Together, they created a process that slowed everything the company was trying to do.

When we removed most of those steps, the organization did not lose control. It gained speed.

History's Harsh Lessons

Complexity is not just an internal nuisance that makes a manager's day more difficult. Left unchecked, it can quietly weaken even the most successful organizations. History is full of companies that dominated their industries, employed thousands of talented people, and still lost their position because their systems became too heavy to adapt.

Consider Blockbuster. At one time, it was the undisputed giant of home entertainment, with thousands of stores, a powerful brand, and millions of loyal customers. The company had access to the same technologies and trends that eventually gave rise to streaming. In fact, the opportunity was right in front of them. But their business had become structured around a massive network of physical stores, late fees, and internal processes designed to protect that model. Decisions moved slowly, and experiments were difficult to approve. By the time the organization recognized how quickly the market was changing, Netflix had already rewritten the rules.

Kodak tells a similar story, though in an even more ironic way. Kodak engineers actually invented the first digital camera in the 1970s. The technology that would eventually replace film was born inside the company itself. But bringing it forward meant challenging the existing business, which revolved around film sales, chemical processing, and a vast manufacturing infrastructure. Layer upon layer of internal interests, priorities, and decision processes slowed the company's ability to act. The invention that should have secured Kodak's future became something the organization hesitated to embrace.

General Motors faced its own version of complexity in the early 2000s. Over decades, the company had accumulated brands, divisions, overlapping engineering groups, and long chains of decision making. Instead of clarity, the organization carried weight. Product development stretched longer than competitor's. Costs rose as similar work was repeated in different parts of the company. Quality issues became harder to resolve because responsibility was scattered across the system. The company still had immense resources, but the structure surrounding those resources made progress painfully slow.

These companies did not collapse because people stopped working hard. They struggled because the systems they had built became too complicated to move quickly in a changing world.

Complexity does not just slow an organization down. Eventually, it can make adaptation almost impossible.

That is when competitors who are simpler, faster, and more focused begin to pull ahead.

Lean: The Antidote to Complexity

If complexity is the force that slowly weighs organizations down, Lean is the discipline that helps lift that weight. At its core, Lean is not a collection of tools or slogans. It is a way of looking at work and asking a very simple question: what truly creates value for the customer, and what is simply getting in the way?

Most organizations have never taken the time to examine their processes through that lens. Over the years, layers of activity accumulate until the difference between value and motion becomes blurred. Meetings multiply, reports expand, approvals increase, and systems become harder to navigate. Everyone is busy, but not all of that effort is moving the business forward.

Lean challenges that reality.

It asks leaders and teams to step back and look at the work with fresh eyes. What steps actually matter to the customer? Which ones exist only because they were added at some point in the past? Which decisions require more coordination than they should? Which processes slow people down instead of helping them succeed?

When organizations begin asking those questions honestly, something interesting happens. Waste becomes visible. Bottlenecks reveal themselves, and activities that once felt unavoidable start looking optional. Instead of accepting complexity as part of doing business, people begin removing it piece by piece.

That is why Lean often feels so different from the management fads that come and go every few years. It does not depend on clever slogans or temporary enthusiasm. It depends on understanding how work really happens and improving it continuously.

And unlike many approaches that are tied to a specific industry or moment in time, Lean has proven remarkably adaptable. It has helped manufacturers stabilize production lines, hospitals reduce patient wait times, logistics companies speed up deliveries, and office teams eliminate frustrating administrative work. Wherever processes exist, the principles apply.

As you move through the next chapters of this book, you will encounter several of the practical tools that make this possible. Techniques such as value stream mapping, policy deployment, standard work, and kaizen are not theoretical exercises. They are ways to expose complexity and remove it so the organization can move faster, think more clearly, and serve customers better.

Lean is commonly associated with trimming organizations for the sake of efficiency. Yes, it does help improve efficiency, but I want you to see it as a means to restore clarity to the way work is done.

Once that clarity begins to emerge, many of the problems that seemed unavoidable start to look surprisingly solvable.

Case Study: Harley-Davidson, from Chaos to Control

If Lean is the antidote to complexity, Harley-Davidson offers one of the clearest examples of what that antidote can do when a company commits to it seriously.

Today, the Harley-Davidson brand is associated with craftsmanship, pride, and a loyal community of riders. But that reputation was not always secure. By the late 1970s and early 1980s, the company was in serious trouble. Japanese manufacturers such as Honda, Yamaha, and Kawasaki were producing motorcycles that were often cheaper, more reliable, and delivered to customers faster. Harley-Davidson, meanwhile, was struggling with quality problems, inefficient factories, and processes that had grown far more complicated than they needed to be.

Customers felt it first. Some motorcycles arrived with defects that required immediate rework. Delivery times were long and unpredictable. Inside the factories, employees were working hard, but the system around them was cluttered with delays, unclear workflows, and outdated practices.

In many ways, Harley-Davidson was experiencing the same symptoms we discussed earlier in this chapter. The organization had become weighed down by complexity.

Leaders at Harley realized that simply working harder was not going to solve the problem. The company needed to fundamentally rethink how its operations functioned.

That realization led them toward what we now recognize as Lean thinking.

A Different Way of Running the Factory

Rather than chasing quick fixes, Harley-Davidson began focusing on simplifying the system that produced their motorcycles. The goal was straightforward: build better bikes faster, with fewer defects and less waste.

Several key changes played a role in the transformation.

Creating order with 5S

The first step was surprisingly simple. Workspaces were reorganized so that tools, materials, and parts were easy to find and easy to use. Through the 5S method of sorting, setting in order, shining, standardizing, and sustaining, clutter was removed, and the shop floor became easier to navigate. This did more than improve appearance. It reduced wasted motion, improved safety, and helped employees focus on the work itself instead of searching for what they needed.

Understanding the flow of work

Harley-Davidson teams began mapping how motorcycles actually moved through the factory. Value stream mapping exposed delays, bottlenecks, and steps that added no value to the customer. Processes that had existed for years were suddenly questioned. Some were simplified. Others were removed altogether.

Empowering employees through kaizen

Improvement was not left to managers alone. Teams across the company began participating in **kaizen events:** short, focused efforts to improve specific parts of the process. Engineers, supervisors, and line workers worked side by side to identify problems and test solutions. This shift was powerful because the people closest to the work often understood the issues best.

Producing only what was needed

Inventory practices also changed. Instead of keeping large stockpiles of parts sitting idle, Harley-Davidson moved toward just-in-time production. Materials arrived closer to the moment they were needed. This reduced storage costs, freed up cash, and made problems easier to see when they occurred.

Keeping equipment reliable

The company also adopted Total Productive Maintenance (TPM), encouraging employees to take an active role in maintaining their equipment. Machines were no longer someone else's responsibility. Operators were trained to notice early warning signs and prevent breakdowns before they interrupted production.

If some of these terms are new to you, don't worry. We will explore many of these tools later in the book. What matters here is the principle behind them: simplify the system so people can do their best work.

The Results

The changes did not happen overnight, but the results were unmistakable.

Quality improved dramatically as defects were addressed earlier in the process. Production became more predictable, which meant customers no longer had to wait months for motorcycles to arrive. Costs began to stabilize as waste was removed from the system. Just as important, employees became more engaged because they could see how their ideas improved the work.

Harley-Davidson regained control of its operations and began rebuilding its reputation.

The Real Lesson

Harley-Davidson's story is not just a motorcycle story. It illustrates what happens when an organization decides to confront complexity instead of accepting it.

The company did not succeed because it discovered a single brilliant solution. It succeeded because it simplified its processes, involved its people, and committed to continuous improvement.

In other words, it embraced the same principles that define Lean.

And the lesson applies far beyond the motorcycle industry. Any organization that is struggling with delays, quality problems, or frustrated employees can benefit from the same approach.

Complex systems can be improved.

But only when leaders decide to *simplify* them.

Why This Book Exists

When I first sat down to write this book, the idea was fairly simple. I imagined something practical and concise: a kind of Lean field manual that a manager could keep nearby and open whenever a problem appeared on the shop floor. A quick reference. A collection of tools and techniques that could help teams remove waste and improve the way work was done.

But as the writing progressed, something became clear: Real transformations rarely happen because someone discovers a new tool or checklist. They happen because leaders begin seeing their organizations differently. They notice the patterns behind the daily frustrations. They start asking why simple things feel so hard. And they begin questioning processes that have quietly grown more complicated over time. That realization changed the direction of this book.

Instead of writing a short manual, I found myself writing about the journey organizations take when they decide to simplify their operations. The tools still matter, of course. Lean provides powerful ways to expose waste, stabilize processes, and improve performance. But tools alone are not enough. What truly drives change is the mindset behind them: the willingness to look honestly at the system and improve it step by step.

Stories help with that. Real examples make the lessons stick. Structure helps leaders see how today's challenges connect to tomorrow's results. So, the book grew into something larger than I originally planned.

What you are holding is not just a collection of Lean concepts. It is a roadmap for simplifying how organizations work and building operations that are faster, clearer, and more resilient.

Simplicity does not appear by accident. It is the result of decisions made by leaders over time. Every process, every approval, every report, and every meeting either adds clarity or complexity. When organizations begin questioning those layers, asking whether they still serve a real purpose, they often discover opportunities that were hiding in plain sight. That is where meaningful improvement begins.

In the chapters ahead, we will walk through the path that many successful turnarounds tend to follow. We will start by looking honestly at why operations become difficult to manage and why improvement efforts so often stall. From there, we will move into the practical work of simplifying processes, stabilizing performance, and making problems visible.

Along the way, we will talk about the role leaders play in developing people who can improve the system, not just operate inside it. And toward the end of the book, we will step back and consider how these ideas help organizations remain strong in a world that is becoming more complex and unpredictable.

This is not meant to be a theory book.

It is meant to help you see your organization more clearly and to give you the confidence to begin improving it. Immediately.

Your Role Starts Now

By this point, you may already be thinking about your own organization.

Perhaps you are the owner or CEO trying to keep your company competitive in a market that seems to move faster every year. Maybe you are a COO or operations leader responsible for fixing processes that no longer work the way they should. You might be a department head who knows the team could achieve much more if the system around them were simpler. Or perhaps you are someone inside the organization who simply refuses to accept that frustration and inefficiency are normal.

Wherever you sit, one reality remains the same: Transformations do not begin with tools. They begin with people who decide that the current situation can be better. They are the change agents.

That decision often starts quietly. A leader begins asking different questions: *Why does this step exist? Why does this decision take so long? Why do our best people spend so much time navigating the system instead of improving it?* Those questions are powerful because they shift the focus from blaming individuals to understanding the system itself.

If you read this book casually, you will likely come away with useful ideas. But if you read it actively, with pen in hand, reflecting on your own organization, working through the "Reflection and Action" sections, you will begin forming something much more valuable: *a plan*.

A plan to simplify the way work is done.

Many readers will recognize some of the concepts in this book. Lean has been discussed, studied, and applied for decades. Yet, in many organizations, it has been reduced to isolated tools, temporary programs, or initiatives that faded once the initial enthusiasm passed. The approach in this book is different.

Over the years, I have seen that real progress comes from focusing on what the business actually needs, not on what happens to be fashionable at the moment. Every organization has constraints, and improvement becomes meaningful when efforts are directed at the problems that truly matter.

Understanding complexity is the first step. But understanding alone does not change anything. The question leaders eventually ask is simple: *If complexity is the problem, what actually helps remove it?* For decades, one of the most effective answers has come from an unexpected place: Manufacturing. More specifically, from the principles that became known as "Lean."

Lean is not a collection of tricks or short-term fixes. At its best, it is a disciplined way of simplifying work so that problems become visible and people can solve them. Organizations that apply these principles thoughtfully often discover that improvements they once thought would take years can begin happening much sooner.

Over time, I have come to believe that most operational problems are not caused by a lack of effort or intelligence. They are caused by systems that have quietly become too complicated.

When leaders begin removing that complexity, performance improves in ways that often surprise them. That is what this book is about: not adding another layer of management tools but helping you make the work clear, manageable, and effective again.

In other words, learning how to *manufacture simplicity.*

Reflection and Action

1. What are the greatest pain points in your organization? Be specific.
2. Where do you see the most complexity in your operations? Map out a few key processes using the tools you already know, such as a flow diagram.
3. How is complexity impacting your employees? Talk to them. What are their frustrations? What do they think should be simplified?
4. How is complexity affecting your customers? What feedback are you receiving? How would customers benefit from a streamlined process? What customer satisfaction metrics will improve once you streamline your internal processes?
5. What are the potential consequences of inaction? What will happen if you don't address these issues?

The situations described in this chapter are rarely abstract. Most leaders recognize them immediately because they have lived through them. The purpose of the questions below is not to judge your organization but to help you see it clearly. Before jumping to solutions, take a few minutes to reflect on how complexity may already be affecting the way your business operates.

1. Where does complexity show up most often in your organization?
Think about the frustrations people mention repeatedly. Are decisions slow? Do projects stall? Do teams spend more time coordinating work than doing it?

2. What processes feel heavier than they should?
Identify workflows that require too many approvals, too many handoffs, or too much rework, as they are often the first places where simplification can make a real difference.

3. Where are your best people spending their time?
Are they improving the business or navigating systems that slow them down?

4. What problems have become "normal"?
Every organization develops habits that people stop questioning. Delivery delays, recurring defects, long meetings, or reports no one reads may simply be accepted as the way things are.

5. If you could remove one layer of complexity tomorrow, what would it be?
Sometimes, a single improvement can reveal how much easier work can become.

6. What would your business look like a year from now if complexity wasn't holding you back?
Just imagine how your business would look if you fixed some, most, or all of the pain points you uncovered in the questions above.

The goal is not to solve everything at once. It is to begin seeing the system clearly.

By honestly answering these questions, you'll begin to uncover the root causes of your organization's challenges and lay the foundation for a successful Lean transformation. This is the first step towards escaping the complexity trap and building a thriving, sustainable business.

Don't worry about employing the right words of formats. As thoughts and ideas come to mind, write them down. Don't hold back. No one is judging you, and I fully expect that, as you learn more, you may refer back to your notes to tweak things or add content.

At the end of every chapter, you will find a blank page to jot down your answers, thoughts, and action plans. Take your time to *reflect and act*, and you will get the most out of this publication. It is important that you not only reflect on the pain incurred by not taking action but also think of how much better life will be once things change. Combining these two opposing forces, "the need to avoid the pain" with the "desire to move towards a more pleasant place," will motivate you to take action and transform your organization as well as your career.

Chapter 1: Personal Plan & Insights

CHAPTER 2

The Lean Advantage: *A Path to Sustainable Growth*

Several years ago, a large customer approached a company I was helping with an interesting request. They wanted a new product manufactured in two different facilities.

The idea made sense from the customer's perspective. One plant, located on the East Coast, would supply customers across the eastern half of the United States. The other, on the West Coast, would cover the western states. Splitting production would shorten delivery times, reduce transportation costs, and give them a built-in backup if one facility ever ran into trouble.

For the organization I was working with, it seemed like a straightforward opportunity. Both plants belonged to the same corporation. Both had capable people, similar equipment, and access to the same corporate resources.

But there was one important difference.

Each facility was managed locally. That's how that corporation managed its businesses. Plant managers had significant autonomy in how they ran their operations. Corporate leadership set the goals and approved budgets, but the day-to-day systems, decision processes, and culture were shaped inside each plant.

At first, the project looked identical in both places. Engineering teams reviewed specifications, production planners built schedules, and quality groups prepared validation plans. Everyone wanted to make sure the new product launch went smoothly.

But as the weeks passed, the two facilities began moving in noticeably different directions.

At the first plant, the work quickly became complicated. Meetings multiplied as departments tried to coordinate their responsibilities. Questions that could have been resolved on the shop floor traveled up and down chains of approval. Small issues, such as an unavailable part, a process adjustment, or a documentation change, required emails, discussions, and revised plans.

No one was doing anything wrong. People were trying to be careful and thorough. Yet the system made progress slower than it needed to be. Every new problem triggered another layer of coordination.

Across the country, the second facility faced the same challenges but approached them differently. This plant had spent several years developing Lean practices and strengthening the way work flowed through the factory. The team was used to mapping processes, clarifying responsibilities, and involving employees directly in solving problems. Tools such as value stream mapping, standard work, and visual management were not special projects; they were simply how the operation functioned. So, when the new product was introduced, the response was practical.

The team walked through the process together, identifying where the product would move, how it would be assembled, and where potential delays could appear. Operators contributed insights about equipment and material flow. Engineers refined the sequence of steps. Supervisors focused on keeping communication simple and visible.

Because the system was already organized around clarity and flow, incorporating the new product was far less disruptive than many people expected. Issues still appeared, as they always do with new products, but they were easier to see and quicker to resolve. Instead of creating more meetings and approvals, the process itself guided the team toward solutions.

The contrast between the two facilities became increasingly clear. Both had skilled employees. Both worked hard. Both wanted to serve the customer well. But one plant relied on coordination to manage complexity. The other relied on a system designed to prevent complexity from taking over in the first place.

That difference is what Lean is really about. Lean did not emerge as a management trend or a theoretical framework. It developed as a practical way to simplify work, expose problems early, and help organizations improve continuously.

When companies truly embrace those principles, the results can be dramatic.

Where Lean Actually Came From

When people first hear the word "Lean," they often assume it refers to cutting costs, reducing staff, or squeezing more output from the same resources. In reality, Lean began as something very different.

It emerged from a simple challenge: how do you build high-quality products efficiently when resources are limited and customer expectations are rising?

After the Second World War, Japanese manufacturers faced exactly that situation. Companies like Toyota did not have the financial strength, factory scale, or domestic market that American manufacturers enjoyed at the time. They could not afford large inventories, long production runs, or massive inefficiencies hidden inside their processes. They had to find another way.

Rather than copying the dominant mass-production systems of the era, Toyota engineers and leaders began studying the flow of work itself. They asked questions that now seem obvious but were radical at the time.

Why should parts sit in storage, waiting to be used?
Why should defects be discovered only after a product is finished?
Why should employees simply follow instructions instead of improving the process?

Over time, these questions led to a very different production system, one designed to make problems visible rather than hide them.

Machines were arranged so work flowed smoothly from step to step. Inventory was reduced so issues appeared quickly instead of staying buried. Workers were encouraged to stop the process when something went wrong so the root cause could be addressed immediately. The goal was not simply efficiency. The goal was learning. Every problem became an opportunity to improve the system.

This approach eventually became known as the **Toyota Production System**, and many of the principles developed there later spread across the world under the name "Lean."

But something important often gets lost in translation. Lean is not defined by its tools. It is defined by the thinking behind them.

Value stream maps, kanban systems, standard work, visual boards, and kaizen events are useful, but they are not the destination. They are ways of helping organizations see their work clearly and improve it continuously.

When Lean works well, the organization becomes easier to manage, not more complicated. Problems surface earlier. Decisions become clearer. Employees feel more involved because their insights help shape the way work is done.

In other words, Lean helps companies do exactly what we saw in the second facility of the opening story. It simplifies the system so people can succeed.

What Lean Is Not

By the time most leaders encounter the word "Lean," they already have an opinion about it.

Some believe it is a program focused on cost-cutting. Others associate it with consultants, workshops, and colorful charts that appear for a few months before fading away. In some organizations, the term has even become something employees quietly dread because they assume it means doing more work with fewer people.

None of those interpretations captures what Lean is actually meant to accomplish.

Lean is not a short-term initiative designed to impress leadership or produce quick savings. Organizations that treat it that way usually see the same pattern repeat itself. The first round of projects generates enthusiasm. A few improvements are made, and some metrics move in the right direction. Then attention shifts to something else, and the old habits slowly return. The system never really changes.

Lean is also not a collection of isolated tools. Many companies try to adopt Lean by selecting a few techniques they have heard about. They run a kaizen event, introduce visual boards, or reorganize a work area using 5S. These activities can produce real improvements, but if they are introduced without a clear understanding of the system, they often become disconnected efforts.

People attend the workshops, and the charts go up on the wall. For a while, things look different. But eventually, the organization drifts back to familiar routines because the underlying complexity was never addressed.

Lean is not about working faster, either. In fact, one of the surprising things new practitioners discover is that Lean often slows things down at the beginning. Teams take time to understand the process, clarify responsibilities, and properly solve problems rather than rushing past them. That deliberate pace can feel uncomfortable in environments used to constant urgency, but it is often what allows real improvement to take hold.

Most importantly, Lean is not about removing people. When companies approach it that way, they damage the very resource that makes improvement possible. The insight needed to simplify work rarely comes from a spreadsheet or a distant office. It comes from the people who interact with the process every day.

Organizations that succeed with Lean learn to see their employees differently. Instead of asking them only to follow procedures, they invite them to help improve those procedures. Problems become discussions rather than accusations. Ideas begin coming from places leadership may never have expected. This is where Lean starts to reveal its real purpose.

At its best, Lean is a way of designing work so that complexity cannot quietly take over. It creates systems that make problems visible, encourage learning, and enable teams to continuously improve their processes. In other words, Lean is not another layer of management. It is a way of removing the layers that no longer belong.

The Few Ideas That Change Everything

Lean becomes much easier to understand when you stop thinking of it as a toolkit and start seeing it *as a way of thinking about work*.

That may sound abstract, but it is actually the most practical thing about Lean. Tools come and go, terminology changes, and software evolves. But the underlying logic stays remarkably consistent, and it works for a simple reason: it is designed to remove unnecessary complexity from how work gets done.

When Lean is applied well, your operation starts feeling different. Not louder or more frantic, but quite the opposite. It becomes calmer, clearer, and more predictable. The firefighting does not disappear overnight, but it stops being the default mode. People spend less time coordinating, chasing, and guessing and more time producing, solving, and improving.

That shift happens because Lean rests on a few core ideas. They are not complicated, but they are demanding because they force you to see reality and simplify the system.

1. Start with value, not activity.

Most organizations measure activity because activity is easy to see. People are in meetings. Reports are generated. Emails are answered. Projects are launched. The operation looks busy, and busyness feels like progress. Lean challenges that assumption by asking a more disciplined question: *where is value actually being created?*

Many publications define "value" as something the customer is willing to pay for. In Lean terms, value is added only when material or information is transformed in a way that directly produces what the customer has requested. If a step changes the product or service to better reflect customer needs, it adds value. If it does not, then it is either necessary support work or waste.

This distinction matters. Customers may be willing to pay for inspections, compliance checks, or expedited shipping. But inspections do not transform the product. They verify it. Reports do not change the product. They describe it. Meetings do not alter material or information in a way the customer experiences. They coordinate the people doing the work.

That does not mean those steps are always useless. Some are necessary *under current conditions*. But they do not add value in the strict sense.

A practical way to apply this principle is to walk through a process and label each step with honesty:

- Does this step transform the product or the information in a way the customer cares about?

- Or is it something we do because our internal system requires it?
- If this step disappeared tomorrow, would the customer notice?

When leaders begin viewing work through that lens, something powerful happens. They stop confusing effort with value. They begin separating true value creation from the layers that surround it.

That is often the first real step toward simplification.

2. Understand where complexity hides.

Once you begin looking at work through the lens of value, another reality becomes impossible to ignore: a large portion of what organizations do every day does not actually add value. We have measured it in several companies and usually under 5 percent of the time is spent adding value.

In Lean thinking, any activity that does not transform material or information in a way that directly reflects what the customer wants is considered **non-value-added**. These activities consume time, effort, and resources, yet they do not move the product or service closer to what the customer requested. We call these activities **waste**.

The word may sound harsh at first, but it is not meant as a criticism of people. Most waste does not arise from employees being careless or inefficient. It appears because systems evolve over time. Processes grow more complicated. Workarounds accumulate. Safeguards are added to compensate for earlier problems. Over the years, layers of coordination, checking, waiting, and rework begin to surround the actual value-creating work.

Eventually, the organization becomes preoccupied with managing the system rather than delivering value through it.

One of the most useful contributions of Lean thinking is that it provides a simple way to identify where waste tends to appear. Traditionally, seven major categories of waste are used to describe the most common patterns. Practitioners often remember them using the acronym **TIMWOOD**.

Each letter represents a type of activity that consumes resources without creating value.

Transportation refers to the unnecessary movement of materials or products between locations. Every extra transfer, forklift trip, or shipment increases cost and risk without improving the product itself.

Inventory refers to materials, work in process, or finished goods that sit idle awaiting the next step. Inventory often hides deeper problems such as unstable processes, long setup times, or poor coordination between departments.

Motion describes unnecessary movement by people. Searching for tools, walking long distances between workstations, or reaching awkwardly for parts may seem minor individually, but over time, these movements slow work and create fatigue.

Waiting occurs whenever work stops because something else is not ready. A machine waits for parts. A technician waits for instructions. A customer waits for approval. Waiting is one of the most visible forms of waste because it stretches lead times and disrupts flow.

Overproduction happens when more is produced than the customer currently needs or earlier than required. This is often considered the most damaging waste because it creates other waste, such as excess inventory, additional handling, and hidden defects. Some companies call overproduction the "mother of all waste."

Overprocessing refers to doing more work than the customer actually requires. Extra polishing, redundant approvals, unnecessary reporting, or overly complex procedures fall into this category.

Defects are errors that require correction, rework, or replacement. Defects consume time, materials, and attention while delivering no value to the customer.

Over time, practitioners recognized another form of waste that deserved attention as well. Many organizations fail to use the full capability of their people. Employees see problems every day and often have ideas for improvement, yet those insights remain untapped because the system does not encourage participation. For this reason, many Lean practitioners speak of an **eighth waste: the waste of unused human potential**. When people are treated only as operators of the system rather than contributors to its improvement, the organization loses an enormous source of insight.

Understanding these categories is not meant to turn every employee into a waste inspector. The purpose is to help leaders and teams recognize patterns that quietly drain performance.

Once waste becomes visible, *Lean tools and techniques* begin to make much more sense. Value stream mapping helps reveal waiting and unnecessary steps in the flow. Standard work reduces variation that leads to defects and rework. Pull systems reduce overproduction and excess inventory. Visual management quickly exposes delays and coordination problems. Each tool exists for a reason. They are not random techniques collected over time. They are practical responses to the different ways waste appears in real operations.

Consider a common situation in many manufacturing environments.

A customer places an order for a product that should take less than an hour of *actual processing time* to produce. The work itself is not complicated. Materials are available, the equipment is capable, and the operators know the process well. Yet the customer is told the order will ship in two weeks. Where does the time go?

When leaders walk the process step by step, the answer becomes surprisingly clear. The product spends most of its life waiting. It waits in a queue before the first operation begins. After processing, it sits on a pallet until a forklift driver becomes available. It waits again before inspection, then waits for documentation to be completed. Eventually, it joins a larger batch scheduled for packaging at the end of the week. Yet, when they add the individual cycle times for each operation, the total is measured in minutes, not weeks.

None of those delays improve the product. They simply accumulate because the system allows them to.

Now imagine looking at that same process through the lens of the eight wastes.

- The queues between operations reveal **waiting**.
- The palletized batches waiting for transport show **inventory**.
- The extra forklift trips represent **transportation**.
- Repeated paperwork approvals introduce **overprocessing**.
- If defects are discovered during inspection, **rework** appears as well.

The process did not look inefficient at first glance. Machines were running, people were working, and reports showed respectable utilization numbers. But once the work was viewed through the lens of waste, the true picture became obvious.

Most of the lead time had nothing to do with *creating value* for the customer.

This is the moment when Lean thinking becomes powerful. The goal is not to push people to work harder or faster. The goal is to redesign the system so that the unnecessary delays, movements, and complications disappear.

When that happens, the same people using the same equipment often produce dramatically better results. And as waste is gradually removed, processes become easier to understand, decisions become clearer, and work begins to flow more naturally. The system becomes simpler.

Once leaders begin recognizing waste in this way, a new question usually follows: if the sources of inefficiency are so visible, why do they persist in so many organizations?

Most companies are not blind to their problems. Managers know where delays occur. Employees recognize unnecessary steps, and customers occasionally point out the consequences through missed expectations or complaints. Yet these patterns often remain in place for years.

The reason is not a lack of awareness. It is that removing waste requires changes in how the system is managed. Processes must be redesigned, priorities must be clarified, and leaders must be willing to question habits that once felt necessary. This is where many Lean journeys encounter their first real test.

3. See the whole flow, not isolated departments.

Most complexity lives in the handoffs. When one department finishes its work and another begins, that boundary becomes a breeding ground for delays, rework, blame, and confusion. Each group may be efficient inside its own walls, yet the end-to-end process moves slowly.

Lean forces you to look at the entire journey, from request to delivery. Not the process map that lives in a binder but the real flow of work as it happens today.

This is why value stream thinking is so powerful. It exposes truths that are invisible when each department is only optimizing itself.

Here is a common example.

A factory may proudly report that each work cell is hitting its internal output goals, yet customers still complain about long lead times. When you map the flow, you discover the product spends most of its time waiting: waiting for parts, waiting for inspection, waiting for a decision, waiting for paperwork, and waiting for an engineer to respond. Or the parts may just be sitting in inventory.

The operation is not slow because people are slow. It is slow because the work spends too much time not moving.

When leaders begin managing the system as a flow, not as silos, complexity starts losing its hiding places.

4. Make work flow so problems cannot hide.

Flow is the opposite of batching, piling up, and pushing work forward in big chunks. In a complex operation, you often see large batches everywhere because batching feels efficient. Run a huge lot to reduce changeovers. Build extra inventory just in case. Process the paperwork in weekly piles. Inspect everything at the end so you do not interrupt production. The cost is that problems hide inside the batch.

If you produce five thousand units and inspect them later, you can create five thousand defects before you learn anything. If you build two months of inventory, you can mask instability for weeks. If you process orders once a week, you guarantee long lead times even if the actual work only takes minutes.

Lean aims to shorten the distance between cause and effect: smaller batches, shorter queues, clearer sequences, tighter feedback loops.

When flow improves, issues surface earlier. That can feel uncomfortable at first because problems appear more frequently, but the reality is the problems were already there. Flow simply stops hiding them. This is one of Lean's most important simplification moves: it reduces the places where dysfunction can hide.

5. Replace "push" with "pull."

Many organizations operate in push mode without realizing it. They forecast demand, build schedules, and push work into the system to keep everyone busy. Work piles up, priorities shift, and teams spend enormous energy sorting what matters most.

Pull works differently. Pull means you produce based on real demand and real capacity. You replenish what was actually used. You pace the system so work enters only when the next step is ready. The goal is not to keep every machine busy. The goal is to deliver value quickly and predictably.

A simple way to think about pull is this: **the downstream process should signal what it needs, when it needs it, in the quantity it needs.**

That idea changes everything.

It reduces overproduction, which is often the most expensive waste. It reduces inventory, which hides problems. It reduces scheduling chaos because the system becomes more self-regulating. Now, that's *simplification.*

In practical terms, pull can be implemented with kanban systems, supermarkets, and clear replenishment rules. But the deeper principle is this: Stop building complexity into the schedule. Instead, build clarity into the flow.

6. Build quality into the process, not at the end.

In many operations, quality is treated like a gate. Work is done, then quality checks it, and then we discover what went wrong. This approach almost guarantees rework, delays, and conflict because defects are discovered after the cost has already been incurred.

Lean takes a different stance: **quality should be built into the process, as close to the point of work as possible.** That does not mean inspectors are bad. It means the system should be designed so that defects are prevented or detected immediately, not weeks later.

Practical examples include:

- Mistake-proofing devices that prevent incorrect assembly.
- Simple go/no-go checks at the station.

- Clear acceptance criteria, visible where work happens.
- Stop-and-fix behaviors when something is off.
- Root-cause problem-solving instead of repeated containment.

This is where simplification becomes very real. The simplest quality system is the one that prevents defects rather than managing them downstream.

7. Standard work is not rigidity; it is the baseline for improvement.

Standard work scares some leaders because they associate it with bureaucracy. In reality, the absence of standard work creates a different kind of bureaucracy: constant interpretation, constant debate, and constant "it depends."

Standard work is simply the best-known way to perform a task today, written and taught so it can be repeated. The keyword is "today."

In Lean, standard work is not a rule carved in stone. It is the current baseline, which means it can be improved tomorrow. Without that baseline, you cannot tell whether a change made things better or worse.

Standard work also simplifies leadership. If you expect a supervisor to manage a process, they need a clear understanding of what "normal" looks like. If "normal" varies by operator, shift, or mood, the supervisor becomes a referee instead of a leader.

Well-designed standard work reduces variation, makes problems visible, and creates stability. Stability creates room for improvement.

This is why mature Lean operations feel calmer. They are not calm because problems do not exist. They are calm because work is clear.

8. Visual management turns confusion into clarity.

In a complex organization, information is often trapped. It lives in spreadsheets, meetings, email threads, or one person's head. When things go wrong, leaders spend time hunting for the truth.

Visual management is the opposite. It brings reality into the open.

The point is not to decorate the wall. The point is to make it obvious, at a glance:

- Are we winning or losing today?

- What is the problem?
- Who owns it?
- What is the next action?
- When will we check again?

When visual management is done well, it reduces the need for status meetings because the status is visible. It reduces the need for escalations because teams can act sooner. It reduces confusion because priorities are clearer. That is simplification in its purest form: fewer conversations to get to the same truth.

9. Respect for people is not a slogan; it is a design choice.

This is where many Lean efforts succeed or fail. A company can install tools and still fail if the culture treats people as hands instead of minds.

Respect for people in Lean is practical. It means designing work so people can succeed. It means listening to the people closest to the work because they see problems first. It means building a system where raising a problem is safe and valued.

When the culture is right, something important happens. People stop hiding problems. They stop working around them quietly. They start surfacing issues early and participating in solving them.

This goes beyond engagement, creating a system where performance becomes easier to achieve. A system that depends on leaders seeing everything will always be limited. A system that enables everyone to see and improve can scale.

10. Continuous improvement is a routine, not an event.

Many organizations "do Lean" through events. Events can be useful, especially early on. But if Lean lives only in events, improvement will always be episodic. The organization improves when it schedules improvement, and it drifts when it does not.

The mature version of Lean is a daily habit. Problems are surfaced, and their causes are explored. Countermeasures are tested, learning is captured, standards are updated, and leaders coach rather than rescue.

This is why the earlier chapters of *your* book matter so much. Lean is not a poster. It is an operating system. And operating systems work only when they are used consistently.

Pulling It All Together

If you step back, you will notice something.

Every one of these principles reduces complexity:

- Value reduces distraction.
- Flow reduces waiting and hidden problems.
- Pull reduces chaos and overproduction.
- Built-in quality reduces rework and blame.
- Standard work reduces variation and confusion.
- Visual management reduces meetings and guesswork.
- Respect for people reduces silence and workarounds.
- Continuous improvement reduces drift.

Lean is not complicated. It is disciplined. And the reason it works is that it makes the system simpler, clearer, and easier to run.

That is why Lean remains relevant across industries and across decades.

Because complexity is still the enemy.

And simplicity is still the advantage.

Why Lean Efforts So Often Disappoint

If Lean is built on such practical and enduring principles, why do so many organizations claim they "tried Lean" and saw little lasting impact?

The answer is rarely that Lean does not work. More often, it is that the organization never truly changed the way it operated.

In many companies, Lean begins with energy. Leaders attend a workshop or visit another facility and return inspired. A transformation is announced. Teams are trained. Visual boards appear. A few kaizen events generate visible improvements. Metrics move in the right direction. There is momentum. And then, slowly, daily reality begins to reassert itself.

Production pressure rises, urgent customer issues demand attention, managers fall back into familiar routines, and meetings crowd out reflection. Improvement activities are postponed "just this once." The visual boards remain on the wall, but they are no longer updated with the same discipline. The enthusiasm fades, not because people stopped caring, but because the underlying management system never changed.

Lean, in those environments, was treated as something added on top of the existing structure. That is where many efforts go wrong.

Lean cannot survive as a project layered over a complex system. When it competes with daily operations, daily operations will always win. Improvement becomes an initiative with a start date and, eventually, an end date.

Organizations that sustain Lean make a different choice. They stop treating it as an initiative and begin treating it as the way the business runs. Visual management becomes how performance is reviewed, not a side exercise. Standard work becomes how leaders coach, not a document stored in a binder. Problem-solving becomes part of the daily rhythm, not something reserved for special events.

Lean fails when it is extra. It succeeds when it becomes normal.

Another common reason for disappointment lies in leadership behavior. In some companies, Lean is delegated to a specialized team. A group of trained experts is assigned to "drive the transformation." Improvement becomes their responsibility.

But complexity does not live in one department. It lives in policies, priorities, reporting structures, and decision chains. It lives in how leaders respond when production targets conflict with quality concerns. It lives in whether problems are surfaced or quietly worked around.

When senior leaders continue operating the same way while asking others to simplify the system, the contradiction becomes visible very quickly. Employees are encouraged to remove waste, yet new layers of reporting are introduced. They are told to stop processes when something goes wrong, yet they are measured only on output.

Lean requires something far more demanding than delegation. It requires *visible leadership participation*: Leaders who spend time where work happens. Leaders who ask why a step exists. Leaders who tolerate short-term discomfort in order to solve root causes instead of masking them.

Without that shift, Lean becomes vocabulary rather than transformation.

There is another subtle reason Lean efforts stall. Many organizations attempt to apply advanced tools before establishing stability. They introduce pull systems into processes that are inconsistent, create visual dashboards without clear ownership, and standardize work that has never been properly understood.

When the foundation is unstable, new tools amplify the instability rather than resolve it. Frustration follows. Teams conclude that Lean is complicated or impractical when, in reality, the sequence was wrong.

Lean works best when leaders first stabilize processes, then improve flow, and only then refine coordination and scheduling. Skipping that order creates noise where clarity was intended.

Perhaps the most uncomfortable reason Lean efforts falter is this: *simplifying a system requires questioning past decisions*. It may require removing approvals that once felt essential. It may require redesigning reports that leaders have grown accustomed to reading for years. It may reveal that certain structures were built to solve yesterday's problems and are now creating new ones.

That kind of reflection demands *humility*. But avoiding it allows complexity to remain in place.

Organizations that succeed with Lean are not flawless. They still encounter problems, and they still make mistakes. The difference is that they *remain committed* after the initial excitement fades. They understand that Lean is not a burst of activity. It is a disciplined way of running the business.

Over time, that discipline produces something noticeable. The operation feels lighter, conversations become clearer, decisions require fewer layers, and problems surface earlier and are solved closer to their source.

Not because people are working harder, but because the system is no longer working against them.

Before You Improve Anything, You Must See Clearly

After learning about Lean principles, many leaders feel an immediate urge to start fixing things. The problems in their organizations are often obvious. Delays frustrate customers, work piles up between departments, and meetings multiply while decisions take longer. People work hard, yet progress feels slower than it should.

The natural instinct is to begin improving immediately, but one of the most important lessons in Lean is surprisingly simple: before improving a system, you must first understand it.

Organizations often attempt improvement without this clarity. A new reporting structure is introduced. Software is implemented, departments are reorganized, and procedures are rewritten. Each change is meant to solve a problem, yet many of these efforts add new layers without addressing the underlying causes. The result is familiar: complexity grows while the original frustrations remain.

Lean approaches improvement differently. Instead of jumping directly to solutions, it begins by observing the current reality with discipline and humility. Leaders step back from assumptions and look closely at how work actually flows through the organization.

What truly happens between the moment a customer places an order and the moment the product or service is delivered?

Where does the work slow down?

Where do problems appear repeatedly?

Where are people compensating for weaknesses in the system?

These questions sound simple, but they require something that many organizations rarely practice: honest observation.

In many companies, the official description of a process and the actual process are two very different things. Procedures describe how work is supposed to happen. The shop floor, the office, and the daily interactions between teams reveal how it actually happens. Lean insists on understanding that reality before attempting to improve it.

This is why the next step in any serious transformation is assessment. Not a superficial review or a collection of opinions, but a structured effort to see the system clearly. Leaders examine the flow of work, the decisions that guide it, and the cultural habits that shape daily behavior.

The goal is not to assign blame. It is to understand how the system produces the results it currently delivers.

Once that understanding is achieved, improvement becomes far more focused. Instead of attacking dozens of disconnected issues, leaders begin addressing the structural causes that create them.

In other words, clarity replaces guesswork, and that clarity is where meaningful simplification begins.

The next chapter will guide you through this process. Before you attempt to redesign workflows, introduce Lean tools, or launch improvement initiatives, you will learn how to step back and examine your organization with fresh eyes.

Because the most effective transformations do not start with action; they start with understanding. And that's what we will cover in Chapter 3.

Putting It to Work [Bonus Section]

In the early stages of Lean implementation, I like to run what I call "waste workshops" to teach the organization and help them identify the various kinds of waste. Why? Because it's almost impossible to apply Lean tools effectively if people can't recognize waste in the first place.

The setup is simple: we bring in small groups, explain each type of waste, and then send them back into their work areas for thirty to sixty minutes with one mission: hunt for waste. To guide the exercise, we hand out a simple "waste collection form" where employees can jot down what they see. I added a simple example below.

When they return, the room is buzzing. Forms are full, ideas are flowing, and employees see their workplace with fresh eyes. This discovery exercise doesn't just teach; it transforms perspective. Once you see waste, you can't unsee it, and that's exactly the point.

I'll never forget one of my earliest workshops when I was general manager of a large fastener manufacturing business. A tool room employee, someone who had worked in the same area for almost twenty years, came back with a mix of amazement and disgust. He told me:

"I've been running these two lathes all this time with a table placed between them. Every cycle, I remove the finished part from one machine, load the next, then walk around the table to do the same on the second lathe. Back and forth. All day. Every day. For almost two decades. And today, I suddenly realized how much motion I've been wasting just walking around a table."

That's the moment we aim for: the "waste awakening." Once he saw it, he couldn't unsee it.

I asked him to take me to the gemba, the actual workplace, and show me. Sure enough, the waste was obvious. But instead of telling him what to do, I asked questions: "What would make this easier? How could we arrange this better?"

Within minutes, he suggested moving the table aside to create a straight path between the two lathes. Then, after a pause, he said: "Wait, what if we moved the machines closer? I wouldn't need to walk as much at all."

One idea led to another. Soon, he and I had a list of improvements. We called in maintenance, and within a couple of hours, the changes were made.

This simple adjustment, something overlooked for twenty years, was solved in one afternoon once the waste was visible. The result? Less walking, faster cycles, reduced fatigue, and a proud, motivated employee.

That's the essence of Lean: Teach people to see waste. Engage them in solving it. Act quickly so improvements feel real.

The outcome isn't just better processes. It's an energized workforce that knows they can make a difference. And that cultural shift is far more powerful than any single improvement.

The Waste Workshop

If you like the idea of running events like the waste workshops, you can create simple forms, like the one below, that attendees can use in their "waste walk":

Waste Type	Example You Observed	Impact	Your Recommendation/Idea
T – Transportation			
I – Inventory			
M – Motion			
W – Waiting			
O – Overproduction			
O – Overprocessing			
D – Defects			
Unutilized Talent			

This form helps employees identify different types of waste in their work areas. Use it during a "waste walk" exercise, then regroup to discuss findings and brainstorm improvements. Of course, you do the waste walk *after* you teach them about the eight kinds of waste.

Instructions

1. Walk through your work area with this sheet in hand.
2. Observe carefully. Look for examples of the seven (plus one) types of waste.
3. For each observation, write down:
   - Where you saw it
   - Description of the waste
   - Impact (time, cost, quality, frustration, etc.)
   - Your recommendation/idea (even if small or unfinished)

Remember: Don't fix it yet; just see it. Improvement comes after awareness.

Workshop Reflection Questions (Optional, for debrief)

- Which type of waste did you see most often?
- Which waste has the biggest impact on customers?
- Which idea do you believe would be easiest to implement quickly?
- Which idea, if implemented, would create the greatest long-term improvement?

Next Steps

☐ Share your findings in the group debrief.
☐ Select one quick win to implement immediately.
☐ Log remaining ideas for prioritization in the Lean action plan.

Reflection and Action

Understanding Lean intellectually is useful, but it becomes powerful only when leaders and practitioners begin applying its lens to their organizations. The purpose of this section is not to test your knowledge of Lean concepts. It is to help you begin seeing your operation differently.

Before moving on to the next chapter, pause and reflect on how the ideas discussed here might appear in your own environment.

Reflection

1. **Where does value actually get created in your organization?**
   Think about the processes that deliver products or services to your customers. At which steps are material or information truly transformed into what the customer requested?

2. **Where does work slow down or accumulate?**
   As you picture the journey from customer request to delivery, where do waiting, handoffs, or queues appear?

3. **Which types of waste seem most visible in your operation?**
   Reflect on the eight forms of waste discussed in this chapter: transportation, inventory, motion, waiting, overproduction, overprocessing, defects, and unused human potential. Which ones appear most often?

4. **How often do employees surface problems or improvement ideas?**
   Are people encouraged to raise issues and suggest improvements, or do they tend to work around problems quietly?

5. **When problems occur, how does your organization typically respond?**
   Does the response focus on addressing the immediate symptom or on understanding the system that allowed the problem to occur?

These questions are not meant to produce perfect answers. Their purpose is to help you begin observing your organization with the same mindset that drives Lean thinking.

Action

Choose **one process** in your organization that affects customers directly. It could be a manufacturing process, an order-to-delivery workflow, a service interaction, or an internal process that supports customers.

Take a few minutes to sketch the journey of that process from beginning to end.

As you review the steps, ask yourself three simple questions:

- Where is **value actually created**?
- Where does **waste appear** in the form of delays, rework, or unnecessary steps?
- Where might the **knowledge of employees** closest to the work help simplify the process?

Do not worry about fixing the process yet. The goal of this exercise is simply to begin seeing the system more clearly.

In the next chapter, we will take this observation further by learning how to assess an organization systematically. Instead of relying on intuition alone, you will develop a structured way to examine processes, leadership behaviors, and operational systems.

Because meaningful improvement begins with understanding how the system really works.

Once again, Lean is a journey, not a destination. By consistently asking these questions, applying the principles, and empowering your team, you can unlock the Lean advantage and create a path for sustainable growth in your organization.

Feel free to go back to the answers you gave in Chapter 1. Build upon them. *Each chapter is designed to build upon what you learned in previous chapters*. As long as you follow our guidelines, at the end of this "simplification manual," you will end up with your Lean transformation plan, with some gains along the way.

Chapter 2: Personal Plan & Insights

CHAPTER 3

Assessing Your Current State: *The Treasure Hunt for Opportunities*

A Monday Morning Reality Check

It's your first morning in your new role.

You arrive early, hoping for a quiet hour to review notes and get your bearings. That hope disappears the moment you walk through the door.

Your phone starts buzzing before you even sit down. A customer's delivery is late. Production missed its numbers again last week. A supervisor wants approval for overtime work. Finance is asking why scrap is up. Someone from sales is waiting outside your office with their arms crossed, clearly frustrated.

You glance around. The place looks busy but not productive. People are moving fast, yet nothing seems to flow. Pallets are stacked where they shouldn't be. Some whiteboards are filled with numbers no one appears to use, while others are just not updated. You overhear the same problems being discussed in three different corners of the building, each with a different explanation and a different sense of urgency. Everyone wants answers, and they want them now.

You ask a simple question: "What's the biggest issue we're trying to fix this week?"

You get five different answers.

One manager points to staffing. Another blames scheduling. Someone else says the equipment is unreliable. A veteran operator quietly tells you, "We've tried fixing all of this before."

As the morning goes on, the pressure builds. You are expected to improve results immediately, yet it's clear that jumping straight to solutions would be guesswork at best. Every instinct tells you that reacting too fast will only add more noise, more initiatives, and more confusion.

You realize something important: before you can fix anything, you need to understand everything.

Not through reports alone and not through dashboards that already contradict each other but by seeing the work, hearing the unfiltered truth, and connecting the dots between symptoms and root causes.

This is when many leaders rush ahead, armed with tools and good intentions, and unintentionally make things worse.

This chapter is about choosing a different path.

Instead of guessing, you assess. Instead of reacting, you observe. Instead of fixing symptoms, you search for causes.

This is where the real work begins.

Chapters 1 and 2 laid the groundwork, exposing the insidious nature of complexity and introducing the powerful philosophy of Lean as the cure. Now it's time to roll up your sleeves and get practical. This chapter is where the rubber meets the road. This is your guide to conducting a thorough assessment of your current operations, uncovering hidden inefficiencies, and identifying the goldmine of opportunities for simplification that lies within your organization.

Know Thyself: The Importance of a Thorough Assessment

Before you can embark on a Lean transformation, you need to understand where you stand. It's like planning a road trip without a map; you might have a destination in mind, but you'll likely get lost along the way. A comprehensive assessment is your map, guiding you toward the most promising opportunities for improvement. You will take a hard, honest look at your current processes, identify areas of waste and inefficiency, and understand the root causes of your challenges.

Imagine you're a doctor diagnosing a patient. You wouldn't just randomly prescribe medication, would you? You'd start with a thorough examination, gather data, analyze symptoms, and identify the root cause of the problem. Assessing your current state, in a Lean transformation, is much the same. It's not about grabbing a toolbox and randomly applying techniques; it's about understanding the "why" behind your challenges and charting a course toward lasting improvement. But before we dive into the specifics of "how" work is done, we need to understand the *bigger picture,* the overall health and direction of the organization.

At this stage, many leaders instinctively want to move directly into the factory, the service process, or the workflow they believe needs fixing. That impulse is understandable. After all, Lean is strongly associated with improving processes. But jumping straight into process analysis without understanding the broader business environment can lead to solving the wrong problems.

Processes do not exist in isolation. They are shaped by the company's strategy, the pressures of the market, financial constraints, leadership priorities, and even the culture of the organization. A scheduling problem might actually be a product-mix problem. A quality issue might trace back to unclear strategic priorities. A chronic overtime problem might reflect demand volatility rather than operational inefficiency.

For that reason, the first step in a serious assessment is not to study the process itself but to understand the *business landscape in which that process operates.* Before examining how work flows through the organization, we must first understand the forces that shape that work.

I. A Holistic View: Understanding the Business Landscape

Before focusing on processes and tools, I like to assess the broader context. This involves gathering information from various sources and perspectives to understand the organization's current state from a business perspective.

1. **Interviews: Voices from All Levels**

    - **Emphasis on Diverse Perspectives:** Conduct interviews with a representative sample of employees at all levels, from front-line workers to managers and owners. These conversations should be confidential to encourage open and honest feedback.

- **Key Questions:**

    - **Owners/Leadership:** "What is your vision for the company?" "What are your strategic priorities?" "What are your biggest challenges and opportunities?" "What are your expectations for this assessment and the Lean transformation?"

    - **Managers:** "What are your team's biggest challenges?" "What are your key performance indicators?" "What resources do you need to improve performance?" "What are your thoughts on the current culture?"

    - **Front-Line Employees:** "What are your biggest frustrations with your job?" "What prevents you from being more productive?" "What ideas do you have for improvement?" "What do you enjoy most about your work?"

    - I always like to ask managers and front-line employees, "What would you do if you were the owner of this company?"

    - I recommend you cross-check some of the information across levels. As an example, I like to ask the executive team about their strategy and how it is deployed. Often, I hear different "versions" of the strategy among members of the executive team. Usually, they say they communicated the strategy well to the organization, so I like to ask people at all levels specific questions about the strategy. In addition, as a bonus, I like to ask: "How much did you work on the strategy today/this week/this month?"

    - As you uncover issues and opportunities during interviews, ask the interviewees about them. This is the time to uncover the truth.

2. **Discovering the Pain Points**

    - **Systematic Approach:** Use the interviews and observations to identify the key **pain points**, the areas where the organization is experiencing the most significant challenges. These could be related to efficiency, quality, customer satisfaction, employee morale, or any other area impacting performance. Note that you will hear a mix of problems, causes, myths, and ideas for solutions. At this point, take it all in and ask clarifying questions. Don't recommend solutions yet. Just listen!

- **Sort Through and Prioritize:** Not all pain points are created equal. Prioritize them based on their impact on the business and their feasibility for improvement. Depending on the amount of information collected, you may want to use a large language model (LLM) to help you sort through all the interview forms, create categories, and identify similarities and connections. Don't blindly trust any LLM, as they are prone to hallucinations. Make sure you check the results and confirm they align with what you heard during the interview process. Of course, this step should not be performed during the interview process. Consolidate it on your own after you finish the interviews.

3. Company Direction and Strategy

- **Strategy:** Does the company have a clearly defined mission, vision, and strategy? What's the three-to-five-year goal? If they do have a good strategy, is it effectively communicated and understood by all employees? If not, this is a critical gap that needs to be addressed.
- **Alignment:** Are the company's goals and objectives aligned across different departments and functions? Is everyone working towards the same vision? How is this alignment evident? Are there metrics that gauge the strategy attainment?
- Both the existence of a strategy and the organizational alignment can be assessed by the interview questions, along with postings and metrics throughout the business.

4. SWOT Analysis

- **Comprehensive View:** Conduct a Strengths, Weaknesses, Opportunities, and Threats (SWOT) analysis to get a comprehensive view of the organization's strengths, weaknesses, opportunities, and threats. This provides a valuable framework for understanding the internal and external factors that are impacting the business.

- **Most companies already have a SWOT analysis.** Use what they have, challenge it, and validate it. If they don't have one, help create one. You can have a SWOT analysis done over lunch with management.

5. Financial Status and Projections

- **Key Metrics:** Review the company's financial statements to understand its current financial health. Analyze key metrics such as revenue, profitability, cash flow, and debt. Look at trends over time. Understand the key drivers for performance. Most of the time, you will find there are concerns with cash, revenues, and/or costs. Understand what costs are out of line, why the company is not able to sell more, as well as their cash constraints.

- **Projections:** What are the company's financial projections? Are they realistic and aligned with the company's strategic goals? Does the company have credible plans to achieve its projections?

6. Growth and Market Analysis

- **Market Trends:** What are the key trends in the company's industry? Is the market growing or shrinking? What are the competitive dynamics? What is keeping the company from dominating the market? Are there emerging disruptive technologies? How's the product development pipeline?

- **Growth Strategy:** Does the company have a clear growth strategy? How does it plan to achieve its growth objectives?

7. Employee Engagement and Turnover

- **Metrics and Drivers:** Assess employee engagement levels. High turnover can be a symptom of deeper issues. Analyze turnover rates, reasons for leaving (if available), and potential drivers of disengagement. In addition, figure out why people stay, as this may shed light on what the company is doing right.

- **You should be able to sense employee motivation and engagement as you go through the interview process.** How does the interview inputs match what you hear from HR?

8. **Quality Issues and Customer Feedback**

   - **Data and Insights:** Review data on quality metrics, such as defect rates and customer returns. Gather customer feedback through surveys, interviews, or online reviews. Understand what customers value and where the company is falling short. Look at trends, too. Are things getting better or worse over time?

   - **Internal Quality:** Understand what is measured internally. Look for scrap rates, non-conformance logs, and closure timing. If they measure first-pass yield, it may signal an intention to do things right the first time around. What is the quality of their root-cause analysis? Do they measure their effectiveness? Are there repeat issues? If some customer complaints are related to internal issues, it means the organization is letting quality slip.

II. The Assessment Process: From Big Picture to Specific Actions

This section builds upon the holistic view established in Part I.

1. **Define the Scope and Objectives**

   - **Based on Holistic View:** Based on the information gathered in Part I, refine the scope and objectives of the Lean assessment. Which areas are most critical to address to achieve the company's strategic goals and address the most pressing pain points?

2. **Assemble the Team**

   - **Focus on Key Players:** In a small business, the team might be smaller, but it's still essential to have representation from key areas. Top management or the owners themselves should be actively involved.

3. Gather Data and Insights (Targeted)

- **Focus on Key Areas:** Given the scope and objectives, focus data collection on the most relevant processes and areas. Don't try to assess everything at once.

4. Analyze and Identify Opportunities (With Business Context)

- **Connect to Business Goals:** When analyzing data and identifying opportunities, always connect them back to the company's strategic goals and the pain points identified in Part I. How will these improvements contribute to the overall success of the business?

5. Prioritize and Select Tools (Strategically)

- **Match the Approach to Business Needs:** Choose techniques and Lean tools that are appropriate for the specific problems being addressed and that align with the company's needs, resources, and capabilities.

6. Document and Report (Actionable and Relevant)

- **Focus on Key Findings:** The report should focus on the holistic assessment key findings, prioritized opportunities for improvement, and recommended solutions. It should be concise, actionable, and relevant to the management or owners' priorities.

- **Lean Rollout Plan:** Include a Lean transformation plan with the recommended sequence of events. At this stage, it is hard to come up with the proper timing, as you may not know the company's commitment and resource availability.

The Lean Toolkit: Not a Checklist, a Set of Lenses

During an assessment, it's tempting to grab a Lean checklist and start using scoring tools. Don't do that.

Lean tools are not "requirements," and they're not badges. They are *lenses*. Each one helps you see a different part of how the business truly works: how work flows, how stable the process is, how decisions get made, how problems get solved, and whether the organization has the discipline to sustain improvement.

Also, not every company is at the same point in its Lean journey. Some have never used the language of Lean. Others have banners on the wall and a few kaizen binders, but no day-to-day habits. A few have real systems that run even when leaders are not watching.

So, the goal of this section is not to "grade Lean." The goal is to quickly answer questions like these:

- Where is the waste really coming from: flow, quality, reliability, planning, or leadership behaviors?
- Is the operation stable enough to improve, or is it trapped in firefighting?
- Does the company have building blocks in place (standard work, basic visual controls, team problem-solving)?
- If we invest effort, will it stick, or will it fade after the initial push?

With that in mind, here are the core tools and methods I use as part of a Lean "treasure hunt." I'm not recommending you implement all of them during an assessment. I'm recommending you use them selectively to diagnose reality, prioritize opportunities, and shape a practical transformation plan.

How to Use the Toolkit During an Assessment (The Playbook)

Here's a simple way to guide your thinking:

Step 1: Start wide, then narrow.

- Begin with tools that show **flow and system constraints** (VSM, PQPR, basic planning approach).
- Then zoom in to tools that show **process stability and discipline** (standard work, 5S, TPM).
- Finally, look at tools that show **quality prevention and change capability** (poka-yoke, SMED, kaizen habits).

Step 2: Look for evidence, not slogans.

Lean is one of the easiest things to "pretend." Posters, training certificates, "Lean teams," and kaizen photo collages do not prove capability. Evidence is different:

- Work is stable day to day.
- Problems are visible quickly.

- The same problems don't repeat for months.
- Improvements are standardized and sustained.
- Leaders ask consistent questions and follow up.

Step 3: Use each tool to answer: "So what?"

A tool is only useful if it changes your diagnosis or your priorities. Every tool should answer one of these:

- What is the biggest constraint to flow?
- Where are we losing capacity?
- Why is quality escaping?
- Why can't we keep a schedule?
- Why are people firefighting?
- What prevents learning and sustaining?

Step 4: Translate findings into "first moves."

You need to turn observations into action. For each tool, it's helpful to connect it to:

- What it usually signals when it's missing.
- What the first improvement move might be.
- What not to do (common traps).

That's what the sections below are designed to do.

Value Stream Mapping (VSM): Seeing the End-to-End System

What it is and why it matters:
VSM is a structured way to see the full flow of value, from customer demand to delivery, including both material flow and information flow. During an assessment, VSM is less about drawing boxes and more about exposing the truth of how the business performs:

- Where time is spent (processing vs. waiting)
- Where inventory hides problems
- Where handoffs create delays, errors, and rework
- Where priorities change because the system is unstable

What it reveals during an assessment:

- The true lead time (often shocking compared to "touch time")
- The biggest queues and bottlenecks
- Scheduling and planning behaviors (push vs. pull)
- Where firefighting is coming from: demand changes, quality, downtime, shortages, or decision making

How to do it (assessment version):

1. Pick one **representative product family** (high volume, high margin, or strategic).
2. Map the **current state** at a high enough level to capture flow, but not so detailed it becomes a poster project.
3. Capture **key data** quickly: cycle times, changeover times, uptime, WIP levels, queue time, batch sizes, and information triggers.
4. Sketch a **future state** as a direction, not perfection. It should show what you intend to fix first: flow, leveling, pull signals, or stability.

What to look for (evidence):

- Large WIP piles, long waits, batching, and expedites
- Many schedules and priority lists floating around
- "We can't build to plan" as a daily norm
- Quality checks that happen late, not at the source
- Unclear triggers: Who decides what to run next?

Questions to ask:

- What causes the schedule to change during the day?
- Where do you see the most frequent expediting?
- If you had to reduce lead time by 30 percent in ninety days, where would you attack first and why?

Common trap:
A VSM that becomes a workshop deliverable but doesn't change how decisions are made. During an assessment, keep it crisp and diagnostic. (You can go deeper later, in your transformation phase.)

Process Mapping: Understanding How Work Actually Happens

What it is and why it matters:
Process mapping zooms in on a single process and makes every step visible: actions, decisions, handoffs, waits, and rework loops. It's one of the fastest ways to uncover hidden complexity and non-value-added work.

What it reveals during an assessment:

- Why a "simple" process takes so long (handoffs, waiting, approvals)
- Where errors originate and how they propagate
- Where workarounds live (a key sign the process is broken)
- Where the process depends on tribal knowledge

How to do it (assessment version):

1. Pick a process that matches the pain: quoting, planning, receiving, changeovers, a test procedure, picking/packing, or customer return.
2. Walk it with the people who do it. Don't map from a conference room.
3. Capture: steps, decision points, wait time, rework loops, and where information gets lost.

What to look for (evidence):

- "It depends" steps that rely on one person
- Multiple re-entries of data
- Long wait times for approvals or QA release
- Steps that exist only because downstream doesn't trust upstream

Questions to ask:

- What step frustrates you the most and why?
- If you left for two weeks, could someone else run this process without calling you daily?
- Where does the process break most often?

Common trap:
Mapping too much detail too early. During an assessment, map enough to expose root causes and handoffs, then stop.

5S: Workplace Discipline You Can See

What it is and why it matters:
5S is a workplace organization method, but the deeper purpose is discipline. A truly "5S-able" environment usually has better safety, quality, and predictability because standards are visible and followed. You are not implementing 5S during an assessment. Instead, you're using it as a readiness indicator.

What it reveals during an assessment:

- Whether the organization can establish and follow standards
- Whether problems are visible or hidden
- Whether leaders notice abnormalities

How to assess it (practical scoring approach):
Walk the operation and score a few zones using a simple rubric:

- **Sort:** Clutter removed, obsolete items not present
- **Set in Order:** Locations labeled, tools and materials have homes
- **Shine:** Basic cleaning, leaks addressed, floors and machines cared for
- **Standardize:** Visuals and standards exist and match reality
- **Sustain:** Leaders reinforce it, and it remains without "inspection panic"

What to look for (evidence):

- Clear aisles, labeled locations, and shadow boards where relevant
- Visual limits (min/max, WIP limits)
- Clean, well-lit work areas
- Standards posted and actually followed

Questions to ask:

- Who owns this area? How do you know?
- What happens when something is out of place?
- How often do leaders walk this area, and what do they look for?

Common trap:
Treating 5S as a cosmetic cleanup. In your framing, 5S is a proxy for discipline and leadership consistency.

SMED: Changeover Reality Check

What it is and why it matters:
SMED (Single-Minute Exchange of Dies) is a method used to reduce changeover time and increase flexibility. During an assessment, it tells you whether the factory is forced into large batches because changeovers are painful or whether it can respond to demand smoothly.

What it reveals during an assessment:

- Whether batching is a choice or a forced constraint
- Whether capacity is lost to poor setup practices
- Whether operators have a method to improve setups

How to assess it:
Observe at least one real changeover. Don't rely on "it takes about..." Ask to see:

- Setup start/finish timestamps.
- What triggers the changeover.
- How much searching, waiting, and "figuring it out" happens.

Then classify activities:

- **Internal:** Must occur while stopped
- **External**: Can occur while running or before shutdown

What to look for (evidence):

- Tools not staged
- No checklist or standard sequence
- Adjustments that depend on one expert
- Cleanup and searching embedded into setup time

Questions to ask:

- What part of this setup is most unpredictable?
- What preparations could be made before the machine stops?
- If you had to cut this time in half, where would you start?

Common trap:
Thinking SMED is only "fast hands." In reality, it's planning, staging, standard work, and eliminating adjustments.

TPM: Reliability, Predictability, and Ownership

What it is and why it matters:
TPM (Total Productive Maintenance) is a technique used to maximize equipment reliability and availability. It improves predictability and performance while building operator ownership. During an assessment, it is a leading indicator of whether the plant is run proactively or reactively.

What it reveals during an assessment:

- Whether downtime is controlled or accepted as "normal"
- Whether basic maintenance is systematic or heroic
- Whether operators and maintenance work as one team or as adversaries

How to assess it:
Look for:

- Preventive maintenance plans that are current and executed.
- Visual maintenance boards and daily checks.
- OEE tracking (or at least downtime categorization).
- Root cause follow-up after major failures.

Also look for "autonomous maintenance" signals:

- Operators doing routine cleaning, inspection, lubrication.
- Simple visual standards are posted at the machine.

Questions to ask:

- What are the top three downtime causes?
- When you fix a breakdown, how do you prevent it from returning?
- How do operators report abnormalities?

Common trap:
Measuring "maintenance activity" instead of "equipment reliability." TPM isn't about doing more PM. It's about fewer surprises.

Kaizen: The Company's Improvement Metabolism

What it is and why it matters:
Kaizen is a Lean practice of making small, frequent improvements to processes, usually by involving the people closest to the work. It can be a workshop, but the deeper idea is daily improvement. During an assessment, kaizen tells you whether the business learns and improves as a habit or only improves during special events.

What it reveals during an assessment:

- Whether improvement is integrated into daily work
- Whether people feel safe raising problems
- Whether leaders follow through or improvements die quietly

How to assess it:
Ask for:

- A list of improvements in the last three, six, and twelve months.
- Who led them and who participated.
- Before/after results (even simple ones).
- How improvements were standardized and sustained.

What to look for (evidence):

- Visual improvement boards that reflect the current reality
- Small improvements happening without fanfare
- A pipeline: ideas, prioritization, execution, sustainment
- People who can clearly describe recent improvements

Questions to ask:

- What was the last improvement you personally made?
- How do you decide which ideas get worked on?
- What happens when a kaizen creates a new standard?

Common trap:
Kaizen that creates temporary change but not new standards. Kaizen without standardization becomes "activity," not capability.

Standard Work: The Baseline for Improvement

What it is and why it matters:
Standard work defines the best-known method to perform a task today. It stabilizes performance, reduces variation, and creates a baseline for improvement. Without it, every improvement becomes opinion-based.

Standard work is not always built "from takt time" in the early stages. Sometimes, you establish basic best practices first, then evolve it to align with demand.

Simply put, **takt time** represents the specific pace your team must maintain to fulfill customer orders on time without creating excess inventory. In other words, takt time is the pace at which a process must produce one finished unit in order to match customer demand.

What it reveals during an assessment:

- Whether the process is stable enough to improve
- Whether training is systematic or tribal
- Whether leaders manage through standards or personalities

How to assess it:
Look for standard work in a few places:

- Operator work instructions
- Material replenishment steps
- Quality checks
- Changeover checklists
- Admin processes (order entry, planning, release)

Then verify: Do people follow it? Do leaders audit it? Is it updated?

Questions to ask:

- If performance drops, what standard do you reference?
- How do new employees learn the job?
- When a problem occurs, do you adjust the standard?

Common trap:
Treating standard work as a document library. It should be alive: visible, taught, audited, improved.

Poka-Yoke: Designing Errors Out of the Process

What it is and why it matters:
Poka-yoke is a Lean method used to prevent errors from happening or to make them immediately obvious before they create defects. It prevents errors by making defects difficult or impossible. During an assessment, it is one of the strongest indicators of whether the business fights quality with inspection and training or prevents defects at the source.

What it reveals during an assessment:

- Whether quality is reactive (detect and rework) or preventive
- Whether engineering and manufacturing collaborate to eliminate causes
- Whether recurring defects are treated as "normal"

How to assess it:
Start with the top defect or top customer complaint and trace:

- Where it originates
- How it was detected
- What was done after detection
- Whether recurrence prevention exists (not just training)

What to look for (evidence):

- Simple fixtures that prevent misassembly
- Sensors that prevent wrong part selection
- "Go/no-go" gauges for critical features
- Process interlocks that stop bad output

Also, look for the feedback loop:

- Does the organization learn or repeat?

Questions to ask:

- What defects do you see repeatedly? Why?

- Is the countermeasure "be careful," or is it a design/process change?
- How quickly does a defect trigger investigation and standard updates?

Common trap:
Over-relying on training. Training matters, but defects should be engineered out whenever possible.

Kanban: Controlling Flow and Inventory with Signals

What it is and why it matters:
Kanban is a pull system that controls inventory and replenishment using visual signals. During an assessment, your goal is not to judge whether they use "true kanban," but whether they control material flow in a stable way.

What it reveals during an assessment:

- Why shortages happen (poor signals, poor discipline, poor planning, supplier issues)
- Why inventory is high (fear, uncertainty, batching, poor reliability)
- Whether replenishment is driven by consumption or by forecasts alone

How to assess it:
Look for how they trigger replenishment:

- Kanban cards/bins
- Min-max
- Two-bin systems
- ERP/MRP signals

Then evaluate discipline:

- Are signals followed?
- Are visual limits respected?
- Are shortages common anyway?

Questions to ask:

- What do you do when you run out of material?
- How often do you expedite suppliers?
- Where do you carry "just in case" inventory, and why?

Common trap:
Believing kanban automatically reduces inventory. It doesn't at first. It stabilizes control. Inventory reduction follows improvements in reliability, quality, and flow.

Heijunka: Leveling the Mix and Volume to Reduce Chaos

What it is and why it matters:
Heijunka is a Lean method used to smooth out the mix and volume of work instead of producing in large batches or reacting to demand spikes. It levels production to match demand patterns, reducing swings that create overtime, shortages, and expediting. During an assessment, Heijunka tells you how much of the chaos comes from demand variation vs. internal instability.

What it reveals during an assessment:

- Whether scheduling is reactive or structured
- Whether the plant can run small batches reliably
- Whether changeovers, quality, and reliability support flexibility

How to assess it:
Review:

- Demand patterns (by week/month, product mix)
- How the schedule is created and changed
- Actual adherence to plan
- Batch sizes and their drivers (setup time, quality, capacity)

Questions to ask:

- How often does the schedule change? Why?
- If demand is stable, why isn't production stable?
- What prevents smaller batches?

Common trap:
Trying to level load before fixing the basics (quality, downtime, long changeovers). Heijunka works best when the system is stable enough to respond predictably.

Teamwork: Collaboration as a Capability, Not a Value Statement

What it is and why it matters:
Teamwork in Lean is not motivational talk. It is a practical operating capability: people across functions work together to solve problems at the source, quickly, and without politics. *Most* operational dysfunction is not caused by bad people. It's caused by poor coordination, unclear ownership, and conflicting incentives.

What it reveals during an assessment:

- Whether departments cooperate or protect themselves
- Whether problems get solved end-to-end or bounced around
- Whether leaders align goals and drive shared accountability

How to assess it (practical):
Watch and listen:

- Do production, quality, maintenance, engineering, and planning speak as one system or as separate camps?
- When a defect happens, do people collaborate or blame?
- Are goals shared (lead time, delivery, first-pass yield), or is each function optimized separately?

Look for structural signals:

- Co-location (or frequent joint routines)
- Shared metrics and daily review
- Clear escalation paths and follow-up discipline

Example:
A business implements a focus factory, where support functions (quality, engineering, maintenance, supply chain) are physically embedded with manufacturing teams and share the same daily targets. During an assessment, the strongest sign isn't the seating chart, it's behavior: problems are solved in real time, with joint ownership, and countermeasures don't die after the meeting.

Questions to ask:

- When production misses the plan, who owns the recovery plan?
- What happens when quality blocks output? Is it a war or a collaboration?

- Tell me about the last problem solved by a cross-functional team. What changed permanently?

Common trap:
Calling it "teamwork" while metrics and incentives still drive functional conflict. If the system rewards silo performance, teamwork won't show up consistently.

Automation: Making It Earn Its Place

What it is and why it matters:
Automation means using machines, software, or technology to perform work with minimal human intervention. Automation can remove manual work, reduce defects, and improve throughput. But it can also lock in complexity, create fragile systems, and waste capital. The Lean principle is simple: **simplify first, stabilize second, automate third.** We will discuss this topic in more depth later in the book.

What it reveals during an assessment:

- Whether the company solves problems through process thinking or through spending
- Whether processes are stable and standardized enough to be automated successfully
- Whether automation is improving flow or creating new bottlenecks

How to assess it:
For any major automated process, look for:

- Clear business reason: capacity, quality, safety, labor constraint, customer requirement
- Stable standard work upstream and downstream
- OEE or uptime data and downtime categorization
- Maintenance capability and spare parts strategy
- Operator competence and simple troubleshooting routines

Also watch for red flags:

- Frequent manual overrides
- People working around the automation
- Automation creating batching because it's inflexible

- Quality issues moving downstream because the inspection was automated poorly

Example:
A company automates a repetitive inspection step only after stabilizing the upstream process and defining clear defect criteria. Result: fewer escapes and less rework. In contrast, companies that automate too early often end up with "high-tech firefighting," where only a few people can keep the line running.

Questions to ask:

- What problem were you trying to solve when you automated this step?
- What had to be true for this automation to work well? Was it true at the time?
- How often do you bypass it? Why?

Common trap:
Automating variability. If inputs are unstable, automation will magnify the pain. You end up with downtime, scrap, and expensive frustration.

PQPR (Product-Quantity-Process-Routing): Exposing Structural Complexity

What it is and why it matters:
PQPR is a structured way to understand the structural complexity of a manufacturing operation by analyzing four fundamental dimensions:

- **Product:** What you make
- **Quantity:** How much of each product you make
- **Process:** Which processes are required to make each product
- **Routing:** The sequence and path that those processes take through the factory

Most factories struggle not because they lack effort or talent, but because they operate with excessive and poorly understood complexity. PQPR makes that complexity visible. It allows you to separate what is driven by true customer requirements from what has accumulated over time through incremental decisions, special cases, and a lack of standardization.

What it reveals during an assessment:

- Which products dominate volume and revenue (the "vital few")

- Which products create disproportionate disruption (the "troublemakers")
- Where routings diverge and why (true requirements vs. historical habit)
- Opportunities for product family grouping, standardization, and flow design

How to do it (assessment version):

1. Pull a product list with volumes (monthly or annual) and key attributes.
2. Add routings: major process steps and special operations.
3. Sort by volume and cluster by routing similarity.
4. Identify:
   - High-volume families (best candidates for VSM and flow improvements)
   - Low-volume, high-complexity products (often where lead time and schedule pain live)
   - Special cases that might need separate strategies

Example:
You discover that 70 to 80 percent of volume flows through a small number of common routings. That lets you choose a representative family for VSM and avoid mapping the entire factory at once. You also discover a long tail of low-volume products with unique steps that constantly disrupt scheduling. That often becomes a key simplification opportunity: standardize routings, reduce variation, or separate the long tail into a different production strategy (cells, dedicated days, or engineered-to-order lanes).

Questions to ask:

- Which products cause the most schedule disruption and why?
- How many routings do you truly need vs. how many exist historically?
- If we simplified routings by 20 percent, what would that change in planning and lead time?

Common trap:
Assuming complexity is unavoidable. Some is real (customer requirements). Much of it is self-inflicted (options proliferation, lack of product family strategy, inconsistent engineering decisions).

After reviewing these tools, it's worth stepping back and addressing an important question: how do you know whether a company is truly ready for Lean, beyond the presence of tools and terminology?

Recognizing True Lean Maturity: What to Look for Beyond the Tools

As you assess a business, you will quickly notice that Lean maturity cannot be measured by the number of tools in use. Some companies proudly display Lean terminology yet struggle daily with the same problems. Others use little formal Lean language but operate with remarkable clarity and discipline.

Rather than asking, "Which tools are implemented?" I encourage you to ask a more revealing question:

How does the organization behave when things don't go as planned?

Over time, I have found that truly Lean organizations consistently demonstrate the following signals, regardless of industry or size.

1. Standards exist and are actually followed.
Work is performed in a consistent way, and deviations are visible. When performance drops, leaders and teams refer to standards rather than opinions.

2. Abnormalities are visible quickly.
Problems do not hide for days or weeks. Visual controls, metrics, and routines make issues obvious early, when they are still small and manageable.

3. Leaders respond consistently to problems.
When an abnormality appears, leaders react in a predictable way. They ask questions, support problem-solving, and follow up. They do not ignore issues or jump straight to blame.

4. Root causes are addressed, not recycled.
Problems are investigated to prevent recurrence. The same issues do not resurface month after month with different explanations.

5. Improvements become the new normal.
When a better way is found, it is documented, trained, and embedded into standard work. Improvement does not depend on memory or motivation.

6. Teams solve problems across functions.
Problems are owned end-to-end. Quality, production, maintenance, engineering, and supply chain work together rather than protecting silos.

If you observe most of these behaviors, the organization is likely ready to absorb and sustain deeper Lean improvements. If you observe a few of them, your initial focus should not be on advanced tools. It should be on stability, clarity, and leadership routines.

This perspective helps you avoid a common pitfall: launching sophisticated Lean initiatives into an organization that is not yet prepared to sustain them.

III. Preparing for the Assessment and Setting the Stage for Success

A well-prepared assessment is a successful assessment. Rushing in without a solid plan is a recipe for missed opportunities and inaccurate conclusions. Here's a comprehensive checklist for preparing for your assessment to ensure you and the company get the most out of the assessment:

1. Define Clear Objectives:

Before you even set foot on site, define the *specific* objectives of the assessment. What questions are you trying to answer? What are the desired outcomes? Make these objectives measurable whenever possible. For example, instead of "Improve manufacturing efficiency," aim for "Identify opportunities to reduce lead time by 20 percent." Ensure that your objectives are directly aligned with the client's goals and priorities. This will ensure that your assessment is relevant and valuable to them.

2. Gather Preliminary Information (Pre-Data Gathering):

Before the on-site visit, gather as much information as possible from publicly available sources (e.g., industry reports, competitor analysis) and any materials the client provides (e.g., website, brochures, annual reports). This will give you a better understanding of the business and its context. Have preliminary conversations with the client (owners/key personnel) to clarify the scope of the assessment, confirm their priorities, and gather any initial data they can provide (e.g., organizational charts, financial statements, sales figures).

3. Develop an Assessment Plan:

Create a detailed schedule for the on-site visit, including specific times for interviews, gemba walks, and other activities. Share this schedule with the client in advance so they can prepare. Work with the client to identify the key individuals you need to interview. Ensure that these people are available during the assessment period. Plan your gemba walks in advance. Identify the specific areas you want to observe and the key questions you want to ask. Consider having a "waste walk" checklist prepared. Prepare any data-collection tools you will need, such as interview guides, observation checklists, and document review templates.

4. Communicate the Plan:

Communicate the purpose and scope of the assessment to all employees in advance. Explain why the assessment is being conducted and how it will benefit the organization. Address any potential concerns or anxieties about the process. (Work with the owners to craft this message.) Clearly communicate that all information gathered during the assessment will be kept confidential. This will encourage employees to be more open and honest in their feedback.

5. Arrange Logistics and Confirm Resources:

Arrange travel and accommodation if necessary. Confirm the availability of meeting rooms, access to relevant areas, and any other resources you will need on-site (e.g., Wi-Fi, projector, easel pads). Prepare all necessary materials, such as notebooks, pens, a camera (for documentation), and any assessment templates or checklists.

6. Ready the Team (If Applicable):

If you are working with a team of assessors, clearly define the roles and responsibilities of each team member. Ensure that all team members are aligned on the assessment objectives, methodology, and communication plan. Provide any necessary training or guidance.

7. Develop Initial Hypotheses (Based on Pre-Assessment Info):

Based on the preliminary information you have gathered, develop some initial hypotheses about the potential challenges and opportunities. This will help you focus your assessment efforts and ask more targeted questions. (These are *starting points*, not conclusions.)

8. Prepare Your Mindset:

Approach the assessment with an open mind and a spirit of curiosity. Be prepared to listen, observe, and learn. Strive to be objective in your observations and analysis. Avoid making judgments or drawing conclusions prematurely. Keep your focus on identifying opportunities to create more value for the client and their customers.

I strongly recommend a pre-assessment meeting with the owners or top management before the assessment day to request data, agree on the objectives, and set up the agenda and logistics. By thoroughly preparing for the assessment, you will ensure you make the most of your time on site, gather the most relevant information, and be well positioned to provide valuable recommendations to your client. This preparation also demonstrates your professionalism and commitment, building trust and rapport with the client.

IV. Conducting the Assessment: A Systematic Approach to Uncovering Opportunities

Once the groundwork is laid, it's time to conduct the actual assessment. This phase is crucial, as it allows you to gather real-time data, observe processes in action, and engage with employees to uncover inefficiencies.

The extent of the assessment will depend on the time and resources allocated. A one-person, one-day assessment may not include items such as VSM and time studies and would be heavily focused on interviews and data gathering instead. The key is to follow a structured approach while remaining flexible enough to adapt based on findings.

1. Start with Gemba Walks: Observing the Reality

The best way to understand how a process truly operates is to see it firsthand. A **gemba walk** involves going to the actual place where work happens and observing with a critical yet open mind. Key steps in an effective gemba walk include:

- **Follow the Flow**: Walk through the process from start to finish, tracing how work moves from one stage to another.
- **Ask, "Why?" Repeatedly**: Use the **five whys technique** to uncover the root causes of inefficiencies.
- **Engage with Operators**: Employees performing the tasks are your best source of insights. Ask them about bottlenecks, frustrations, and improvement ideas.

2. Conduct Time and Motion Studies: Measuring Productivity

A Lean assessment requires quantifiable data to validate observations. **Time and motion studies** help establish:

- How long tasks take and where delays occur.
- Non-value-added activities, such as waiting, excessive movement, or redundant checks.
- Opportunities to streamline processes for better flow.

3. Gather Data from Multiple Sources

Relying solely on observation is not enough. A well-rounded assessment includes:

- **Operational Metrics**: Cycle times, defect rates, productivity KPIs.
- **Employee Feedback**: Surveys and interviews to capture workforce perspectives.
- **Customer Complaints and Returns**: Indicators of inefficiencies in product or service delivery.
- **Financial Impact Analysis**: Understanding how inefficiencies translate into costs.

4. Identify Waste Using the Eight Wastes Framework

Every organization has waste, but identifying it systematically ensures nothing is overlooked. Assessors should categorize findings into the **eight wastes of Lean**:

- **Defects**: Errors requiring rework or scrap
- **Overproduction**: Producing more than needed
- **Waiting**: Idle time due to slow approvals, handoffs, or system delays

- **Unused Talent**: Employees' skills are underused
- **Transportation**: Unnecessary movement of materials or products
- **Inventory**: Excess stock tying up capital
- **Motion**: Excessive movement by workers
- **Extra Processing**: Redundant steps that add no value

5. Conduct a Value Stream Mapping (VSM) Exercise

A **value stream map** provides a visual representation of how value flows through a process. This tool helps pinpoint:

- Steps that add value vs. those that don't
- Process inefficiencies, such as delays or bottlenecks
- Opportunities for Lean improvements

6. Summarize Findings with a Priority Matrix

Not all identified inefficiencies are equally impactful. Use a **priority matrix** to categorize findings into:

- **Quick Wins:** High impact, low effort
- **Strategic Projects:** High impact, high effort
- **Low-Hanging Fruit:** Low impact, low effort
- **Avoid:** Low impact, high effort

By systematically executing these steps, the assessment will uncover actionable insights that directly contribute to Lean transformation.

V. Reporting: Communicating Insights and Driving Action

1. Structure the Assessment Report for Maximum Clarity

The effectiveness of an assessment depends on how well the findings are communicated. A structured report should include:

- **Executive Summary**: A concise overview of key findings and recommended actions
- **Assessment Methodology**: How data was gathered and analyzed
- **Key Observations**: Summarized insights categorized by Lean principles
- **Waste Analysis**: Detailed breakdown of the eight wastes identified

- **Value Stream Mapping Summary**: Before-and-after process flow visualizations
- **Priority Actions**: Clear recommendations with expected benefits and timelines

2. Use Data Visualization to Highlight Key Points

Charts, graphs, and process maps help leaders quickly grasp complex data. Consider using:

- **Heatmaps** to show problem areas in workflows
- **Pareto Charts** to highlight the most significant inefficiencies
- **Before-and-After VSM Diagrams** to illustrate the impact of recommended changes

3. Present Findings in a Way that Drives Action

A well-structured presentation can ensure leadership buy-in and mobilize teams for change. Best practices include:

- **Focusing on Business Impact**: Link findings to cost savings, customer satisfaction, and operational efficiency.
- **Storytelling with Data**: Combine metrics with real-world examples from the gemba walk.
- **Highlighting Quick Wins**: Show immediate actions that can deliver results within weeks.
- **Assigning Responsibilities**: Clearly define who will lead each improvement initiative.

4. Conduct a Debrief and Alignment Session

After presenting the report, discuss with key stakeholders how to:

- Align on priorities
- Address concerns or resistance
- Gain leadership commitment for the next steps
- Define timelines and accountability measures

5. Develop an Implementation Roadmap

The final output of the assessment should be a **Lean Transformation Roadmap**, detailing:

- **Short-Term Actions** (0–3 months): Quick wins with immediate impact
- **Mid-Term Actions** (3–12 months): Process optimization projects
- **Long-Term Actions** (12+ months): Cultural and systemic changes

This chapter is packed with information, and I know it can feel like a lot to take in. We've touched on many powerful tools and techniques, and you might be thinking, *Where do I even start?* That's perfectly understandable. Each of these tools could easily fill its own manual, and many do!

The goal here isn't to make you an expert in everything, but rather to give you a broad overview of the possibilities. If you're unfamiliar with some of these concepts or if value stream mapping feels a bit daunting, please don't worry. There are countless resources available online and in bookstores to help you deepen your understanding. We're also building a library of helpful materials on our website, www.manufacturingsimplicity.com, specifically designed to support you on your Lean journey. We're in this together.

Reflection and Action

1. As you look back at the points we made in this chapter, what aspects can you extract and apply to assess your business, or at least your area of responsibility?
2. Develop a custom assessment for your business or area of responsibility. Feel free to adapt, add, and delete the few points brought up in this chapter. The assessment must be relevant to your company and support of the overall strategy, direction, and vision.
3. Choose one process in your organization that you think could be improved. Conduct a mini value stream map of that process. Refer back to your answers in Chapter 1; they should serve as your guide for which processes need to be addressed first.
4. Identify three specific examples of waste in that process using the TIMWOOD framework. Be specific!
5. For each example of waste, propose at least one potential solution.

6. What tools or techniques from this chapter could you use to further analyze this process and identify additional opportunities for improvement?
7. What is the potential impact of improving this process? How will it benefit your team, your customers, and your organization?
8. What other Lean tools have you heard of that we did not list in this chapter and you would like to know more about? How will you learn about them?

Chapter 3 Reflection and Action Answers

CHAPTER 4

Building a Lean Culture: *Engaging Your Workforce at The Heart of Your Lean Transformation*

The Rumor

It began the way most damaging things do inside a company. Quietly. Not with a confrontation, not with an announcement, and not with a crisis meeting. Just a sentence spoken in passing, in the hallway, as two people walked out of the break room.

You didn't hear the full sentence. You only caught the last part and the way their voices dropped when they noticed you. One of them stopped mid-thought, and the other looked away too quickly, as if staring at the floor would make them invisible. You kept walking, but you felt it immediately. Something was moving through the building.

That morning, you had already been carrying the weight of the turnaround. A customer had escalated late orders the day before. Finance had sent you an updated forecast that was uglier than anyone wanted to admit. You had a board update coming in two weeks, and you could already hear the questions in your head: *What changed since last month? What is the plan? Why should we believe it will work?*

You were walking from one meeting to the next, trying to keep your pace steady, when you heard the whisper.

You didn't stop. You didn't turn around. You didn't confront anyone. You did something simpler and more deliberate. You made a note in your phone, one sentence, so you wouldn't forget it later.

"Rumor. Break room. People went quiet."

It was a small leadership habit you had learned over time: When something feels off, don't rely on memory. Capture it. Because if you ignore those signals, they don't disappear. They grow.

Later that morning, you met with a supervisor to review performance. You expected the usual. A machine issue. A schedule problem. A material shortage. Instead, he hesitated when you asked what was driving the dip in output. He leaned forward and lowered his voice.

"People are distracted," he said.

"Distracted by what?" you asked.

He paused, as if deciding whether he should say it at all. Then he said, "They think layoffs are coming."

You felt that sharp drop in your stomach. Not because layoffs were coming. They weren't. The business had problems, yes, but you were focused on stabilizing the operation, not shrinking it. You needed people. You needed engagement. You needed everyone pulling in the same direction. The last thing you needed was fear.

You asked him where it came from.

He shrugged. "I don't know. Someone heard something. It's spreading."

That afternoon, you walked the gemba. The operation was running, but it didn't feel the way it had felt a few weeks earlier. People were working, but the energy was different. Less eye contact, less conversation, no casual humor, and no small talk. It wasn't chaos. It was something colder. It was withdrawal.

You stopped at a work cell that had been doing well. Just a few weeks ago, that team had been proud of a change they'd helped implement. They had reduced changeover time dramatically. They had been engaged. They had even asked you when the next improvement workshop would happen.

This afternoon, one operator looked up and asked the question directly.

"Are we getting laid off?"

You paused.

Not because you didn't know how to answer. You did. The answer was simple, but you could tell by his face that he wasn't really asking for information. He was asking whether it was safe to believe anything he'd heard. You didn't answer him from across the aisle.

Instead, you stepped closer, lowered your voice, and asked him to walk with you for a minute. Not because you wanted privacy for yourself, but because you wanted to give him dignity. Because when fear is spreading, people don't just need facts. They need to feel seen.

"No," you said once you were out of earshot. "We're not planning layoffs."

He nodded slowly, but the nod didn't carry relief. It carried uncertainty. He wanted to believe you, but something had already shifted. The rumor had already taken hold, and once it has, it doesn't behave like a normal piece of information. It behaves like a story. It grows. It adapts. It fills gaps. It becomes the explanation for everything people don't understand.

By the next day, the story had evolved. It wasn't "Layoffs might be coming." It was "They're already planning it." By the end of the week, it had become, "They're bringing in consultants to decide who stays." Then, like clockwork, it turned into the most damaging version of all.

"They're doing Lean so they can cut jobs."

That was the moment you realized the rumor wasn't just distracting people. It was poisoning the future. Because, even if you corrected it, even if you addressed it head-on, it would leave residue. People would remember that fear. They would remember how fast it had spread. They would remember how long it had taken leadership to respond. They would remember the silence. And the worst part was that it didn't start because of a bad person. It started because something real happened that no one explained.

A corporate leader visited unexpectedly. A finance manager walked the floor with a notebook. A conference room was booked for a full day. A few managers looked tense. Someone saw a spreadsheet. Someone overheard a sentence out of context. No one knew what it meant, and no one asked openly. They asked each other instead. And when an organization fills gaps with speculation, it rarely fills them with optimism.

Over the next few weeks, performance slipped. Not dramatically at first. Just enough to feel it. The work still got done, but it became heavier. Problems weren't raised as quickly. People stopped volunteering ideas. They stopped experimenting. They stopped sticking their neck out. They did their job, and they protected themselves.

When people are afraid, they don't become lazy; they become cautious. And caution is one of the most expensive emotions in a business.

A few months later, you launched the Lean transformation. You did what every leader does. You prepared the kickoff, explained the purpose, spoke about building a culture of continuous improvement, talked about empowerment, engagement, and making work easier. You asked for participation, and you asked for ideas. And you were met with polite silence.

People listened, nodded, then returned to their stations and waited.

Not because they were against improvement. But because they had already learned something deeper: that leadership messages can change quickly and that the safest move is to keep your head down until you know what is really happening.

Years later, you would still remember that moment. Not the question or the rumor. Not even the performance dip. You would remember the look in that operator's eyes when he asked it. Because it wasn't just fear. It was disappointment.

That's the tragedy of culture. Once trust is damaged, it doesn't stay contained. It spreads into everything. It changes how people interpret your words. It changes how they respond to requests. It changes whether they tell you the truth. It changes whether they believe new programs are real. It changes whether they invest emotionally.

And rebuilding that trust is not quick. It doesn't take a speech or a town hall. It takes consistency, follow-through, and visible behavior, week after week, long after the urgency fades. In some organizations, the recovery takes years. In others, it never fully happens.

That is why culture is not a soft topic. It is not an HR topic. It is not a nice-to-have.

Culture is the system that decides whether your Lean transformation becomes real or another initiative people learn to survive.

I. Introduction
Lean Is a Team Sport: Why Culture Beats Strategy When Things Get Hard

In Chapter 1, we explored how complexity silently undermines organizational success, creating hidden costs, confusion, and inefficiencies. Complexity often arises not just from processes or products but from unclear expectations, disengaged teams, and ineffective communication. Building a Lean culture directly counters this complexity by creating clarity and simplicity. Employees clearly understand their roles, expectations, and contributions to overall success.

A Lean culture thrives on simplicity. It encourages open dialogue, transparency, and continuous learning, reducing organizational noise and friction. Employees who clearly see how their daily activities contribute to larger goals are empowered to identify unnecessary complexity and proactively eliminate it. This simplicity, embedded culturally, doesn't just streamline processes; it enhances morale, innovation, and responsiveness.

Throughout this chapter, we'll explore how developing this kind of culture, one rooted in simplicity and employee engagement, is essential to lasting Lean transformation. We'll discuss practical steps to engage your teams effectively, reinforcing behaviors that continuously simplify processes and create a more responsive, agile organization.

In my work turning around or simply improving businesses, I've witnessed firsthand the power of Lean done right, as well as the devastating consequences of Lean gone wrong. The list of companies that have stumbled while trying to implement Lean is, unfortunately, a long one.

Too often, I see a familiar pattern, like this case I saw in the U.S. Midwest: an executive reads a book, hires a consultant (often inexperienced), and then focuses obsessively on a single tool or technique, usually 5S. They drill it into the workforce for years, even when the technique doesn't align with the company's immediate needs. The employees get fed up with being told to stop everything to clean and organize, and the management team gets frustrated with the ongoing consulting fees without seeing bottom-line impact. Eventually, the whole initiative collapses.

In South America, I encountered another company proudly proclaiming its Lean journey. But when we went to the gemba (the place where the work happens, in this case, the shop floor), it was clear they were far from being Lean. Inventory was piled high, employees seemed to be doing everything but adding value, and despite struggling with unreliable suppliers, machine downtime, and quality issues, they'd chosen to implement kanban with ridiculously high inventory levels at each "supermarket."

The employees I spoke with were understandably frustrated; they were already fighting daily operational fires, and now they had to wrestle with a confusing new kanban card system that was not adding any value. I do realize kanban is a great tool, and I have implemented it many times. My point here is that there is a right timing for each technique to be implemented.

These stories, though from different continents and industries, share common threads. The Lean implementations were tool-focused, not culture-focused. The chosen tools weren't aligned with the company's most pressing needs. Most critically, the workforce wasn't trained, motivated, or engaged. Both companies mentioned, by focusing on the doing rather than the being of Lean, not only failed in their transformations but also gave Lean a bad name, making my subsequent work that much harder.

This introduction is not meant to point fingers; the intention is to highlight that you don't *do* Lean; you *become* Lean. This requires a fundamental shift in mindset and behavior at every level.

Think about the people in your organization who typically identify problems, develop solutions, and drive improvements. Chances are, it's a small group. These "problem solvers" are invaluable, but they often become overwhelmed, working long hours, burning out, and ultimately becoming a bottleneck for change.

Now imagine a different scenario: what if every employee in your company could identify waste? What if they were equipped with Lean tools and knew how to use them? What if they were constantly measuring relevant metrics and taking action when things went wrong? What if they proactively formed teams to make things better and celebrated their successes? What kind of results would you see?

That's the power of a true Lean culture. It's contagious, rewarding, and achievable. This chapter will explore how to build that culture, the very heart of any successful Lean transformation.

II. Leadership's Role in Cultural Transformation

The Shift from Traditional Manager to Lean Leader: From Stagnation to Engagement

The success or failure of a Lean transformation is ultimately determined by leadership behavior. Not strategy, not tools, not the quality of the consultants, but leadership behavior repeated every day, especially when things are difficult.

Most organizational stagnation is not caused by bad intentions or poor character. It is perpetuated, often unintentionally, by a traditional management mindset that views leadership as an administrative function. In this model, leaders spend most of their time behind a closed door, managing through emails, dashboards, and reports. Decisions are made far from the work itself. Problems are discovered late, filtered through layers of explanation, and often addressed only after they have grown large enough to demand attention.

This way of leading is understandable. Many managers were promoted because they were strong individual contributors. Others learned to protect themselves by staying close to data and far from conflict. Over time, this creates a leadership style that feels busy and responsible yet disconnected from reality.

The cost of this distance is high. Bottlenecks form because decisions take too long. Innovation slows because ideas must travel uphill before they are heard. Teams learn that leadership engagement is episodic, often triggered by crises rather than by curiosity. The message, though rarely spoken, becomes clear: *Solve problems quietly; don't bother leadership unless it's urgent.*

Why Most Traditional Managers Behave the Way They Do

It's important to pause here and clarify something.

Most traditional managers do not lead the way they do because they are disengaged, lazy, or resistant to change. In my experience, the opposite is usually true. Many are deeply committed, work long hours, and genuinely want their teams to succeed.

So, why does traditional management persist?

In many organizations, managers are promoted because they are technically strong. They are the best engineers, the most experienced operators, or the most reliable problem solvers. When something goes wrong, they are the ones who step in and fix it. Over time, this problem-solving ability becomes their identity.

Then their role changes.

As managers, they are suddenly responsible for many processes, people, and decisions at once. Meetings multiply. Emails never stop. Performance reviews, forecasts, escalations, and compliance demands fill the day. Being busy becomes a proxy for being effective.

In this environment, distance from the shop floor is rarely intentional. It is a survival mechanism.

Many managers also carry a sincere belief that staying close to the work means micromanaging. They worry that frequent presence will be interpreted as a lack of trust. So, they stay in their offices, relying on reports and second-hand information, believing that giving teams space is a form of respect.

Others have learned, often through painful experience, that visibility comes with risk. When leaders react emotionally to bad news, people adapt by hiding problems. Over time, managers receive filtered information rather than reality. Decisions are made later than they should be, based on incomplete data, reinforcing a reactive cycle.

None of this makes managers bad people. But it does create a system where leadership unintentionally reinforces distance, firefighting, and stagnation.

Lean leadership challenges this pattern, not by demanding more effort but by redefining what effective leadership actually looks like.

A Lean leader represents a fundamental shift away from this model.

This shift is not about working harder or being everywhere at once. It is a shift from being a spectator of the operation to becoming the team's most committed coach and champion. It moves leadership from control to coaching, from isolated analysis to direct observation, and from mandating change to creating the conditions where improvement is inevitable.

Where the traditional manager asks for updates, the Lean leader goes to see.
Where the traditional manager solves problems personally, the Lean leader develops others to solve them.
Where the traditional manager reacts to fires, the Lean leader works systematically to prevent them.

This difference in behavior is not subtle. It is felt immediately by the organization.

The Two Leadership Archetypes

Over the years, I've found it helpful to describe this contrast using two archetypes. Most leaders will recognize elements of themselves in both. The goal is not to label but to reflect.

Traditional Manager (Stagnation): The traditional manager focuses primarily on maintaining the status quo and reacting to problems as they arise. Firefighting becomes normal. Most time is spent in the office, relying on reports, meetings, and email to understand what is happening. Communication flows largely in one direction, through instructions and requests for explanations.

Employees are viewed as people who execute tasks, and when problems occur, accountability is often pushed downward. Feedback feels threatening, conflict is avoided, and improvement initiatives are treated as additional work layered onto an already full agenda.

Lean Leader (Engagement): The Lean leader is focused on continuous improvement and proactive problem-solving. Rather than waiting for problems to escalate, they spend significant time at the gemba, observing work as it actually happens. Communication is two-way and frequent, centered on listening, coaching, and asking thoughtful questions.

Employees are seen as the collective genius of the organization and therefore the primary source of solutions. Feedback is welcomed, the status quo is challenged, and motivation is built by helping people succeed in their daily work.

These two archetypes create very different cultures, even when operating under the same strategy and using the same tools.

The Personal and Professional Rewards of Lean Leadership

Making the transition from traditional manager to Lean leader is not only a strategic imperative for the business. It is often deeply rewarding for the leader as well.

If you are a manager who genuinely wants to drive change, I invite you to pause for a moment and imagine a different work life. Imagine fewer surprises late in the day. Imagine problems surfacing early, when they are still manageable. Imagine teams that come to you with solutions instead of excuses. Imagine spending less time reacting and more time building capability.

If you are a change agent, your role is slightly different but just as important. Learn these leadership behaviors deeply. Model them yourself. Use them as a lens to coach, challenge, and support the leaders in your organization. Cultural transformation does not start with authority. It starts with example.

The transition to Lean leadership is not always comfortable. It requires visibility. It requires patience. It requires consistency, even when results are not immediate. But for those who make the shift, leadership becomes less about survival and more about purpose.

And that is where real transformation begins.

Why the Shift Feels Hard at First and Then Becomes Addictive

For many leaders, the idea of becoming more visible, present, and engaged can initially feel overwhelming. The calendar is already full. The inbox never stops. The pressure to deliver results is constant. Adding "Lean leadership" can sound like adding one more responsibility to an already unsustainable workload.

What most leaders don't realize is that the transition to Lean leadership often has the opposite effect.

In the short term, it changes how leadership feels.
In the long term, it changes what leadership makes possible.

Short-Term Benefits: The Momentum Boost

One of the first changes leaders notice is a renewed sense of purpose and energy.

Traditional management roles often drift toward abstraction. Days are spent reviewing reports, attending meetings about meetings, and reacting to issues long after they have already caused damage. Over time, this creates a sense of detachment. Leaders begin to feel like administrative gatekeepers rather than drivers of progress.

Lean leadership reverses that dynamic quickly.

By spending time at the gemba and engaging directly with real problems, leaders reconnect with the reason they stepped into leadership in the first place: making things better. Problems are no longer theoretical. Improvements are no longer delayed. You can see the impact of your actions in real time. That visibility creates momentum, and momentum is energizing.

Many leaders are surprised by how quickly burnout begins to fade when their work produces immediate, visible value.

Another early benefit is rapid skill acquisition.

Instead of learning Lean concepts in isolation or through formal training alone, leaders develop competence by applying ideas immediately to real situations. Coaching replaces commanding. Questions replace directives. Structured problem-solving replaces emotional reactions. Over time, leaders become more confident, not because they have all the answers, but because they know how to guide others toward them.

This shift also improves skills that many leaders were never formally taught: coaching, conflict resolution, and constructive confrontation. These are not abstract competencies. They are practiced daily, in short interactions on the floor, where the stakes are real and the learning is fast.

And then there are the wins.

When leaders empower teams and remove obstacles instead of absorbing every problem themselves, progress accelerates. A longstanding issue gets resolved. A process becomes simpler. A metric moves in the right direction. An employee steps up and solves a problem that had been ignored for months.

These moments matter.

They create immediate, positive reinforcement. They remind leaders that change is possible. Just as importantly, teams notice the difference. When leaders show up consistently, listen genuinely, and follow through, appreciation is not abstract. It is expressed directly, often in simple, human ways. That appreciation fuels commitment on both sides.

Long-Term Benefits: The Growth Trajectory

While the short-term benefits restore energy, the long-term benefits reshape a leader's trajectory.

As leaders spend more time understanding how work actually flows through the organization, their perspective changes. Daily decisions begin to connect naturally to broader objectives. Trade-offs become clearer. The relationship between strategy and execution stops being theoretical.

This is where Lean leadership becomes a catalyst for exponential personal growth.

Leaders develop a systems-level understanding of the business. They learn to see patterns instead of isolated events. They become more effective at aligning teams around a shared direction, which is the practical foundation of policy deployment, even if the formal terminology comes later.

Over time, something more profound happens.

The leader stops being the bottleneck.

Instead of being the person everyone waits for, the leader becomes the person who develops others to act. Capability spreads. Decisions move closer to the work. The organization becomes more resilient because it no longer depends on one person's heroics.

This shift creates space.

Leaders who once spent their days fighting fires find time to think, plan, and lead. The work becomes less reactive and more intentional. That is not only good for the organization; it is deeply satisfying on a personal level.

Finally, there is the professional impact.

Leaders who successfully drive cultural and operational transformation stand out, not because they talk about Lean, but because they deliver results that last. Reduced costs, improved quality, higher engagement, and lower turnover are not abstract achievements. They are measurable outcomes that follow leaders wherever they go.

Over time, these leaders are recognized not just as competent managers but as builders of capability and agents of sustainable change. That reputation opens doors. More importantly, it creates confidence that no matter the context, they know how to lead transformation the right way.

Turning Managers into Champions: Why Buy-In Is Passive and Ownership Changes Everything

Every Lean transformation ultimately rises or falls with management.

You will hear a lot about "buy-in." Buy-in is necessary, but it is not sufficient. A manager who buys in may agree in principle, attend meetings, and avoid openly resisting the change. But buy-in is passive. It does not move an organization forward when pressure mounts.

What you need are champions.

Champions are leaders who do not simply understand Lean but *own it*. They talk about it when you are not in the room. They defend it when results dip. They model it when no one is watching. They stop waiting for permission and start shaping the environment so improvement can happen.

The difference between buy-in and ownership is the difference between spectators in the stands and coaches on the field. And just like in sports, the team takes its cues from the coaches.

If you want Lean to take root, management must move first.

This does not happen through persuasion alone. It happens through relevance, experience, and success.

Connecting Lean to What Truly Matters

The fastest way to lose a manager is to speak about Lean in abstract terms.

Most managers are already overwhelmed. They are measured relentlessly. They live under the weight of KPIs, targets, budgets, and commitments. When Lean is presented as "another initiative," their instinct is to protect themselves and their teams from overload.

This is why your first responsibility is not to teach Lean. It is to understand their world.

Before you ever ask a manager to support a Lean effort, take the time to answer a few basic questions. What are they accountable for? What numbers define success or failure for them? What problems consume their time and drain their energy? What keeps them awake at night?

When you approach Lean from this angle, the conversation changes.

Instead of sounding like someone adding work, you sound like a partner offering relief.

This is also where policy deployment naturally enters the picture. Lean is no longer a philosophy. It becomes a mechanism for achieving what the organization already says is important. Strategic objectives stop living in slide decks and start translating into daily actions.

And when you talk about benefits, be concrete.

Managers do not respond to vague promises. They respond to clarity. If Lean can reduce lead time, say by how much. If it can improve on-time delivery, connect it to customer retention. If it can free up capacity, translate that into cost, revenue, or sanity.

Whenever possible, let managers take the credit. Allow them to be the heroes of the story. Ownership grows fastest when success is personal.

One simple habit helps keep this grounded: always ask, "So, what?"

- So, what does this improvement change for your team?
- So, what does it free up?
- So, what becomes easier tomorrow?

When managers can visualize a better future that solves *their* problems, curiosity replaces resistance.

Planting the Seed: Sparking Curiosity Before Commitment

Few managers become champions because they were convinced in a meeting. Most become champions because they became curious.

Stories are powerful here.

Sharing examples of other organizations that have succeeded with Lean, especially in similar industries, helps managers lower their guard. Focus less on tools and more on outcomes. What changed? What pain went away? What became possible that wasn't before?

Just as important, connect Lean to their personal journey.

Managers are people. They want to feel competent, respected, and successful. Many quietly hope to grow, to be recognized, to leave something better behind than they inherited. Lean can be positioned not just as a business system but as a leadership accelerator.

At the same time, resist the temptation to overwhelm.

Introduce Lean in small, digestible pieces. Short articles. Brief videos. Focused discussions. Think of these as "Lean bites." The goal is not mastery. It is familiarity and interest.

It is also essential that management stay slightly ahead of the organization in Lean understanding. Not as experts but as informed guides. When managers feel confident enough to ask questions, challenge ideas, and support experiments, they naturally step into a coaching role.

And then there is the case for change.

Whether the company is struggling or performing well, complacency is always a risk. If the business is under pressure, Lean becomes a path out of pain. If the business is successful, Lean becomes a way to stay ahead and avoid decline.

The message changes, but the urgency remains.

From Understanding to Action

Understanding Lean intellectually is not enough. Managers become champions when they *experience* it.

This is why well-designed workshops are so effective.

Rather than lecturing, create environments where managers can see and feel the impact of Lean principles. Simple simulations using paper, blocks, or basic materials can demonstrate flow, imbalance, and variability far more effectively than slides ever could. These moments are often eye-opening. They replace skepticism with insight.

Gemba walks are equally powerful when done with intent.

Do not send managers to "observe." Give them a purpose. Teach them what to look for. Introduce the concept of waste and provide a simple template to guide their observations. Ask them what they see, what surprises them, and what feels unnecessary.

Then close the loop.

Back in the room, discuss what they observed. Ask how the operation would feel if those wastes disappeared. Help them connect what they saw to the metrics they care about. This reflection turns observation into ownership.

Pilot Projects: Where Belief Becomes Commitment

Champions are not created in conference rooms. They are created through results.

This is why pilot projects matter so much.

Choose pilots carefully. Do not try to transform everything at once. Select an area aligned with management priorities, where pain is real and improvement is visible. Define the scope clearly. Set a small number of measurable targets.

Then execute with discipline.

When the pilot delivers results, celebrate them publicly. Share the story. Highlight what changed and why it mattered. Make sure management is visible in the success, not as sponsors but as engaged leaders.

This is the moment where belief turns into conviction.

Once managers experience firsthand that Lean works, not in theory but in their own operation, they stop being asked to support it. They start demanding it.

That is when champions are born.

The Pilot as a Learning Engine, Not a Test of Perfection

Too many organizations treat pilots as evaluations. The pressure is high, the expectations are unrealistic, and failure is quietly punished. When that happens, pilots become performative. People do what they think leadership wants to see, not what actually needs to be learned.

A Lean pilot should be the opposite.

A well-designed pilot is a **safe place to learn**.

From the very beginning, it must be made clear that the goal is not perfection or immediate success. The goal is learning. Learning what works. Learning what doesn't. Learning how the organization responds when things are tried, adjusted, and tried again.

This framing alone changes everything.

When people know they are allowed to experiment, pressure drops. Fear recedes. Creativity increases. Work becomes lighter, even when the problems are serious. Teams stop worrying about getting it "right" and start focusing on making it better.

The way you select the pilot area matters. Choose a place where pain is visible but where leadership is open. Choose a team that is representative of the organization, not an elite group of high performers. The pilot should feel relatable, not exceptional. That way, success feels transferable.

Equally important is how you build the pilot team.

The most effective pilots bring together a small, cross-functional group: operators, supervisors, engineers, maintenance, quality, planning. Not everyone full-time, but everyone engaged. This creates shared ownership and accelerates learning. Problems are solved faster because the people who understand them are in the room.

As the pilot progresses, something subtle but powerful happens.

Early improvements begin to show. A process flows better. Fewer surprises appear. Metrics start to move in the right direction. At first, people are cautious. They assume it's temporary. Then, slowly, the realization sets in: *This is actually working.*

That moment is the cultural inflection point.

The team no longer needs convincing. Pride replaces skepticism. Confidence replaces hesitation. What started as an experiment becomes a reference point.

At that stage, the pilot naturally evolves into something more.

It becomes a **training ground**.

Other leaders visit. Engineers observe. Operators from other areas ask questions. The pilot team begins to teach, often without realizing it. They explain why decisions were made, what failed, and what they would do differently next time. Learning spreads horizontally, not through mandates but through curiosity.

The pilot is then refined, documented, and stabilized. Not frozen but clarified. What worked becomes standard. What didn't is openly acknowledged. This transparency builds trust.

From there, replication becomes possible.

Not as a copy-paste exercise, but as an informed adaptation. Each new area takes the principles, the lessons, and the confidence gained from the pilot and applies them to its own reality.

In this way, the pilot stops being a project and becomes a catalyst.

From Chaos to Calm

Early in my career, I was asked to take responsibility for a struggling production department at a tier 1 automotive manufacturer in the Southern U.S. The team was rapidly falling behind on key performance metrics. Demand was climbing fast, but the operation wasn't keeping up. Long changeover times, frequent equipment breakdowns, and a young, inexperienced workforce had created a perfect storm.

Overtime had become normal. Weekends were no longer exceptional. Morale was sliding, quality was inconsistent, and frustration was building across the team. People were working hard, but the system was working against them.

It didn't take long to see where the pain was coming from.

Equipment downtime was killing output, and changeovers were so long that the line spent more time waiting than producing. If we were going to make progress, we had to stabilize the equipment and regain flexibility. That meant TPM to address reliability and SMED to attack changeovers.

When I met with the team, I didn't lead with Lean terminology. I led with their reality.

I explained that if we could reduce downtime, weekends could disappear. That single sentence changed the tone of the room. There was skepticism, of course. People had heard promises before. But there was also just enough hope to try.

We chose the worst-performing line, known simply as "Line B," as our pilot.

That decision raised eyebrows immediately.

Other lines joked about it. Shutting down production for cleaning and inspection felt reckless to many. Even some senior leaders questioned whether we had lost our minds. Stopping a struggling line to clean machines didn't look like progress. It looked like failure.

But we stayed the course.

The TPM kickoff was not glamorous. We cleaned. We inspected. We fixed things that had been ignored for years. We learned the equipment together, with operators, maintenance, and supervisors side by side. For many on the team, it was the first time anyone had asked them what they thought was wrong with the machines.

Once the line was restarted, the difference was immediate.

We began tracking output hourly. Every miss was visible. And when a miss occurred, the TPM team didn't wait for blame or escalation. They jumped in. Causes were addressed quickly. Small adjustments were made. Stability began to return.

Within weeks, something important happened.

Weekend work stopped.

That was the moment when skepticism turned into belief.

As equipment reliability improved, another constraint became impossible to ignore: changeovers. What used to take three days, yes, days, became the next target. Using SMED principles, we broke the process down, challenged assumptions, and shifted work offline. Changeovers dropped from days to hours, then to minutes, and eventually reached a point where they occurred within the production cycle time of six seconds, with no lost output.

Along the way, 5S emerged naturally.

Tools needed to be where people expected them. Searching became waste. Organization became a necessity, not a directive. We didn't "roll out 5S." The team pulled it in because it made their work easier.

That sequence mattered.

We didn't start with 5S. We started with pain. TPM addressed downtime. SMED addressed flexibility. 5S supported sustainment. The right tools were pulled in at the right time.

Within a few months, Line B had gone from being the worst performer to the benchmark. Work was easier. Knowledge exploded. Pride returned. The line didn't just perform better. It felt different.

And then something even more interesting happened.

Other lines started asking when it would be their turn.

They didn't ask because they were told to. They asked because they saw what was possible. They wanted the same relief, the same stability, the same ownership.

Lean hadn't been mandated. It had been invited.

That is the kind of momentum you want to build in your organization.

Culture didn't change because we talked about Lean. It changed because people experienced a better way of working.

Sustaining the Transformation: From Champions to Coaches

Early success in a Lean transformation is exhilarating. Metrics move. Problems shrink. Energy returns. Leaders who were once skeptical become enthusiastic champions. It feels like the hardest part is behind you.

It isn't.

In reality, this is the moment where most transformations quietly stall.

The reason is simple: early success is often driven by attention. Leaders show up. Teams feel supported. Barriers are removed quickly. But as results stabilize, attention drifts. Meetings fill the calendar again. Old priorities resurface. Without realizing it, leaders begin to step back just as the organization needs them most.

Sustaining a Lean transformation requires a deliberate shift in leadership behavior. Champions must become coaches.

The Subtle Shift from Driving Change to Developing Capability

In the early stages, leaders often drive improvement directly. They attend events, remove obstacles, and push momentum forward. This is necessary at first. But if it continues too long, leaders become the engine instead of the enabler.

Sustainment begins when leaders focus less on *doing* Lean and more on *developing others* to lead it.

This requires ongoing training and coaching, not as a one-time investment but as a continuous process. Leaders must be equipped not only with Lean concepts but with the leadership skills required to support them: asking better questions, coaching problem-solving, managing conflict constructively, and resisting the urge to jump in with solutions.

This is why management must always remain a few steps ahead of the rest of the organization.

When leaders understand what is coming next, when they have practiced the upcoming techniques, and when they feel confident rather than exposed, they are far more willing to lead from the front. Uncertainty breeds hesitation. Confidence breeds ownership.

As a change agent, this is one of your most important responsibilities. You are not just teaching tools. You are building leadership confidence.

Communication as Reinforcement, Not Noise

As transformations mature, communication often degrades into reporting. Updates are sent. Slides are presented. Numbers are reviewed. The narrative is lost.

Effective communication during a Lean transformation is more about intention than volume.

Leaders need regular, structured communication that reinforces why the transformation matters, what progress looks like, and where learning is happening. Success stories should be shared not as self-congratulation but as proof that improvement is possible. Challenges should be discussed openly, without defensiveness, as part of the learning journey.

This is where a thoughtful communication plan becomes invaluable.

Not a generic plan but one that evolves with the transformation. Early on, communication builds the case for change. As pilots mature, it reinforces learning and momentum. Later, it aligns the organization around what comes next. Cadence, audience, message, and ownership all matter.

When communication is consistent and honest, trust deepens. When it becomes sporadic or sanitized, skepticism returns.

Empowerment Is Earned Through Capability

Empowerment is often misunderstood.

Delegating responsibility too early feels like abandonment. Delegating too late creates dependency. The balance is delicate.

As managers grow more comfortable with Lean, responsibility must be transferred intentionally. Leaders who once relied on direction should be trusted to drive improvement themselves. This reinforces ownership and signals that Lean is not a program being managed but a way of leading.

This transition does not happen automatically. It requires patience, coaching, and reinforcement. Cultural change does not follow a project plan. It follows human learning curves.

The Human Side of Sustainment

Sustaining culture is a relational exercise.

Strong relationships with key leaders are not a nice-to-have. They are essential. When pressure mounts, people fall back on trust. If trust is weak, support evaporates.

Different leaders learn differently. Some need data, while others need stories. Some thrive in workshops. Others learn best by doing. Tailoring your approach is not favoritism. It is respect.

And throughout all of this, leadership behavior matters more than messaging.

When leaders say the right things but behave differently, credibility collapses. When leaders consistently show up, ask thoughtful questions, and follow through, culture solidifies. People do not need speeches. They need examples.

Shared Vision, Psychological Safety, and Servant Leadership

At its core, Lean requires a shared vision of a better way of working.

This vision must be compelling, concrete, and personal. People need to see how Lean benefits the organization, but they also need to understand how it benefits them: fewer surprises, less firefighting, more pride in their work.

For that vision to take hold, psychological safety is non-negotiable.

People must feel safe to speak up, to challenge the status quo, and to admit problems without fear of blame or reprisal. Without safety, improvement becomes theater. With safety, learning accelerates.

This is where servant leadership becomes more than a concept.

Servant leaders do not remove accountability. They remove obstacles. They prioritize the needs of the team and create conditions where others can succeed. In a Lean environment, this alignment is natural. Leaders serve the system so the system can serve the customer.

Transparency reinforces all of this.

Open communication, honest discussion of problems, and visibility into decisions build trust. Trust is the currency of sustainment.

Protecting the Transformation

Even with the right intent and structure, Lean transformations are not smooth sailing.

There will be moments when expertise is missing, progress stalls, or internal capability is not yet sufficient. Seeking external guidance during these phases is not weakness. It is prudence. The goal is not independence at all costs but capability over time.

There will also be resistance.

Some resistance is natural and temporary. It deserves patience and coaching. But there are cases where resistance becomes active sabotage. Allowing a few people to undermine progress is not fair to the rest of the organization. It sends a message that commitment is optional and effort is negotiable.

When resistance persists despite support and clarity, it must be addressed decisively. Difficult decisions are sometimes necessary to protect the integrity of the transformation. Avoiding them does more damage than making them.

Culture is shaped by what leaders tolerate.

Resistance to Change

Why It's Normal, Predictable, and Often a Sign You're on the Right Path

At some point in every Lean transformation, momentum slows.

The early excitement fades. The pilot is working. Results are visible. Leaders are engaged. And yet, resistance begins to surface. Sometimes quietly. Sometimes openly. Sometimes in ways that feel confusing or even personal.

This is the moment where many transformations lose their footing.

Not because resistance appears, but because leaders misinterpret what it means.

Resistance to change is often treated as a problem to eliminate. In reality, it is a **signal to understand**. When approached correctly, resistance becomes one of the most valuable sources of information in the transformation.

When approached poorly, it becomes a wedge that divides teams and undermines trust.

Why Resistance Is Not a Character Flaw

One of the most damaging assumptions leaders make is that resistance is caused by laziness, negativity, or unwillingness to improve. In my experience, that assumption is almost always wrong.

Most resistance has rational roots.

People resist Lean because change threatens something important to them, even if they can't always articulate what that something is. Sometimes, it's status. Sometimes, it's competence. Sometimes, it's predictability. Sometimes, it's safety.

Consider the experienced operator who has mastered a process over twenty years. Lean arrives, and suddenly, their deep knowledge is questioned. Standard work replaces personal judgment. Visual boards make performance visible. What feels like "improvement" to leadership can feel like exposure to the operator.

Or consider the supervisor who has survived for years by firefighting. Their value has been measured by how quickly they respond to problems. Lean begins to remove the fires. Their role feels unclear. Their identity feels threatened.

In these moments, resistance is not rebellion. It is self-preservation.

Understanding this changes everything.

Resistance as a Natural Phase of Learning

Lean transformations force people through a learning curve they didn't ask for.

At first, there is curiosity. Then comes discomfort. Old habits stop working, but new ones aren't fully formed yet. This is the most dangerous phase. People feel clumsy. Insecure. Slower than before.

This is often when resistance shows up.

People question the need for change. They point out flaws. They compare the present discomfort to a past that now seems better than it actually was. This is not sabotage. It is a predictable human response to uncertainty.

Organizations that expect resistance and plan for it move through this phase more swiftly. Organizations that react emotionally get stuck in it.

The Hidden Cost of Ignoring or Crushing Resistance

When resistance appears, leaders often respond in one of two unproductive ways.

Some ignore it.

They hope it will fade. They focus on the willing and bypass the skeptics. Over time, resistance doesn't disappear. It goes underground. People comply publicly and disengage privately. Improvement becomes fragile.

Others confront resistance aggressively.

They label people as blockers. They escalate quickly. They apply pressure without understanding. This may produce short-term compliance, but it damages trust. People learn that honesty is risky. Silence becomes safer than contribution.

Both responses weaken the very culture Lean requires.

What Resistance Is Really Telling You

Resistance always carries information.

It may be telling you:

- The purpose of the change is unclear.
- The pace is too fast.
- The skills gap is too large.
- The workload feels unfair.
- Trust has not yet been earned.

Lean leaders learn to listen for these signals without becoming defensive.

This does not mean accommodating every objection. It means understanding what sits underneath it. When leaders treat resistance as feedback instead of opposition, conversations shift from confrontation to collaboration.

This mindset becomes critical as you move into the next phases of the transformation.

Because unleashing the collective genius of the organization requires people to speak honestly.
Creating engagement requires people to feel safe.
Tapping into ideas requires people to believe their input matters.
Cross-functional collaboration requires trust across boundaries.

None of those are possible if resistance is treated as a threat.

When Resistance Is a Sign of Progress

One of the paradoxes of Lean is this:

Resistance often increases when change is working.

As long as Lean is theoretical, it's easy to agree with. When it starts to affect daily routines, expose problems, and challenge old assumptions, emotions rise. That's when the real work begins.

If no one is uncomfortable, you are probably not changing anything meaningful.

The goal is not to eliminate resistance. The goal is to **move through it deliberately**, without losing momentum or dignity.

Setting the Stage for What Comes Next

Understanding resistance at this level prepares leaders for the work ahead.

- You cannot unleash the collective genius of your workforce if people feel unheard.
- You cannot build engagement if fear dominates.
- You cannot harness ideas if speaking up feels risky.
- You cannot form effective cross-functional teams if blame still exists.

Resistance is the doorway you must pass through to reach those outcomes.

In the sections that follow, we will focus on how to channel energy productively: equipping people, creating engagement, building trust, and turning resistance into participation.

Later, we will return to resistance again, this time with a practical leader's guide for addressing it decisively when necessary. But first, we need to build the conditions in which resistance naturally softens.

Because the most powerful way to overcome resistance is not to fight it.

It is to make it unnecessary.

III. Unleashing the Collective Genius

A Lean transformation cannot be driven by mandates alone. At best, mandates create compliance. At worst, they create quiet resistance. Sustainable improvement requires something very different: a groundswell of engagement.

Every organization already contains an enormous amount of intelligence, creativity, and practical insight. The challenge is not the absence of ideas but the absence of conditions where those ideas can surface and be acted upon. The people closest to the work see the problems first. They live with the inefficiencies. They adapt every day. When given the opportunity, they are also the most capable problem solvers in the organization.

Unleashing this collective genius is more than motivation posters or suggestion boxes alone. You must **shift people from observers to owners**.

From Observers to Owners

One of the most common mistakes in Lean transformations is waiting too long to involve employees. Leaders design plans, select tools, and define roadmaps, then present the result to the workforce. Even when the plan is solid, the message is clear: *This was decided without you.*

Engagement works very differently.

When employees are involved early, even before plans feel complete, something powerful happens. People stop evaluating the change and start contributing to it. They move from asking, "What is this program?" to asking, "How can we make this work?"

This is where communication matters deeply. A clear case for change, shared openly and repeatedly, gives people context. It explains *why* the organization is changing and *why now*. When people understand the reason for the journey, participation becomes voluntary rather than coerced.

Gemba walks are one of the most effective tools for making this shift real.

When leaders go to the floor and ask sincere, open-ended questions, something changes in the dynamic:

- "What frustrates you most during your day?"
- "Where do you lose the most time?"
- "If this were your business, what would you fix first?"

These questions signal respect. They say *your experience matters*.

That said, visibility must be intentional. In organizations where leaders rarely walk the floor together, a sudden group gemba walk can create anxiety or rumors if it's not communicated properly. A simple explanation beforehand, why we're here, what we're looking for, and what will happen next, prevents misunderstandings and builds trust.

True ownership begins when employees are not only encouraged to identify problems but are supported in solving them.

One question I often ask is simple:
"What would you do if this business were yours?"

That question shifts thinking immediately. People stop limiting themselves to their job description and start seeing the system as a whole. They start to weigh factors that go beyond their department or area of expertise. As a leader, your role then becomes one of coaching, not rescuing.

Over the years, I've learned the importance of setting boundaries clearly and kindly. When someone says, "They should do something about this," I pause and ask, "Who is 'they'?" After the silence that usually follows, I explain that there is no "they." *We* are "they."

Then I ask another question:
"Do you know how to fix this? And what would you need to do it?"

Most of the time, the answer is yes. And more often than not, when I return later, the problem has been solved by the very person who raised it. Public praise follows. That combination, clear responsibility followed by positive reinforcement, is one of the most powerful culture-shaping mechanisms I know.

Ownership grows when people are trusted to act.

This also means encouraging experimentation. Within clear safety and boundary conditions, employees should be encouraged to try ideas, test changes, and learn. Failure, when treated as learning, becomes fuel rather than fear.

Equipping the Lean Army

Empowerment without capability creates frustration. Capability without empowerment creates waste. The two must grow together.

Before launching training, it's important to understand what people actually need to learn. Skill levels vary. Learning styles vary. Some employees may already be familiar with continuous improvement concepts. Others may be encountering them for the first time.

Even those with prior experience should be included in training. Shared language and a common approach matter more than individual expertise. Just knowing the Lean tools is not enough. They have to be employed the same way, for the same purpose, across the organization.

Training works best when it is phased and problem-driven.

Foundational concepts such as waste, flow, and value provide a common base. More advanced tools should be introduced when they help solve real problems, not because they appear on a roadmap. Tools must serve strategy and business needs, not the other way around.

Hands-on learning is essential.

The most effective training does not stay in the classroom. Teaching a concept and then immediately applying it in the gemba anchors learning in reality. People leave not only with knowledge but with results and pride.

Over time, developing internal trainers becomes a force multiplier.

Most organizations rely on a handful of experts to drive improvement. Imagine instead an organization where hundreds of people have the skills and confidence to improve their own work. This is how autonomy is built. This is how Lean scales.

It's important to remember that this does not happen all at once.

You do not need to train everyone immediately or build a Lean university overnight. Start where you are. If you begin with a pilot, your training scope is the pilot. As the transformation expands, you will naturally identify people who show curiosity, aptitude, and passion. Invest in them. Over time, you can reshuffle roles, free up capacity, and build a network of internal change agents.

Communication Planning

The purpose of communication is to **create shared understanding**.

Clear channels matter. So does consistency. But most importantly, communication must be two-way; otherwise, you are just informing. If people cannot ask questions, raise concerns, and be heard, communication becomes noise.

Transparency builds trust. Share progress honestly, celebrate wins, acknowledge setbacks, and tell stories more than statistics. Humor helps. Real moments resonate. People remember what made them feel something.

Visual communication is especially powerful. Before-and-after pictures anchor reality, and they remind people how far they've come when memory fades. I've lost count of how many times skepticism disappeared the moment someone saw what "normal" used to look like.

How to Keep the Transformation Alive

If a Lean transformation fails, it is rarely because the tools are ineffective. More often, it fails because leadership stops reinforcing the purpose, direction, and discipline behind the effort.

At the beginning, communication is easy. There is energy and urgency. Leaders are visible, the teams are curious, and people feel the shift. Even skeptics pay attention because something is happening. Then real life shows up.

A customer crisis hits, a popular manager quits, a production schedule slips, a product complaint escalates, someone has to work overtime, a corporate project lands on your desk, a new ERP requirement appears out of nowhere, and slowly, the Lean transformation stops being "the work" and becomes "something extra." At this point, communication becomes the difference between momentum and fade.

Because, in every organization, there is a silent battle happening every day:

- Between the urgent and the important
- Between truth and comfort
- Between leadership intent and daily reality
- Between discipline and drift

If you don't actively manage the conversation, the conversation will manage you, and the default conversation inside most struggling organizations is not improvement. It is survival. That is why communication planning is a leadership system. It keeps people aligned, engaged, and emotionally invested long enough for the culture to change.

What a Communication Plan Really Is

Your monthly newsletter is not your communication plan. Those posters and slogans alone are not your communication plan, either. And it is definitely not leadership talking at employees while calling it "transparency." A real communication plan is a deliberate system for creating shared understanding, week after week, especially when the business is under pressure.

It answers five questions clearly:

1. What are we trying to accomplish?
2. Why does it matter right now?
3. What is changing, and what is not changing?
4. What do we expect from leaders, managers, and employees?
5. How will we know if we are winning?

If those questions are not answered consistently, people fill the gaps themselves, and when people fill gaps, they rarely assume the best. They assume layoffs, blame, politics. They assume the initiative will fade or that leadership is not being honest. They assume the company is in trouble.

That is not because people are negative, but because humans hate uncertainty.

A strong communication plan reduces uncertainty, and uncertainty is one of the biggest drivers of resistance.

Why Communication Is a Culture Tool

Culture is built by what employees hear repeatedly. This means that one all-employee town hall meeting is not enough. Culture is what gets reinforced and what survives pressure.

Every Lean transformation asks people to change habits that feel safe. Even if the habits are inefficient, they are familiar. People know how to survive inside the old system. They know how to protect themselves. They know how to avoid getting blamed, and Lean threatens that survival strategy by asking people to expose problems, stop hiding, admit they don't know, experiment, hold each other accountable, and trust.

You cannot demand that with a kickoff meeting. You earn it by managing communication like a discipline.

The Three Levels of Communication in a Lean Transformation

A mistake many leaders make is thinking communication is one thing. It is not. There are three different layers of communication you must manage simultaneously.

Level 1: Strategic Communication (Leadership Intent)

This is the "why."

It answers:

- Why are we changing?
- What happens if we don't?
- What does success look like?
- What are the non-negotiables?

Strategic communication should come primarily from the CEO, COO, plant manager, or site leader. It cannot be delegated. People need to hear the commitment from the top. This communication should be simple, repetitive, and consistent. The message cannot change every month.

Level 2: Operational Communication (Daily Reality)

This is the "what's happening."

It answers:

- What are we working on right now?
- What did we improve last week?
- What is broken today?
- What are we doing about it?
- What is the next step?

This communication must happen at the gemba, through visual boards, daily huddles, and real problem-solving. This is where Lean becomes believable.

Level 3: Emotional Communication (Trust and Belief)

This is the layer most leaders ignore.

It answers:

- Is leadership serious?
- Is it safe to speak up?
- Will I be punished for raising problems?
- Does my opinion matter?
- Will this disappear like the last initiative?

This communication is not done through speeches but through behavior. You still must manage it intentionally because people interpret silence as meaning. When leaders stop talking about the transformation, employees do not assume it is "going well." They assume it is dying.

The Most Common Communication Failures (And How to Avoid Them)

Let's be brutally honest: most organizations do communicate during transformations, but they just communicate poorly. Here are the most common failure patterns.

Failure #1: One-Way Communication

Leaders announce while employees listen, and no one asks questions. People don't give feedback. This creates compliance but not commitment. The culture we want to create requires two-way communication. If employees cannot speak, the organization cannot learn.

Failure #2: Corporate Language

When leaders use vague phrases like:

- "We are on a journey."
- "We are streamlining."
- "We are transforming our culture."
- "We are becoming world-class."

People tune out because they've heard it before. The more pressure employees feel, the more they crave plain truth. So, please use real language.

Say things like:

- "We are losing money, and we need to fix it."

- "Our customers are waiting too long, and they may leave us."
- "Our quality escapes are unacceptable, and they compromise our future."
- "We are wasting too much time and burning out our best people."

Truth builds trust.

Failure #3: Overpromising

If you promise a perfect future too early, people will stop believing you. A Lean transformation is messy, and it includes mistakes, setbacks, and tons of learning. Don't sell perfection. You need to sell discipline.

Failure #4: Silence During Bad Weeks

This is the biggest one. When performance drops, leaders often go quiet because they don't want to "make things worse." But silence is not neutral; it creates fear. In bad weeks, communicate more, not less. Even if the message is:

"This week was rough. We missed the schedule. Here's what happened. Here's what we learned. Here's what we're doing next."

That kind of honesty is rare. And when employees experience it, they remember it.

Communication Planning Starts Before the Kickoff

A communication plan is not something you create after the transformation starts. It is something you establish during the staging phase, before the kickoff. In fact, in my experience, the communication plan is one of the most important elements of staging. It is the mechanism that turns a Lean transformation from a leadership idea into a shared movement.

A well-designed communication plan does five things at once:

1. Creates a clear case for change
2. Explains the transformation in a way people can understand
3. Builds energy and belief
4. Provides direction and alignment
5. Creates structured, two-way communication so people can contribute

You want to avoid the perception that the transformation is something leaders "do" instead of something the organization owns.

What a Real Communication Plan Includes

When people hear "communication plan," they often think about posters, newsletters, or corporate messaging. That is not at all what we mean here. A Lean transformation communication plan is a practical schedule of meetings, messages, and engagement routines, starting before kickoff and extending all the way into sustainment.

It defines:

- Message
- Audience
- Speaker
- Cadence
- Expected outcome
- Feedback loop

In other words, it is standard work for leadership communication.

The Transformation Communication Arc (From Staging to Sustainment)

A good plan follows a predictable arc:

Phase 1: Staging (Before Kickoff)

Purpose: build understanding and readiness.

This is where leaders:

- Align on the real problems
- Agree on the case for change
- Define the "why" and the "why now"
- Choose a clear transformation structure
- Define what will be different this time

Phase 2: Kickoff (Launch Week)

Purpose: create clarity, energy, and seriousness.

This is where you:

- Introduce the transformation
- Explain the approach
- Set expectations
- Describe what people will see in the next thirty days
- Invite participation

Phase 3: Execution (First 90–120 Days)

Purpose: make Lean visible and credible.

This is where communication becomes tightly connected to:

- Daily huddles
- Visual boards
- Kaizen events
- Leader standard work
- KPI reviews
- Action tracking

Phase 4: Expansion and Stabilization

Purpose: prevent drift and expand capability.

This is where you:

- Show progress
- Connect wins to business results
- Scale the operating rhythm
- Train internal leaders
- Build the improvement funnel

Phase 5: Sustainment

Purpose: make improvement the normal way of working.

This is where the communication plan becomes less about "the Lean transformation" and more about "how we run the business."

The Lean Communication Cadence

The easiest way to keep communication alive is to create a predictable rhythm. This will turn it into a habit. Here is a cadence that works extremely well.

Daily: Gemba Communication

- Tier huddles
- Visual boards
- Problem escalation
- Short, focused, factual

The goal is not motivation. It is *clarity*.

Weekly: Leadership Review Communication

- Review KPIs
- Review improvement actions
- Highlight abnormal conditions
- Celebrate real wins
- Communicate priorities for next week

This is where *alignment* is reinforced.

Monthly: Transformation Story

Once a month, communicate the "big picture" story:

- What have we improved?
- What are we working on next?
- What did we learn?
- What obstacles are we removing?
- What help do we need?

This can be done through:

- A short all-hands meeting
- A simple newsletter
- A video message
- A town hall
- A plant-wide stand-up meeting
- Several small-group meetings covering the entire organization

The format matters less than the **consistency**.

What to Communicate (The Five Topics That Always Work)

If you don't know what to say, use these five topics. They work in every company.

1) Customer Reality

- Late orders
- Complaints
- Lead time
- Delivery performance
- Market pressure

2) Progress and Wins

- Before/after
- What changed
- What was removed
- What got simpler
- What got faster

3) Problems and Learning

- What didn't work
- What surprised us
- What we learned
- What we are doing differently

4) Expectations and Standards

- Leadership behavior
- Meeting rhythms
- Standard work
- Escalation rules
- What "good" looks like

5) Recognition

Recognition is not fluff; it is reinforcement, and Lean cultures are built through reinforcement.

Celebrate:

- People who surfaced problems
- People who simplified a process
- People who helped another department
- Teams that ran a kaizen and updated standard work
- Leaders who showed up consistently

A communication plan is the leadership standard work that makes sure the organization understands:

- Why change is necessary
- What the transformation is
- What is expected from each level
- What progress looks like
- How people will be involved
- How Lean will be sustained when the excitement fades

At the end of the book, I have included a "Templates" section. There, you will find one for the Lean transformation communication plan. Use this template to build a complete communication plan before kickoff and to keep it alive through sustainment.

6) The "Lean Communication Calendar" (Twelve-Month Skeleton)

This is the part most companies never do, and it's why they drift.

Build a calendar that spans the full transformation.

Month 0 (Staging)

- Leadership-alignment meeting
- Supervisor briefing
- Kickoff agenda + messaging
- Launch visual boards
- Define huddle cadence

Month 1

- Kickoff
- First-tier huddles
- First weekly KPI review
- First kaizen event
- First report-out

Months 2–3

- Stabilize cadence
- Two to four kaizens
- Monthly all-hands
- Recognition system begins

Months 4–6

- Expand tier meetings
- Train internal facilitators
- Begin sustainment audits
- Strengthen KPI discipline

Months 7–12

- Expand to office value streams
- Strengthen policy deployment
- Shift from "Lean program" to "CI operating system"

7) Ownership Rules (So It Doesn't Collapse)

This is critical:

Site Leader (CEO/COO/Plant Manager)

Owns:

- The message
- The tone
- The seriousness
- The monthly all-hands
- The reinforcement of standards

Managers

Own:

- The weekly rhythm
- The escalation system
- Removing blockers
- Protecting improvement time

Supervisors

Own:

- Daily huddles
- Frontline engagement
- Surfacing problems
- Coaching behavior

CI Leader

Owns:

- Structure and templates
- Training and coaching
- Audits and sustainment
- Facilitation support

The continuous improvement (CI) leader does not own the transformation. Leadership does.

8) The Feedback Loop (How You Prevent "Fake Communication")

A communication plan is only working if information flows upward, not just downward.

Use at least one of these mechanisms:

- Anonymous pulse surveys (three questions, monthly)
- A "top-five questions" board, updated weekly
- Skip-level listening sessions
- Structured gemba walks with a question list
- Open Q&A during all-hands meetings

If you communicate without listening, you don't have communication. You have broadcasting.

Final Reminder

Your Lean transformation will not be sustained by the quality of your kickoff; it will be sustained by the discipline of your cadence. And your cadence will only survive if communication is treated as a system. Not a speech, a poster, or a newsletter. A system.

Metrics (How Will We Know Communication Is Working?)

- Employee engagement participation
- Number of improvement ideas submitted
- Number of problems surfaced
- Attendance consistency
- Survey pulse checks (simple)

The Final Rule: Communication Must Match Reality

Don't say "Lean is about people" while ignoring people, or you will erode your efforts. A sure way to destroy credibility is to talk about improvement while canceling the meetings. Don't communicate only when things are going well. Communication is not what you say but what the system teaches people to believe.

So, if you want a Lean culture, treat communication like a process. Standardize it, make it visible, review it, and improve it. And most importantly: keep it alive long enough for the culture to change.

Creating a Culture of Engagement

Engagement grows when effort is noticed.

Recognition does not have to be monetary. In fact, it often shouldn't be. A sincere thank-you, delivered thoughtfully, can carry more weight than a bonus.

Knowing your people matters. Some thrive on public recognition. Others prefer quiet acknowledgment. One practice I've seen work beautifully is writing a heartfelt letter to someone important in the employee's life, describing their contribution. It must be authentic. And no, this is not something to delegate or automate.

Autonomy also fuels engagement.

When employees are trusted with clear expectations, the right tools, and the freedom to act within defined boundaries, most rise to the occasion. Autonomy builds pride, and pride builds performance.

Growth opportunities reinforce this further. Training without application is wasted. Assignments that allow people to apply what they've learned deepen both competence and confidence.

And always connect work to purpose.

When people understand how their daily efforts contribute to the broader mission, work becomes meaningful. Policy deployment, when done well, gives everyone a reason to start the day with intent. Chapter 6 is dedicated to policy deployment.

At the end of the day, happy employees stay longer, contribute more, and care more deeply. Engagement is not a perk. It is a competitive advantage.

Tapping into the Power of Ideas

Ideas are the visible expression of engagement.

Make it easy for people to contribute. Visual boards work well because they allow ideas to be seen, discussed, and improved collectively. Digital tools can help, too. The mechanism matters less than the message: ideas are welcome.

Responsiveness is critical.

If ideas disappear into a void, participation stops. Even when ideas cannot be implemented, thoughtful acknowledgment preserves trust.

I am cautious about paying individuals for ideas. Over time, monetary rewards tend to shift motivation from contribution to transaction. A healthy Lean culture encourages ideas because people care, not because they are paid per suggestion. Team-based success and shared rewards reinforce the right behaviors.

When ideas flow freely, prioritization becomes necessary.

Not every idea can be implemented immediately. A simple impact-versus-effort matrix helps the organization focus. Quick wins build momentum. Larger initiatives build credibility. Both are needed.

Cross-Functional Teams Break Down Silos

Many organizations are still structured in functional silos that unintentionally slow improvement.

Moving toward focused factories, or value-stream-aligned teams, brings people together around shared outcomes. Quality, planning, engineering, purchasing, and production working side by side to develop deeper product knowledge and stronger relationships.

In this environment, accountability shifts.

Teams no longer optimize for functional goals alone. They share responsibility for safety, quality, delivery, inventory, and cost. Trade-offs become visible. Collaboration replaces escalation.

When objectives are clear, support is available, and facilitation is thoughtful, cross-functional teams become engines of creativity and execution.

IV. Extending the Culture Beyond the Walls

A Lean culture does not stop at the edge of your organization.

Once internal behaviors begin to shift, once people take ownership, solve problems collaboratively, and focus relentlessly on value, something important happens. The way the organization interacts with the outside world begins to change as well.

Suppliers, customers, and even the surrounding community start to feel the difference.

This stage of the transformation should not be rushed. Extending Lean beyond your walls only works once internal maturity has been established. Attempting to "teach" Lean to others before you live it yourself will damage credibility and trust.

But when the foundation is solid, extending the culture outward becomes a strategic advantage.

From Transactions to Partnerships: Rethinking Supplier Relationships

No organization operates in isolation. Suppliers are a critical part of the value stream, and their performance directly affects your ability to deliver quality, cost, and service. Lead times, defects, shortages, and variability often originate upstream, long before materials arrive at your dock.

A Lean organization recognizes this reality and responds by changing the nature of supplier relationships.

Instead of adversarial negotiations and price-driven transactions, Lean organizations move toward partnership. The goal is no longer to extract value from suppliers but to **create value together**.

This shift begins with open, honest communication.

Key suppliers need to understand *why* you are embracing Lean and *what it means* for the relationship. It must be made clear early that the objective is not price squeezing. The objective is waste elimination, stability, quality improvement, and long-term competitiveness for *both parties.*

While some resistance is inevitable, many suppliers respond positively, especially those who have already witnessed your internal transformation. Seeing Lean in action builds confidence. It signals seriousness and maturity.

From there, a shared vision can be developed.

What does a Lean supply chain look like for both of you? Shorter lead times. Fewer surprises. Better quality. Lower total cost. Mapping the combined value stream together is one of the most effective ways to make this vision tangible. It allows both parties to see bottlenecks, delays, and handoffs that neither could fully understand alone.

Trust is the cornerstone of this work.

Without trust, suppliers will protect information, limit transparency, and resist collaboration. Trust is built through consistency, fairness, and long-term intent.

It grows when suppliers see that improvements benefit them as well, not just your bottom line.

Engaging Suppliers in the Lean Journey

True engagement goes beyond conversation.

Inviting key suppliers into your Lean journey is often a powerful first step. Offering Lean training or involving suppliers in kaizen events within your own operation helps create a shared language and shared understanding. It also demystifies Lean.

Suppliers see how problems are discussed, how people are treated, and how learning happens. This exposure builds comfort, appreciation, and often genuine excitement.

Joint improvement activities deepen the relationship further.

Conducting kaizen events together, focused on shared pain points, transforms the dynamic. Waste is no longer "your problem" or "their problem." It becomes "*our* problem." Solutions are developed collaboratively. Ownership is shared.

As maturity grows, some organizations establish supplier councils.

These are not negotiation forums. They are partnership platforms. Supplier councils bring representatives from key suppliers together to discuss common challenges, share best practices, and explore joint improvement opportunities. This step typically comes later, once trust is established and Lean behaviors are stable internally.

Extending value stream mapping across the supply chain, from your suppliers' suppliers to your own customers, often reveals opportunities that were previously invisible. Delays, batching, and misaligned incentives become clear. Improvement becomes systemic rather than local.

Choosing the Right Approach for Different Suppliers

Not all suppliers require the same level of engagement.

Strategic, long-term partners deserve deeper collaboration. These relationships benefit most from joint improvement, shared planning, and long-term alignment. Helping these suppliers succeed strengthens your own competitiveness.

Transactional suppliers require a different approach.

Clear expectations, simplified processes, and performance-based agreements are often sufficient. Even here, internal simplification matters. Streamlining how your organization interacts with all suppliers reduces waste and friction on both sides.

A tiered approach allows you to focus energy where it matters most while maintaining discipline across the entire supply base.

Creating Engagement Through Shared Success

Supplier engagement increases when benefits are mutual.

Lean collaboration must improve the supplier's business, not just yours. Reduced rework, smoother demand, clearer communication, and more predictable planning all contribute to supplier health.

Sharing success reinforces this.

Publicly recognizing supplier contributions, celebrating joint wins, and communicating a long-term commitment to Lean signal that this is not a passing initiative. It is a direction.

Suppliers, like employees, invest more when they believe the relationship has a future.

Avoiding Common Pitfalls

Extending Lean beyond your walls is not without challenges.

Lack of trust will stall progress quickly. Transparency, fairness, and taking the first step, sometimes even without data sharing, help break the ice.

Conflicting priorities are common. Understanding what matters most to your suppliers allows you to identify improvement opportunities that serve both sides.

Resistance to change is natural. You cannot force Lean on suppliers. But consistent partnership and visible success often bring reluctant suppliers along over time.

Smaller suppliers may lack resources. Technical support, phased expectations, or targeted assistance can make participation feasible.

Communication breakdowns undermine everything. Clear channels and regular contact prevent misunderstandings from escalating.

Addressing these challenges proactively preserves momentum and credibility.

Beyond Suppliers: Customers and Community

A mature Lean culture naturally extends further.

Customers feel the difference when organizations focus relentlessly on value. Shorter lead times, better quality, and more responsive service build loyalty and advocacy. Involving customers in improvement efforts, listening to feedback, and incorporating their needs closes the loop between value creation and delivery.

The surrounding community benefits as well.

Organizations that truly embrace Lean often give back by teaching improvement methods, supporting local education, offering internships, and promoting environmental responsibility. Lean thinking encourages respect for resources, people, and the environment.

At this stage, Lean is no longer an operational approach. It is part of the organization's identity.

When managing a business based in the U.S. Southeast, our performance improved so much that our largest customer recognized our company as their best supplier. We were continually invited to teach their teams, and we were also invited as guest speakers for many activities, including annual supplier conferences.

V. Measuring and Sustaining the Culture

Making the Invisible Visible and the Temporary Permanent

One of the most common mistakes in Lean transformations is assuming that culture, once established, will sustain itself. Early success creates momentum. Engagement increases. Behaviors improve. And then, quietly, attention shifts.

Culture does not erode overnight. It drifts.

Sustaining a Lean culture requires the same discipline as sustaining a Lean process. You must make it visible, review it regularly, and improve it deliberately. Measurement, when used correctly, is not about control. It is about alignment, learning, and focus.

The goal is not to measure culture for reporting purposes. The goal is to **reinforce the behaviors you want to see, every day, at every level of the organization**.

What You Measure Shapes What You Get

Culture cannot be measured directly, but it leaves clear footprints.

The behaviors you care about, engagement, ownership, problem-solving, learning, all produce observable outcomes. The key is to select indicators that reflect *how* work is done, not just *what* is produced.

Some useful cultural indicators include:

- Employee engagement measures, such as engagement surveys or employee Net Promoter Score (eNPS)
- Participation rates in suggestion or improvement systems
- The number and quality of kaizen events conducted
- Critically, the impact generated by improvement activities

One of the most powerful metrics I've used over the years is the **value of the kaizen funnel**.

Almost every improvement can be translated into financial impact, whether through cost reduction, capacity release, inventory reduction, quality improvement, or avoidance of future expense. When teams learn to quantify the impact of their ideas in currency, something important happens.

Improvement stops being abstract.

Teams begin to see that their ideas matter. Leaders gain a tangible way to set goals, track progress, and compare year-over-year improvement. The organization develops a shared understanding of what "better" really means.

We are not trying to turn Lean into an accounting exercise. This gives the improvement a **palpable target** that reinforces seriousness and credibility.

Review Cadence Is Where Culture Is Reinforced or Undermined

Measurement without review is noise. Review without action is theater.

The power of Lean measurement lies in **where and when** it is reviewed.

The most effective reviews happen at the **point of impact**, as close to the work as possible and as soon as possible after performance is known.

At the production level, I strongly advocate for hourly reporting where it makes sense. Output, defects, downtime, and safety issues become visible in near real time. This allows supervisors, engineers, and support teams to respond immediately, while recovery is still possible.

Finding out the next day that a line struggled is already too late. That is not feedback. That is history.

Daily huddles then create the next layer of reinforcement.

Held at the start of the day, these short, focused meetings allow teams to:

- Review the previous day's results
- Discuss lessons learned
- Identify issues that need escalation
- Set a clear mission for the day

These huddles are not status meetings. They are alignment moments. Everyone leaves knowing what success looks like today.

Daily huddles are also an ideal place for short, targeted learning. One-point lessons, quick reminders, or brief reflections reinforce learning without overwhelming people.

At the next level, weekly reviews allow focused factory teams to step back and look at trends. Dashboards are reviewed not to explain misses but to identify opportunities for improvement. Patterns replace anecdotes. Learning replaces blame.

Monthly policy deployment reviews then connect operational performance to strategic objectives. Leaders assess whether the business is progressing toward its goals and where adjustments are needed.

Finally, at the executive level, quarterly reviews provide strategic course correction. In a world of constant geopolitical, economic, and market volatility, this cadence ensures that strategy and execution remain aligned.

Each level of review serves a different purpose. Together, they create a **management system** that sustains culture through behavior, not slogans.

Improving the Culture Itself

Just as processes are continuously improved, culture must be as well.

This requires humility.

No cultural model is perfect. What works in one organization may not translate cleanly to another. Even within the same company, practices must evolve as the business grows, markets shift, and people change.

Feedback is essential.

Leaders should regularly ask:

- Where are people disengaging?
- Where are improvements slowing?
- Where does fear still exist?
- Where are old behaviors resurfacing?

These questions should be explored openly, without defensiveness. Culture improves when leaders model curiosity rather than certainty.

It is also important to remember that you do not need to implement everything at once.

Many of the practices described in this book are meant as starting points, not prescriptions. Some will fit immediately. Others will need adaptation. Some may come much later, once the organization is ready.

What matters most is not completeness but commitment.

Start. Learn. Adjust. Improve.

Over time, as capability grows and confidence increases, you can layer in additional elements. Culture matures through iteration, not perfection.

The Leader's Responsibility

Ultimately, sustaining culture is a leadership responsibility.

Not through speeches. Not through mandates. But through daily choices:

- What gets reviewed
- What gets followed up
- What gets tolerated
- What gets celebrated

Culture is sustained by what leaders pay attention to, especially when pressure is high.

If you are consistent, patient, and intentional, culture becomes resilient. If you are distracted or reactive, culture erodes quietly.

The difference is rarely dramatic. But over time, it is decisive.

A Final Reflection Before Moving Forward

If you take nothing else from this section, take this:

Culture is not sustained by good intentions.
It is sustained by disciplined routines that reinforce the right behaviors.

In the next sections, we will bring all of this together by focusing on leadership judgment: how to respond when resistance persists, how to protect momentum, and how to ensure Lean becomes a lasting part of how your organization operates.

VI. A Leader's Guide to Overcoming Resistance

Navigating Human Reality Without Losing Momentum

Resistance is not a failure of your Lean transformation. It is evidence that something meaningful is changing.

Any initiative that challenges habits, power structures, comfort zones, or long-held assumptions will generate resistance. This is not unique to Lean. It is human. The role of leadership is not to eliminate resistance but to **understand it, work through it, and prevent it from derailing progress**.

Handled well, resistance becomes fuel for learning.
Handled poorly, it becomes a silent killer of momentum.

Understanding Resistance Before Reacting to It

Most resistance does not come from bad intentions. It comes from uncertainty.

People worry about what change means for them personally: *Will my job change? Will I look incompetent? Will I lose control? Will this be another program that fades away after a year, leaving me exposed for having supported it?*

Past experience matters. Many employees have lived through initiatives that were announced with enthusiasm and abandoned quietly. Each failed attempt leaves scar tissue. Cynicism is often learned behavior.

Resistance also emerges when people feel change is being done *to* them rather than *with* them. A perceived loss of autonomy can trigger defensiveness even among otherwise engaged employees.

Good leaders resist the urge to label these reactions as negativity. Instead, they treat them as signals.

Turning Skeptics into Participants

The most effective way to address skepticism is not persuasion. It is involvement.

Start by listening. Truly listening.

Create spaces where people can speak openly without fear of reprisal. Acknowledge concerns without dismissing them. You don't have to agree with every objection to show respect for it. Empathy builds credibility far faster than logic alone.

Education matters, but education without context rarely works. Explaining Lean tools is less important than explaining *why* the organization must change and *what happens if it doesn't*. Data helps, but stories help more.

Involvement changes the conversation.

When people help design solutions, they stop seeing themselves as victims of change and start seeing themselves as owners of it. This is why pilot projects are so powerful. They allow people to experience improvement rather than debate it.

Quick wins matter here, not as marketing but as proof. When employees see processes improve, frustrations reduce, work becomes easier, and skepticism weakens naturally.

Leadership visibility is critical.

Nothing undermines credibility faster than leaders who talk about Lean but remain absent from the work. Gemba walks, training participation, report-outs, and follow-up actions send a clear signal: this matters, and it's not optional.

When Setbacks Occur (And They Will)

No transformation unfolds exactly as planned.

Processes break. Data is messy. Resources are constrained. External forces intervene. Momentum dips. These moments are not exceptions. They are part of the journey.

What separates successful transformations from stalled ones is not the absence of setbacks but the *response to them.*

Ignoring setbacks erodes trust. Overreacting to them creates fear.

Effective leaders acknowledge issues openly, analyze them rigorously, and adjust without drama. Root-cause analysis should focus on systems and decisions, not people.

Adaptation is not weakness. It is leadership.

Plans should evolve as learning increases. Teams should be encouraged to experiment within clear boundaries. Failure, when contained and analyzed, becomes learning rather than liability.

Communication during setbacks is essential.

Silence creates rumors. Transparency builds resilience. When leaders explain what happened, what was learned, and what will change, they reinforce psychological safety even under pressure.

Protecting Momentum Without Burning People Out

Early success creates excitement. Sustaining it requires discipline.

Small victories should be recognized, but recognition should be proportional. Not every improvement requires a ceremony. Not every milestone needs a reward. When recognition is unexpected and authentic, it carries more meaning.

Avoid transactional thinking. Improvement should not become a game where people only act when rewards are guaranteed. The deeper goal is intrinsic motivation: pride in work, ownership of outcomes, and shared success.

Reinforce the long-term vision consistently.

During difficult moments, remind people why the journey started. What future are you building? What problems are you leaving behind? Vision anchors effort when energy dips.

Knowing When Resistance Becomes a Leadership Issue

Not all resistance is equal.

Most resistance is passive, rooted in uncertainty, and responsive to engagement. Some resistance, however, is active and persistent. It shows up as undermining behavior, constant negativity, or deliberate obstruction.

This is where leadership judgment matters.

Allowing a few people to sabotage progress sends a damaging message to everyone else. It tells the organization that commitment is optional and effort is not protected.

Engage first. Coach second. Be patient.
But if resistance persists despite clarity, support, and opportunity, leaders must act.

This is not punishment. It is stewardship of the culture.

Protecting the momentum of the many is more important than accommodating the unwilling few.

When to Seek Outside Help

There is no shame in seeking support.

Lean transformations are complex. They challenge habits, structures, and identities. External expertise can accelerate learning, provide objectivity, and help leaders avoid common traps, especially in the early stages.

The key is to use external help as a capability builder, not a crutch.

Ultimately, ownership must remain inside the organization.

A Final Word on Resistance

Resistance is not your enemy.
Complacency is.

Handled thoughtfully, resistance sharpens thinking, strengthens engagement, and improves outcomes. Handled poorly, it stalls progress and drains energy.

Strong leaders don't fear resistance.
They **navigate it deliberately**, with empathy, clarity, and resolve.

VII. Building a Sustainable Lean Culture

From Transformation to Identity

A sustainable Lean culture is not something you "install."
It is something you grow.

It is not a project, a program, or an initiative. It is a long-term commitment that reshapes how people think, lead, and work together. Organizations that succeed with Lean understand one fundamental truth:

Culture change is not linear, and it is not fast.

It moves in waves. There are periods of acceleration and periods of fatigue. Moments of excitement and moments of doubt. Breakthroughs followed by plateaus. Progress followed by setbacks. This is not failure. It is the natural rhythm of transformation.

Leaders who expect a smooth journey burn out their organizations.
Leaders who prepare for a long journey build something that lasts.

Playing the Long Game

Sustainable culture is built when leaders stop thinking in quarters and start thinking in years.

Short-term wins matter. Momentum matters. But durability matters more.

Real cultural change requires patience because it involves changing habits, beliefs, and identity. People are not machines. You cannot reprogram them with a memo, a training session, or a new KPI. Culture shifts through repetition, experience, and consistency.

This means resisting the temptation to chase quick fixes.

Organizations often fall into the trap of implementing tools rapidly without allowing behaviors to stabilize. The result is activity without depth. Motion without meaning. Eventually, people disengage because nothing feels permanent.

Sustainable Lean cultures move differently. They prioritize rhythm over speed, consistency over intensity, and learning over appearance.

They focus on:

- Reinforcing purpose
- Embedding learning
- Stabilizing routines
- Making Lean part of daily life rather than a special event

When Lean Becomes "How We Work"

Lean becomes sustainable when it stops being a separate initiative and becomes the normal way work is done.

This happens when Lean thinking is woven into:

- Daily routines
- Standard work
- Management systems
- Performance discussions
- Leadership development
- Strategic planning

At that point, Lean is no longer something people *do*.
It becomes something they *are*.

Decision-making becomes data-driven.
Problem-solving becomes structured.
Improvement becomes expected.
Learning becomes continuous.
Ownership becomes natural.

Lean stops being a methodology and becomes an operating philosophy.

The Role of Measurement in Sustainability

Measurement plays a role here, but not as control.

Metrics sustain culture by reinforcing focus and alignment.

When improvement is visible, tracked, and reviewed, it becomes real. When it disappears into reports and dashboards that no one uses, it fades into noise.

Sustainable cultures use measurement to:

- Guide behavior
- Reinforce priorities
- Support learning
- Anchor decision-making

They use data to ask better questions, not assign more blame.

They adapt KPIs as the organization matures. What mattered in year one may not matter in year three. Cultural maturity requires measurement maturity.

Leadership as the Anchor

No culture outgrows its leadership.

If leaders disengage, culture weakens.
If leaders drift, culture drifts.
If leaders compromise, culture fractures.

Sustainability begins with leadership behavior.

Leaders must remain visible in the work, not just in meetings.
They must continue to coach, not just manage.
They must protect time for improvement, not just production.
They must remove barriers, not just set targets.

Resources matter. Support matters. Training matters. But **presence** matters more than all of them.

People do not follow strategies.
They follow behavior.

Developing future leaders becomes essential at this stage. A Lean culture that depends on a few individuals is fragile. A Lean culture that builds leadership depth becomes resilient.

Sustainability is achieved when the next generation of leaders does not "adopt" Lean, but inherits it.

Adaptability as a Cultural Strength

A sustainable Lean culture is not rigid.

Markets change. Technology evolves. Customer expectations shift. Organizations grow, merge, and restructure. A healthy Lean culture adapts without losing its core principles.

The principles remain stable.
The practices evolve.

This adaptability is what allows Lean to remain relevant across decades, industries, and business cycles.

Organizations that treat Lean as doctrine become brittle.
Organizations that treat Lean as thinking become resilient.

The Quiet Mark of Success

You will know a Lean culture is sustainable when:

- People solve problems without waiting for permission.
- Improvement happens without being announced.
- Learning happens without being mandated.
- Leaders coach without being prompted.
- Employees speak about "our system," not "the program."

At that point, Lean no longer feels new.

It feels normal.

And that is the real sign of success.

Closing Reflection

Building a sustainable Lean culture is not about perfection but direction.

Not speed, but consistency.
Not intensity, but endurance.
Not tools, but mindset.
Not compliance, but belief.

The organizations that succeed are not the ones that implement the most tools.
They are the ones who build the deepest ownership.

Lean, at its highest level, is not operational excellence.
It is organizational maturity.

It becomes your identity.

VIII. Making Sense of a Big Chapter with a Simple Starting Point

This chapter is long by design.

Culture is not a single tool, workshop, or leadership speech. It is a system of beliefs, habits, decisions, and structures that reinforce one another over time. I intentionally showed many situations, choices, and tensions so you would have a reference map, not a slogan.

Some parts of this chapter read more like explanation than instruction. That, too, is intentional. Culture must be understood before it can be taught, and taught before it can be owned.

If this feels like a lot, that's because it is.

Dissecting just this chapter could easily fill a book on its own. Don't try to memorize it. Use it as a guide when you face real moments on the floor, in meetings, and with suppliers or customers. When you're unsure what to do, return to the basics: clarity of purpose, respect for people, and learning every day at the gemba.

You don't need a master plan to begin. You need a starting point.

A Simple Way to Begin

Pick one area.
Choose a pilot where problems are visible, customers are feeling pain, and the local leader is open to trying something new. Name the area. Make it explicit. Post it where the work happens.

State a plain target.
Write one sentence in numbers. For example, reduce changeover time on line twelve from a hundred minutes to forty minutes in eight weeks while holding quality. Real numbers beat percentages every time. Post the target at the point of use.

Make truth visible.
Create a small board showing plan versus actual, first-pass yield, and the top reasons for misses. Update it by the hour in production or at least twice a day in office work. Visibility changes behavior faster than any speech.

Teach, then use.
Teach one concept in the morning and apply it that afternoon. Seven wastes. SMED basics. One-point lessons. Keep the teaching short and the practice real.

Build a daily rhythm.
Run a ten-minute stand-up at the board. Review yesterday's results. Set today's plan. Call out today's risks. Ask what help is needed. Thank one person for a specific behavior. Make announcements last, not first.

Ask better questions.
On every walk, use three questions: What do you see? What is the impact? What would you try by Friday? After each walk, write down one commitment you will personally keep.

Capture proof.
Post one before-and-after photo each week. Pictures settle arguments and remind people how far they've come, especially when memory fades.

Share the load.
Co-locate at least one support role with the team for sixty days. Give them the same goals and the same stand-up. Watch how quickly decisions improve.

Close the loop on ideas.
Use a simple board with four columns: *"New," "In Review," "Doing," "Done."* Respond to every idea within five working days. Keep at least two quick wins moving while larger items are analyzed.

Celebrate proportionally.
Small wins deserve a quick thank you at the board. Breakthroughs deserve a real moment. Recognition should feel earned, not scripted.

Signals You're on the Right Track

You'll know the culture is shifting when people say "we" instead of "they."
Misses are discussed in facts, not blame.
Leaders keep their gemba time.
Ideas move across the board.
Customers notice steadier delivery and fewer surprises.
New hires learn the language on day one.

These are quiet signals, but they are reliable.

Common Detours and Simple Corrections

If meetings grow and action shrinks, shorten the agenda and move decisions to the gemba.
If tools multiply without impact, return to the target and choose the tool that fits the problem.
If resistance rises, ask what people fear losing and address it directly with training, clearer boundaries, and faster support.

One Last Ask

In your first week, pick one idea from this page and act on it. Next week, pick another.

Small, steady steps will do more for your culture than any large announcement ever will.

Keep the work visible.
Keep the conversations honest.
Keep learning.

That's how a Lean culture takes root.
And that's how it lasts.

Reflection and Action

This chapter asked a lot of you on purpose.

Culture is not something you can delegate, announce, or install. It is shaped daily by what leaders do, what they tolerate, and what they reinforce. Before moving on, take time to reflect honestly. The value of this chapter is not in agreement but in application.

Use the questions and exercises below selectively. You do not need to do all of them at once. Choose the ones that create discomfort, because those are usually the ones that matter most.

1. Cultural Reality Check

Describe your organization's current culture as it actually operates today, not how it is described in presentations.

- How do people react when problems surface?
- Where do decisions really get made?
- What behaviors are rewarded, even unintentionally?
- What behaviors are discouraged, even if never stated?

Now ask yourself:
Which of these cultural patterns help your business perform, and which quietly undermine it?

Write down three cultural strengths and three cultural constraints you observe regularly.

2. Leadership at the Gemba

Schedule at least two intentional leadership gemba walks over the next two weeks.

Go alone or with one other leader. Do not turn this into a tour.

Observe:

- How often do leaders interact directly with operators and staff?
- Are doors open or closed?
- Do conversations feel curious or corrective?
- Are problems discussed openly or carefully avoided?

After each walk, write down:

- One leadership behavior you want to reinforce.
- One leadership behavior you personally need to change.

Be specific. Vague intentions do not change habits.

3. Alignment Between Strategy and Reality

List your organization's stated strategic objectives.

Next to each one, list the KPIs your leaders are currently measured on.

Ask yourself:

- Do these KPIs reinforce the strategy or compete with it?
- Would a frontline employee be able to explain the strategy in their own words?
- If not, what signal does that send?

If you asked five employees today, would they give you roughly the same answer?

If the answer is no, alignment work comes before tool deployment.

4. The "So What?" Discipline

Choose one recent Lean initiative, improvement effort, or proposed change.

With your leadership team, ask, "So, what?" five times:

- So, what does this improve?
- So, what pain does it remove?
- So, what becomes easier tomorrow?
- So, what changes for the customer?
- So, what happens if we don't do this?

If you cannot clearly connect the initiative to something leaders care about deeply, resistance is predictable, not surprising.

5. Designing Your First or Next Pilot

Identify one area where:

- Problems are visible.
- Customers feel pain.
- The local leader is open, not perfect.

Define:

- One clear, numeric target
- One small set of metrics
- One cross-functional support structure

Before you start, answer this question honestly:
Is this pilot being positioned as a learning engine or as a performance test?

The answer will determine how people behave.

6. Capability Before Empowerment

Assess your organization's current Lean capability.

- Who understands the basics?
- Who can coach others?
- Who applies tools correctly, not just frequently?

Identify the three most important skills your teams need in the next six months, not the next three years.

Design training that is:

- Short
- Practical
- Immediately applied

Remember: Empowerment without capability creates anxiety. Capability without empowerment creates frustration.

7. Communication That Builds Trust

Review how Lean is currently communicated.

- Is communication mostly one- or two-way?
- Are challenges discussed openly or sanitized?
- Are stories told, or just numbers shared?

If you had to reduce communication by 50 percent, what would you keep?

That answer usually reveals what actually matters.

8. How Resistance Shows Up in Your Organization

Identify the most common forms of resistance you see today.

Do they include:

- Silence
- Compliance without ownership
- Skepticism based on past failures
- Passive delay

For each form, ask:
What might people be afraid of losing?

Do not answer defensively. Resistance handled well strengthens culture. Resistance ignored weakens it.

9. Cross-Functional Reality Check

Identify one problem that has persisted because it sits between functions.

Form a small cross-functional team and give them:

- A clear objective
- Shared metrics
- A defined time window
- Leadership protection

Watch closely:
Do silos dissolve when accountability is shared, or do they reassert themselves?

That observation tells you more about culture than any survey.

10. Extending Lean Beyond Your Walls

Choose one key supplier or partner.

Ask yourself:

- Do we treat them as a cost to manage or a system to improve together?
- Where does variability originate?
- Where does trust break down?

Even a simple conversation about shared waste can open doors if your internal culture is mature enough to support it.

11. Sustaining the Culture

Answer this question honestly:
If you stepped away for six months, would Lean continue to strengthen or slowly fade?

If it would fade, why?

- Is leadership behavior inconsistent?
- Is improvement still event-driven?
- Is learning still optional?

Sustainment is not about intensity. It is about routines that survive distraction.

12. Your Personal Commitment

Finally, turn the lens inward.

Write down:

- One behavior you will stop
- One behavior you will start
- One behavior you will reinforce in others

Commit to practicing these for the next thirty days.

Culture does not change because leaders agree.
It changes because leaders consistently behave differently.

Closing Thought

If this chapter did its job, it did not give you comfort. It gave you clarity.

You do not need to do everything described here.
You do need to start somewhere, deliberately.

Culture is built the same way Lean is built:
one visible problem,
one honest conversation,
one better habit at a time.

And once it starts moving, it becomes very hard to stop.

Chapter 4 Reflection and Action Answers

CHAPTER 5

Seeing the Whole:
The Power of the Value Stream

You arrive at the plant before sunrise. The parking lot lights still hum, and inside, you can already hear forklifts moving, pallets scraping, people rushing. Everyone is working. Everyone is busy. And yet, nothing seems to move.

You walk the floor, and the same patterns greet you. A supervisor juggling five fires before 8 a.m. A line waiting for parts that were "just released." A meeting about backorders that produces another spreadsheet instead of a solution.

You feel it in your chest, that familiar mix of frustration and restless energy. This is not laziness. It is not incompetence. People care. People are trying. But effort keeps piling up without results to match.

It's motion without progress.

At some point, usually quietly, a thought surfaces:
We can't keep working this hard for so little flow.

That moment matters. Many turnarounds don't start with a project or a consultant. They start with that realization. Something deeper is broken, and pushing harder isn't fixing it.

Over the next few weeks, you do what good leaders are taught to do. You tighten controls. You raise expectations. You reorganize a department or two. For a while, things improve. Meetings run faster. Charts look better. Output increases in pockets.

And yet, customers still wait. Lead times remain stubborn. Inventory grows where you least expect it. Quality improves in one area, while delivery slips somewhere else.

That's when the irony becomes impossible to ignore. Every function claims success, but the system keeps failing.

Each department is doing what it was asked to do. Each team is optimizing its own world. But the whole never gets better.

Eventually, the pattern reveals itself. You're improving pieces of a system you've never actually seen as a system.

This is the trap nearly every organization falls into. Local efficiency masking global dysfunction. Activity replacing progress. Metrics telling comforting stories while customers keep waiting.

And beneath it all, a quiet question begins to surface:
How does work really flow through this business?

Why Seeing the Whole Changes Everything

Most leaders manage what they can see. Metrics. Dashboards. Departmental results. What they can't see, and what no spreadsheet ever truly shows, is flow.

Flow is how value actually moves. From order to delivery. From raw material to customer. From idea to cash.

When flow is broken, leaders unknowingly fight symptoms instead of causes. They speed up individual steps while the system stays slow. They reward utilization while lead time grows. They add controls where clarity is missing.

This is why so many improvement efforts stall. Teams optimize islands. Leaders chase numbers. Firefighting becomes normal.

Value stream mapping (VSM) exists to break that cycle.

VSM is not a documentation exercise. It is not a Lean artifact. And it is not about drawing boxes and arrows. At its core, VSM is a way to make the invisible visible.

It forces leaders to confront a simple truth: **you cannot manage what you cannot see.**

When you map a value stream, something important happens. Conversations change. Assumptions get challenged. Long-held beliefs fall apart under the weight of facts collected at the gemba.

People stop debating opinions and start looking at reality.

Inventory that "has always been there" suddenly shows up as weeks of waiting. Delays blamed on other departments reveal their true causes. Information paths, often ignored, emerge as major constraints.

And once that picture exists, once everyone can see the same flow, leadership changes.

You stop reacting and start guiding.
You stop managing people and start managing flow.
You stop pushing and start stabilizing.

This is why organizations that truly adopt VSM often describe it as a turning point. Not because the map itself fixes anything, but because it changes how leaders and teams understand their system.

The map is not the goal. Shared understanding is.

What This Chapter Will Give You

This chapter is written as a manual, not theory. Its purpose is twofold.

First, it will help you understand **why value stream mapping is necessary**. Why effort alone is not enough. Why local improvements fail. Why seeing the whole is a leadership responsibility, not an engineering task.

Second, it will give you a **practical, step-by-step method** to run a VSM event yourself. The same approach I have used across industries and geographies, mapping from customer back to supplier, grounded in real data and real work.

If you are planning a VSM event soon, read on carefully. The mechanics matter. If you are not ready yet, that's fine. Mark this chapter and come back when the timing is right.

What matters most is this: once you learn to see flow, you cannot unsee it. And once you can see, real change becomes possible.

From Insight to Discipline

Why Value Stream Mapping Comes First

Seeing the whole changes how you think. But insight alone does not change results.

This is where many organizations stumble. Leaders recognize that something deeper is wrong. They feel the drag in the system. They sense that local improvements are not adding up. And yet, when it comes time to act, they default to familiar patterns: projects, metrics, reorganizations, and isolated fixes.

VSM exists precisely to interrupt that reflex.

Before tools, before kaizen events, before layout changes or automation, VSM forces a pause. It asks leaders and teams to slow down just enough to understand how value actually moves through the organization. Not how it is supposed to move. Not how it is documented. How it truly moves, today, under real conditions.

This is why VSM is not optional in a serious Lean transformation. It is the foundation.

Without it, improvement efforts are often guesses. With it, they become deliberate.

When a value stream is mapped properly, several things happen at once. First, assumptions are exposed. Teams often discover that what they believed was a capacity problem is actually a waiting problem. What they blamed on quality turns out to be scheduling. What they thought was a supplier issue is really an internal batching decision.

Second, conversations change. The map gives people a shared language. Instead of debating opinions, teams look at the same facts. Instead of defending departments, they examine flow. Blame loses its power when reality is visible.

Third, leadership shifts. Leaders stop managing activities and start managing systems. The focus moves from utilization to lead time, from output to flow, from effort to results.

This is the real advantage of value stream mapping. Not the drawing itself, but the clarity it creates.

However, that clarity only emerges when VSM is done with discipline.

A rushed map becomes decoration. A poorly scoped map becomes noise. A map created without gemba data becomes fiction. And a map created by one person at a computer becomes a missed opportunity for learning.

That is why VSM follows a deliberate sequence. Each step builds the conditions for the next. Skipping steps weakens the outcome. Doing them in order strengthens understanding and accelerates improvement.

We begin not with symbols or sticky notes, but with focus.

Before You Map: Choosing What to See

Product Quantity and Process Routing (PQPR)

Most organizations do not suffer from a lack of improvement ideas. They suffer from a lack of focus.

Walk into almost any factory or operation and you will hear the same concerns: too much inventory, long lead times, quality issues, firefighting, expediting. All of them are real. All of them matter. But trying to address all of them at once usually guarantees that none are solved well.

Value stream mapping works when it is applied to a *specific* flow serving a *specific* customer need. That requires a choice.

This is where Product Quantity and Process Routing, or PQPR, comes in.

PQPR is not a Lean formality. It is a thinking exercise. Its purpose is to help you decide which value stream to map first, based on facts rather than opinions.

Most companies produce multiple products or services. Volumes vary. Routings differ. Some products run daily, others weekly or monthly. Some flow through shared resources, others through dedicated lines. Mapping each part number individually would be overwhelming and pointless. Mapping everything at once would be chaotic.

Instead, value streams are mapped by **product family**.

A product family is a group of products that follow a similar process routing through the operation. The key word here is "similar," not "identical." The goal is not perfection. The goal is to capture a representative flow that reflects how value is created for a meaningful portion of the business.

PQPR helps you identify those families.

OK, but what does it look like? I'm glad you asked… See FIGURE 1 below.

	PARTS QUANTITY				PROCESS ROUTING									
	Part #	Demand Qty	% of Total	% Cumulative	Guillotine	Splicer	Table Tape	Press	Router	Sander	1 Cut	Cut	Fire Rated	Rack
1	Architectural Panel	10,050	28%	28%	1	2	3	4	5	6				7
2	Resale	9,790	28%	28%										1
4	Laminate	6,800	19%	19%				1	2					3
5	Architec 4x10 Ply	3,500	10%	10%	1	2	3	5	6	7	4			8
6	Express Panel	2,890	8%	8%				1	2	3				4
7	Blueprint	1,000	3%	3%	1	2	3	5	6	7		4		8
8	Door Skin	600	2%	2%							1			2
9	Architec on Medite	370	1%	1%	1	2	3	5	6	4 7				8
10	Fire Rated	200	1%	1%									1	2
11	2 Sheets	150	0%	0%				1						2
	TOTAL	35,350	100%											

Example of a Product Quantity and Process Routing (PQPR)

A PQPR helps identify product families by showing product volume alongside the process routing each product follows. This allows teams to choose a representative value stream before mapping.

The exercise is simple but powerful.

You begin by listing all products or services produced by the organization. This list should be complete, even if some items are low volume or infrequent. Next, you sort that list by volume, usually annual demand. Volume matters because high-volume products consume the majority of capacity, inventory, and attention. Improvements made there will have the greatest impact.

Across the top of the list, record the major process steps each product flows through. These are not detailed work instructions. They are the primary operations: fabrication, assembly, testing, packaging, approval, release, shipment, or their equivalents in service and administrative processes.

As this matrix takes shape, patterns emerge. Products that share similar routings naturally cluster together. These clusters are your product families.

This visibility is critical. Without it, teams often choose value streams based on convenience, politics, or the loudest problem of the week. With PQPR, the decision becomes objective.

Once families are identified, leadership can make an informed choice: which value stream best represents current demand, strategic importance, and opportunity for improvement?

At the end, your PQPR should look something like what you see in FIGURE 2 below:

	PARTS QUANTITY				PROCESS NAME									
	Part #	Demand Qty	% of Total	% Cumulative	Guillotine	Splicer	Table Tape	Press	Router	Sander	1 Cut	Cut	Fire Rated	Rack
1	Architectural Panel	10,050	28%	28%	1	2	3	4	5	6				7
2	Architec 4x10 Ply	3,500	10%	38%	1	2	3	5	6	7	4			8
4	Architec on Medite	370	1%	39%	1	2	3	5	6	4 7				8
5	Express Panel	2,890	8%	48%				1	2	3				4
6	Laminate	6,800	19%	67%				1	2					3
7	2 Sheets	150	0%	67%				1						2
8	Resale	9,790	28%	95%										1
9	Fire Rated	200	1%	95%									1	2
10	Blueprint	1,000	3%	98%	1	2	3	5	6	7		4		8
11	Door Skin	600	2%	100%							1			2

Product Quantity and Process Routing (PQPR)

PQPR brings focus to value stream mapping. Instead of guessing where to start, leaders can see which product families drive volume, complexity, and opportunity.

At a glance, PQPR turns a complex product mix into a clear decision.

That is the value stream you map first.

It is worth emphasizing that PQPR is not about analysis for its own sake. It is about setting the conditions for learning. By choosing a representative family, you ensure that what you learn from the map will generalize. The insights gained will apply elsewhere. The patterns uncovered will repeat.

Only after this choice is made does value stream mapping truly begin.

From here, the work shifts from deciding *what* to see to understanding *how* value flows.

From this point forward, we will move into the practical execution of VSM, walking step by step through how to map the current state from customer back to supplier, how to capture both material and information flow, how to calculate lead time and identify the true constraints in the system, and how to design a future state that replaces chaos with rhythm.

The purpose is not to create a perfect map. The purpose is to see clearly enough to lead differently.

And that work begins at the customer.

Mapping the Value Stream: A Practical, End-to-End Method

Value stream mapping is not an abstract exercise. It is a hands-on investigation of how value actually flows through your operation. When done well, it replaces assumptions with facts and opinions with evidence. Once the product family has been chosen, VSM moves from focus to observation. This is where the real learning begins.

Again, all the steps in this section apply to the **product family** you selected.

This section is written so that you can either **lead a VSM event yourself** or **confidently guide a team through it**, even if this is your first time.

Do not rush this process. Speed comes later. Clarity comes first.

Step 1: Clearly Define the Value Stream Boundaries

Before you map anything, you must define what is included and what is not. Ambiguity at this stage creates confusion throughout the event.

The **right boundary** of the value stream is the customer. This is where value is realized. Be explicit. Are you mapping to shipment, delivery, or customer acceptance? Choose one and state it clearly.

The **left boundary** is the supplier shipping point for the chosen product family. This is not where material is received internally but where it leaves the supplier.

Everything in between is part of the value stream.

Next, define the **time window** you will observe. If demand is relatively stable, choose a typical production day. If demand is uneven, choose a representative week. Avoid peak or atypical days unless the purpose of the map is to understand those extremes.

Write these boundaries at the top of your mapping area so everyone agrees on the scope.

Step 2: Start with the Customer and Establish Takt

Value stream mapping always begins with the customer. This is not symbolic. It is practical.

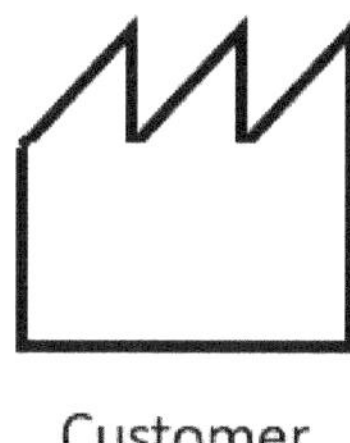

Customer

At the customer, collect the facts that define demand:

- Average daily or weekly demand
- Delivery frequency
- Typical order quantity or pack size

- Required lead time
- Service level expectations
- Quality requirements or defect tolerances

Do not estimate. If you do not know, stop and find out.

Once demand is known, calculate **takt time**.

Takt time equals available production time divided by customer demand over the same period. For example, if you have twenty-seven thousand seconds of available time per shift and customer demand is nine hundred units per shift, takt time is thirty seconds.

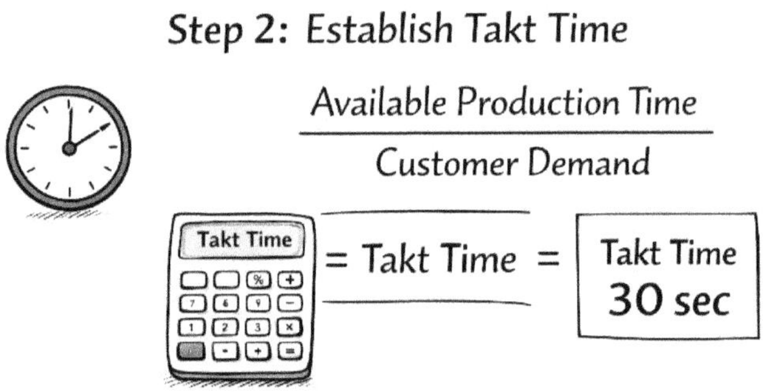

Step 2: Establish Takt Time

Available Production Time / Customer Demand = Takt Time = Takt Time 30 sec

Write the takt time clearly on the map.

Takt time is not a target, and it is not a performance metric. It is a reference that allows you to compare how each process behaves relative to customer demand.

Many teams skip this step or treat it casually. That is a mistake. Without takt, the rest of the map lacks context.

Step 3: Walk the Process from Customer Back to Supplier

With the customer defined, the team now physically walks the value stream **from right to left**, starting at shipping and moving upstream toward receiving.

This walk must happen at the gemba.

As you walk, observe work as it is actually performed. Do not rely on procedures, routings, or ERP data. Those describe how the process was intended to work, not how it works today.

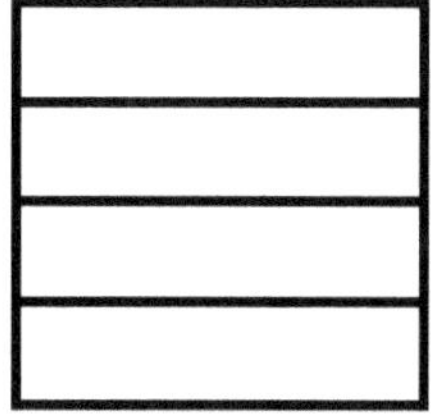

Process Box

At each process, ask operators three simple questions:

1. What do you do?
2. How do you know what to work on next?
3. What happens when something goes wrong?

Watch carefully. Many of the most important insights come from what people do not say.

Time cycles with a stopwatch. Count inventory by hand. Follow information back to its source. If someone says, "The system tells us," ask to see it.

Capture both **material flow** and **information flow**. If you do not understand how information triggers production or movement, you do not yet understand the process.

Step 4: Draw the Current State in Real Time

Draw the map as you go. Use sticky notes or markers so changes can be made easily.

Each process is represented by a **process box**, with a **data box** underneath it. In the data box, record:

- Average cycle time (measured)
- Changeover time
- Number of operators
- Uptime or availability
- Scrap rate or first-pass yield
- Batch or pack size
- Working time per shift

Do not over-analyze. Use averages. The goal is to understand flow, not statistical variation.

Between processes, draw **inventory triangles** and record:

- Quantity of material waiting.
- Approximate days or hours of waiting time.

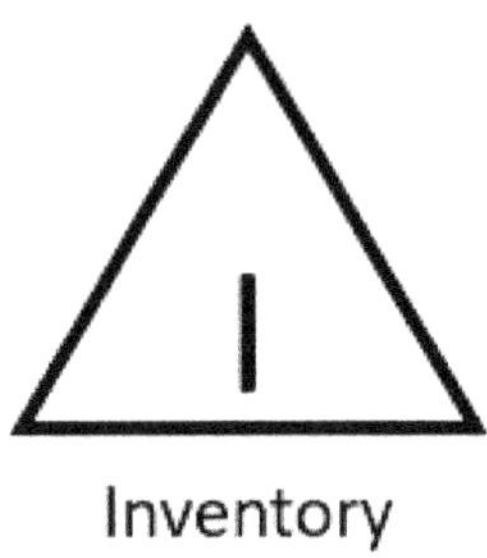

Arrows show how material moves. Jagged arrows or labeled arrows show how information flows. If information arrives by phone call, email, paper, or informal conversation, capture it.

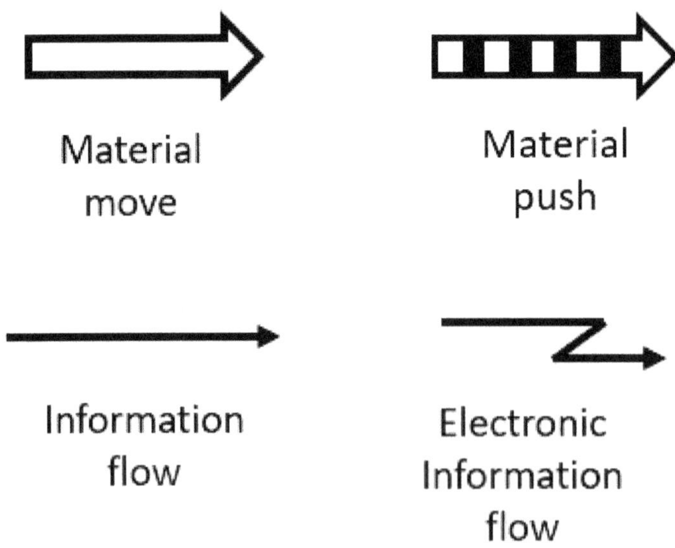

If the map looks messy, you are doing it right.

Step 5: Identify Push, Pull, and Flow Explicitly

As the map develops, make it explicit how each process is triggered.

If a process runs because it is scheduled independently, mark it as **push**.

If it produces in response to consumption from a downstream process, mark it as **pull**.

If two processes are directly linked and produce one unit at a time, mark it as **flow**.

This distinction matters because most overproduction originates at push points.

If every process is scheduled separately, capture that honestly. This is not a failure. It is insight.

Where supermarkets, FIFO lanes, or kanban loops exist, draw them and record their rules:

- Maximum capacity
- Replenishment trigger
- Who owns the decision

A Word About Symbology

There are standard symbols for all these options. I have added a few examples throughout this chapter, and you can easily find them online. I encourage you to search for them and use those standardized options. Some people choose to develop their own symbols, and the truth is, when you do, the VSM will work fine. The problem is that, when people come from outside your organization, they are likely to be familiar with the standard notation. This means that people from outside your organization, now and in the future, will have to learn your symbology, adding a level of complexity you don't need.

Step 6: Identify the Pacemaker Process

In every value stream, one process sets the pace for the rest. This is the **pacemaker**.

The pacemaker is usually the process closest to the customer, where:

- Mix and volume can be leveled.
- Output can be scheduled reliably.
- Downstream demand is clearly understood.

Only the pacemaker should receive the schedule.

Once identified, calculate **pitch**. Pitch equals pack size multiplied by takt time. Pitch defines the rhythm at which work is released or completed at the pacemaker.

Write the pacemaker and pitch clearly on the map. This will become critical when designing the future state.

Step 7: Build the Timeline and Calculate Lead Time

At the bottom of the map, draw two horizontal bars.

The top bar represents **processing time**. Add up all the cycle times.

The bottom bar represents **waiting time**. Add up all the inventory delays, transport, queues, and approvals.

Write the totals clearly:

- Total processing time
- Total lead time
- Percentage of value-added time

For most organizations, value-added time is shockingly small. This realization often changes the tone of the room.

Step 8: Validate the Map at the Gemba

Before moving on, validate the map with the people who do the work.

Stand in front of the map and ask:
"Is this what really happens on a busy day?"

Encourage corrections. Make them immediately.

This step builds credibility and ensures the map reflects reality, not perception.

Step 9: Design the Future State at a High Level

Only after the current state is fully understood should the team sketch a future state.

The future state is not detailed engineering. It is a conceptual design that answers a few critical questions:

- Where can flow be created?
- Where is pull necessary?
- What should the pacemaker control?
- How should information flow?
- What improvements are required to make this possible?

Limit improvement opportunities to a small number. Three to five is ideal. Mark them clearly on the map.

Focus beats ambition.

Step 10: Translate the Map into Action

A value stream map is only complete when it leads to action.

Each improvement opportunity becomes an action with:

- A clear problem statement
- A target condition
- An owner
- A timeline

These actions are reviewed regularly at the gemba and tracked visually.

The map stays visible. It becomes part of how the system is managed.

Value stream mapping does not solve problems by itself. What it does is far more powerful.

It teaches leaders and teams how to see. Once people can see the system, improvement stops being reactive and starts becoming intentional.

That is the difference between activity and progress.

Worked Examples: Making the Map Tell the Truth

Value stream mapping only works when the map reflects reality. Not averages pulled from a system. Not how the process is supposed to work. What actually happens on a normal, busy day.

This is why two teams can map the same process and come away with completely different conclusions. One map tells the truth. The other tells a comforting story.

The difference is usually in the details.

What a Good Process Data Box Looks Like

A **process data box** exists to describe behavior, not capability. Its purpose is to help the team understand how the process actually performs under real conditions.

A good data box contains just enough information to support decisions about flow.

Here is an example of a **useful process data box**:

- **Process:** Assembly Cell A
- **Cycle Time (C/T):** 42 sec (measured over 10 cycles)
- **Changeover Time (C/O):** 18 min
- **Operators:** 2
- **Uptime:** ~85%
- **Scrap / FPY:** 4% scrap
- **Batch Size:** 50 pieces
- **Working Time:** 7.5 hrs. / shift

This data box immediately tells a story.

The cycle time can be compared to takt. The changeover time explains batching. The uptime hints at instability. Scrap explains hidden rework and delays. Batch size explains inventory accumulation.

Most importantly, this data came from observation, not assumption.

Now compare that to a **poor data box**:

- **Cycle Time:** 30 sec (standard)
- **Efficiency:** 95%
- **Output:** 1,200 units/day

This data is nearly useless for VSM.

It does not explain variation. It does not reflect downtime. It does not show batching behavior. It hides scrap and rework. And worst of all, it creates false confidence.

A simple rule applies: if the operator cannot recognize themselves in the data box, the data is wrong.

How Much Data Is Enough?

Teams often ask how precise the data needs to be. The answer is simple: precise enough to reveal flow problems.

You are not doing time studies. You are not certifying processes. You are trying to understand where time is spent and why work waits.

Use averages. Use ranges when helpful. Write notes next to the box if something unusual happens.

Truth beats precision every time.

Worked Example: Information Flow That Looks Fine but Is Broken

Information flow is where many value streams quietly fail.

On paper, it often looks clean. Orders are entered. Schedules are released. Systems are updated. Everyone believes they know what to work on.

At the gemba, a different story emerges.

Here is an example of **bad information flow**, even though it appears structured:

- Customer orders are entered weekly into the ERP system.
- Production Control generates a weekly schedule for each department.
- Schedules are emailed to supervisors.

- Supervisors interpret priorities and relay them verbally to operators.
- Expedite requests override the schedule multiple times per day.

On the map, this shows up as:

- Multiple information arrows from Production Control to individual processes.
- Different frequencies (weekly schedules, daily updates, hourly expedites).
- Informal verbal signals replacing formal ones.

This is a classic symptom of push production. Every process is being told what to do independently. No one owns flow. Overproduction and firefighting are inevitable.

Now compare this with **healthy information flow**:

- Customer demand is received daily.
- One schedule is released to the pacemaker process only.
- Upstream processes replenish based on consumption signals.
- Visual controls make priorities obvious.
- Exceptions are handled explicitly, not constantly.

On the map, this appears simpler. Fewer arrows. Clear pull signals. Defined supermarkets. A visible pacemaker.

The paradox of VSM is that better systems look simpler on paper, even though they are more disciplined in reality.

If your information flow looks complicated, the system probably is.

Seeing the Hidden Factory Through the Timeline

One of the most powerful moments in a VSM event happens when the bottom timeline is completed.

Teams add up cycle times and are often pleased with how little processing time is required. Then they add up waiting time.

This is when the room goes quiet.

For example:

- **Total Processing Time:** fourteen minutes
- **Total Lead Time:** twelve days

Less than 1 percent of the lead time is value-added.

This realization changes the nature of improvement discussions. Instead of debating how to shave seconds off cycle time, teams start asking why work sits untouched for days.

The timeline does not argue. It simply shows.

This is why the timeline must always be built by hand and written clearly. It is one of the strongest teaching tools in Lean.

Advanced VSM Applications: Going Beyond the Basics

Once teams understand how to map a current state and design a future state, value stream mapping becomes much more than a one-time event. It becomes a way of thinking.

This chapter goes deeper on purpose. These applications are not optional in complex organizations. They are necessary.

Mapping Information Flow as a First-Class Citizen

In many value streams, information is the primary constraint, not material.

Administrative delays, approvals, handoffs, and rework loops often dominate lead time, even in manufacturing environments.

Advanced VSM treats information flow with the same rigor as material flow.

This means:

- Mapping decision points explicitly
- Showing approval loops and rework paths
- Capturing waiting time for information
- Identifying where decisions are pushed versus pulled

When information flow is mapped honestly, it often reveals that work is waiting for permission, not capacity.

VSM in Service and Administrative Processes

Value stream mapping is just as powerful in non-manufacturing environments, sometimes more so.

In service and administrative processes:

- Inventory becomes work-in-process (cases, orders, requests).
- Transport becomes handoffs.
- Motion becomes searching, re-entering data, or following up.

The principles remain the same.

Start at the customer. Define demand. Walk the process. Measure waiting. Map information flow. Build the timeline.

The biggest mistake in service VSM is mapping departments instead of flow. Processes almost always cut across functions. Mapping them vertically hides waste. Mapping them horizontally exposes it.

VSM Across the Supply Chain

Once internal flow is understood, VSM can be extended upstream and downstream.

Supply chain VSM reveals:

- How supplier batch sizes drive internal inventory
- How customer ordering behavior creates instability
- Where information delays amplify variability

This type of mapping requires trust and collaboration. It should be done selectively and deliberately. But when done well, it often produces the largest gains.

One caution applies: never map beyond your control without agreement. Visibility without alignment creates frustration.

Using VSM to Drive Strategy, Not Just Improvement

At an advanced level, value stream mapping becomes a strategic tool.

Leadership teams can use VSM to:

- Decide where to invest
- Prioritize improvement initiatives
- Evaluate automation opportunities
- Test whether a strategy is operationally feasible

If a future-state map cannot support the strategy, the strategy is theoretical.

This is one of the most underutilized aspects of VSM. It bridges the gap between boardroom intent and shop-floor reality.

When Value Stream Mapping Is Truly Working

You will know VSM has taken root when:

- Teams talk about flow instead of output
- Leaders ask about lead time before efficiency
- Schedules become fewer, not tighter
- Problems surface earlier, not later

At that point, the map itself becomes less important. The way of seeing remains.

That is the ultimate goal of value stream mapping. Not better drawings. Better decisions.

By the Book

There is a book called *Learning to See: Value Stream Mapping to Add Value and Eliminate Muda*, by John Shook and Mike Rother. This book is a step-by-step guide that clearly describes how to develop a value stream map. It is where I learned this methodology. Neither I nor my company, Manufacturing Simplicity, LLC, are associated with the authors or the publisher.

Mini Case Studies: How Value Stream Mapping Changes Decisions

Value stream mapping becomes real when leaders see how it plays out in actual organizations. The following short case studies are drawn from real situations across manufacturing and service environments. Details have been simplified, but the patterns are common and repeatable.

Each case illustrates a specific lesson about how VSM reveals truth and redirects effort.

Case Study 1: The Fast Line That Made Everything Slower

Lesson: Cycle time improvements without flow make lead time worse

A consumer products manufacturer was proud of its assembly line. Over several years, the team had invested heavily in automation and line balancing. Cycle time had been reduced by more than 30 percent. Utilization was high. Output metrics looked strong.

Customers, however, were still complaining about long lead times and missed deliveries.

When the value stream was mapped, the surprise came quickly. Assembly was fast, but upstream processes ran in large batches to "keep the line fed." Finished goods accumulated in front of final test and packaging, which operated on a different schedule.

The timeline told the real story:

- **Processing time:** twenty-two minutes
- **Total lead time:** eighteen days

Less than one-tenth of one percent of the lead time added value.

The team had optimized the most visible process, unintentionally destabilizing the rest of the system. Assembly had become the source of overproduction.

The future-state map shifted the pacemaker downstream, reduced batch sizes, and introduced pull between test and assembly. Assembly slowed slightly. Lead time dropped by more than 60 percent.

The insight was uncomfortable but powerful:
Speed without flow is waste.

Case Study 2: The ERP System That "Controlled Everything"

Lesson: Bad information flow hides behind good systems

A medical device manufacturer believed its ERP system provided full control of production. Schedules were generated weekly. Reports were reviewed daily. Expediting was common but was accepted as part of the business.

During the VSM event, the team mapped information flow in detail.

What emerged was a spiderweb of signals:

- Weekly schedules from Planning
- Daily updates from Customer Service
- Hourly emails from Sales
- Verbal overrides from supervisors

Operators admitted they had ignored the schedule by mid-morning and were waiting for verbal direction.

On paper, the system looked sophisticated. On the map, it was chaos.

The future state simplified information flow dramatically. Only the pacemaker process received a schedule. All upstream processes replenished based on consumption. Visual controls replaced emails.

Expediting dropped sharply. Not because people worked harder, but because priorities no longer changed every hour.

The key realization was this:
A system can be digital and still be uncontrolled.

Case Study 3: The Perfect Data Box That Lied

Lesson: System data often hides instability

An industrial equipment company prepared extensively for a VSM event. Data was pulled in advance. Standard cycle times, efficiencies, and outputs were neatly documented.

During the gemba walk, the team timed the process anyway.

Actual cycle times were consistently 20 to 40 percent longer than the standards. Downtime was frequent but unrecorded. Operators had developed workarounds that were invisible to the system.

When the team replaced system data with observed data, the map changed completely. The supposed bottleneck moved. Inventory patterns suddenly made sense.

The lesson was clear:
Standards describe intent. Observation reveals reality.

From that point forward, the team treated system data as a hypothesis, not a fact.

Case Study 4: The Service Process That Looked Efficient

Lesson: In services, waiting hides in approvals

A financial services organization mapped its loan-approval process. Each department believed it was efficient. Turnaround times at each step were measured in hours.

The value stream map showed something else.

Between steps, work sat untouched for days waiting for review, clarification, or sign-off. Work-in-process was high. Rework loops were common.

The timeline told the story:

- **Processing time:** six hours
- **Lead time:** twenty-seven days

Most delays were not caused by workload but by unclear decision rules.

The future state focused less on speed and more on clarity. Approval criteria were simplified. Decision authority was pushed closer to the work. Several approvals were eliminated entirely.

Lead time dropped by more than half without adding resources.

The insight surprised leadership:
Most service delays are decision delays, not capacity problems.

Case Study 5: The Supply Chain Map That Changed a Strategy

Lesson: VSM exposes strategic misalignment

A mid-sized manufacturer planned to expand capacity to support growth. Before approving capital spending, leadership asked for a supply chain VSM.

The map revealed that supplier batch sizes drove internal inventory far more than internal constraints. The proposed expansion would have increased output but also increased inventory and lead time.

Instead of investing in capacity, leadership worked with key suppliers to reduce batch sizes and improve delivery frequency. Internally, supermarkets were resized, and information flow was simplified.

The growth target was met without expansion.

The strategic takeaway was simple:
If the value stream cannot support the strategy, the strategy must change.

Why These Cases Matter

These examples all share a common thread. The problems were not invisible because they were complex. They were invisible because no one had stepped back far enough to see the whole.

Value stream mapping did not provide answers. It provided clarity. The answers followed naturally.

That is why VSM remains one of the most powerful tools in Lean. Not because it fixes things, but because it changes how leaders and teams understand their system.

Once that understanding exists, better decisions become unavoidable.

Common Failure Modes in Value Stream Mapping

Why Good Intentions Often Produce Weak Maps

Value stream mapping is simple in concept and unforgiving in execution. Most failed VSM efforts do not fail because teams lack intelligence or commitment.

They fail because small, seemingly reasonable shortcuts quietly undermine the purpose of the exercise.

Understanding these failure modes in advance dramatically increases the odds that your map will lead to real change instead of another round of frustration.

Treating VSM as a Documentation Exercise

One of the most common mistakes is approaching VSM as a way to document the current process rather than understand it.

Teams focus on drawing clean maps, aligning symbols, and capturing every step exactly as it appears in a procedure. The map becomes tidy, detailed, and ultimately useless.

Value stream mapping is not about accuracy for its own sake. It is about insight. A rough map that reveals where time is lost is far more valuable than a perfect map that hides it.

If your team spends more time debating symbols than discussing flow, the exercise has already drifted off course.

Mapping from Memory Instead of the Gemba

Another frequent failure mode is building the map in a conference room based on experience, reports, or assumptions.

This approach feels efficient. It is also deeply misleading.

What people remember is rarely what actually happens, especially in unstable systems. Workarounds, informal signals, and rework loops are almost always invisible unless you observe the process directly.

A simple test applies: if the map was not drawn while physically walking the process, it is not a value stream map. It is a theory.

Using System Data Instead of Observed Data

ERP systems, standards, and reports are seductive. They are clean, readily available, and authoritative.

They are also often wrong.

System data reflects intent, averages, and delayed feedback. VSM requires observed reality. Timing cycles with a stopwatch, counting inventory by hand, and tracing information back to its source are not optional steps. They are the core of the learning.

When teams rely on system data, the map looks impressive and explains nothing.

Skipping or Rushing PQPR

Many teams jump directly into mapping because they are eager to get started. Product family selection is treated as a formality.

This almost always leads to confusion.

Mapping with too broad a scope produces bloated maps with no clear improvement focus. Mapping with too narrow a scope produces local insights that do not generalize.

PQPR exists to force a disciplined choice. When it is rushed or skipped, the value stream map inherits that lack of focus.

If the team cannot clearly explain why this value stream was chosen, the map will struggle to produce meaningful action.

Ignoring Information Flow

Material flow is visible. Information flow is not. As a result, many maps underrepresent or oversimplify how decisions are made.

This is a serious error.

In most organizations, information flow drives behavior far more than material flow. Schedules, priorities, approvals, and exceptions determine what actually happens day to day.

Maps that show material but not information tend to blame people or equipment for problems that originate in planning and decision-making.

If information flow looks simple on the map but feels chaotic in reality, it has not been mapped honestly.

Confusing Activity with Flow

Some teams focus heavily on what people are doing and too little on how work moves.

They document every task, every motion, every handoff. The map becomes dense with detail and thin on insight.

Flow is about waiting, accumulation, and pacing. It is about where work stops, not where it moves.

If the map does not clearly show where time is lost, it is missing the point.

Overemphasizing Cycle Time and Ignoring Lead Time

Cycle time is intuitive. Lead time is uncomfortable.

As a result, teams often fixate on cycle time differences between processes while ignoring the waiting time that dominates the system.

Value stream mapping exists to reveal lead time. The bottom timeline is not an accessory. It is the punchline.

If the timeline is rushed, incomplete, or treated as an afterthought, the most important insight of the entire exercise is lost.

Designing a Future State Without Understanding the Current State

A tempting failure mode is jumping to solutions too early.

Once problems become visible, teams naturally want to fix them. Improvement ideas start flying. The map becomes a brainstorming session.

This is premature.

Without a deep understanding of the current state, future-state designs are guesses. They often replicate existing problems in new forms.

Discipline matters here. The current state must be fully understood and validated before any serious future-state design begins.

Creating an Overly Ambitious Future State

When teams finally design the future state, another trap appears: ambition.

Maps become idealized. Everything flows. Inventory disappears. Schedules vanish. The future state looks beautiful and impossible.

A useful future state is not perfect. It is directional. It focuses on a small number of changes that can realistically be implemented and tested.

If the future state requires dozens of simultaneous improvements, it will not survive contact with reality.

Treating the Map as the Outcome

Perhaps the most damaging failure mode is treating the completed map as the result of the exercise.

Teams admire it. Leaders praise the effort. The map is hung on a wall. And then nothing happens.

A value stream map that does not lead to action is unfinished.

The map is a means, not an end. Its purpose is to drive better decisions, clearer priorities, and disciplined follow-through.

If actions are not clearly defined, owned, and tracked, the map has failed, regardless of how insightful it appears.

Losing the Leadership Thread

Finally, many VSM efforts fail because leadership treats the exercise as a technical activity rather than a leadership responsibility.

Value stream mapping changes how work is seen. That change must be reinforced by leadership behavior. If leaders continue to reward local optimization, expedite constantly, or override the system, the map becomes irrelevant.

VSM does not replace leadership judgment. It sharpens it.

When leaders model patience, curiosity, and discipline during the mapping process, the organization follows.

A Final Warning and a Final Encouragement

Most VSM failures are not dramatic. They are quiet. The map gets done. The workshop ends. Life resumes.

The difference between success and failure often comes down to whether the team used the map to challenge its own assumptions or simply confirm them.

Approached with humility and discipline, VSM is one of the most powerful learning tools available to leaders.

Approached casually, it becomes another artifact.

The choice is yours.

Reflection and Action

Reflection: How Well Do You See the Whole?

Think about your organization as it operates today.

- When problems arise, do leaders instinctively look for local causes, or do they ask how the system is behaving?
- How often do improvement efforts focus on making people faster instead of making flow smoother?
- If you were asked to explain your end-to-end lead time from customer order to delivery, could you do so confidently, without looking it up?

Now consider visibility.

- Do leaders and teams share a common understanding of how value actually flows, or does each function see only its own part?
- How often are decisions made based on reports rather than direct observation at the gemba?
- When priorities conflict, is there a clear reference point tied to customer demand, or do the loudest issues win?

VSM exposes these patterns quickly. The discomfort it creates is not a sign of failure. It is a sign that reality is finally visible.

Reflection: Information Flow and Leadership Behavior

Information flow reflects leadership intent.

- How many different signals tell your teams what to work on each day?
- Who controls priorities in practice: the system, the schedule, or the last escalation?
- When plans change, is the reason clear and visible, or does it arrive as a surprise?

Now reflect on your own behavior.

- When you intervene, are you reinforcing the system or bypassing it?
- Do your actions make information flow clearer or more chaotic?
- If you mapped information flow honestly, what would it reveal about how decisions are really made?

Culture is not what is written in values statements. It is what the system teaches people to do when things get hard.

Reflection: Where Time Is Truly Lost

Think about lead time, not activity.

- Where does work wait the longest in your value streams?
- Are delays caused by capacity or by batching, approvals, and unclear decisions?
- How much of your total lead time is truly value-adding?

Now think about improvement priorities.

- Are you spending most of your energy optimizing processes or reducing waiting?
- Do your metrics reward output or flow?
- If you improved lead time by half, which customer problems would disappear immediately?

Value stream mapping shifts attention from effort to impact. That shift changes how improvement is chosen and justified.

Action: Prepare to Map Your First Value Stream

If you have not yet conducted a value stream mapping event, use this chapter to prepare deliberately.

Start by answering the following questions in writing:

1. **Which product family or service flow should be mapped first, and why?**
   Base your answer on volume, strategic importance, and pain, not convenience.

2. **Who must be involved for the map to reflect reality?**
   Include people who do the work, not just those who manage it.

3. **What customer demand facts are currently assumptions rather than facts?**
   Identify what you must verify before mapping begins.

4. **What leadership behaviors might undermine the exercise if left unchecked?**
   Be honest. VSM will surface them anyway.

This is not planning for a workshop. It is preparing for learning.

Action: Use the Map as a Leadership Tool

Once a value stream map exists, its real work begins.

Commit to the following:

- Use the map to guide conversations, not defend positions.
- Review actions at the gemba, not just in meetings.
- Ask about lead time before asking about efficiency.
- Treat the map as a living reference, not a one-time artifact.

Most importantly, resist the urge to fix everything at once. Focus on the few changes that will most improve flow. Let learning guide the next step.

Building Your Lean Transformation Plan

As you move through the remaining chapters of this book, your Lean transformation plan should begin to take shape.

From this chapter, capture:

- The value streams that matter most to your business
- The systemic constraints that limit flow
- The leadership behaviors that must change to sustain improvement

These elements will connect directly to strategy, daily management, capability building, and culture in the chapters ahead.

Lean transformation does not begin with tools. It begins with seeing clearly enough to lead differently.

Value Stream Mapping gives you that vision.

The responsibility to act on it is yours.

Chapter 5 Reflection and Action Answers

CHAPTER 6

Turning Seeing into Direction: *Policy Deployment as the System That Keeps Strategy Alive Every Day*

The Missed Handoff

It's Monday morning again, and you walk in with something you didn't have before: clarity.

You've been to the gemba. You've mapped the value stream (Chapter 5). You can see where time is lost, where work waits, where information breaks down, and where decisions create instability. The system is no longer a mystery.

For the first time in a long time, you can point to the real causes of performance, not just the symptoms.

And yet, by mid-morning, the familiar pattern begins to reassert itself.

Customer Service escalates a late order. Production pushes back, citing the schedule. Planning adjusts priorities. Quality stops a process. Engineering launches a fix. Someone calls it a "quick workaround." Someone else says it's "just for this week."

By noon, everyone is busy again.

You walk the floor and feel the disconnect. People are working hard but not together. Each function is acting rationally within its own world. Nobody is lying. Nobody is lazy. Everyone is doing what they believe is right.

And still, the customer is waiting.

This is one of the most frustrating moments in leadership.

Not because the team failed.
But because the organization is behaving exactly as it was designed to behave.

You now see the system clearly. But the system is still pulling people in ten directions at once.

This is the moment when many Lean transformations stall. Not because the tools don't work, but because visibility alone does not create alignment. In fact, once problems become visible, the noise often gets louder. Everyone brings you their favorite fix. Every department has a priority. Every metric has its own emergency.

Clarity reveals opportunity, but it also reveals overload.

This is where policy deployment enters the story.

Complexity does not arrive as chaos. It arrives as good people optimizing their slice. Strategy deployment is how you pull everyone back toward the same priorities, the same direction, and the same definition of success.

When the goals are visible and the path is clear, decisions speed up and wasteful work falls away. The question shifts from "Who is right?" to "Does this move us toward the goal?" If not, we stop. If yes, we simplify and go.

From Seeing to Choosing, and from Choosing to Sustained Focus

As seen in Chapter 5, value stream mapping is one of the most powerful ways to understand how your organization creates value. It reveals flow. It exposes waste. It shows you where the system is truly constrained. For many leaders, it becomes the turning point where assumptions collapse and reality becomes visible. But VSM is not your strategy.

VSM is a diagnostic tool. It shows you what is happening in the value stream you mapped at the moment you mapped it. That information is incredibly valuable, and it often provides critical input into what the business should prioritize next.

Policy deployment is something broader. Policy deployment (PD) is the system that keeps strategy alive every day. It is how an organization decides what matters most, translates that into a small number of measurable priorities, and then ensures that every level of the organization is aligned and engaged in executing them.

It is the bridge between leadership intent and daily work.

Without it, even the best strategy becomes a slide deck. Even the clearest diagnosis becomes a list of disconnected projects. Even the most motivated teams drift back into firefighting, because urgent work always finds a way to dominate important work.

Policy deployment solves a different problem than VSM.

- VSM helps you see and understand the system.
- Policy deployment helps you focus, align, execute, measure, and respond.

It ensures that:

- The organization does not chase everything at once.
- Improvement work is connected to strategy.
- Progress is visible.
- Problems surface early.
- Countermeasures happen quickly.
- People at every level know what winning looks like.

Although the VSM exercise provides valuable input into your strategy, policy deployment is not simply a tool to prioritize a value stream map.

PD is the operating system that prevents the organization from losing focus, even when the pressure rises, even when the day gets messy, and even when the work is hard.

And once it is in place, it becomes the structure that turns Lean from improvement activity into transformation.

This chapter will show you how to build it.

I. Introduction

One of the most powerful outcomes of effective strategy deployment is organizational simplification. As we explored earlier in Chapter 1, complexity is an invisible but costly drain on organizational resources, productivity, and employee morale. A clearly defined, well-communicated strategy serves as an antidote, creating focus and clarity across all organizational levels.

When strategic goals are ambiguous or poorly communicated, teams naturally drift into complexity. Conflicting priorities emerge, duplicate efforts arise, and unclear decision making slows progress. On the other hand, when every team member clearly understands the overarching strategic objectives and how their daily actions contribute, wasteful complexity dissolves. Tasks and initiatives that do not align with strategic goals become transparently unnecessary and can be confidently discarded.

Moreover, strategic alignment empowers teams at all levels to make simpler, quicker decisions. Rather than awaiting instructions or navigating bureaucratic layers, employees can evaluate choices against clearly articulated goals and ask, "Does this action align with our strategy?" If the answer is no, they have immediate justification to simplify by eliminating or adjusting the task accordingly.

Ultimately, strategic alignment clarifies priorities, removes confusion, and accelerates decision-making, fostering an environment where simplicity becomes a natural state. Throughout this chapter, you'll learn how to clearly articulate your strategy, cascade it effectively through your organization, and sustain alignment to ensure complexity is consistently minimized and simplicity continuously embraced.

Companies often get caught up in doing things, many things, to improve. They chase new projects, try to cut costs, or boost sales without really asking, "Why are we doing this?" It's like everyone's running around, but no one knows where the finish line is.

Think of it this way. If every department is doing its own thing, without considering the company's overall goals, you run the risk of ending up with chaos. You might have one team that's super-efficient at their small part, but they're creating problems for the next team in line. This means wasted time, resources, and frustrated customers.

I often employ the analogy of an orchestra. Imagine dozens of excellent musicians, each playing their instrument flawlessly. When they are all playing the same song, that is a beautiful experience. But what happens if each musician is playing a different song? Although individually they may be outstanding musicians, the end result is still chaos.

It is depressing to think about how many businesses we engaged in improving or turning around that had such misalignment as the root cause of their problems. Typically, people and their departments work hard, doing their best within the confines of their respective areas, but overall, the business still declines. Often, someone's efforts are cancelled out by another area marching in a different direction.

Can you think of examples of this happening in your company? I usually see things such as Manufacturing working to improve efficiency and reducing two operators with the goal of cutting costs while Quality Control adds three people to modify procedures, increasing the regulatory burden in Manufacturing, where they just reduced personnel. In this example, it does not matter who is right or who is wrong, but clearly, the teams are not working in concert.

When you have strategic alignment, everyone understands the big picture. They know how their work contributes to the company's success. This means you use your resources wisely, everyone's efforts are focused, and communication flows smoothly. Decisions get easier because you're always asking, "Does this help us reach our goals, or is it moving us away from our goals?" And when things change, as they always do, you can adapt quickly because everyone's on the same page.

Now let's bring in the Lean initiatives. Lean is fantastic for improving efficiency and cutting waste. Although your Lean projects will bring benefits no matter what, they shouldn't exist in a vacuum. As I said many times before, they need to support the company's strategic goals.

When you connect Lean to your strategy, you turn those big, abstract goals into real, tangible results. Lean helps you execute your strategy. You become more competitive because you're cutting out unnecessary costs and improving quality. You build a culture of continuous improvement, where everyone is working towards the same vision.

And here's the best part: Lean gives you data. You can track your progress and see how your efforts are helping you reach your goals. Plus, Lean focuses on the customer. So, when you improve your processes, you're also improving the customer's experience.

In this chapter, you will see that Lean is more than making things faster or cheaper. Lean will help you build a company that's focused on delivering real value to both your customers and your employees. And that happens when everyone is aligned with the company's strategic direction.

So, we've talked about why aligning your Lean efforts with the company's strategy is so important. How do you actually *do* that? That's where hoshin kanri comes in.

Before we jump in, let me ask you a question. Who in your company is in charge of implementing the company's strategy? Don't read on until you answer this. Do all the employees even know what the strategy is? Please pause to reflect on this point. What have you or your team done today to implement the company's strategy? Who is implementing it right now? How far into the implementation is your company?

Hoshin kanri, sometimes just called "hoshin," is a Japanese term that translates to "policy deployment," and we often use it interchangeably with "strategy deployment." It's a strategic planning and management system that was developed in Japan in the 1960s, largely influenced by the work of W. Edwards Deming and Joseph M. Juran. You've probably heard their names before; they're the grandfathers of quality management.

This process ensures everyone in the organization knows and understands the strategy. In addition, everyone knows the role they play in the implementation of the strategy. Every day starts with a mission, and people know that if they meet their goals, they have contributed to the achievement of the company's vision. This is rewarding and powerful. It makes the work meaningful.

Think of hoshin kanri as your company's GPS. It's a way to make sure everyone's heading in the same direction and that you're actually going to reach your destination. It's a system that helps you take those big, long-term strategic goals and break them down into smaller, more manageable, actionable steps. Just to refer back to the orchestra analogy, the policy deployment process ensures everyone plays to the same sheet of music.

Here are the key principles behind hoshin kanri:

- **Strategic Alignment:** Like we just discussed, this process makes sure everyone's efforts are aligned with the company's overall strategy.
- **Participation:** Hoshin kanri involves everyone, from top management to frontline employees. It's about getting input from everyone and making sure everyone's on board.
- **Focus:** It drives focus on a few key goals rather than trying to do everything at once. You know how it is: if you try to chase too many rabbits, you catch none.
- **Communication:** Hoshin kanri fosters clear and consistent communication. Everyone needs to know what the goals are and how they're progressing.
- **Review and Action:** Regularly reviewing progress and taking action to make sure you're on track is part of the routine. Monthly, weekly, daily, and yes, at times, hourly.

Now, you might be thinking, *Okay, that sounds interesting, but how does this connect to what I'm doing every day?* That's where **daily management** comes in.

Daily management makes sure that your daily operations are aligned with your strategic goals. You should not just do things for the sake of doing them. Instead, you should be doing things that are actually helping you achieve your goals.

Think of it this way. Your strategic goals are like your long-term travel plans. You know where you want to go, and you have a general idea of how you're going to get there. But your daily operations are like your day-to-day driving. You need to make sure you're staying on the right roads and not getting lost.

Hoshin kanri helps you connect your strategic goals to your daily operations by:

- Breaking down goals into smaller, actionable steps.
- Ensuring the lowest level goals support the goals of the next level up, that they support the next level up, etc., all the way to the top where the strategy was generated and deployed.
- Assigning responsibilities and timelines.
- Establishing key performance indicators (KPIs) to track progress.
- Conducting regular reviews to make sure you're on track.

II. The Strategy Deployment Process

Before jumping into the detailed explanation of the strategy deployment process, let me ask you one thing. What is a strategy? Pause and think about it before reading on.

A company I worked for defined the strategy as the answer to two questions:

1. **What game are we playing?**
2. **How do we win?**

That's an easy and straightforward way to think about it, so let's complicate it a little.

Let's define strategy as:

- **A plan of action designed to achieve a long-term or overall aim.**

However, it's more than just a plan. In strategic planning, you make choices and allocate resources to gain a competitive advantage. Here's a more nuanced breakdown:

- **A Set of Choices:**
  - A strategy involves making deliberate choices about what to do and, equally important, what *not* to do.
  - It focuses resources on the activities that will have the greatest impact.

- **A Path to Achieve a Goal:**
  - A strategy provides a roadmap for achieving a specific objective.
  - It outlines the steps that will be taken to reach the desired outcome.

- **A Source of Competitive Advantage:**
  - A good strategy helps an organization differentiate itself from its competitors.
  - It creates a sustainable advantage that allows the organization to thrive.

- **A Framework for Decision Making:**
  - A strategy provides a consistent framework for making decisions at all levels of the organization.

    - It ensures that everyone is working toward the same goals.

- **A Dynamic Process:**
    - A strategy is not a static document. It must be adapted and updated as circumstances change.
    - It must be able to change with the market.

In essence, a strategy includes:

- Where you want to go (your goal)
- How you plan to get there (your actions)
- Why you believe your approach will work (your rationale)

I hope this brief explanation puts us on the same page. Now, let's move on.

A. Developing the Strategic Plan:

So, let's pretend you believe me and you've decided you need a strategic plan. Great. But where do you even start? We are not just going to sit in a boardroom, pulling ideas out of thin air. We need to do some listening, analyzing, and then chart a course.

1. Capturing the Voice of the Customer (VOC):

First and foremost, you've got to understand what your customers actually want. Not what you *think* they want but what they *really* want. I've seen too many companies make assumptions, and it always backfires.

How do you do this? You get out there and talk to them. Conduct surveys, hold focus groups, analyze customer feedback, and even go to industry events and listen to what people are saying. Use every tool at your disposal.

And don't just listen to the good stuff. Dig into the complaints, the frustrations, the areas where you're falling short. That's where the real gold is. If you want bonus points, also assess the market trends and the emerging technologies. Talk to your technical people and have them scrub articles, go to universities, and find out what disruptive technologies could help or hinder your industry.

Meet with the executive team along with key people and conduct brainstorming sessions, asking, "In what other ways could we satisfy our customers? If we were not allowed to make our product anymore, how else could we deliver what the customer needs?" Ask out-of-the-box questions to force breakthrough thinking. Use the voice of the customer as an input.

Once you've got that data, translate it into actionable insights. What are the key customer needs? What are their pain points? How can you deliver more value? What other products should you make? How should you modify your offerings? Keep the questions flowing, aiming at becoming a drastically better company in the future. Paint a positive, innovative, picture, focusing on building a sustainable business by overwhelming your customers with service.

2. Identifying Long-Term Vision and Goals:

Now you've got to figure out where you want to be in, say, three to five years. What's your big, audacious goal? What's your "north star?" This is the beginning of the top-level part of this process, where the vision, strategy, top-level initiatives, etc. are set. Later in the process, we will explain how.

Don't focus solely on making money. Continue to work with the executive team and use this practice to define your purpose, your company's reason for being. What impact do you want to have on your customers, your employees, and the world?

Keep in mind, the strategy will be communicated and deployed to the entire organization. You want to give the organization their purpose, their "why." Make it compelling and motivating. As a matter of fact, be proud of your vision and share it not only with your employees but with all stakeholders, including customers, suppliers, the community, and investors.

Companies do this in different ways. Some hold visioning workshops, some bring in outside experts for guided sessions, and some just have a few key leaders lock themselves in a room until they figure it out. The important thing is that it's a collaborative process. Everyone needs to buy into the vision, and the wider the participation is in building the vision, the greater the buy-in will be.

Once you've got your vision, you can start setting some long-term goals in support of it. Teams often struggle to transition from a vision, which is usually subjective, to something measurable. Well, you have to make it measurable. These goals should be specific, measurable, achievable, relevant, and time bound (SMART). They should be ambitious, but not so ambitious that they're impossible to achieve.

How do you make something subjective measurable? Visions often include statements such as *"a satisfied customer"* and *"a great place to work."* These are too generic and unmeasurable. To assign a metric and a goal, I usually ask the team, "How do you know the customer is satisfied?" or "What does it mean when you say a workplace is great?"

As you engage the team in the conversation and brainstorm with them, ideas will start to emerge, and you can establish metrics, such as Net Promoter Scores or repeat purchase rates to measure customer satisfaction, and employee turnover rates or employee satisfaction scores to support your vision of a great place to work. Do not be limited to existing metrics. If you need to create a new, more relevant metric in support of your vision, do it.

Let's pick an example to walk you through these next steps. Let's say the vision, or three-to-five-year breakthrough objectives, include doubling the size of the company in five years. If your current annual revenue is $50 million, then you know you have arrived at your established vision when you achieve $100 million.

3. Chunking Your Vision:

At this point, you know what you want your company to look like in three to five years. That is a long time, and it will be hard to keep everyone motivated if they continue to work on a five-year goal. The initiatives become too big, and efforts are diluted over time. In addition, things are likely to change, especially when you consider external factors that are outside your control. If you are locked into a five-year plan, halting and modifying large-scale projects becomes hard.

The solution is to chunk it down. This means breaking your long-term strategic goal into annual increments. Be especially aggressive in year one! Don't "hockey stick" it! The question is, "How much of the three-to-five-year objective will we meet in year one?"

Using the example above, how much of the $100 million revenue will be achieved in year one? Aim high. Let's say the team agrees with $75 million, and that is what we will call the "annual breakthrough objective." Note that, unless you know exactly how to get there, don't put $75 million in the budget. I recommend you follow the budget process as you normally do and keep the conservative growth estimates. In the policy deployment process, you want to drive breakthroughs by going way above budget estimates.

4. Analyzing the Current State and Identifying Gaps:

All right, now you know where you want to go (your vision), you quantified it in a measurable way, and you know how much of the long-term goal you will pursue in year one. But what does the organization have to do to achieve its ambition? It is necessary to understand where you are starting from. You've got to take a hard look at your current situation.

This means analyzing your internal processes, financial performance, market position, and competitive landscape. You've got to be brutally honest with yourself. Where are you strong? Where are you weak? What are your opportunities and threats?

Tools like SWOT analysis and value stream mapping can be really helpful here. You're looking for the gaps between where you are and where you want to be. What's holding you back? What needs to change?

This step is important because it will help you identify the improvement priorities. The **improvement priorities** are the initiatives the company must work on and what processes must change so that you reach the annual breakthrough objectives. These initiatives will be the mechanism to move from where your company currently is toward your year-one objectives, which will, in turn, allow you to achieve the three-to-five-year objectives.

In our example, let's say the team will implement a new sales process and, in addition, will deploy a new phone system with call monitoring as the improvement priorities for this specific breakthrough objective.

5. Establishing Improvement Priorities' Targets:

So, each initiative you have to work on in order to close the gap we call an "improvement priority." If you select the right improvement priorities, once they are successfully completed, they should ensure you meet your annual objectives and get you closer to your vision. The question then is: "How do you know each improvement priority is on track?" Since these improvement priorities are the initiatives that will drive the implementation of your strategy, you want to make sure they stay on track, right? So, you must establish a way to ensure all your improvement priorities are successful. The solution is your **targets to improve**, or TTIs.

What are the TTIs? They are metrics you need to establish for each improvement priority. All improvement priorities must be accompanied by at least one TTI that will keep you honest. Ask the following question for each improvement priority: "How do I know when this initiative is succeeding or failing?"

Finally, each improvement priority must have one person who is responsible for its implementation. Note that I didn't say a "group," "team," or "department." I said "person." Give this individual the authority and resources commensurate with the accountability and hold them responsible to get it done. When you assign a group or anything other than one person to lead an initiative, it becomes a "group project," and you run the risk that someone does the work while others watch. In the end, you end up with finger pointing while the initiative remains unfinished.

Let's clarify something that often causes confusion. Aren't the targets to improve the same metrics as the annual breakthrough objectives? Not necessarily. Actually, more often than not, they are not the same metric. The annual breakthrough objective is how you are measuring your progress toward the vision. For example, if you established you will double the revenue from $50 million to $100 million in five years, you may have established an annual breakthrough objective of $75 million for next year.

How are you going to get there? Let's say that through your workshops and based on your sales process, you know that the revenue growth is given by how many phone calls your sales team makes each day. So, to increase the sales by 50 percent (going from $50M to $75M), you want to increase the daily calls for each salesperson by 50 percent, going, say, from ten calls a day to fifteen calls a day per person. *This* becomes your target to improve the number of daily calls, because your improvement priority is to increase the number of calls. This is a metric every salesperson can track; you can log them daily, and that is the metric that will show if the team is on track.

See it in the form below. This form has many names, and it varies a bit from business to business. It is called the **PD matrix**, where "PD" stands for policy deployment. Other names include the "strategy deployment matrix," "X matrix," and "wire matrix." See FIGURE 3 below:

Top Level Policy Deployment

Owner:	Joanna CEO
Revision Date:	

Top Level Improvement Priorities	Reduce time to market for new products from 28 months to 16 months	Free up $7M in cash	Increase revenue from $50M to $75M	Improve the sales processcertification for sales associates from 12% to 90%	Increase the average number of sales calls per salesperson from 10 to 15	Increase cash flow from $5M to $7M	Reduce the average times for stage gate 1 from 92 days to 30 days, and 88 to 20 in stage 2.	Petros	Muhammed	Olivia	Geraldo
Implement ProdEx System	●						●			●	
Working capital initiative		●				●					●
Deploy phone system with call monitoring			●		●				●		
Implement ABCtoXYZ sales process			●	●				●			

3-5 Year Breakthrough Objectives	Reduce time to market for new products from 28 months to 16 months	Free up $7M in cash	Increase revenue from $50M to $75M
Increase revenues by 100%			●
Free up $10M for investments in growth		●	
Reduce time to market for new products by 60%	●		

Matrix quadrants: Top Level Improvement Priorities; Targets To Improve; 3-5 Year Breakthrough Objectives; Annual Breaktrhough Objectives

Key

●	Primary Responsibility
❍	Support

Note that the *"owner"* of the top-level matrix is the CEO; in this case, her name is Joanna. You can see the owner's name in the upper-right corner of the matrix. At the heart of the matrix, you will find an "X" dividing it in four quadrants. At the bottom, you will find the *"3–5 Year Breakthrough Objectives."* The most important objectives are the ones closer to the center of the "X." In this case, *"Increase revenue by 100%"* is the most important objective, followed by *"Reduce lead times by 50%"* and, finally, *"Reduce time to market for new products by 60%."*

Let me direct you to look at the left quadrant, where the *"Annual Breakthrough Objectives"* are. The objective closest to the center is *"Increase revenue from $50M to $75M."* This objective is linked to the *"3-5 Year Breakthrough Objective"* by a black dot "•." The black dots link objectives, priorities, and targets to improve throughout the matrix.

Now look at the top quadrant, and you will see there are two improvement priorities in support of the revenue growth. They are *"Implement ABC to XYZ sales process"* and *"Deploy phone system with call monitoring."*

The last quadrant, the one on the right, shows the targets to improve, where you will find the target *"Increase the average number of sales calls per salesperson from 10 to 15."* Go further to the right, and you will see the people responsible for each improvement priority. In the case of our example, Muhammed is the person responsible for making this happen.

Now step back and look at the entire top-level matrix. In one page, you can see the company's direction, how much of it will be conquered in the next year, the actions that need to be taken to realize the strategy, how they will be measured, and who is responsible for them. This is a powerful document that good leaders can use to inspire and motivate the entire workforce. It should be posted everywhere and discussed at every opportunity.

6. Action Plans:

Stay with me now.

So far, you have led your company through the process of establishing a **vision** and the **breakthrough objectives** to get you there in three to five years.

Then you broke those objectives down in annual increments, establishing a target for next year, and they are called **annual breakthrough objectives**.

After that, you determined **improvement priorities** for each of the annual objectives, where the team agreed on which initiatives will be implemented to get to the annual objectives.

Consequently, you established the **targets to improve**, a way to measure the success of each improvement priority. You also assigned one person to lead and be responsible for each improvement priority.

At this point, there are a few initiatives you call improvement priorities, along with the metrics and targets to achieve by year end or earlier. Now the folks responsible for the improvement priorities must get their team together and plan what they will do to achieve their TTI by year end. This means they must develop an action plan.

I recommend they produce a Gantt chart containing the tasks required to implement the improvement priority, the timing associated with each task or when they are due, who is accountable for completing each task, and what the *impact* of each task is expected to be once it's implemented. I will bring up the impact again shortly…

By the way, you can build all these forms, including one for the action plan, using your preferred, appropriate software. You can also download them from our site: www.manufacturingsimplicity.com.

Oh, wait a minute. Do you know what a Gantt chart is? If you do, skip to "7" below; otherwise, read on.

So, you know how when you're planning a big project, you have a bunch of tasks you need to get done? And you need to know who's doing what and when it's all supposed to happen? That's where a **Gantt chart** comes in.

Think of it like a visual timeline for your project. It's a bar chart that lays out all the tasks, their start and end dates, and who's responsible for each one.

Here's the breakdown:

- **Tasks on the Side:** Down the left side of the chart, you'll see a list of all the tasks in your project. Each task gets its own row.
- **Timeline Across the Top:** Across the top of the chart, you'll see a timeline, usually broken down into days, weeks, or months, depending on how long your project is.

- **Bars Representing Tasks:** Each task is represented by a horizontal bar that stretches across the timeline. The length of the bar shows how long the task is expected to take.
- **Dependencies (Sometimes):** Some Gantt charts also show dependencies between tasks. This means that some tasks can't start until others are finished. These dependencies are usually shown with arrows connecting the bars.
- **Who's Doing What:** Often, the chart will also show who's responsible for each task.

Why is this useful?

- It gives you a clear picture of your project's timeline. You can see at a glance when tasks are starting and ending and how they overlap.
- It helps you identify potential bottlenecks. If you see that a lot of tasks are scheduled to happen at the same time, you know you might have a problem.
- It helps you track progress. As tasks are completed, you can mark them on the chart so everyone can see how things are going.
- It is a great communication tool.

In short, a Gantt chart is a simple but powerful tool for planning and managing projects. It helps you keep everyone on the same page and ensures that your project stays on track.

7. The Review Process:

Hang on. We are almost there.

Now it is time to establish a review frequency for these **top-level improvement priorities**. The question is who will review what, and how often? At this level, I recommend a monthly review. The executive team should be present, and the leaders for each improvement priority should report the status of their projects. In the presentation, the leaders must explain how they are progressing according to the action plan. In addition, they must bring their bowler and their countermeasures, if necessary.

If you are not familiar with this process, your first question might be, "What in the world is a bowler?" The **bowler**, or bowling chart, is a visual tool used to track the performance of each TTI. It contains the pre-established targets leading to the end-of-the-year goal, as well as the actual results achieved each month.

A key point I want to discuss is how the monthly targets are established. By now, you know that by the end of the year, it is expected that each improvement priority, or initiative, will be fully implemented. That will allow the company to achieve its annual breakthrough objectives. The leaders of each initiative work with their teams and develop an action plan that includes, among other things, the expected **impact** of each task as it is implemented.

Each metric should gradually improve throughout the year, allowing the achievement of the goal at the end or earlier. To illustrate this, let's go back to our example where, in order to support the revenue growth goal, each salesperson should increase their daily calls from ten to fifteen. Let's say that they start the year at ten calls and that is the goal for January. But the team is working on a system that will allow the sales personnel to improve productivity by 10 percent (the **impact**), and this system will be in place by the end of February. This means that the following month, March, the sales personnel will be making eleven calls a day and that should be the target.

The bowler would look something like FIGURE 4:

Target To Improve	**Responsibility**	**Units of Measure** **Start Point**	PD Target **Actual**	**Jan**	**Feb**	**Mar**	**Apr**	**May**	**Jun**	**Jul**	**Aug**	**Sep**	**Oct**	**Nov**	**Dec**
Improve number of daily sales calls from 10 to 15 by year end.	Maria	Number of calls	Target	10	10	11									
		10	**Actual**												

The team should continue setting monthly targets based on the expected impact from the action plan. In this fictitious example, the bowler will end up looking like FIGURE 5:

Target To Improve	Responsibility	Units of Measure Start Point	PD Target Actual	Jan	Feb	Mar	Apr	May	Jun	Jul	Aug	Sep	Oct	Nov	Dec
Improve number of daily sales calls from 10 to 15 by year end.	Maria	Number of calls	Target	10	10	11	11	12	12	12	14	14	15	15	15
		10	Actual												

As the teams present their progress to the executive team, they should show their bowlers, including the targets and the actual results for each month. A good practice is to color the *"Actual"* cells green if the metric is on target and red if it is not. Note that there is no yellow, amber, light red, etc. The metrics are either on target or they are not. In the example below in FIGURE 6, the metric was on target all the way through April, and then the team missed the goal in May:

Target To Improve	Responsibility	Units of Measure Start Point	PD Target Actual	Jan	Feb	Mar	Apr	May	Jun	Jul	Aug	Sep	Oct	Nov	Dec
Imrove number of daily sales calls from 10 to 15 by year end.	Maria	Number of calls	Target	10	10	11	11	12	12	12	14	14	15	15	15
		10	Actual	10	10	11	11	11							

This is a critical part of the process. The leader of the team is now accountable for developing a countermeasure to bring this initiative back on track.

The **countermeasure** is extremely critical, and the review team, in this case the executive team, must ensure it is done correctly. The person accountable for the metric must explain the factors that led to the miss. In addition, this person must present a good root-cause analysis, along with the actions to address it, who will be implementing the actions, when they are due, and the impact of those actions on the metric. The actions must bring the metric back to target as soon as possible.

The countermeasure sheet looks like FIGURE 7:

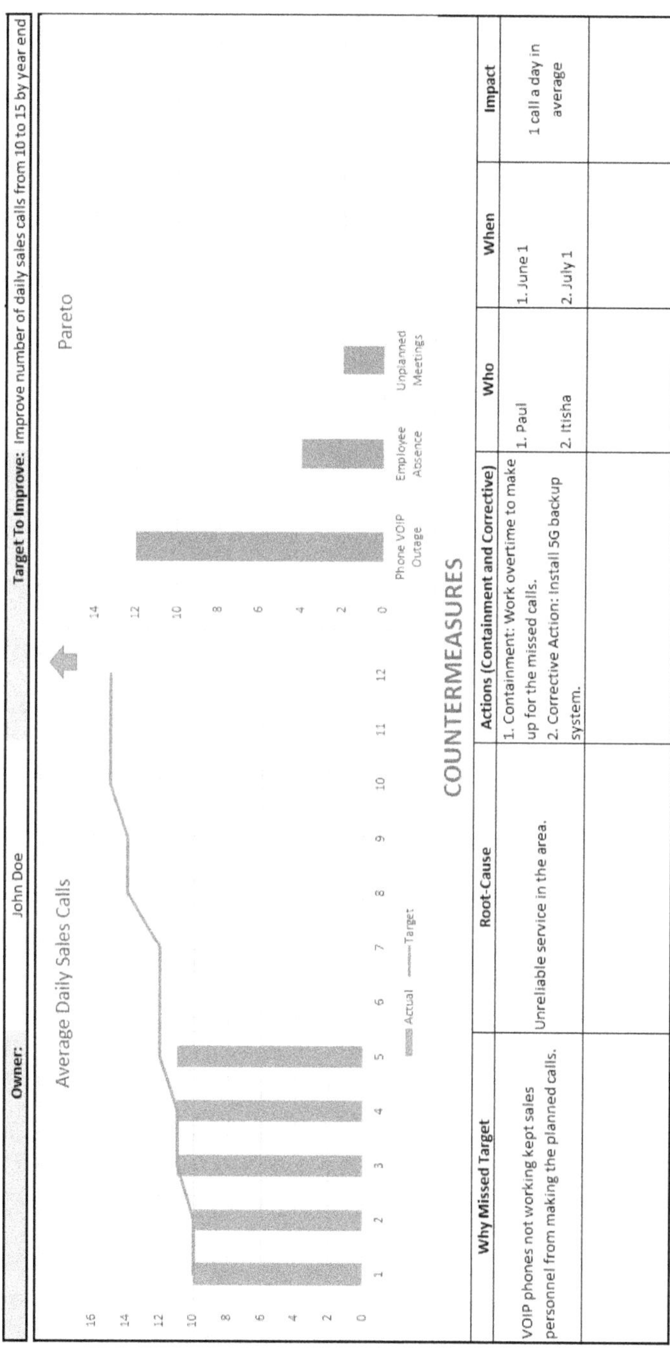

Why Missed Target	Root-Cause	Actions (Containment and Corrective)	Who	When	Impact
VOIP phones not working kept sales personnel from making the planned calls.	Unreliable service in the area.	1. Containment: Work overtime to make up for the missed calls. 2. Corrective Action: Install 5G backup system.	1. Paul 2. Itisha	1. June 1 2. July 1	1 call a day in average

In one page, the team can see the progress towards the goal, the reasons for the miss, and the actions, including the thought process, to bring the metric back to target. In this example, the team found several causes and decided to work, as they should, on the reason with the most impact.

The countermeasure review is a tremendous opportunity for management to guide the teams to perform effective problem-solving, ensuring solid countermeasures are put in place to keep the problem from reoccurring. In this fictitious example, the team decided to work overtime to make the necessary number of calls until the permanent corrective action could be put into place. This decision will bring the metric to target immediately.

And remember, this isn't a one-time thing. You've got to regularly review and adjust your plan as you go. The world is constantly changing, and your strategy needs to be able to adapt.

B. Cascading the Strategic Plan:

1. Deployment

When taken seriously, this process is extremely powerful, especially when you cascade, or **deploy**, the plan to the entire organization. Up to this point, we've covered how to create a strategy and how to break it down all the way to the high-level initiatives and their respective owners. We also discussed the review process. This is still at a high level, though. An important part of the process is ensuring everyone in the organization is aligned with the strategy and work every day.

The policy deployment matrix we discussed is the top-level or Level I matrix. This implies there are other levels as well, and there are.

Let's refer back to the top-level matrix. On the far-right side, you will find the *"Resources,"* or people at the executive level who are responsible for the implementation of the *"Top Level Improvement Priorities"* along with their correspondent *"Targets to Improve."* These executives, the **Resources**, will now involve their teams in the deployment of the strategy.

Let's now use Geraldo as an example. You can find him in the top-level matrix. He is responsible for implementing the *"Working capital initiative,"* and his target to improve is to increase cash flow from $5M to $7M.

Geraldo will go back to his team and present the top-level matrix to them. He will probably even bring Joanna, the CEO, to explain the strategy, detailing how great the company will be in three to five years, how much will get done in year one, the top-level initiatives, and the importance of the role his team will play in realizing the strategy. When done right, this part of the policy deployment process should engage the next level down, Level 2 or Level II. At this point, the Level 2 team is motivated, and they will work on developing their own improvement priorities in support of their boss's (Geraldo's) goals.

2. Level 2

Geraldo now meets with his team to work on the Level 2 matrix. They will start with a blank matrix template. The 3–5 Year Breakthrough Objectives quadrant disappears, replaced with the Annual Breakthrough Objectives, straight out of the top-level matrix. These objectives are listed in the same order as in the top-level matrix, with the most important ones placed closer to the center. In the left quadrant, Geraldo will list the Top-Level Improvement Priorities, just like they were in the top quadrant of the top-level matrix. This portion of the matrix will then look like this:

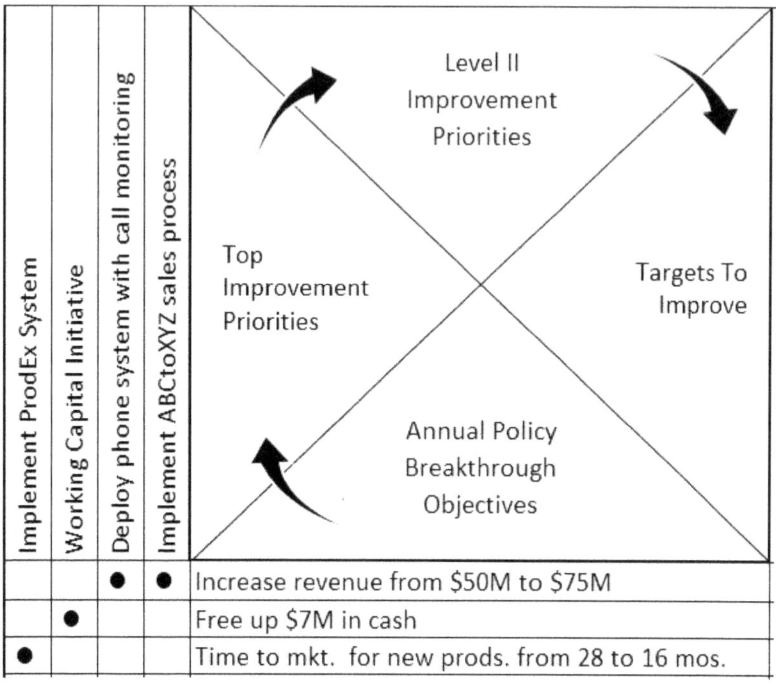

Although these forms are a great tool, the contents, along with the diligence and team involvement, are the most important part of the policy deployment. The team now understands the company's direction and the role they will play in its achievement. Next, Geraldo and his team will brainstorm ways to drive the Working capital initiative to free up $7 million in cash for the year.

Let's suppose they will implement a kanban system to control inventory levels. In addition, they will negotiate with the suppliers to increase payment terms. They will measure the success of the kanban initiative through inventory turns, which becomes the TTI for that initiative. They will also measure average payment terms to track the progress of the negotiations with the suppliers. They may also consider adding balanced metrics to ensure nothing else is compromised. For example, they may choose to track PPV, or purchase price variance, to ensure prices are not going up as a consequence of increased payment terms.

The Level 2 matrix will end up looking something like FIGURE 8:

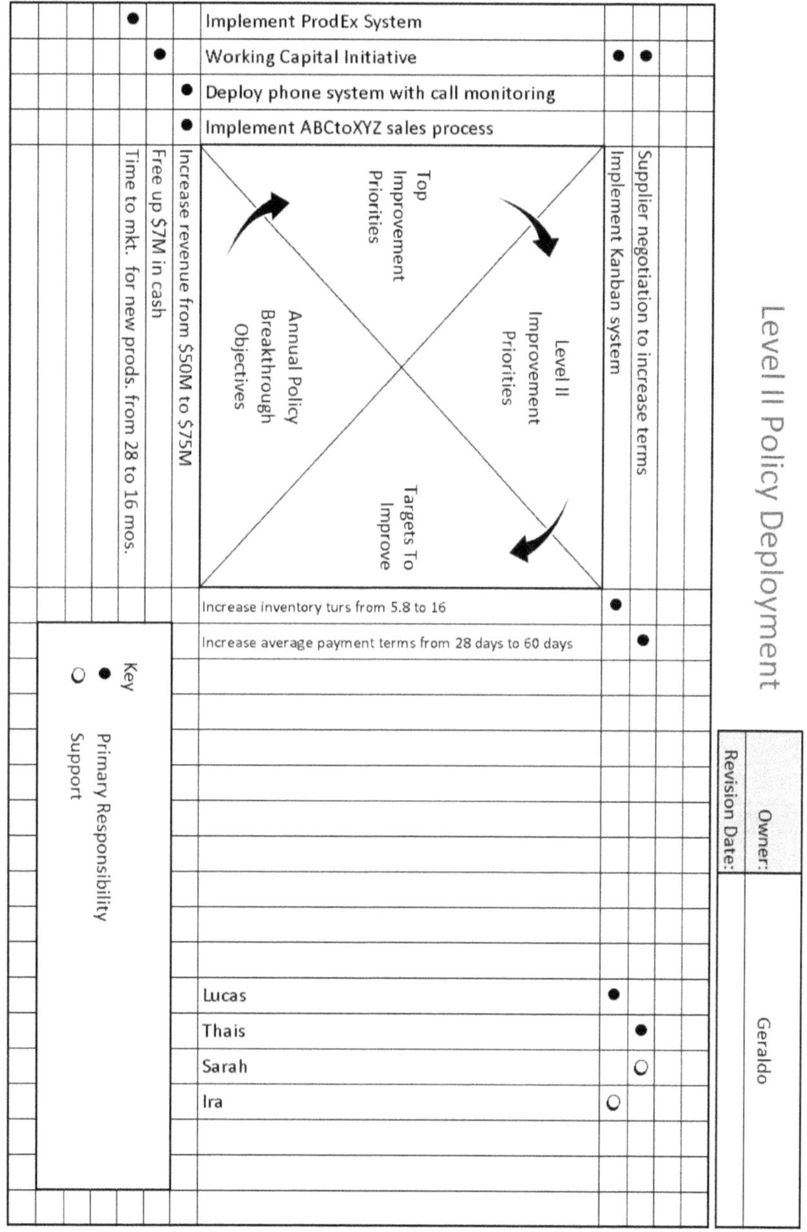

The rest of the process is the same as discussed previously. Geraldo's team will develop the Level 2 bowler, have regular reviews, and apply countermeasures when metrics are missing the target. These reviews should take place *before* the top-level reviews, allowing Geraldo to be ready to present his piece to the executive team at the top-level review meeting.

So far, we've only mentioned Geraldo, but if you look back at the top-level matrix, other people are responsible for other improvement priorities. They will do exactly the same thing as Geraldo: involve and motivate their teams, develop their own matrices, bowlers, etc.

I would now like to bring your attention to the keys that link resources to the improvement priorities and their metrics. Until now, we have used a solid black dot. To this, we have added an empty circle, which symbolizes support rather than direct responsibility. I recommend that the entire team be listed under resources. Sometimes, there aren't enough improvement priorities for everyone on the team, but you can assign people to support them. This helps focus the teams, and no one feels left out.

3. Full Rollout

In mature organizations, the policy deployment does not end at Level 2. Instead, the Level 2 resources will meet with their teams and develop the Level 3 matrix, bowler, etc. As we did in Level 2, the quadrants will rotate counterclockwise once again. In this case, the Top Improvement Priorities move to the bottom quadrant, and the Level II Improvement Priorities move to the left quadrant, leaving room at the top for the Level III Improvement Priorities. The right quadrant is open for the new TTIs and resources.

Ideally, this process repeats itself, adding levels until *all* employees are affected and everyone understands the company direction and the role they play in the achievement of the company's strategy. Level 2 is not *duplication*. It is *translation*.

Stop for a moment and think about how powerful this is. Everyone in the organization knows and understands the strategy. They understand the company's direction and how the team will get there, and they know what they need to do to support it! Day in, day out. That's like an entire army marching in the same direction. Everyone speaking the same language. The priorities are clear. You will start witnessing the teams' conversations as they make decisions and ask themselves, "Is this action moving us closer or further away from the goal?"

The numerous reviews keep the teams engaged, motivated, and on their toes. Although the top-level metrics are reviewed quarterly or monthly, all others, from Level 2 and below, are reviewed at least monthly. On my production lines, we record them hourly and address out-of-control conditions on the spot. Every morning, each department reviews the previous day's performance, addresses any issues, and plans how to catch up in case they fall behind. On a weekly basis, each focus factory reviews the trends, makes sure they are on plan, and looks for ways to improve further. Monthly, each department reports progress to the plant manager or general manager. The frequency changes based on the metric, the point of impact, and the reaction time needed. And it is all in support of PD.

Pitfall: People make the forms a priority over the content. This has happened a lot as we've helped organizations implement the PD process. Executives fall in love with forms and want to show how much they know about how the forms work. It is truly great when management embraces the PD process and becomes familiar with the tools, as long as they don't neglect the substance. Communication, team involvement, rigorous reviews, and other aspects of PD are critical factors for success. The forms are merely a guide and a way to present and display the substance.

4. Overcoming Challenges and Ensuring Success

Deploying strategy effectively across an organization is not without obstacles. Anticipating the challenges, and proactively addressing them, is essential to your Lean transformation's long-term success. Here are some common pitfalls you may encounter, along with practical strategies to overcome each one:

4.1 Addressing Resistance to Change

Challenge: People naturally resist change, especially when the benefits aren't immediately clear. Employees may feel threatened, uncertain, or skeptical about new initiatives.

Solution:

- Communicate the "why" clearly and frequently.
- Help people "see" what the future will look like.
- Engage employees early in the process and invite their input.
- Provide specific examples of how strategy deployment will positively impact their roles.

- Celebrate early successes publicly to build momentum and buy-in.

4.2 Maintaining Alignment and Focus

Challenge: Organizations can easily lose sight of their strategic priorities, slipping back into old habits and fragmented initiatives. Policy deployment, like many other initiatives, will be tested once it faces the "real world." Unless management is diligent and makes it a priority, daily urgencies, combined with resistance to change, tend to interfere, and eventually, PD will fade away.

Solution:

- Regularly communicate strategic objectives at all organizational levels.
- Use visual management tools (e.g., dashboards, visual boards) to keep goals visible.
- Hold regular review meetings to reinforce alignment and quickly address deviations.
- Stick to the schedule and have all PD-related events on time as planned.
- Hold people accountable for their deliverables regardless of other events.
- Empower employees to question actions that don't align with the stated strategy.

4.3 Sustaining the Strategy Deployment Culture

Challenge: Initial enthusiasm can fade quickly, causing strategic alignment efforts to weaken over time. Therefore, it is imperative that management stay on course and continue holding regular meetings and communications.

Solution:

- Embed strategy deployment into your organization's routine, such as regular check-ins, job descriptions, performance reviews, and leadership discussions.
- Include policy deployment in the new employee induction package.
- Continuously invest in employee training on strategic concepts and alignment tools.
- Visibly recognize and reward sustained alignment and results.
- Frequently refresh and communicate strategic messaging to maintain energy and focus.

4.4 Overcoming Communication Gaps

Challenge: Miscommunications or incomplete messages lead to confusion and misaligned actions across teams.

Solution:

- Establish multiple, clear, consistent communication channels to keep the message alive.
- Explain the link between each victory with the teams' efforts.
- Simplify strategic language, ensuring it's clear, concise, and easily understood.
- Encourage feedback loops to ensure messages are accurately received and understood.
- Use visual management and standard templates for consistent messaging.

4.5 Preventing Strategic Drift

Challenge: Teams gradually veer away from core objectives, adopting lower-priority activities or reacting impulsively to short-term issues.

Solution:

- Use clearly defined metrics and regular reviews to quickly identify deviations.
- Reinforce the strategy with strong leadership commitment, regular updates, and clear, compelling messaging.
- Encourage teams to regularly reflect on whether current activities align with long-term strategic goals.

4.6 Avoiding Overly Ambitious Objectives

Challenge: Setting unrealistic goals can lead to frustration, loss of credibility, and burnout within teams.

Solution:

- Break strategic objectives into smaller, achievable milestones.
- Engage cross-functional teams to reality check goals and timelines.

- Later, we will discuss **play catch**, which is relevant to addressing this specific challenge.
- Regularly review and adjust goals based on real-world progress and challenges.

4.7 Ensuring Consistency Across Departments

Challenge: Different departments may interpret strategic objectives differently, resulting in fragmentation and inefficiencies.

Solution:

- Ensure all the executive team members are on board with the objectives set, along with the reasons behind each objective. When the executive team understands what is behind each goal and the importance of achieving it, they tend to work together. Their teams see this and do the same. This behavior is also deployed throughout the organization.
- Create cross-departmental forums or steering groups to maintain consistency.
- Develop standardized tools, templates, and definitions used by everyone.
- Facilitate frequent discussions among departments to ensure cohesive interpretation and application.

4.8 Maintain Leadership Engagement

Challenge: Leaders can unintentionally disengage, shifting focus to urgent day-to-day tasks rather than strategic alignment.

Solution:

- Clearly define leadership roles in strategy deployment.
- Schedule regular leadership reviews focused exclusively on strategic alignment.
- Hold leaders accountable through performance metrics explicitly tied to strategy execution.
- The goals set during the leaders' performance review should be in support of the PD goals. Executive bonuses should also be tied to the achievement of the PD objectives.

4.9 Allocating Adequate Resources

Challenge: Insufficient time, personnel, or financial resources can derail strategic alignment initiatives.

Solution:

- Proactively identify and secure required resources before launching initiatives.
- Include resource allocation in strategic planning to ensure it is adequately prioritized.
- Regularly assess resource utilization, adjusting as needed to maintain alignment and momentum.
- Note that a company does not necessarily need to add resources to implement PD. They can simply stop doing other less-important things or the busy work, diverting resources to drive the implementation of the strategy. The team can also place the activities that free up resources early in the process and use the freed-up resources in the implementation of subsequent improvement priorities.

4.10 Keeping Motivation and Morale High

Challenge: Sustained strategic alignment requires high motivation, which can wane if employees lose sight of progress or recognition.

Solution:

- Continuously highlight progress through regular updates, stories, and visible metrics.
- Celebrate small wins frequently and publicly.
- Foster a culture of appreciation, consistently recognizing the people and teams who contribute to strategic success.

5. Real-World Example

The reason this section is included is to show that the implementation of PD or any other program doesn't always go as planned. This is why understanding the fundamentals is important, as it allows you to change course and adapt as needed.

I was once hired by a medium-sized company as their head of U.S. operations. As usual, there were many things that needed to be fixed, and quickly, it became obvious that many of their problems were rooted in cultural issues. Each of the many corporate executives were doing "their own thing" based on what they thought was right for their own areas of responsibility regardless of the company's needs.

A weak CEO, combined with an equally ineffective board of directors, had allowed incompetence to flourish over the years. They would openly go to extremes to avoid confrontation. In that culture, the legacy executives, the ones who had been with the company for a long time, retained all the knowledge, and they would blatantly disregard any direction. Since the upper level was afraid of losing them, they did whatever they wanted. These legacy executives wanted to retain the power of decision-making to continue to feel important. The outcome was that people were frequently waiting for the "busy executives" to make a decision. In addition, each executive would blame another area for the poor results.

This corrosive culture led to a lot of time wasted, and the operational and financial results were dismal. Each department would follow the direction set by their respective leaders. Since each leader was usually moving in different directions, arguments and disagreements were routine. The executives would speak evil of other areas to their teams, and as a result, the departments were constantly clashing. What was deployed was not strategy, but disdain and disrespect.

The physical layout was a reflection of their culture. The executives were constantly behind closed doors, and there were plenty of walls compartmentalizing departments and separating the various teams. Even the cubicle walls were high, further isolating people.

I could go on and on describing the environment, as well as all the operational issues and inefficiencies. I could explain the poor service and deliveries or the quality concerns, but that's not the point I am trying to make, and I think you get the picture. The message here is that the lack of alignment, compounded by a self-destructive culture, was clearly affecting the company's results. When combined with a leadership team that did not hold people accountable, it created a perfect storm.

They hired me to fix their operational issues. A week after I started, I met with the global head of operations, who was my boss at that time and the CEO. I said I had some findings, and he was surprised that I wanted to meet so quickly. He expected an operational analysis, which I had, but you can't imagine his surprise when I explained that the company's issue was cultural.

In that session, I explained the PD process to the CEO, and he fell in love with it. In my naiveté, I misjudged how bad the culture was and thought the rigorous PD process would align everyone, allowing the teams to focus on the higher priority. The negative signs that would eventually prove me wrong were evident early on.

In preparation for the meeting where we would decide on the strategy and all other activities leading to the top-level matrix, we all agreed on a set of deliverables each member of the executive team should bring. Most of the deliverables revolved around the voice of the customer. At the kickoff meeting, no one bothered to bring the required, agreed-upon information. The worst part was that there was absolutely no consequence for ignoring the CEO's request. Regardless, we did the best we could with what we had, which was mostly limited information and people's perceptions. Yeah, not a good start.

After some discussion and give-and-take, we finally agreed on a strategic direction. We made the top-level matrix and agreed on the goals for the upcoming year, along with the improvement priorities and TTIs. If nothing else, I hoped to have a common direction for the company, and since we had established a cadence of metrics reviews, I was looking forward to driving the right attitudes and initiating a culture of teamwork and accountability.

As you might expect, the U.S. operations, which were under my responsibility, developed Levels 2 and 3 matrices and all the bowlers, and we did a textbook rollout, engaging and motivating all employees. The bowlers were displayed, and teams started to form to tackle challenges and drive performance. We had good KPI review cadence.

The manufacturing operations saw a marked improvement in the first three months. Metrics such as on-time delivery went from 53 percent to over 90 percent, customer complaints dropped to zero, and rejection rates were cut in half, and these are only a few examples. Of course, I realize the results were not yet world-class, but they signaled a marked improvement, and the financial statements for the U.S. operations started to improve rapidly.

On the other hand, when I went to the monthly executive team PD reviews, although I presented my results, including countermeasures to the metrics that were not on target, it was evident that other areas were not engaged in the process at all. Some, even months after the kickoff, had not bothered to implement or present their results, and still, there were no consequences.

But then something interesting started to develop. Not with the executives, but some people in their teams started to notice how engaged, motivated, and, frankly, happy the operations team was. They felt the energy, fast pace, and fun environment we created. In time, some employees started to join the operations team in projects and, of course, in the celebration of results. We also went out of our way to thank and recognize them.

At one point, the board of directors also noticed the rapid improvement in results in the U.S. operations and requested that they have a board meeting in the U.S. facility. They invited me to participate in the board meeting and explain what we were doing. I explained the process and took them on a tour, where some team members explained what they were doing.

It was contagious. The board members were overwhelmed with joy and asked the CEO why no one else was following the same process. Bingo! That's when the tides started to turn. The CEO tried to explain, and he was not convincing at all. He ended up promising to use policy deployment.

With people in other areas already joining the operations team in projects and now, with pressure from the top, the management team was squeezed from both ends and started asking for help in implementing the "system" in their areas. We were more than glad to help them. In this situation, I did not force anyone to follow the process. Instead, we were the ones helping the executive team deliver on a requirement from the board.

In summary, it was a rocky two or three years in the beginning, but eventually, the PD process became better and better, and today, I am glad we did not stop doing it when we faced the initial challenges. Not long after this situation, the CEO was terminated. The new CEO came from a company that had historically embraced PD, and then we flourished.

6. Lean

You may be wondering: *Where does Lean fit into all this?* Another question you may have is: *The entire policy deployment process seems complex, so what is it doing in a book written to foster simplification?* Good questions! I'm glad you asked them.

First, the policy deployment process *is* part of the Lean toolbox. So, even by itself, PD is part of Lean. But let's dig a bit deeper. Many aspects of the PD process, from teamwork to problem-solving, count on Lean tools. The metrics and the process of driving continuous improvement to achieve goals will also drag in the various tools in the Lean toolbox. PD counts on the Lean tools by using them to help the various teams achieve their goals.

Allow me to illustrate this point. Let's pretend a team is missing its cost-reduction goals. Since they are not on target, the team must develop a countermeasure. To do that, they have to apply problem-solving techniques, including the use of the five whys to get to the root cause. Once they get to the root cause, the team will have to develop the actions to address it. In most cases, the root cause will be addressed by employing Lean tools, such as poka-yokes in case of defects, kanban and heijunka in case of inventory issues, SMED, line-balancing, and many other tools in case of productivity issues, etc.

As the facilitator of the Lean transformation, initially, you should guide the teams and teach them about the right tools to address the root causes of the issues they are coming across. Gradually, as tools are employed and people learn to apply them, they will remember and use them again when needed next time they find themselves in similar situations.

Regarding the second question, is PD adding complexity? At first glance, it may seem that way, but in fact, it is quite the opposite. It is a new process and comes with forms and meetings, which seem to add complexity. However, once adopted, it brings order to the daily chaos, allowing the teams to focus on fewer but more relevant tasks. Furthermore, PD brings the Lean simplification tools along at the right time, in concert with the implementation of the strategy, and the systemic application of these tools will drive simplification.

Reflection and Action

Turning Strategy Deployment into Your Turnaround Control System

This chapter introduced a truth that most organizations learn too late:

Hard work does not create results. Alignment does.

Policy deployment is the system that creates alignment, keeps strategy alive every day, and forces fast reaction when performance goes out of control.

If your goal is to lead a turnaround, your objective is not to "implement PD." Your objective is to **build a management system that makes winning inevitable**.

Use the questions and exercises below to turn this chapter into your own working plan.

Part 1
Reality Check: Do You Actually Have a Strategy?

1) Clearly identify your strategy (two sentences).
Write your company's strategy in two sentences:

- What game are we playing?
- How do we win?

If you cannot write this clearly, your employees cannot execute it.

2) Conduct a strategy alignment test.
Ask five people in different functions:

- What is the company's top priority this year?
- What does success look like?
- What are we doing differently because of it?

Write their answers word-for-word.
If the answers do not match, you do not have alignment. You have activity.

3) Conduct a strategy drift test.
List the five initiatives currently consuming the most time in your organization.

For each one, answer:

- Does this directly support the strategy?
- If not, why are we doing it?

This exercise alone will often reveal the hidden cause of overload.

Part 2
Your Turnaround Direction: Define the Breakthrough

A turnaround cannot succeed with twelve priorities.

It requires a few outcomes that force the system to change.

4) Choose one to three breakthrough objectives.
Write one to three measurable outcomes for the next twelve months.

Use this format:

- **Metric:** (Lead time, OTD, COPQ, Cash, Output, etc.)
- **Baseline:**
- **Target:**
- **Deadline:**

If you write more than three, you have not prioritized.

5) Write the trade-offs (the "no list").
List three things your company must stop doing or deprioritize to make space.

This is the hardest part of strategy.
It is also the most honest.

Part 3:
Build the Top-Level X-Matrix (Level 1).

Now you will build the skeleton of your deployment system.

Do not aim for perfection. Aim for clarity.

6) Draft your Level 1 matrix.
Using a blank template, fill in:

- Three-to-five-year breakthrough objectives
- Annual breakthrough objectives (year one)
- Improvement priorities
- Targets to improve (TTIs)
- Owners (one name per improvement priority)

Rule: Every improvement priority must have at least one TTI.
Rule: Every TTI must have a clear definition and a baseline.

7) Perform the "diagonal integrity check."
Read the matrix diagonally and ask:

- Does every annual objective clearly support a three-to-five-year objective?
- Does every improvement priority clearly support an annual objective?
- Does every TTI clearly measure the success of an improvement priority?

If you cannot answer "yes" immediately, simplify.

Part 4:
Convert the Strategy into Execution (Bowler + Reviews)

A strategy is not real until it is reviewed.

8) Build your first bowler (one page).
Create a bowler with:

- TTIs as rows
- Months as columns
- Target and actual
- Owner
- Red/green status (no yellow)

If your organization is in crisis, do this weekly.

9) Establish the review cadence.
Schedule these meetings for the next ninety days:

- Level 1 monthly review (executive team)
- Level 2 monthly reviews (department or value stream)
- Weekly working reviews for TTIs in trouble

Write the date, time, and attendees.
Put them on calendars now.

A system that is not scheduled is not a system.

Part 5:
Create Your Countermeasure Discipline

This is where PD becomes a turnaround engine.

10) Define what "out of control" means.
Pick three critical metrics and define:

- What is the threshold for escalation?
- Who must be notified?
- How fast must a countermeasure be created?
- What does "back on track" look like?

11) Build your countermeasure template.
Create a one-page sheet with:

- Problem statement
- Target vs. actual
- Root cause hypothesis
- Immediate containment (if needed)
- Permanent countermeasure
- Owner
- Due date
- Expected impact on the metric

Then commit to one rule:

Every red metric must have a countermeasure within a defined time window.

This is how you stop firefighting from becoming normal.

Part 6:
Cascading: Generate Level 2 Without Losing the System

The purpose of Level 2 is engagement.

If Level 2 becomes paperwork, PD will die.

12) Select one improvement priority to cascade first.
Do not cascade everything at once.

Pick the most important improvement priority and deploy it into Level 2.

13) Run the Level 2 workshop.
In a two-to-three-hour session, the Level 2 team must produce:

- Level 2 improvement priorities
- TTIs
- Owners
- First bowler

Rule: Level 2 is translation, not duplication.
They must answer:

"What do we control that will make Level 1 succeed?"

Part 7:
Your Turnaround Plan Artifact (Save This)

By the end of this chapter, you should have created:

1. Your strategy in two sentences
2. One to three breakthrough objectives with baselines and targets
3. Level 1 X-matrix draft
4. First bowler (even if incomplete)
5. Countermeasure template
6. Ninety-day review cadence
7. Plan to deploy Level 2 for the most important priority

These are not academic exercises.

They are the beginning of your turnaround control system.

Closing Reflection (The Leadership Question)

Finally, answer this honestly:

If you disappeared for two weeks, would the organization still execute the strategy?

If the answer is no, you do not yet have policy deployment.
You have leadership heroics.

And heroics do not scale.

Chapter 6 Reflection and Action Answers

CHAPTER 7

Standard Work and Visual Management: *Creating Clarity and Consistency*

I. Introduction: Why Clarity and Consistency Matter

In Chapter 6, we discussed how strategy deployment creates powerful organizational alignment, ensuring everyone understands their role in driving the company's strategic objectives. However, even the best strategies can quickly fall apart if clarity and consistency of execution are missing. Without clearly defined standards and robust visual management systems in place, complexity inevitably returns, quietly eroding the gains made through strategic alignment.

Policy deployment tells the organization what matters most and where to focus. **Standard work** then defines how the work must be done to deliver those priorities consistently, and **visual management** makes it immediately obvious whether the work is being done as intended. Together, they turn strategy into something you can manage daily, not just review monthly.

Consider this: a strategic plan might map your long-term vision perfectly, but unless every team member knows exactly what to do and how to do it, the day-to-day actions will drift. Employees may revert to old habits, creating unintended variation and inconsistency. This, in turn, breeds inefficiency, frustration, and a subtle but damaging return to complexity.

This chapter introduces two powerful tools: standard work and visual management. These tools bridge the gap between strategic intent and everyday actions. Standard work clearly outlines the best-known method of completing tasks, ensuring consistency and quality across operations. Meanwhile, visual management makes these standards intuitive, visible, and easy to follow.

Together, these methods embed clarity and consistency deeply into your operations, significantly reducing complexity, improving efficiency, and helping sustain the gains from your Lean transformation.

In short, standard work and visual management are the critical connectors between your high-level strategy and everyday operational excellence. This is key to daily management. More on that will come later.

Before diving into the details, let's define what we mean by standard work and visual management, two foundational elements of any successful Lean transformation.

Standard Work

At its core, standard work refers to the documented best-known method of performing a task or process. More than just a set of instructions, it's a precisely defined approach designed to achieve consistent results, reduce variability, and eliminate waste. By establishing a clear, repeatable method for performing work, organizations ensure that everyone understands exactly how tasks should be completed. This clarity enables all employees to consistently produce high-quality outputs, simplifies training, and makes it easier to spot and correct issues when deviations occur. In short, standard work ensures everyone does the right thing, the right way, every time.

Visual Management

Visual management complements standard work by making standards visible and intuitive to everyone involved. It uses visual signals, tools, and cues, such as clearly marked indicators, status boards, color-coded systems, or simple signs, to communicate important information at a glance. The purpose is straightforward: reduce confusion, quickly highlight abnormalities, and support immediate corrective actions without relying on complicated explanations or detailed instructions. When done effectively, visual management transforms workplaces into environments where the right information is always easily accessible, allowing everyone to quickly understand current performance, identify deviations, and take appropriate action.

Why Standard Work and Visual Management Are Critical to Avoiding Complexity

As we discussed early in this book, complexity is a hidden but costly enemy in every organization. It slows processes, increases errors, and frustrates employees and customers alike. Without clear standards and visual cues, tasks tend to become overly complicated, often relying on people's memories or informal "tribal knowledge." This dependence creates significant variation, inconsistency, and inefficiency, and that is exactly what Lean transformation aims to eliminate.

Standard work and visual management are your frontline defenses against this complexity. Standard work creates simplicity by defining a clear, repeatable, and efficient method for tasks. With clear instructions, employees spend less time guessing and more time performing value-added activities. Visual management further reinforces simplicity by making these standards instantly visible and understandable. Employees don't need to hunt for instructions or rely on complex explanations. Everything they need is clearly displayed and easy to follow.

Together, these two tools systematically remove complexity by ensuring consistency, clarity, and ease of understanding in every aspect of daily operations. This approach not only simplifies processes but also reduces stress, minimizes errors, and significantly boosts productivity, allowing your Lean transformation to thrive in a genuinely simple and clear environment.

II. Understanding Standard Work

Definition

As mentioned earlier, standard work is the established, documented method for performing a specific task or set of tasks. It represents the best-known way, at a given point in time, to complete a task efficiently, compliantly, consistently, and safely, with minimal waste. More than just step-by-step instructions, standard work sets clear expectations, defines responsibilities, and provides a reference point for measuring and continuously improving performance.

Standard work is built around three essential elements:

- **Takt Time:** The pace at which tasks must be completed to meet customer demand.
- **Work Sequence:** The precise steps and order of actions required to execute a task effectively.
- **Standard Inventory:** The minimum quantity of materials or resources needed to complete tasks efficiently. In service work, this often translates to **standard WIP**, or the minimum information/tools required to complete the task without interruption.

Establishing standard work creates clarity, reduces errors, ensures consistency, simplifies training, and serves as the foundation for continuous improvement. It's about making sure everyone knows exactly what to do, how to do it, and when to do it every time.

Real-World Example

Think about a hospital emergency room (ER). The stakes are incredibly high, as even small errors or delays can significantly impact patient outcomes. Hospitals use standard work in ERs through clearly defined and documented protocols for common procedures, such as patient check-in, triage, diagnosis, and treatment.

Consider the patient check-in process: the receptionist follows a standard procedure designed to quickly and accurately capture critical information, such as name, age, symptoms, and medical history, ensuring patients are correctly prioritized for immediate care. This standardization helps medical teams rapidly understand each patient's situation, make quick and accurate decisions, and move efficiently to provide treatment.

Standard work ensures that every patient experiences the same high-quality process regardless of who's on duty or how busy the ER is. It simplifies training for new staff, reduces uncertainty, accelerates decision making, and, most importantly, improves patient safety and satisfaction. Just picture the opposite. What would happen if each employee did what they thought was best?

The Playbook

The Importance of Playbooks: Preparing for Real-World Scenarios

Standard work provides the foundation for consistent and efficient operations under ideal conditions. But we all know that real-life rarely cooperates with our perfect plans. Markets fluctuate, employees call in sick, equipment breaks down, customer demands change, or suppliers fail to deliver. Without preparation, even minor disruptions can quickly escalate into chaos, causing delays, confusion, frustration, and increased complexity.

That's why an integral element of truly effective standard work is what we call the "playbook." A **playbook** is a set of pre-defined contingency plans developed specifically for predictable deviations from ideal operating conditions. Just like a coach's playbook in sports, it outlines the actions your team should take under various common scenarios to quickly adapt and maintain productivity and quality, no matter what happens.

What Exactly Is a Playbook?

Think of the playbook as your "Plan B," "Plan C," and even "Plan D." It clearly defines how to adjust standard operations when specific variables change. Instead of improvising or panicking during disruptions, your teams have pre-documented, pre-validated, well-thought-out "plays" they can quickly execute.

A good playbook addresses questions like:

- What should we do if customer demand suddenly increases or decreases (changing takt time)?
- How do we adjust operations if several team members unexpectedly don't show up for work?
- What happens if critical equipment breaks down?
- What adjustments should we make if certain raw materials are delayed or unavailable?

By anticipating these scenarios in advance, your teams will know precisely how to respond, minimizing downtime, confusion, and mistakes.

Developing an Effective Playbook

Here's how you build a strong, practical playbook for your operations:

1. Identify Common Scenarios

Start by brainstorming potential disruptions that could realistically occur. Focus on scenarios most likely to significantly impact your operations. Common examples include:

- Significant demand increase/decrease (takt time changes)
- Unexpected staffing shortages
- Equipment downtime
- Materials shortages or supplier delays
- Quality or safety incidents

2. Develop Clear, Specific Response Plans

For each scenario, outline the precise actions your team should take. This should include:

- Clear alternative workflows
- Adjusted work sequences or tasks
- Staffing reallocations or reassigned responsibilities
- Emergency contacts or notification procedures
- Criteria for when to trigger each play

3. Document and Standardize the Plays

Create clear, visual documentation of each scenario and corresponding response plan. Store these plans where teams can easily access and reference them. Incorporate visual tools, such as flowcharts or diagrams, to improve clarity.

4. Train and Validate

Regularly train your employees on each scenario and corresponding response plan. Conduct periodic drills or simulations to ensure the team can execute each play quickly, confidently, and effectively. If you are in a highly regulated industry, such as pharmaceutical or aerospace, you may have to run validation and verification for each scenario in the playbook.

5. Regularly Review and Update

Revisit your playbook periodically. As your processes, personnel, or market conditions change, the playbook must stay relevant and accurate. This ongoing maintenance ensures that your playbook remains a reliable tool rather than becoming outdated paperwork.

Trigger Points: When the Playbook Activates

One of the most common reasons playbooks fail is that they exist but nobody knows when to use them. Teams wait too long, hoping the problem will "work itself out," and by the time they react, the situation has already escalated into chaos. In a turnaround, you cannot afford delayed reactions. You need clear trigger points.

A trigger point is a simple, predefined condition that tells the team: *Stop improvising and run the play.*

Good trigger points are:

- **Objective** (based on facts, not opinions)
- **Easy to detect** (visible at a glance)
- **Time bound** (so the team acts early, not late)

Here are a few examples:

- If staffing drops below **X operators**, activate the staffing shortage play.
- If a critical machine is down for more than **ten minutes**, activate the downtime play.
- If hourly output falls below target for **two consecutive hours**, activate the recovery play.
- If a key material is not received by **a specific time**, activate the alternate material or rescheduling play.

Trigger points are not about control. They are about speed. They eliminate hesitation, protect quality, and keep the team aligned under pressure.

Normal vs. Abnormal: The Missing Piece

Standard work is designed for normal conditions. It assumes that the process is stable, the right people are present, materials are available, and equipment is running. But in most struggling operations, "normal" is the exception, not the rule. The organization spends most of its time operating in abnormal conditions, and that is exactly why firefighting becomes the default way of working.

This is where the playbook becomes a turning point in a turnaround. It does not replace standard work. It protects it. It gives teams a clear, pre-agreed response for predictable disruptions so the organization can respond quickly, without improvising, panicking, or creating a new workaround every time.

If you want a simple way to think about it, use this rule:

- **Standard work is the best-known method when conditions are normal.**
- **The playbook is the best-known response when conditions are abnormal but predictable.**

When you put these two together, you stop depending on heroic individuals and start building a system. And that is one of the most important shifts in any turnaround: moving from "people saving the day" to "the process preventing the crisis."

A Practical Example of a Playbook in Action

Put yourself in a situation where you're managing a manufacturing line that typically operates with a takt time of sixty units per hour. Your standard operations, which include the workstation layout, staffing, work sequence, etc., are optimized for this rate. But suddenly, customer demand increases significantly, requiring your team to produce seventy-five units per hour instead.

Instead of scrambling and improvising, your team turns to your playbook. The playbook clearly outlines the adjusted work sequence, reallocates tasks between operators to balance workload, and identifies where temporary staff or additional resources are needed. Since your team previously practiced this scenario, they smoothly implement the adjustments with minimal disruption, quickly achieving the increased output without compromising quality or safety. "Back in the day," each scenario was a tab in a binder, and this method is still in use today, although the playbooks are more frequently done electronically these days.

Benefits of Using a Playbook

- **Reduced Stress and Confusion**: Teams respond calmly, confidently, and effectively.
- **Minimal Downtime**: Quick and efficient responses minimize disruptions.

- **Improved Customer Service**: Your team can flexibly respond to customer needs and market shifts.
- **Increased Morale**: Employees feel empowered and are allowed to operate autonomously, knowing they are well prepared to handle challenges.
- **Consistency Under Pressure**: Maintains high standards of quality and productivity even during disruptions.

III. Steps to Implement Standard Work

Step 1: Identify and Document Current Processes

Implementing effective standard work always begins with understanding precisely where you currently stand. Before creating new standards or procedures, your first task is to clearly identify and document exactly how your processes work today. No guesses, no assumptions, just objective facts.

Documenting your existing processes accurately is about pinpointing your organization's current operational reality, providing clarity, and laying a strong foundation for future improvements.

Why Start with Current Processes?

The objective of this step is to uncover what actually happens every day instead of what managers and engineers think is happening or what written procedures might claim happens. The most common failure is writing standard work in a conference room and forcing it onto people. That creates compliance theater, not stability. There's often a significant gap between ideal or assumed processes and real-world practices. Without accurately capturing this reality, you risk creating standard work that isn't feasible, relevant, or sustainable.

Documenting the current state provides:

- **Objective Baseline**: Establishes an unbiased reference point from which future improvements are measured.
- **Visibility into Variations**: Highlights inconsistencies, waste, or hidden complexity in your existing workflows.
- **Employee Engagement**: Involves the people doing the actual work, making them active participants in the improvement process.

How to Identify and Document Current Processes

Here are practical, actionable steps for documenting your current processes clearly and thoroughly:

1. Assemble Your Team

- Gather employees who directly perform the tasks. They have firsthand knowledge of the actual steps and variations that occur daily.
- Consider involving supervisors, engineers, quality personnel, and sometimes even customers or suppliers if their inputs directly affect the process.

2. Clearly Define the Scope

- Clearly establish which processes you'll be documenting. Be specific to avoid confusion or excessive scope creep. For example:
    - "Final assembly of product XYZ"
    - "Customer service complaint handling"
    - "Inventory replenishment in warehouse A"

3. Observe the Process Directly (Go to Gemba)

- The best way to document your current state is direct observation. Go to the work area ("gemba" in Lean terms) and watch the process as it unfolds. Since you are involving the people who work in that area, they are well informed and will perform their tasks as they normally do, without any fear, at their normal speed. This is critical because you are gathering real data.
- Avoid relying solely on existing documentation or managers' descriptions. Watch and document real people performing real tasks in real time. As you did during the VSM, use paper and pencils. For the same reasons, avoid the technology at this step.

4. Record Each Step in Detail

- Take detailed notes on each step, including the actual time required, equipment used, personnel involved, inventory levels, and any noticeable problems, variations, or interruptions.
- Capture exact task sequences, documenting any rework, waiting time, or idle periods. Note safety concerns or ergonomic issues as well.

5. Create a Visual Process Map

- Using the detailed notes from your observations, create a visual representation of the current process. Tools like flowcharts, swim lane diagrams, or spaghetti diagrams can clearly illustrate the actual sequence and relationships between steps. Select the best representation for the situation. Make it easy to understand and follow and standardize the approach throughout the operation.
- Highlight wasteful steps, unnecessary movement, delays, or redundant tasks clearly within your visual documentation.

6. Validate the Documented Process

- Share your documentation with employees who perform the tasks regularly. Have them verify accuracy and completeness. This ensures your captured processes reflect reality and builds team buy-in.
- Many regulated industries will require proper validation for each scenario. In that case, follow the required protocols.
- Adjust your documentation based on team feedback and validation.

Real-World Example: Documenting a Customer Service Process

Let's illustrate this step with a common non-manufacturing scenario: customer service at a call center.

Suppose you manage a call center handling customer complaints. You've noticed significant variation in response times and customer satisfaction, and you want to establish standard work to improve consistency.

Here's how you would document your current process:

- **Observe Real Calls**: Listen directly to numerous actual calls from beginning to end. Take notes on each step representatives take when handling complaints.
- **Record Key Steps and Variations**: Document steps like answering calls, customer verification, complaint understanding, troubleshooting, escalation procedures, and final resolution. Note variations, how different reps handle similar issues, where delays or bottlenecks occur, and where rework happens (e.g., multiple calls from the same customer). Highlight best practices.

- **Create a Flowchart**: Illustrate your observations clearly in a visual flowchart. Highlight redundancies or frequent points of confusion or delay.
- **Employee Validation**: Review the flowchart with call center reps to confirm accuracy and uncover hidden insights or challenges.

2. Document the Current Best Practices

Once you've thoroughly observed and understood the process, the next critical step is systematically capturing and documenting the current best practices, along with key observations and insights. Your goal at this stage is to turn your detailed observations into a clear, structured record, highlighting what works well and identifying the most effective approaches to performing each task.

Key Actions:

- **Review Your Observations Carefully:**
  Begin by organizing your notes, video recordings, and any visual materials you've gathered during the observation stage. Look for patterns and consistently efficient actions performed by experienced operators.

- **Extract and List the Best Practices:**
  Clearly define the methods that repeatedly lead to high-quality results, safety, efficiency, and consistency. Best practices might include optimized task sequences, effective tool usage, ergonomic handling, and efficient work pacing.

- **Include Important Nuances and Tips:**
  Pay close attention to the subtle but important details you captured during observations. For example, note how an experienced operator positions materials to minimize unnecessary movements or how tools are set up to enhance efficiency.

- **Clearly Outline Task Sequences:**
  Using a clear format, such as a flowchart, bullet points, or numbered steps, document each task sequence step by step. Each step should explicitly detail actions, necessary tools, time expectations, safety considerations, and quality checks.

- **Highlight Common Issues and Inefficiencies:**
  In addition to documenting best practices, record frequently observed inefficiencies, bottlenecks, or challenges. This documentation serves as valuable input for future improvements and continuous refinement of standard work.

- **Create Visual Aids:**
  Include photos, diagrams, or simplified sketches alongside the documented steps to clearly illustrate how each task should be performed. These visual aids help workers quickly grasp the standardized processes and minimize errors or misunderstandings.

- **Validate and Refine Documentation:**
  After initially drafting your best practice documentation, review it with experienced operators and key stakeholders. Solicit their input to confirm accuracy, clarity, and completeness. Make revisions based on their feedback, ensuring the documentation reflects practical, real-world scenarios.

Real-World Example:

Imagine you're documenting standard work for the front desk operations at a busy medical clinic. After observing various receptionists during peak hours, you extract key best practices such as greeting each patient within ten seconds, using a specific script for answering common patient questions, managing patient flow efficiently by promptly checking availability, and quickly communicating updates to medical staff. You document these best practices step by step, including small but valuable tips, such as positioning the computer monitor for easy patient interaction or placing frequently used forms within arm's reach to reduce unnecessary movements.

3. Create Clear and Simple Documentation

At this stage, your goal is to translate the extracted best practices, observations, and critical insights into straightforward, practical, and user-friendly standard work documents. The clarity and simplicity of this documentation are key to ensuring that all employees, from experienced workers to new hires, can easily understand and consistently execute the defined processes.

Key Actions:

- **Choose a Suitable Format:**
  Select a format that clearly communicates the steps, requirements, and expectations. Common formats include:
  - **Standard Work Sheets:** Clearly outline task sequences, cycle times, tools required, safety measures, and quality checkpoints.
  - **Visual Job Aids:** Combine concise text instructions with visual elements, such as photographs, diagrams, or icons, for enhanced clarity.
  - **Checklists:** Simple, sequential lists that workers can quickly reference to verify that they have completed each required step.

- **Use Concise and Direct Language:**
  Avoid technical jargon and unnecessarily complex language. The documentation should be written using short, clear sentences, with action-oriented instructions such as, "Place tool A in position B," rather than vague descriptions like, "Prepare to position equipment appropriately."

  I like to use what some call "the janitor's test." If a janitor walked into the area tomorrow and had to run the process safely and correctly using only your standard work, could they do it? If the answer is no, your standard is not clear enough. This is not an insult to anyone's intelligence. It's a reminder that great standard work is designed for clarity, not for expertise. It should remove ambiguity, reduce interpretation, and make the correct method obvious.

- **Incorporate Visual Management Principles:**
  Leverage visuals to convey key steps clearly and intuitively:
  - Include photographs showing the correct positioning of tools, equipment, or materials.
  - Employ color coding or simple graphics to emphasize critical safety points, quality checks, or workflow sequences.
  - Use arrows or icons to indicate the flow of actions clearly and unmistakably.

- **Structure Documentation Logically:**
  Organize the content in a logical sequence that reflects the actual workflow:
  - Begin with preparation steps, follow with action steps, and conclude with final checks or cleanup activities.
  - Clearly delineate each individual step or sub-process.
  - Separate distinct tasks visually, using headings, numbering, or spacing for readability.

- **Highlight Safety and Quality Considerations:**
  Explicitly identify and emphasize critical safety measures, compliance checkpoints, or quality inspection points within each step. Ensure these stand out visually and are not overlooked or treated as optional.

- **Keep Documentation Accessible:**
  Place standard work documents in visible, easily accessible locations at points of use. Examples include posting laminated sheets at workstations, placing checklists on clipboards at critical inspection points, or making digital documents accessible via tablets or screens at workstations.

- **Test for Clarity and Practicality:**
  Have actual operators or employees test the new documentation. Observe them using it and actively solicit their feedback to identify areas of confusion or ambiguity. Refine the documents based on real-world feedback.

- **Regularly Update and Refine:**
  Standard work documentation is dynamic. As processes evolve or new best practices are discovered, regularly revisit and update your documentation to reflect these changes clearly and quickly.

4. Analyze and Improve the Process

Once you've clearly documented the current best practices, it's time to critically evaluate and refine the process itself. Standard work isn't about blindly capturing what you currently do. Instead, it allows you to understand your baseline and systematically improve upon it. This step ensures the standard you're documenting is as efficient, reliable, and effective as possible.

Key Actions:

Identify Waste and Opportunities for Improvement

After capturing the current state, review the documented process thoroughly, looking for opportunities to eliminate waste, unnecessary steps, or redundant activities.

- **Use Lean Analysis Techniques:**
  - **Value Stream Mapping:** Identify which steps add value and which do not.
  - **Waste Analysis (Seven Wastes):** Systematically review the process for signs of overproduction, waiting, unnecessary transportation, excess inventory, excess motion, defects, and overprocessing.
  - **Cycle Time and Takt Time Analysis:** Compare current cycle times against takt time (customer demand rate) to pinpoint inefficiencies.

Engage Frontline Employees

Include workers directly involved in the process in the analysis and improvement phase. They have intimate knowledge of daily operations, potential inefficiencies, and opportunities for simplification. Employee input is invaluable, ensuring realistic, practical improvements and increasing buy-in for changes.

- Conduct brainstorming or kaizen sessions specifically targeted at identifying improvement opportunities.
- Solicit and document feedback on what employees find challenging or redundant in the current process.

Prioritize Improvements

After identifying potential improvements, prioritize them based on their impact and feasibility:

- **High Impact, Easy to Implement:** Prioritize these first; they create quick wins, generate momentum, and build employee support for further changes.
- **High Impact, Difficult to Implement:** Schedule these strategically, providing adequate resources and planning.

- **Low-Impact Changes:** Consider deferring or minimizing attention unless they significantly improve worker morale or process simplicity.

Develop and Test Improvements

Implement improvements through controlled tests or pilot runs:

- Create a trial or pilot to validate the proposed changes, observing closely for improvements or unforeseen issues.
- Adjust based on pilot feedback, refining the standard until it meets expectations.

Update the Standard Work Documents

Once improvements are validated:

- Revise the documented standard to reflect the improved methods clearly.
- Highlight clearly any new changes or updates.
- Communicate updates proactively to all relevant staff to ensure clarity and compliance.

Implement a Continuous Improvement Mindset

Encourage ongoing reflection on processes and empower teams to continually look for improvement opportunities:

- Schedule regular reviews of standard work documentation.
- Foster a workplace culture where employees feel comfortable suggesting new improvements.
- Recognize and reward individuals or teams who propose beneficial changes to reinforce positive behavior.

Step 5: Clearly Document the New Standard

At this stage, you've analyzed your existing processes, implemented improvements, and thoroughly validated them. Now it's critical to clearly document your new standard in a structured, detailed manner, differentiating it explicitly from the original documentation of best practices you created previously. This final documentation will serve as the official guide moving forward, ensuring sustained improvements and consistency across your workforce.

Purpose of the Final Documentation:

- To replace outdated or previous standards with the new, improved method
- To serve as the single, authoritative source that everyone in your organization references to perform the task
- To ensure ongoing consistency, repeatability, and sustainability of process improvements

How to Document the New Standard:

1. Format Clearly for Easy Implementation

Use straightforward, universally understood formats, such as:

Standardized Work Instruction Sheets:

- Clearly outline each step of the task, specifying exact sequences, methods, critical checkpoints, and timings.

Finalized Visual Work Guides:

- Include annotated photographs, diagrams, or sketches that visually communicate exactly how tasks should be performed, especially critical steps.

Definitive Checklists:

- Clearly identify each step to be confirmed, ensuring employees don't miss critical tasks or quality checks.

Process Flow Charts:

- Illustrate the complete finalized workflow visually, making it easy for everyone to understand the overall process.

2. Highlight Improvements Clearly

Indicate and emphasize changes made during Step 3 (Analyze and Improve):

- Explicitly state what was improved, eliminated, or altered compared to the original method.

- Clearly highlight benefits such as reduced time, improved quality, reduced waste, or increased safety.
- Clearly communicate why each change was made, reinforcing the purpose and expected benefit.

3. Detail Clear Roles and Responsibilities

Define specifically who is accountable and responsible at each step, ensuring clarity in execution and accountability:

- Clearly state roles (e.g., "Operator," "Supervisor," "Quality Inspector") alongside each relevant task.
- If needed, clearly state who is responsible for updates and ongoing maintenance of the standard documentation.

4. Incorporate Critical Metrics and Controls

Outline essential metrics or performance measures for consistent tracking of adherence:

- Identify key performance indicators (KPIs) or other metrics used to confirm ongoing compliance and performance.
- Provide specific guidance for when these metrics should be reviewed and by whom.

5. Accessibility and Training

Make sure the finalized standards are accessible and readily available to all involved personnel:

- Post finalized documents visibly in relevant work areas.
- Incorporate the finalized standard into employee training and onboarding processes to ensure future consistency.

Step 6: Implement the Standard Work and Train the Team

At this point, you have clearly documented your improved and validated standard. The next crucial step is implementation, which involves rolling out the new standard across your operation, accompanied by thorough training for all affected employees. This ensures that the process improvements you've meticulously defined actually translate into consistent, repeatable actions in practice.

Why Effective Implementation and Training Matters

A documented standard is extremely valuable, but it's the **implementation and adoption** that truly determines success. Proper implementation ensures:

- **Consistency:** Everyone knows exactly what is expected and how tasks should be performed, reducing variability and increasing predictability.
- **Efficiency Gains:** Clearly defined and trained standards eliminate guesswork, mistakes, and rework.
- **Employee Engagement:** Employees clearly see how their roles contribute directly to improved performance and organizational goals.
- **Sustainability of Improvements:** Effective training helps ensure that changes stick and become the new norm.

How to Effectively Implement and Train

Follow these structured steps for successful implementation and training:

1. Communicate the Change Clearly and Proactively

Before training begins, communicate clearly with your team:

- State why the change is being made (efficiency, quality, safety improvements).
- Highlight expected benefits clearly for the employees and the organization.
- Explain the roles individuals will play in the successful adoption of the new standard.

2. Develop a Training Plan

Create a comprehensive training plan to ensure effective and thorough implementation:

- Define who needs training (operators, supervisors, quality staff).
- Determine when and how frequently training sessions should occur.
- Identify trainers who are knowledgeable and credible.
- Include hands-on training to ensure practical understanding and engagement.

3. Conduct Structured Training Sessions

Deliver clear, engaging training that emphasizes:

- **Understanding the Standard:** Clearly explain each step and why it is important.
- **Hands-On Practice:** Provide practical sessions where employees physically follow the standard to build familiarity and confidence.
- **Clarifying Questions:** Encourage employees to ask questions and address concerns immediately and clearly.

4. Verify Understanding and Competency

Simply training employees isn't enough. You must confirm understanding through:

- Quick assessments or quizzes to validate theoretical understanding
- Supervised practice runs to confirm practical application and adherence
- Clear documentation of training completion and competency to provide accountability

5. Roll Out Implementation Gradually

Rather than deploying across all areas simultaneously, consider:

- **Pilot Areas:** Start implementation in one or two specific areas. This allows you to observe, correct, and refine your approach before a broader rollout.
- **Incremental Expansion:** After confirming effectiveness, schedule and communicate a phased rollout to additional areas, teams, or shifts.

6. Provide Continuous Support

Establish channels for ongoing support and feedback, including:

- Assigning specific individuals as "go-to" experts who can clearly address questions as they arise.
- Maintaining open channels for feedback, clearly encouraging employees to voice questions, concerns, or suggestions about the new standard.
- Conducting follow-up coaching or refresher sessions as needed to reinforce adherence.

7. Recognize and Celebrate Successful Implementation

To build positive momentum, clearly and visibly celebrate successes:

- Highlight early adopters and teams clearly demonstrating excellence.
- Share initial results and improvements clearly across the organization.
- Celebrate milestones publicly to reinforce the importance of the standard.

Step 7: Monitor, Sustain, and Continuously Improve

Now that you've successfully implemented your standard work, the journey doesn't end here. Standard work isn't a one-time activity. To maximize its long-term benefits, it's essential to monitor compliance, sustain improvements, and continuously refine the processes as conditions evolve.

Why Monitoring and Continuous Improvement Matters

If not actively monitored and improved, even the best standards can gradually deteriorate over time as people revert to old, inefficient habits. Regular monitoring and continuous improvement ensure:

- **Sustained Benefits:** Prevent backsliding, maintaining the gains you've achieved.
- **Responsiveness:** Quickly adapt to new challenges, customer demands, or operational changes.
- **Ongoing Engagement:** Keep teams actively involved, fostering a culture of continuous improvement.

How to Effectively Monitor, Sustain, and Continuously Improve

Follow these structured steps to sustain and continually enhance your standard work:

1. Establish Regular Audits and Reviews

Periodic reviews or audits are critical to maintaining adherence and identifying opportunities for improvement:

- Schedule routine audits (daily, weekly, monthly) based on process criticality and frequency of use.

- Assign responsibility for conducting audits to supervisors, leads, or trained operators.
- Use visual tracking tools like audit checklists or standard adherence charts to quickly identify and address deviations.

2. Use Visual Management Tools

Visual management makes it easy for teams to see at a glance whether standards are being followed:

- Clearly display the standard procedures at workstations.
- Use visual indicators, such as color coding, floor markings, and signage, to support compliance.
- Publicly display performance metrics or dashboards to promote accountability and visibility.

3. Create Feedback Loops

Regularly engage employees in discussions about standard work performance:

- Encourage daily or weekly huddles to discuss any issues, changes, or deviations.
- Establish simple channels (whiteboards, suggestion boxes, digital tools) to collect and address employee feedback promptly.
- Foster an environment where team members feel comfortable raising concerns or suggesting improvements.

4. Update Standards Regularly

Standards are dynamic, not static. Be prepared to regularly update them to reflect operational realities:

- Establish a formal schedule (e.g., quarterly or biannually) for reviewing and revising standards.
- Involve process users in reviewing the standards to ensure they remain practical and relevant.
- Quickly update standards following process improvements, changes in customer requirements, or operational shifts.

5. Train Continuously

Training should not happen just once. Reinforce standards through continuous training:

- Provide regular refresher training sessions to maintain high skill levels and consistent adherence.
- Immediately retrain employees following updates to the standard.
- Incorporate training into onboarding to ensure new employees are aligned with established procedures from the start.

6. Recognize and Celebrate Sustained Excellence

Acknowledging teams and people who consistently adhere to or exceed standards is essential for long-term sustainability:

- Celebrate milestone achievements publicly to reinforce positive behaviors.
- Share stories of success and improvement regularly to inspire teams.
- Integrate adherence to standard work into recognition and rewards programs.

7. Embed Continuous Improvement

Build a culture that actively seeks improvements rather than passively accepts the status quo:

- Regularly challenge the standard by asking teams, "How can we do this better?"
- Encourage small, incremental improvements (kaizen) that lead to significant, long-term gains.
- Ensure any improvements identified are documented, validated, and incorporated into the updated standard.

IV. Visual Management: Making Standards Visible

Visual management is a powerful tool that transforms abstract standards and procedures into concrete, actionable guidelines that are easy to follow. It bridges the gap between written documentation and real-world application, ensuring that standard work is consistently executed at all levels of the organization. Just as standard work brings clarity, visual management provides immediate visibility, allowing everyone to quickly identify deviations and maintain alignment with established procedures.

The Importance of Visual Management

Visual management accomplishes three primary objectives:

- **Improves Understanding:** People naturally grasp information better when it is visual. Images, charts, and color coding simplify complex instructions, making standards easy to follow.
- **Promotes Consistency and Compliance:** Clearly displayed visual instructions reinforce adherence, reducing variations in execution and supporting sustained performance.
- **Enables Immediate Detection and Correction:** Visual cues and indicators instantly highlight deviations or abnormal conditions, allowing for swift corrective actions.

Imagine driving a car without any visual indicators. No speedometer, no warning lights, no fuel gauge. Operating under these conditions would be confusing, stressful, and dangerous. Similarly, without visual management, workplaces become cluttered with uncertainty, inefficiencies, and wasteful guesswork.

Visual management is not decoration. It is decision-making at a glance. If a visual does not drive a behavior, it is waste. And if it does not clearly show normal versus abnormal, it is not visual management.

Core Elements of Visual Management

Effective visual management incorporates several key elements, each serving a specific purpose in maintaining clarity and consistency.

1. Visual Instructions and Standards

This includes prominently displayed, concise visuals that depict how a process should be executed, removing ambiguity from written documentation:

- **Standard Work Charts:** Illustrations clearly showing the sequence of tasks, cycle times, and worker movements

- **Step-by-step Process Photos:** Images demonstrating correct methods, setups, and finished product examples
- **Color-coded Instructions:** Highlighting critical steps or actions to ensure immediate recognition

Example:

In fast-food restaurants, posters with clear visual instructions display exactly how to assemble menu items. Employees can instantly follow the correct sequence, ingredient quantity, and presentation, ensuring uniform quality and efficiency even during peak periods.

2. Visual Indicators of Performance

These tools communicate real-time status and progress, allowing teams to easily monitor performance against standards:

- **Performance Dashboards:** Display daily production targets, output rates, quality metrics, and safety statistics prominently on work-area monitors or bulletin boards
- **Bowling Charts and Metrics Boards:** Regularly updated to indicate actual versus planned performance and highlight deviations immediately
- **Andon Lights:** Colored lights or signals alerting workers to machine breakdowns, quality issues, or safety concerns

Example:

In call centers, electronic dashboards display real-time metrics, like average wait times, calls in queue, and service level targets. Agents can immediately see their performance, understand priorities, and adjust their actions accordingly.

3. Visual Controls and Error Prevention

These visual cues ensure operations are executed correctly, reducing human errors and maintaining consistent output:

- **Floor Markings:** Clearly defining walkways, storage areas, and workstations to maintain an organized, efficient flow
- **Shadow Boards:** Tools and equipment silhouettes clearly indicating correct placement and ensuring tools are always returned to their designated location

- **Color-Coding Systems:** Clearly distinguishing equipment, raw materials, or safety zones to minimize errors

Example:

Hospitals often use visual controls, such as clearly marked storage areas for sterile equipment, designated color-coded carts for medication distribution, and shadow boards for surgical instruments, drastically reducing potential errors and enhancing patient safety.

Steps to Implement Effective Visual Management

Building upon the principles and steps defined in Part III for standard work, the following structured approach ensures effective implementation of visual management:

Step 1: Identify Key Areas for Visual Management

Begin by assessing which processes, standards, or areas will benefit most from visual clarity:

- Prioritize high-impact processes or those with frequent errors or variations.
- Select workstations or tasks involving multiple operators or shifts where consistency is critical.
- Involve frontline employees to identify areas where visual management can significantly enhance their work effectiveness.

Step 2: Choose Appropriate Visual Tools

Match visual management tools to specific operational needs:

- Use standard work charts and process photos to clarify procedural steps.
- Apply performance dashboards and metrics displays to communicate progress.
- Install visual controls, such as shadow boards and floor markings, to prevent errors.
- Ensure these tools are intuitive, easy to update, and clearly visible to all relevant personnel.

Step 3: Design and Test Your Visuals

Develop visual aids collaboratively with the teams that will use them:

- Ensure visuals are simple, easily understood, and culturally appropriate.
- Test initial designs on a small scale, gathering feedback and refining visuals for maximum clarity.
- Validate effectiveness by observing process adherence and ease of use.

Step 4: Implement and Communicate

Once finalized, deploy visual management tools across designated areas:

- Provide training sessions to ensure everyone understands the purpose and correct use of each visual tool.
- Explain how visual management supports standard work and why adherence is critical.
- Create a procedure standardizing the use of colors, fonts, and aisle markings, allowing other teams to deploy visual management consistently across the business.
- Continuously reinforce the importance and value of visual standards through frequent team communications.

Step 5: Regularly Audit and Maintain

Consistently monitor the effectiveness of visual tools and maintain them rigorously:

- Regularly inspect visuals to ensure they remain visible, accurate, and relevant.
- Update visuals promptly to reflect changes in standard work or operational conditions.
- Involve employees in regular audits, empowering them to suggest improvements.

Real-World Example (Department Store Chain)

Think about the last time you walked into a large department store you had never visited before. Within seconds, you knew where to go. You did not need a map, an employee, or instructions. Clear signs told you which direction led to clothing, electronics, or home goods. As you moved deeper into the store, the information became more specific: men's versus women's, shoes versus apparel, size ranges, checkout lanes that were open versus closed. At every step, the environment guided your decisions without you having to stop and think.

That is visual management at work.

Nothing about that experience is accidental. The layout, signage, lighting, aisle structure, and even the checkout indicators are designed to make the "normal" flow obvious and deviations immediately visible. If a checkout lane is closed, a light is off. If a section is under renovation, barriers make that clear. You are never guessing what to do next.

Now consider that same store without signs, section boundaries, and visual cues. Employees would constantly be asked for directions, customers would wander, congestion would increase, mistakes would multiply, and frustration would rise quickly. The store would still have rules and procedures, but without visual management, execution would collapse.

The same principle applies in your operation. When standards are visible, people move confidently. When they are not, even good employees slow down, improvise, and create variation. Visual management is what allows large, complex systems to operate smoothly, even under pressure.

Integrating Visual Management into Your Lean Culture

Don't think of visual management simply as posters or charts. It's an essential element in creating a transparent, responsive, and continuously improving Lean culture. By making standards visible and easy to follow, it empowers teams at all levels to maintain alignment, reduce sources of variation, self-correct deviations, and actively contribute to ongoing improvement. As you implement and refine your visual management practices, you'll find your organization becoming increasingly cohesive, agile, and capable of sustained excellence.

Reflection and Action

Build Your Standard Work and Visual Management Starter System

This chapter is not about writing procedures. It is about creating stability. Your goal is to reduce variation, eliminate tribal knowledge, and make execution predictable. By the end of this exercise, you will have the first building blocks of a real operating system.

1) Select the Right Process (Do Not Overthink This)

Pick **one process** that meets all three conditions:

- It happens frequently (daily or multiple times per week).
- It impacts quality, delivery, safety, or cost.
- It shows variation depending on who performs it.

Examples:

- Batch record review
- Line clearance
- Incoming inspection
- Customer complaint handling
- Label printing and verification
- Changeover
- Order picking and staging

Deliverable: Write the process name and why it matters in one sentence.

2) Capture the Reality (Not the Theory)

Go to the gemba and observe the process.

- Watch **at least three people** perform the same task
- Capture differences in sequence, timing, checks, and decision points
- Identify where people "fill in the blanks" with judgment or memory

Deliverable: Create a simple list titled: ***"Top-Ten Sources of Variation in This Process."***

3) Define "Normal" (The Best-Known Method)

Now write the first version of standard work.

Keep it simple:

- The steps in order
- The key quality checkpoints

- The safety points
- The expected time (even if rough)
- What "done right" looks like

Do not write this alone. Involve the people doing the work.

Deliverable: One-page standard work draft

4) Make Abnormal Obvious (Visual Management)

Now apply the most important rule:

If a visual does not drive a behavior, it is waste.
If it does not show normal versus abnormal, it is not visual management.

Add three to five visuals at the point of use. Keep them practical, not pretty.

Examples:

- Posted standard with photos
- Checklist for critical steps
- Red/green status indicator
- Simple output tracking sheet
- Labeled home position for tools and materials
- "Good vs. bad" sample board

Deliverable: A short list titled: ***"My Five Visuals That Make Normal vs. Abnormal Obvious"***

5) Create a Mini Playbook (Predictable Disruptions)

Standard work is for normal conditions. A playbook protects the standard when conditions change.

Pick **three predictable disruptions** that happen in your operation, such as:

- Absenteeism
- Machine downtime
- Material shortages
- Rush orders
- Sudden takt changes
- Quality holds

For each disruption, define:

- What changes in the work sequence
- Who does what
- What gets paused
- What must never be skipped (quality and safety)

Deliverable: A ***"Three-Scenario Playbook"*** (one page is enough)

6) Define Trigger Points (So the Playbook Actually Gets Used)

Playbooks fail when people do not know when to activate them.

Define trigger points that are:

- Objective
- Visible
- Time bound

Examples:

- "If the machine is down for more than ten minutes, run the downtime play."
- "If staffing drops below X, run the staffing play."
- "If output misses target for two consecutive hours, run the recovery play."

Deliverable: A short list titled: ***"My Trigger Points for Each Play"***

7) Create the Sustainment Cadence (So This Does Not Become Wallpaper)

Standard work and visual management only work if leaders reinforce them.

Set a cadence:

- **Daily:** Confirm the process is being followed.
- **Weekly:** Review the visuals and update as needed.
- **Monthly:** Improve the standard based on what you learned.

Also define one simple rule:

When someone deviates from the standard, the response is not to blame. The response is learning.

Deliverable: A simple cadence table:

Cadence	What gets reviewed	Who owns it
Daily	Standard adherence + abnormalities	Supervisor/Lead
Weekly	Visuals + top issues	Area Manager
Monthly	Standard updates + playbook updates	Process Owner

Final Output (What You Should Have After This Chapter)

By the end of this Reflection and Action, you should have:

1. One selected process
2. A top-ten variation list
3. A one-page standard work draft
4. Five visual controls that show normal vs. abnormal
5. A three-scenario playbook
6. Trigger points for each scenario
7. A sustainment cadence and an owner

If you do this for only **one process**, you are already ahead of most organizations. If you do it for **five**, you will feel the operation stabilize. And once stability improves, everything else in your turnaround will become easier.

Chapter 7 Reflection and Action Answers

CHAPTER 8

Driving Rapid Improvements with Kaizen Events

It's 9:12 a.m. when you finally get a chance to go on your gemba walk.

You're not even fully through the door that leads to the shop floor, and you can already feel it. The building has that tired rhythm. People are moving, but nothing is moving forward. You pass the same pallet that was in the aisle yesterday. The same cart parked in the walkway. The same stack of red-tagged parts with no owner and no next step.

A supervisor is talking to someone with his head tilted down, like he's trying to make the conversation smaller. A forklift beeps twice, waits, then backs up again because there's no room to pass. Someone else is hunting for a tool that should have a home but doesn't. You hear a sentence you've heard in every struggling operation you've ever walked into:

"Yeah… we know. We're working on it."

You keep walking.

On the wall near the production area, there's a board with neat columns and yesterday's numbers. Everything is written in marker: targets, actuals, some red circles. It looks like discipline. It looks like control. But you've been doing this long enough to know the truth.

The numbers are not the issue. The issue is that the numbers are telling a story no one wants to deal with.

You stop at the process that's been getting the most attention. It's not the most technical, not the most expensive, and not the most glamorous. It's the "simple" process that should run smoothly every day, yet somehow never does.

One operator is waiting for a label. Another is waiting for a QC check. Someone is walking back and forth between a printer and a workstation like they're pacing in a hospital hallway. A person from materials shows up with a box and asks where to drop it. Nobody answers at first. They are all busy dealing with what is right in front of them.

Then it happens.

A small mistake. Not a dramatic failure. Just one of those tiny things that should not matter, except it always matters.

A document is missing a signature. A container has the wrong cap. A label is printed, but the barcode won't scan. You watch the operator pause. The pause is only a few seconds, but it's loaded with uncertainty. He's deciding whether to ask. Whether to interrupt. Whether to just push forward and hope nobody notices.

He looks around and chooses the option that keeps things moving in the moment. He improvises.

You do not blame him. You've seen this too many times. When the process is unclear, the best people you have will do what they think is best, and they will do it with the best intentions. *That is how variation starts.* That is how defects are born. That is how a good team gets trapped.

A few minutes later, someone notices. Another pause. Another interruption. This time, it becomes a meeting. Not a formal meeting but the worst kind: the spontaneous, urgent meeting where six people gather around a problem that should have been prevented.

You listen to the conversation. It's familiar. Everybody is reasonable. Nobody is lazy. Nobody is trying to do a poor job. And yet, the process is still failing.

A quality person says, "We need to make sure this doesn't happen again."

An engineer says, "We can update the procedure."

A supervisor says, "We just need people to follow the process."

The operator says nothing. He stares at the work. He's thinking, *Which process? The one in the binder? The one we do when the printer works? The one we do when QC is available? The one we do when we're short-staffed?*

You step back and look at the whole scene. It isn't one mistake. It's a system that forces people to make small decisions all day long. Decisions that should not be decisions.

You ask a simple question: "How often does this happen?"

The supervisor shrugs. "A lot."

You ask another: "What do you do when it happens?"

He shrugs again. "We figure it out."

That sentence lands harder than it should. Because "we figure it out" is not a plan. *It's a confession.*

You walk into the manager's office later that morning. He's a decent person, hardworking and smart. He has a calendar full of meetings and a desk full of reports. He has the same strained look you see in leaders who care and feel stuck.

Before you even sit down, he starts explaining.

"We've tried to fix this. We've had meetings about it. We've talked to people. We've asked for ideas. Everyone agrees it's a problem." He pauses like he expects you to congratulate him for awareness.

Then he leans forward and says what he really means: "But nothing changes."

You nod.

You've heard that sentence in plants, hospitals, call centers, labs, warehouses, and offices. It shows up everywhere. And it usually means one thing: the organization is trapped in slow motion.

People are busy. People are competent. People are doing their best, but the business is not improving fast enough to survive.

You ask him, "What's your biggest constraint right now? What's the real reason nothing changes?"

He doesn't hesitate: "Time," he says. "We can't stop. We're always behind. If we pull people off the floor, we lose output. And if we lose output, we fall even further behind."

That fear is real. It's also the trap. It's the same logic that keeps a drowning person from grabbing the lifeline because they're too busy treading water.

You don't argue. You don't lecture. Instead, you ask, "How much time do you spend every day on interruptions, rework, and firefighting?"

He opens his mouth, then closes it.

He knows the answer, even if he's never measured it. Everyone knows it. The business is paying for improvement every day. It's just paying in the most expensive way possible: overtime, stress, defects, lost time, and turnover.

You stand and walk him back out to the floor. You pick a spot where you can see the process from start to finish. You watch quietly for a few minutes.

Then you say, "We're going to run a kaizen."

He looks at you like you just suggested a vacation in the middle of a crisis.

"A kaizen? We don't have time for that."

You smile, not because it's funny, but because it's predictable.

"Exactly," you say. "That's why we're doing it."

You explain it in plain terms: "For five days, we're going to stop pretending this will fix itself. We're going to take the people closest to the work, pull them into one room, and give them the authority to change the process. Not talk about it. Change it. Move things. Simplify steps. Remove approvals that don't add value. Build visuals. Create a standard. Test it. Update it. Train it. And by Friday, this process will run differently than it does today."

He shakes his head. "We've tried workshops before."

You nod again. "I know. And they probably failed for the same reason most kaizen attempts fail. They were treated like brainstorming sessions. People wrote ideas on flip charts, took pictures, then went back to their jobs, and nothing changed."

You point back at the operator waiting for the label. "A real kaizen doesn't end with ideas. It ends with a new way of working."

He looks out at the floor, and you can see the internal debate. The fear of losing output versus the hope of finally breaking the cycle.

"Who would even be on this team?" he asks.

You answer without hesitation. "The operator who lives this problem every day. The supervisor who has to deliver the numbers. Someone from Quality who understands what truly matters and what is just habit. Someone from Materials who touches the handoffs. Someone from Maintenance if equipment is part of the pain. And one strong facilitator who will keep the team moving."

He exhales slowly. "And what happens to production while they do this?"

You keep your voice calm: "We take a short-term hit to remove a long-term wound. And we choose the scope carefully so we can win. We don't try to fix the whole factory. We fix one process that everyone is sick of. We deliver a visible result. Then we repeat."

You let that sit.

Then you add the line that matters most in a turnaround: *"If your people don't see real change soon, they will stop believing change is possible."*

That's the real risk. Not a temporary dip in output. **Loss of belief is what kills turnarounds.**

Later that afternoon, you pull the core group into a quick meeting. Not a long one. You explain the problem in one sentence. You explain the target in one sentence. You explain the rule in one sentence.

Then you say, "On Monday, we start. And by Friday, we will have a new standard, new visuals, a new layout if needed, and we will prove it works."

Some people look skeptical. Some look relieved. One person smiles for the first time all day.

When the meeting ends, the operator who improvised earlier hangs back. He waits until the room clears, then walks up and says quietly: "Are we really allowed to change it?"

You look him in the eye. "Yes. You are."

His shoulders relax slightly, like you just took weight off his back. He nods once, then says something that tells you everything about the culture you're walking into: "Because we've been living with this for a long time."

You nod again. "I know. That's why we're not going to live with it anymore."

And in that moment, you feel it. Not the kind of motivation you get from speeches or posters. The kind you get when a team realizes they're about to stop coping and start improving. That is the real beginning of kaizen.

Not the Japanese word. Not the workshop agenda. Not the flip charts. Not even the posters.

Kaizen begins the first time a team sees a problem they've tolerated for years and fixes it in days.

That's when Lean becomes real. That's when momentum starts.

That's when the turnaround stops being an idea and becomes a method.

I. Introduction: Kaizen as a Catalyst for Simplicity

One of the most powerful tools in your Lean transformation toolbox is the kaizen event. In my career, I have had the opportunity to lead or participate in hundreds of these events. While it might seem like just another improvement initiative, when understood and practiced correctly, kaizen becomes the driving force that turns strategy into results while transforming a culture of complacency into one of ownership, learning, and energy.

As mentioned before, "kaizen," translated from Japanese, simply means "change for better." It drives improvement, but not in the slow, passive sense. Kaizen events are focused, high-impact, and time-bound. In a matter of days, cross-functional teams come together, roll up their sleeves, and tackle a process head-on. They observe it, break it down, find the waste, and fix it right then and there. The results can be dramatic, but more importantly, they're immediate, empowering, and, frankly, satisfying. They give all those involved a tremendous sense of accomplishment, making it a great contributor to cultural change.

What makes kaizen so critical in the context of Lean is that it puts improvement in the hands of the people closest to the work. You're not waiting on a corporate initiative or a consultant to tell you what to do. You're not waiting at all. You're moving fast, learning by doing, and making progress in real time. And when done right, kaizen doesn't just improve the process. It improves the people, the teamwork, and the overall mindset across the business.

Think about everything we've covered up to this point. In Chapter 1, we discussed how complexity quietly undermines a business. Then we looked at the Lean advantage, assessed the current state, created alignment through strategy deployment, and introduced standard work to bring clarity and consistency. Now, kaizen becomes the natural next step. It's how we go from "what should be" to "what is." It's how we fix what we know is broken. It's how we build the bridge from where we are to where we want to be, from current state to future state.

Kaizen doesn't exist in a vacuum. It's tightly connected to your standards. Standard work, as discussed in the last chapter, gives you the starting line. It defines the current best-known method. Kaizen challenges that standard, asking: Can this be better? Can this be faster, safer, simpler, cheaper, or more reliable? Once an improvement is made, the standard work must be updated. That updated standard becomes the new baseline, which then becomes the target for the next round of improvements. And that's how we keep raising the bar.

If standard work is the baseline, kaizen is the mechanism that raises the baseline, week after week, until the business behaves differently.

This chapter is all about making you and your teams confident in running kaizen events. We'll explore what they are, why they matter, and when to use them. You'll learn how to prepare for an event, how to choose the right team, how to facilitate the sessions, and how to implement change immediately, not six or twelve months from now. We'll break down a day-by-day agenda, show you how to track impact, and teach you what to do after the event to make sure improvements stick.

Kaizen is fast, practical, collaborative, and rooted in reality. It's also one of the most energizing parts of the Lean journey. When teams see that they can make a real difference in just a few days, when they're given the trust and the tools to solve problems they live with every day, everything starts to change. Engagement goes up. Ideas flow. Barriers come down. And that's when you know you're building a Lean culture.

So, enough of this intro; let's get into it. This is where Lean becomes real. This is where momentum starts. This is kaizen.

II. What Is a Kaizen Event?

A **kaizen event** is a focused, structured improvement workshop where a small, cross-functional team comes together to solve a specific problem or improve a targeted process. These events typically last between two and five days and are designed to deliver meaningful results right away. Not next quarter, not next year, but by the time the event ends. And while the outcomes matter, what truly makes kaizen events powerful is how they develop people. They give individuals the permission, structure, and support to improve their own work.

This is where Lean becomes visible, hands-on, and fast. Up to this point in the book, we've talked about identifying waste, aligning strategic priorities, documenting standard work, and creating clarity. Kaizen events are the natural next step. They not only generate ideas, but they convert them into action. They give your teams a real way to take part in the transformation, to not just talk about problems but fix them.

Too often, companies get caught up in planning improvements or launching big initiatives that never quite gain traction. A kaizen event breaks through that inertia. You take a manageable slice of a process, gather the people who live it every day, and then fix what's broken. Heck, you can even "fix what is not broken" and just make things better. You test ideas, move equipment, rewrite procedures, build visual tools, train the team, and lock in improvements on the spot. In this practice, you don't just do some brainstorming and then hand off the work to someone else. The team does the work right then and there.

The power of a kaizen event lies in its intensity and focus. For a few days, a team steps away from their normal routine to zero in on a specific challenge. They examine it from every angle, ask hard questions, and experiment quickly. With clear goals and the authority to make changes, the team swiftly gains traction. By the end of the event, the process works better, and the people who own it are the ones who made it better.

Now, let's clarify what a kaizen event is not. It's not a long, drawn-out project that drags on for months. It's not something you assign to a single department and hope for results. And it's not a one-time fix. Kaizen events are part of an ongoing culture of improvement. Each one pushes your organization forward a little more, and the more you do them, the more your people learn how to see waste, solve problems, and raise the bar.

You also need to understand how kaizen fits into the bigger picture of your Lean transformation. Earlier, we introduced the concept of standard work as a starting point. You need that baseline so you know what you're improving. A kaizen event is the main mechanism that challenges and changes that standard. Once you've run the event, the standard work must be updated based on the changes implemented. Then the updated standard becomes the foundation for the next cycle of improvement. This rhythm of observing, improving, standardizing, and repeating is how you build a culture that doesn't settle.

It's also important to know when to use a kaizen event. Not every problem needs a five-day workshop. But when you face a recurring issue, a broken process, or a clear gap in performance, kaizen is often the best tool. It works especially well when there's a need to move quickly or when multiple departments need to work together. And it's incredibly effective when there's no clarity around the root cause. The team figures it out by walking the process, talking to the people doing the work, and trying out changes on the spot.

That's what makes kaizen so real. It doesn't live in a spreadsheet. It doesn't rely on opinions or titles. It lives in the gemba, where the work happens and where problems are most visible. In a world full of meetings and delays, kaizen gives your team a way to act now and win together.

Next, we'll go step by step through how to set up and run a kaizen event. We'll look at how to choose the right focus area, build the team, prepare the space and the data, and move through each day with discipline and urgency. When you finish this chapter, you'll be able to run your first kaizen with confidence, and more importantly, you'll know how to help your team experience what Lean really feels like.

In Lean, improvement happens at different levels, each serving a distinct purpose. Kaizen events are one key tool, but they fit into a broader ecosystem that includes day-to-day continuous improvement and more formal improvement projects. Understanding how these fit together makes every effort more purposeful.

At the heart lies **continuous improvement**, which is a mindset that improvement is not a one-off activity but part of daily work. Colleagues are encouraged to spot small issues and correct them immediately, like rearranging tools for better flow or adjusting a workstation to cut changeover time. This constant, incremental progress becomes part of your team's rhythm. It's not flashy, but its power lies in its consistency and in building a culture where everyone looks for ways to work better.

Kaizen events take that mindset deeper. Think of them as focused workshops where you set aside time, gather a small team, and concentrate on one process. These events, as mentioned earlier, aim for rapid change, often within just a few days. That gives the team time, space, and focus. Problems get mapped, root causes are tackled, ideas are tested, and improvements are made, all within the event's timeframe. Then standards get updated immediately to reflect the new best way.

In contrast, Lean projects or traditional improvement *projects* tend to have broader scope, longer timelines, and a more formal structure. They may involve data-heavy analysis like Six Sigma, multiple departments, or capital investment. These projects are ideal when you're facing complex issues, need rigorous validation, or are planning systemic change across the enterprise. Their downside, though, is that setup and execution can stretch into months before results show up.

Putting it all together, it might help to think of your improvement strategy like three concentric circles. At the center is daily continuous improvement, where small adjustments become second nature. Around that sits the kaizen event circle, where teams jump in for targeted, rapid gains. Finally comes the outer circle of larger improvement projects, which handle deeper or more complex challenges with more planning and resources. When you align all three, you build not just a culture of problem-solving but a system that can quickly improve, adapt, and tackle anything from the simple to the strategic.

Kaizen events thrive when they connect to daily improvement habits and feed into strategic goals. When your teams see how each level links together, they will understand that kaizen events are not optional extras but vital tools in a Lean transformation able to turn small insights into significant, sustainable change.

III. Why Kaizen Fails

The Failure Modes That Kill Momentum (And How to Prevent Them)

Kaizen has a reputation problem in many companies, and it's not because the method is weak. It's because too many organizations run "kaizen" in a way that guarantees disappointment. The worst part is what happens next: people stop believing improvement is real. They show up physically, but they disengage mentally. That loss of belief is expensive, and in a turnaround, it's deadly.

If you want kaizen to be an engine for rapid improvement, you need to understand the common failure modes and design your events to avoid them.

Below are the most common ways kaizen fails, what it looks like when it's happening, and how to prevent it.

Failure Mode 1: Leadership Doesn't Show Up

What it looks like

- A sponsor "kicks off" the event and disappears.
- The team gets blocked by decisions they can't make.
- People learn that improvement is optional.

Why it happens
Leaders treat kaizen like a workshop instead of a priority. They delegate it to "the Lean person" and assume the team can succeed without support.

How to prevent it

- The sponsor must be visible daily, even if only for ten minutes.
- The sponsor's job is to quickly remove barriers, not give speeches.

- Require a daily check-in: "What are you stuck on, and what do you need from me today?"

Turnaround rule: If leadership is not willing to show up, do not run the event yet. You will burn credibility.

Failure Mode 2: No Authority to Implement

What it looks like

- The team generates good ideas, then hears, "We need approval."
- Everything becomes an action item "for later."
- The event ends with slides instead of change.

Why it happens
The organization wants the appearance of kaizen but not the discomfort of decisions. Too many constraints are placed on the team.

How to prevent it
Before the event starts, define what the team is allowed to change immediately, such as:

- Layout within the area
- Point-of-use organization
- Visual controls
- Work sequence within established quality and safety requirements
- Small tooling, fixtures, labeling, checklists, standard work updates

Also define what requires escalation (capital, IT, regulated documentation, validation). Then design the scope so the team can still implement meaningful improvements within the week.

Turnaround rule: A kaizen event must produce visible change by Friday. If it can't, you chose the wrong scope.

Failure Mode 3: Scope Is Too Big

What it looks like

- The team tries to "fix the whole value stream."
- Day 1 and Day 2 disappear into mapping and debate.

- Nothing gets implemented, or changes are chaotic and incomplete.

Why it happens
Leaders pick a problem that is emotionally important, not one that is executable in a week.

How to prevent it
Use this filter:

- Can we observe the entire process end-to-end during the event?
- Can we test changes quickly without waiting weeks?
- Can the team implement at least five meaningful changes within the week?

If the answer to any of these questions is no, shrink the scope until it is yes.

Turnaround rule: Completed smaller scope beats incomplete larger scope. Every time.

Failure Mode 4: No Baseline Metrics (So You Can't Prove a Win)

What it looks like

- Lots of activity occurs, with no clear before/after.
- Leaders argue whether the improvement was "real."
- Finance doubts savings, and future events lose support.

Why it happens
Teams rush into solutions without measuring the current state. Or they measure too many things and lose focus.

How to prevent it
Go into every kaizen with three to five baseline metrics that matter. Examples:

- Lead time (start to finish)
- Cycle time (per step)
- WIP (how much is stuck in the process)
- First-pass yield/defect rate
- Distance walked/motion time
- Changeover time
- On-time completion (for admin processes)

Turnaround rule: If you can't measure the win, the organization won't believe the win.

Failure Mode 5: The Event Becomes a Brainstorming Session

What it looks like

- Sticky notes everywhere
- Lots of opinions, limited testing
- "Great ideas" that never touch the process

Why it happens
Facilitation is too classroom-oriented and not gemba-oriented. The team stays in the room because it feels productive and safe.

How to prevent it
Set the expectation early:

- Observation beats opinion.
- Testing beats debating.
- Change beats analysis.

A good kaizen has a rhythm: gemba → discuss → test → adjust → document → repeat.

Turnaround rule: If the process did not physically change during the week, it wasn't kaizen. It was a meeting.

Failure Mode 6: No Follow-Up (The "Backslide")

What it looks like

- The area looks great on Friday.
- Two weeks later, tools drift, visuals fade, old habits return.
- People conclude: "This stuff never lasts."

Why it happens
The organization treats kaizen as an event instead of a system. Ownership ends when the workshop ends.

How to prevent it
Every event must end with:

- A named owner for each open action (one person, not a department)
- Due dates
- A 30/60/90 review plan
- A simple audit method (weekly at a minimum, early on)

Turnaround rule: The follow-up system is not optional. It is where credibility is built.

Failure Mode 7: Standard Work Doesn't Get Updated

What it looks like

- The team improves the process.
- People keep training from the old documents.
- Variation returns because the baseline never moved.

Why it happens
Documentation feels boring, so it gets postponed. Or Quality/Compliance becomes a gate instead of a partner.

How to prevent it
Make standard work update a non-negotiable deliverable:

- Updated steps
- Updated visuals at the point of use
- Updated training method
- Clear "effective date" so everyone knows what is current

Turnaround rule: No updated standard means no sustained improvement. Kaizen without standardization is temporary relief.

A Simple "Kaizen Readiness" Checklist

Before you schedule an event, confirm these are true:

- **Sponsor is committed** to showing up daily.
- **Scope fits** in two to five days with real implementation.
- **Baseline metrics** are available (three to five, not twenty-five).
- **Team has authority** to make changes within guardrails.
- **Standard work will be updated** before the event closes.
- **Follow-up cadence exists** (30/60/90 + audits).
- **A real process owner** will own the new standard after the event.

If you cannot check these boxes, do not force the event. Fix the setup first. A poorly run kaizen does more damage than no kaizen at all because it teaches the organization that improvement is theater.

The Two Types of Kaizen: Credibility Builders vs. Credibility Killers

In a turnaround, kaizen events are not just improvement workshops. They are trust-building mechanisms.

Every event teaches your organization one of two lessons:

- **Improvement works here.**
  or
- **This is just another program.**

There is no neutral outcome.

That's why I think of kaizen events in two categories: **credibility builders** and **credibility killers**.

Credibility-Builder Kaizen

A credibility builder is an event where people walk away saying:

- "That was real."
- "We actually changed the process."
- "My input mattered."
- "Leadership supported us."
- "This will stick."

These events share a few traits:

- A clear, narrow scope that fits the week
- Baseline metrics and visible before/after results
- Real implementation, not just ideas
- Updated standard work and visuals at the point of use
- A follow-up plan with named owners and due dates
- A sponsor who shows up, removes barriers, and celebrates the team

Even if the results are modest, credibility builders create momentum. They change the culture because they prove that action is possible.

Credibility-Killer Kaizen

A credibility killer is an event where people walk away saying:

- "That was a waste of time."
- "Nothing will happen."
- "We're going to go right back to the old way."
- "Leadership didn't really care."
- "We made posters, not progress."

These events usually include:

- A vague goal ("improve efficiency")
- No baseline metrics, so success is subjective
- Too much analysis and not enough testing
- Endless approval barriers
- Action items that drag on for months
- No updated standard work
- No follow-up, no audits, and no reinforcement

And the damage is real. A credibility killer doesn't just fail to improve the process. It teaches people to stop trying.

A Simple Table to Keep You Honest

Element	Credibility Builder	Credibility Killer
Scope	Narrow and winnable	Too broad and vague
Team	Right people, full participation	Missing key voices
Sponsor	Shows up daily	Disappears
Authority	Team can implement	Team can only recommend
Metrics	Clear before/after	Opinions and guesses
Output	Process changes	Slides and sticky notes
Standard Work	Updated immediately	Left for "later"
Follow-up	Owners + dates + cadence	Action items die quietly

The Turnaround Rule

If your organization is new to kaizen, or if kaizen has failed in the past, your first priority is not the biggest savings. Your first priority is rebuilding belief.

That means your first few events should be selected and designed specifically to become credibility builders. Choose a problem that people feel every day. Choose a scope that allows visible change. Deliver results fast. Then repeat.

Once people believe improvement is real, the pace of change accelerates naturally.

IV. Selecting the Right Kaizen Events

How to Build a Kaizen Pipeline That Supports Your Turnaround

One of the biggest mistakes companies make is treating kaizen events as random bursts of improvement. They run an event when someone is frustrated, when a leader feels pressure, or when the schedule allows. That approach creates scattered wins, inconsistent results, and a team that eventually burns out.

In a turnaround, kaizen must be deliberate. It must be part of a system.

The purpose of kaizen is not just to improve processes. The purpose is to improve the right processes, in the right order, and at the right speed so your business stabilizes and performance improves fast.

This requires a kaizen selection system.

1) Start with Strategy (Policy Deployment) and Reality (VSM)

By now, you have two critical inputs:

- **Policy deployment** tells you what matters most to the business.
- **Value stream mapping** shows you where the waste and delays actually live.

Together, they give you the "where" and the "why."

But they still don't tell you the "how" or the "when."

That is where kaizen selection comes in.

2) The Kaizen Decision Filter: Not Every Problem Deserves a Kaizen

A kaizen event is powerful, but it is not the answer to everything. You need to match the improvement method to the type of problem.

Use this simple decision filter:

Use Daily Continuous Improvement When:

- The issue is small and local.
- One team can fix it immediately.
- It does not require cross-functional coordination.
- It can be solved in hours, not days.

Examples:

- Reorganizing a tool area
- Labeling shelves
- Fixing a recurring documentation annoyance
- Creating a simple checklist

Use a Kaizen Event When:

- The problem is recurring and painful.
- Multiple departments are involved.
- The root cause is unclear.
- Speed matters.
- You can make real changes in two to five days.
- You can implement at least five meaningful improvements inside the event.

Examples:

- Changeover reduction
- Material flow and staging
- A broken inspection process
- A high-defect assembly step
- Order picking and shipping flow
- A CAPA-heavy process with repeated escapes

Use a Larger Project When:

- The scope is enterprise-wide.
- The issue is data-heavy or statistically complex.
- Capital investment is required.
- Validation or IT changes dominate the timeline.
- The solution spans multiple sites or value streams.

Examples:

- ERP implementation
- Equipment replacement
- Major facility redesign
- Global quality system redesign
- New product industrialization system

This prevents one of the most common traps: forcing kaizen onto problems that require a different method.

3) The Kaizen Scoring Model (Simple and Practical)

Once you have a list of candidate kaizen opportunities, you need a way to prioritize them. Otherwise, the loudest voice wins.

A simple scoring model works extremely well.

Score each kaizen candidate on a scale from one to five:

A) Business Impact

- How much will this affect cost, quality, delivery, or safety?
- Will this directly improve a key KPI?

B) Pain Level (Operational Friction)

- How often does this issue disrupt daily work?
- How much frustration does it create?

C) Speed of Payback

- Can you see results quickly?
- Will the improvement be visible within weeks?

D) Cross-functional Need

- Does this require coordination across departments?
- Is a workshop format necessary to align people fast?

E) Executability

- Can the team implement meaningful change within two to five days?
- Or will it be blocked by approvals, validation, or capital?

Your best kaizen events score high on impact, pain, and executability.

In a turnaround, executability matters more than perfection. A smaller win that you can implement now is better than a bigger win that takes six months.

4) The Turnaround Kaizen Sequence (The Right Order Matters)

In a struggling business, not all kaizen events are equal. Some create stability. Some create speed. Some create cost reduction. Some create capability.

A practical kaizen sequence for a turnaround usually looks like this:

Phase 1: Stabilize (Stop the Bleeding)

- Eliminate recurring defects.
- Improve basic flow.
- Reduce rework.
- Reduce chaos and interruptions.
- Strengthen visual management.

These events build trust quickly because people feel relief.

Phase 2: Simplify (Remove Complexity)

- Reduce handoffs.
- Reduce motion and transportation.
- Simplify paperwork and approvals.
- Reduce WIP and queues.

These events create momentum and free up capacity.

Phase 3: Accelerate (Drive Performance)

- Increase throughput.
- Reduce changeover time.
- Improve OEE drivers.
- Reduce lead time.

These events start moving KPIs aggressively.

Phase 4: Scale (Spread and Standardize)

- Replicate successful kaizens across lines and departments.
- Train more facilitators.
- Build a repeatable kaizen engine.

This is how kaizen becomes culture, not a series of isolated wins.

5) Choosing Your First Events (If Kaizen Has Failed Before)

If kaizen has failed in your company before, your first priority is not savings.

Your first priority is credibility.

Choose events that:

- Solve a problem people hate living with
- Can be completed in the event week
- Will produce visible before/after results
- Are mostly within your control (minimal external dependencies)

These early wins rebuild belief.

And once belief returns, the pace of improvement accelerates naturally.

6) Build a Kaizen Pipeline (So Events Don't Become Random)

Kaizen should not depend on a heroic Lean leader or an occasional burst of energy. It should be scheduled and managed like a production plan.

A simple kaizen pipeline includes:

- A running list of kaizen opportunities (a "kaizen backlog")
- Basic scoring and prioritization
- An annual calendar (even if it changes)

- Event charters (scope, target, team, sponsor)
- Post-event tracking (30/60/90)

In other words, kaizen becomes a system.

And once it becomes a system, it stops being optional.

7) The Golden Rule of Kaizen Selection

Never run a kaizen event because someone wants one.

Run a kaizen event because:

- It supports the strategy.
- It solves a real operational pain.
- It can be executed with visible results.

That is how kaizen becomes a turnaround weapon, not a corporate activity.

V. When and Why to Use Kaizen Events

Kaizen events become essential when a process shows serious signs of trouble, like repeated defects, delays, or rising costs. Those issues don't fix themselves, and they only get worse with time. A well-planned kaizen event can deliver targeted, fast results that lighten the load and improve performance.

Another classic trigger is broken flow. If materials pile up, people waste time walking back and forth, or maybe the layout is causing confusion; something is off. Notice that these are causes and the effects end up being one or more of the seven kinds of waste, such as motion or transportation, as discussed earlier in this book. A kaizen event helps teams reconfigure that space, improve flow, and eliminate inefficiency.

Missing standard work is another sign to act. When no one does tasks the same way, inconsistency breeds defects or delays. A kaizen event brings clarity by defining and documenting the best method so everyone can rely on it.

Customer complaints are a powerful signal and require immediate attention. Whether it's delays, quality issues, or missed expectations, a kaizen event helps teams jump on the problem, find root causes, and fix them fast.

Complex handoffs between departments also call for kaizen. Those transition points where work, information, or materials are transferred often break down. Jointly tackling these with a focused event smooths communication and stops waste in its tracks.

Strategic goals offer another clear signal. When your strategy deployment matrix identifies targets like reducing lead time or cutting cost, a kaizen sprint becomes the ideal way to make those targets real in the workplace.

Focused and Open Kaizen Events

Kaizen events can take different forms based on your goals. A **focused kaizen** event zeroes in on a specific objective: cut floor space by 40 percent, eliminate errors in process X, or reduce setup time by half. With that goal in sight, the entire event is built around solutions that directly support reaching it.

In contrast, an **open kaizen** event starts more broadly. The team begins by looking at data for quality, safety, lead times, inventory, or cost. Then they brainstorm where the biggest short-term gain can be made. Days 1 and 2 are about understanding the area, spotting opportunities, and deciding where to focus. From that point, improvement actions start and unfold in the same fast-paced way. Focused events deliver specific outcomes, while open ones uncover hidden opportunities and spark broader engagement.

Why Kaizen Events Matter

These events drive quick outcomes. Teams tackle real issues and put solutions into action within days, not months. They also energize people. When someone sees their idea make a change, their confidence grows. That engagement strengthens Lean culture.

Kaizen events build skills, too. Participants learn practical tools, like root-cause analysis, visual mapping, and many other techniques. That becomes training embedded in real work.

There is also a tangible return. Defects fall, time improves, cost drops. When leaders can see the numbers changing, they invest more in improvement.

Finally, kaizen avoids bureaucracy. Events are empowered and agile. There's no waiting for committees or approvals. You act, document, and move forward.

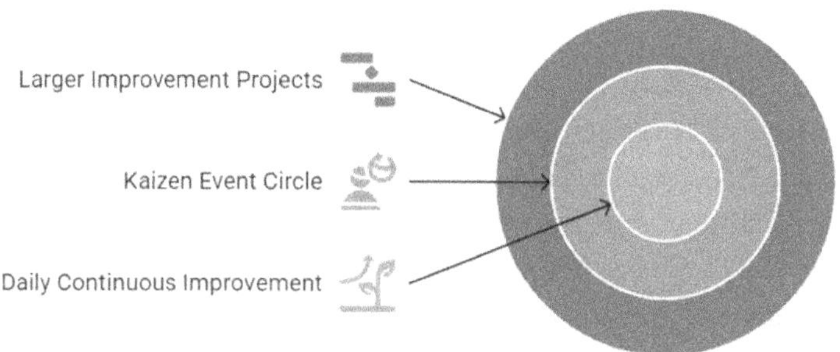

Fitting the Three-Tiered Improvement System

Look again at the picture of a bullseye above. In the center is everyday, continuous improvement with small changes that build habits. Around that circle are kaizen events with fast, focused bursts of improvement. On the outermost ring are larger, formal improvement projects, such as capital investments or organization-wide change programs.

A focused event links directly to strategic targets and clears visible barriers in the process. An open event brings discovery power to teams that may not yet have perfect direction. Both feed back into daily habits and pave the way for bigger project decisions. Together, they form an improvement ecosystem that delivers savings, builds capability, and sustains momentum.

VI. Relationship to Standard Work

Kaizen events and standard work are deeply connected. Standard work establishes a baseline of both what's expected and how work is done under normal conditions. A kaizen event uses that baseline as the launch point to make improvements. In essence, standard work tells us where we are now. A well-run kaizen event helps us move to a better state.

During an event, teams refer to documented sequences, takt times, and work-in-process levels to identify waste, variability, or bottlenecks. They examine each step and ask, "Can this be simplified?" "Can it be safer?" "Can quality improve?" "Can time be saved?" Every improvement passes through a test, and if it proves effective, standard work is updated to reflect new best practices.

For instance, a team might notice that a work sequence requires five steps but includes idle time between steps. They arrange tasks so tools and materials are within reach, reducing movement. The new sequence is then validated for takt time, safety, quality, and ergonomics.

Once it performs reliably across various conditions, such as different times and shifts, standard documents get revised. Picture-based instructions go up at the workstation, and operators get trained and follow them consistently each shift. That revised standard becomes the new baseline, and the next kaizen event looks to improve that, and so on, establishing a cycle of continuous improvement.

To bring this to life, imagine a retail store standardizing shelf stocking:

A team records how employees stock milk and bread. They note each step and how long it takes. During a kaizen event, they recognize redundancies, such as workers walking too much between the cooler and the shelf. They rearrange carts to stay close to shelves, adjust how products are picked, and eliminate unnecessary stocking rounds.

Those changes are tested over a few hours, or even days. Once confirmed, step-by-step visuals with photos and flow diagrams are added to the standard work guide at the shelf for future shifts. When conditions change, like a new shelf layout or a change in sales patterns, they revisit the guide. A quick event can update the steps, tool locations, and photos to match the new reality. In this way, standard work remains relevant and effective.

This iterative cycle of observing, improving, testing, and standardizing ensures that every kaizen event not only brings rapid results but also strengthens the framework for future improvements. A kaizen event follows the **PDCA cycle**. If you are not familiar, that's the Plan, Do, Check, and Act cycle.

Under Plan, you define the target and understand the current state or current standard. In the Do phase, you experiment and implement the changes. Then, in the Check phase, you measure and verify the outcomes. Finally, you Act, addressing what did not work but also updating the standards and sustaining the gains. Each updated standard worksheet is visual, accessible, and part of daily operations. It prevents backsliding and keeps the team on a steady path of continuous, sustainable improvement.

VII. Kaizen in Regulated Environments

How to Move Fast Without Breaking Compliance

If you work in a regulated industry (medical devices, diagnostics, pharmaceuticals, aerospace, food, automotive, and others), kaizen can feel risky. Leaders freeze because they worry that any change, even a small one, could trigger validation work, documentation updates, audits, or nonconformances. The result is predictable: teams stop improving and start coping. They tolerate waste because "compliance" becomes the excuse.

Here is the truth:

Regulation does not prevent kaizen. Poor change control does.

You can move fast and stay compliant as long as you separate *what can change immediately* from *what must go through formal change control,* and you design your kaizen events to work with that reality instead of fighting it.

This section gives you a practical framework you can use to run kaizen safely in regulated environments while keeping momentum high.

1) The Principle: Improve the Process Without Creating Regulatory Risk

In regulated work, the purpose is not to avoid change. The purpose is to ensure that change is:

- Controlled
- Documented at the right level
- Verified or validated when required
- Sustained through training and standardization

When kaizen fails in regulated environments, it is usually because teams treat compliance as a wall instead of a set of guardrails.

Kaizen is still the method. The difference is that you run kaizen with **clear boundaries**, **Quality partnership**, and **a defined path to validation**.

2) The Two-Lane Model: "Immediate Improvements" vs. "Controlled Changes"

The easiest way to keep both speed and compliance is to run your kaizen outcomes in two lanes:

Lane A: Immediate Improvements (Do Now)

These are changes you can implement during the event because they do not alter validated requirements, product specifications, or regulatory commitments. They typically reduce waste, improve flow, reduce errors, or improve clarity.

Common examples:

- 5S and organization (shadow boards, labeled locations, point-of-use storage)
- Visual management (status boards, red/green indicators, clearly posted standards)
- Ergonomic improvements that do not change the process output requirements
- Layout improvements within the area (as long as they don't impact validated environmental controls, segregation rules, or contamination risk)
- Mistake-proofing that prevents known errors (labels, templates, checklists, fixtures) when it does not change product requirements
- Standard work updates that clarify "how" without changing validated parameters
- Training improvements, job aids, onboarding improvements

Key idea: These are often "how we work" improvements, not "what the product is" changes.

Lane B: Controlled Changes (Change Control + Verification/Validation)

These are changes that affect anything the business has committed to in a regulated way. They must go through formal change control and sometimes require verification or validation.

Common examples:

- Changes to product specifications or acceptance criteria

- Changes to materials, suppliers, or critical components
- Changes to validated process parameters (time, temperature, mix rates, sterilization settings, calibration limits, etc.)
- Changes to software, labeling content, UDI systems, or regulated records
- Changes that affect traceability, lot release, sampling plans, or QC methods
- Changes impacting cleanroom classifications, environmental controls, segregation, or contamination risk controls
- Changes to equipment that is validated or qualified (IQ/OQ/PQ type environments)
- Anything requiring regulatory submission or notified body/customer approval (depending on your industry)

Key idea: These are "what must be proven" changes, not just "what seems better."

3) How to Run a Kaizen Without Breaking Compliance

Step 1: Include Quality Early, Not as a Gate at the End

Quality should be a partner in the event setup. If Quality only shows up on Day 4, the team will either:

- Implement risky changes
  or
- Get blocked and demoralized.

Best practice: include a Quality representative as part of the core team or as a daily check-in participant.

Quality's role during kaizen is to help the team answer:

- Is this Lane A or Lane B?
- What documentation must change?
- What evidence is required to sustain this change?

Step 2: Define Guardrails Before Day 1

Before the event starts, define what the team can change immediately, what requires escalation, and who can approve what during the week.

A simple approach:

- **Green zone:** Team can implement during the event.
- **Yellow zone:** Team can test during the event but needs review before full rollout.
- **Red zone:** Change control required before implementation.

This prevents the worst kaizen dynamic in regulated environments: the team works hard all week and then hears, "You can't do any of this."

Step 3: Use "Test Then Lock" Thinking

In regulated environments, you often cannot permanently implement certain changes on Day 3. But you can still move fast by separating:

- **Testing** (learning, pilots, trials, controlled experiments)

from

- **Locking** (full implementation, documentation release, training sign-off).

You can run small, controlled tests to prove the improvement, gather data, and reduce risk. Then you formalize the change through the right pathway.

This keeps kaizen scientific and compliant.

4) How to Keep Momentum When Validation Takes Weeks

This is where many companies lose the culture. The event ends, validation drags on, and the organization feels like nothing happened.

To avoid that, design the event to produce **two types of wins**:

A) Immediate Wins (visible by Friday)

Deliver five to ten improvements that are clearly Lane A and can be implemented immediately:

- Improved visual controls
- Less motion and searching
- Clearer standard work

- Fewer handoffs
- Reduced waiting
- Better organization and flow

These wins rebuild belief and show momentum.

B) Validation Pipeline (started by Friday)

For Lane B changes, your goal is not to complete them by Friday. Your goal is to have a clean, executable path forward with speed and ownership.

Your kaizen deliverables for Lane B should include:

- A written change description (what is changing and why)
- Risk thinking (what could go wrong and how you will detect it)
- The required evidence plan (what data you must collect)
- The owner and due dates
- The change control initiation (started, not "planned")
- A temporary containment plan (how you operate safely until the change is locked)

This turns "validation takes time" into "we are moving with discipline."

The most important leadership move:

Do not let the kaizen end without a follow-up cadence that matches the validation reality.

For example:

- Weekly twenty-minute review until validation is complete
- Visible tracker posted in the area
- Escalation rule if dates slip
- Leadership removes blockers fast (resources, approvals, documentation support)

In regulated environments, the speed of improvement is often determined by the speed of documentation and review, not by the creativity of the team. Leadership must treat documentation work as real work.

5) The Compliance-Friendly Kaizen Checklist (Quick Reference)

Before you run the event, confirm:

- Quality is involved in planning.
- Guardrails are defined (green/yellow/red).
- You know what documentation must be updated.
- You have a way to test safely.
- Lane A improvements are selected to ensure visible wins.
- Lane B changes have a validation path with owners and dates.
- Follow-up cadence is scheduled before Day 5.

If you do this, kaizen becomes a competitive advantage in regulated environments. You do not move slower. You move smarter. You turn compliance into stability and stability into speed.

VIII. Kaizen Roles and Responsibilities

Who Owns What Before, During, and After the Event

A kaizen event is not a workshop. It is a short, intense execution sprint. Like any sprint, it succeeds or fails based on roles and ownership. One of the biggest reasons kaizen fails is that everyone shows up but nobody truly owns the outcome. Below are the core roles you need and what "good" looks like for each.

1) The Sponsor (Leadership Owner)

The sponsor is not a ceremonial kickoff speaker. The sponsor is the person who makes the kaizen real.

Sponsor responsibilities:

- Approve the scope and target before the event starts.
- Ensure the right people are assigned and fully available.
- Provide the authority to implement changes during the week.
- Remove barriers immediately (approvals, resources, conflicts).
- Show up daily (even ten minutes) and reinforce urgency.
- Protect the new standard after the event ends.

What "good" looks like:

- The team never waits days for a decision.
- The sponsor is visible, positive, and decisive.
- The sponsor treats the kaizen as a priority, not an optional activity.

What "bad" looks like:

- Sponsor disappears.
- Team gets blocked.
- Event ends with action items and frustration.

2) The Facilitator (Method Owner)

The facilitator owns the kaizen process. They do not own the content. They own the structure, pace, and discipline.

Facilitator responsibilities:

- Keep the team focused on the scope and target.
- Drive gemba observation and facts over opinions.
- Teach tools as needed, in the moment, not as lectures.
- Maintain momentum and prevent analysis paralysis.
- Ensure the team tests and implements changes.
- Capture actions, decisions, and results daily.
- Ensure standard work updates happen before the event closes.

What "good" looks like:

- The team spends more time in the process than in the room.
- The event produces real changes by Day 3.
- The week ends with results, not just ideas.

3) The Process Owner (Sustainment Owner)

This role is often misunderstood.

The process owner is not the person who "hosts" the event. The process owner is the person who owns the process after the kaizen, when the excitement fades. Usually, they're the leader of the area.

Process owner responsibilities:

- Own the new standard work and visual management.
- Ensure training is completed and maintained.
- Own the follow-up action plan.
- Run the 30/60/90 reviews.
- Ensure the process does not backslide.
- Continue improving the process after the event.

What "good" looks like:

- The process stays improved ninety days later.
- Open actions are closed on time.
- The process owner treats the new standard as non-negotiable.

4) Team Members (Doers, Not Observers)

Kaizen is not a spectator sport.

Team members must come prepared to:

- Observe.
- Challenge assumptions.
- Test ideas.
- Move equipment.
- Rewrite steps.
- Create visuals.
- Implement improvements.

Expectations for team members:

- Be present for the full event.
- Speak honestly about what is happening.
- Prioritize facts over opinions.
- Participate in implementation, not just brainstorming.
- Support the final standard, even if their idea was not chosen.

What "good" looks like:

- Operators lead improvements, not just managers.
- People leave with pride and ownership.

5) Quality and Compliance (Partners, Not Gatekeepers)

In many companies, kaizen dies because Quality is invited too late or because Quality is treated like an obstacle.

Quality is not the enemy of kaizen. Quality is the protector of the standard.

Quality responsibilities during kaizen:

- Help define what can be changed immediately vs. what requires change control.
- Ensure safety, compliance, and risk thinking are embedded in the improvements.
- Support documentation updates and training requirements.
- Help prevent "quick fixes" that create future audit findings.

What "good" looks like:

- Quality enables safe speed.
- Documentation is updated quickly.
- The team leaves with confidence that improvements will stick.

6) Finance (Validation of Savings, Not a Roadblock)

Finance should not "approve" whether kaizen is allowed.

Finance should help:

- Confirm savings are real.
- Avoid double counting.
- Ensure credibility of results.

Finance responsibilities:

- Agree on savings logic early (before the event ends.)
- Help validate before/after metrics.
- Confirm whether savings are hard, soft, or avoided cost.
- Ensure results can be reported consistently.

What good looks like:

- Savings are credible.

- Leadership believes the results.
- Future kaizen events get supported instead of questioned.

IX. How to Conduct a Kaizen Event End-to-End Guide

1. Preparation Phase (Two to Four Weeks Before the Event)

Preparation is the foundation of success and often determines whether a kaizen event delivers meaningful outcomes or fizzles out. It begins with defining a clear problem statement. What is the reason for the kaizen event? Avoid framing challenges as vague symptoms like "too slow" or "inefficient." Instead, identify the core issue, whether it is excessive lead time delaying delivery, frequent operator errors, or safety hazards on the line.

The statement should be tied to a tangible business goal, such as closing a KPI gap or supporting your strategy deployment matrix. If possible, frame the problem in a way that those involved understand the importance of the event, allowing them to realize how the event will help them. Think in terms of "What's in it for them?" For example, if the team is struggling with heavy overtime load because of production inefficiency, frame the purpose of the kaizen as improving productivity, allowing reduction in overtime. Never lie or be deceitful; just help people realize how the improvements will benefit the team as well as the company as a whole.

Once the problem is defined, set a measurable target. If your problem statement concerns lead time, quantify the level of improvement you expect, for instance, reducing it by 50 percent. Clear targets align expectations and provide motivation.

Selecting the right team is critical. Aim for a group of six to ten people that includes process owners, frontline staff who perform the work, upstream and downstream stakeholders, and, ideally, an external or cross-functional voice. This ensures both practical insight and fresh perspectives. If you make the team too small, you lose the opportunity of more perspectives, brainstorming becomes far less powerful, and, of course, there will be fewer hands to do the actual work, from data crunching to the implementation of ideas.

A Lean coach or experienced facilitator leads the event, while a process owner or sponsor provides the authority and resources needed. Keep in mind that every kaizen event is an opportunity to train not only people associated with the process but also people from other areas that you plan to address in the future.

With your team selected, gather baseline data. Capture cycle times, downtime, defect rates, or customer complaints relevant to the problem. Collect any existing process maps or value stream documents. This data provides the reality check you need during the event. Bring the standard worksheets and playbook if they are available as well.

Finally, nail down logistics. Reserve a "war room" where the team can work without interruption, block calendars so everyone is fully present, and stock up on Post-its, flip charts, templates, markers, and stopwatches. Draft and issue an agenda ahead of time, establishing the kaizen hours. Have the presentation material ready and well rehearsed. Be sure to arrange meals, snacks, and periodic breaks. This structure allows the team to focus fully on improvement starting from day one.

Finally, agree on roles and responsibilities ahead of time. The facilitator brings the organization and technique, while the person in charge of the area is the event leader or sponsor, bearing ultimate authority and responsibility for results.

2. Kaizen Event Agenda (Typical Five-Day Format)

The actual agenda for each kaizen event may vary depending on each unique situation, but the days usually flow in line with the proposed, typical agenda below. The events usually run from Monday to Friday, and they are typically long days. In case something does not get done by Friday, the team still has the weekend to catch up, allowing regular work to resume the following Monday.

Day 1: Understand the Current State

The event kicks off with a warm welcome, introductions, and purpose statement. Remind all participants of the goals the team will achieve and why it is important to them and the organization that they achieve them. Follow the welcome and introduction with an overview of kaizen principles, what is expected of the participants and review the agenda.

Then comes the crucial gemba walk, where the team goes to the shop floor or workspace to observe the actual process in real time. This hands-on walk creates shared understanding, reveals hidden waste, and unlocks insight. Encourage the team to take notes of opportunities as they observe. If the organization is not yet familiar with the seven kinds of waste, you may want to incorporate a quick training before the gemba walk, then challenge them to find examples of each category of waste.

Together, the team maps the current state and aligns behind the actual problem, not just the symptoms. Please, take tons of pictures of the current state. Trust me; you will thank me later. I like to tape the floor with an "X" to mark the exact location each picture was taken from. When the work is done, you will take "after" pictures to compare. These before-and-after pictures are great not only for presentations but to be placed on storyboards to remind everyone of how things "used to be."

Day 2: Analyze and Identify Opportunities

Having captured the current layout, opportunities, examples of waste, etc., the team moves to the analysis of the data on hand. They use problem-solving tools from brainstorming to root-cause analysis tools, like the five whys or fishbone diagrams, to uncover deeper issues. Ideas are brainstormed broadly and evaluated by impact and ease of implementation.

Using the outcome of such analysis, the group then creates a future state map, layout, process flow, or whatever represents the new state and may begin small tests to validate ideas before large-scale implementation. This phase may require several trips back to gemba or interviews with the people in the area, and the team may even find the need to pull in additional experts from time to time.

Day 3: Test and Implement

This is where momentum builds. Armed with the prioritized ideas generated in the previous phase, the team conducts rapid experiments, implementing 5S steps, adjusting layouts, fine-tuning ergonomics, or rebalancing work. Operators take the lead in these trials while the teams make adjustments to ensure the work conditions will improve as changes are made. This is not only the right thing to do, but it will also gather additional support and momentum.

The team should simulate real-life events, considering all the various parts and variations that will go through the line or station, in the case of manufacturing, or the various scenarios that a new process will have to address, in case you are leaning up an administrative value stream.

At the Day 3 lunch, you'll often notice a shift in mood. The early fatigue gives way to energy as team members swap stories over sandwiches and snacks. Someone might exclaim, "Oh, so that's why the line kept slowing on Tuesdays!" Seeing the problem from a different angle, along with the midday coffee, often triggers what facilitators lovingly call the "aha" moment.

These shared discoveries deepen understanding and boost connection, setting the tone for an even more productive afternoon. Results are tracked in real time against KPIs to confirm improvements. Each success is recorded visually and becomes a building block for standard work.

Note that it is a best practice to ensure the team addresses safety concerns at every event, adopting a culture where safety issues are addressed in a preventive manner.

Day 4: Finalize Improvements

What worked during testing is now formalized, and it is time to lock in the changes. The team updates work instructions, standard work, and all relevant and required documentation to reflect new practices, sequences tasks correctly, and solidifies visual cues like color coding or shadow boards. Operators are trained and coached on the new methods, and a visual control system or audit routine is put in place to safeguard gains. The more you involve the people who will do the work, the better the chances of success.

Sometimes, not all actions are implemented during the kaizen event. Items with a long lead time need to be ordered, things may need to be fabricated, etc. When actions are planned but not implemented during the event itself, they go on an action plan. This means that, before you call the event "completed," all actions must be implemented.

It is important that every pending action has one clear owner. This owner is not a group, a department, or a team. It is a single person who may work with a team but agrees to ownership of the action and will be held accountable for that action's implementation.

Every action must also have a clear implementation due date. An action is considered implemented when the process is modified and validated, the procedures reflect the changes, and the people are trained on the new way of doing things. The leader of the event should be the person establishing a cadence of meetings to review progress and manage the execution of the pending items until they are all closed.

This part of the kaizen event mirrors the Act phase of Deming's original Plan-Do-Check-Act cycle. By formally reviewing results and locking updated methods into your standards, you complete the cycle: Plan (you set the objective and mapped the current state), Do (you tested the improvements), Check (you measured outcomes against your targets), and Act (you confirmed what worked, updated your documentation, and made the gains permanent). This deliberate mapping back to PDCA reminds participants that kaizen is not random; instead, it is scientific, structured, and built on Deming's methodology.

Day 5: Report Out and Celebrate

The event concludes with a presentation to leadership that highlights before/after metrics and before/after pictures, which tells the story of change. A small celebration reinforces achievement. Participants capture lessons learned and present the action plan. This ensures support from leadership, and it increases visibility and accountability. The atmosphere of success creates relevance and energy for future events. It is important that the facilitator also coach the leadership team, ensuring they are positive and provide the support the team needs.

3. Tips and Tricks for a Successful Event

Scope your event carefully. Attempting to solve too much at once dilutes focus and defeats the purpose. It is better to attack a smaller scope and be successful than to attempt to tackle too much and run the risk of not getting it done. Encourage debate and participation, but progress must be driven toward consensus. At times, the team may have to weigh pros and cons of different approaches, but let the data lead the group towards the right decision.

Start each day with a brief huddle to celebrate small wins, review progress as well as any pending items, and align on goals for the day. Capture photos before, during, and after changes to visually document progress. Include operators in every discussion. They not only know the work best, but their ownership leads to lasting adoption. Maintain high energy through shout-outs, visible success, and short breaks. And most importantly, do not delay implementation, enacting improvements as soon as they make sense.

4. Follow-Up and Sustaining Change

After the event, momentum must be maintained. Use an action tracker to monitor any incomplete improvements and assign responsibility. Continue measuring key metrics over the next thirty, sixty, and ninety days using a bowler chart or scorecard. That transparent tracking keeps the improvements visible and accountable.

A common trap after a kaizen event is that follow-up actions go unfinished and gains begin to erode. To avoid that, document every change, track key metrics consistently, and conduct periodic audits. For example, hold a 30/60/90 day review of action items with accountable owners, reaffirm visual controls on the gemba, and publicly celebrate sustained results. This discipline keeps kaizen from being a one-off event and turns it into a repeatable method for improvement

Conduct standard work audits to check compliance and correct any deviation. Ensure leadership follows up through their daily routines to validate the new procedures. Recognize progress publicly. Every achievement sustains morale and reinforces that the work is worthwhile.

A kaizen event done well transforms not just a process but a team's confidence and capability. It shows tangible results in days, teaches structured problem-solving, and weaves continuous improvement into daily routines. When combined with strong follow-up, effective events become the engine that drives a Lean culture forward

X. Metrics Discipline

How to Prove Results and Avoid "Fake Wins"

Kaizen is fast. That is its advantage. But speed creates a risk: teams can mistake activity for impact.

If you want kaizen to build credibility, you need measurement discipline.

This does not mean complex dashboards. It means choosing a small set of metrics that matter and measuring them consistently before and after the event.

The Rule: Every Kaizen Needs Three to Five Metrics (No Exceptions)

Pick three to five metrics based on the problem. Not fifteen. Not twenty-five. If you measure too many things, you dilute focus and create confusion.

Common kaizen metrics include:

Quality

- First-pass yield
- Defect rate
- Rework hours
- Escapes/complaints

Delivery and Speed

- Lead time (start to finish)
- Cycle time
- Throughput (units per hour/day)
- On-time completion

Cost and Productivity

- Labor hours per unit
- Overtime hours
- Scrap cost
- Productivity rate

Flow and Stability

- WIP levels
- Queue time
- Distance walked/motion time
- Changeover time

Safety

- Ergonomic risk points removed
- Near misses reduced
- Hazards eliminated

Before/After Must Be Apples to Apples

A common kaizen mistake is comparing:

- A good day before
  to
- A great day after

or comparing:

- Different product mix
- Different staffing levels
- Different shift conditions

That creates skepticism and destroys trust.

Best practice:
When possible, measure before and after under similar conditions:

- Same product family
- Same shift
- Same staffing
- Same volume level

If conditions differ, document it clearly so nobody accuses the team of manipulating results.

Avoiding "Fake Savings"

Not all improvements translate into financial savings immediately.

A kaizen event often creates:

- Capacity
- Stability
- Reduced frustration
- Fewer defects
- Faster flow

Those are real benefits, but they must be translated carefully.

To avoid fake savings, categorize results:

Hard savings

- Reduced scrap dollars
- Reduced overtime hours
- Reduced purchased services
- Reduced headcount required for same output

Soft savings

- Time saved that creates capacity but not yet reduced cost
- Productivity gains that allow growth without hiring

Cost avoidance

- Preventing future quality escapes
- Avoiding future capital spend through better flow

All three are valuable, but they must be labeled honestly.

What to Measure Daily During the Event

A kaizen week is not just "before" and "after." It's a learning cycle.

During the week, measure:

- Daily output
- Daily defect counts
- Cycle time changes after experiments
- WIP reduction
- Walking distance reduction (simple step count works)
- Downtime or waiting time removed

These daily measurements help the team learn quickly and prove progress even before Friday.

The Turnaround Rule

If you want leadership to support kaizen, you must show results in numbers, not enthusiasm.

XI. The Follow-Up System

How to Prevent Backsliding and Make Kaizen Stick

The kaizen event is the easy part.

The hard part is what happens after.

Most companies can create improvement for five days. Very few can sustain it for ninety.

That is why follow-up is not a nice-to-have. It is part of the kaizen itself.

A kaizen event is not complete until:

- The new standard is in place.
- The team is trained.
- Open actions are closed.
- Results are sustained.

The Action Plan Rules (Non-negotiable)

Every open action must have:

1. **One owner** (a single person, not a department)
2. **One due date**
3. **A clear definition of "done"**
4. **A follow-up cadence**

If any of these are missing, the action will drift.

Escalation: How You Prevent Silent Failure

In weak cultures, action items die quietly.

In strong cultures, action items are escalated early.

Define a simple escalation rule such as:

- If an action is at risk of slipping, it is raised immediately.
- If an action slips by more than one week, it is reviewed with the sponsor.
- If the slip is due to lack of resources, leadership must decide: provide resources or remove the action.

This prevents the most common kaizen failure: the slow death of follow-up.

The 30/60/90 System (Simple and Powerful)

The purpose of 30/60/90 reviews is not to "check a box."
It is to ensure the process is still running the improved way.

Thirty days:

- Are people following the new standard?
- Are the visuals still being used?
- Are results holding?

Sixty days:

- Are any workarounds returning?
- Are open actions closed?
- Is the process owner reinforcing the standard?

Ninety days:

- Has the improvement become the normal way of working?
- Can the process sustain across shifts and staffing changes?
- What is the next improvement opportunity?

Leadership Reinforcement (The Missing Ingredient)

Kaizen fails when leadership celebrates Friday and disappears Monday.

Leaders must reinforce kaizen through:

- Short gemba visits
- Asking about adherence to the new standard
- Recognizing teams that sustain improvements
- Reacting to deviations as learning, not punishment

The most powerful message a leader can send is this:

"We are not going back."

The Turnaround Rule

If your kaizen does not sustain, the organization learns the wrong lesson.

And in a turnaround, you do not get unlimited chances to rebuild belief.

Templates

I have added three templates to help you get organized during a kaizen event in the Templates section at the end of the book.

XII. Reflection and Action

Part 1: Diagnose Your Current Kaizen Reality

Answer these honestly. Your goal is not to feel good. Your goal is to see clearly.

1. In the last twelve months, how many kaizen events has your organization completed?
2. Of those events, how many produced measurable results within the same week?
3. How many of those improvements are still in place today?
4. If kaizen is rare or inconsistent, what are the real reasons?
   ☐ Leadership does not prioritize it.
   ☐ No one owns the system.
   ☐ People are too busy.
   ☐ Teams lack authority to implement.
   ☐ Quality/Compliance is a barrier.
   ☐ Follow-up is weak.
   ☐ Kaizen has failed before, so people don't believe in it.

Check the top two reasons.

Part 2: Build Your Kaizen Selection System (Your Next Ninety Days)

Kaizen is not random. In a turnaround, it must be deployed intentionally.

1. Identify the **top three value streams** or operational areas where your business is losing the most:

- Quality (scrap, rework, complaints)
- Delivery (late orders, lead time, backorders)
- Cost (labor, overtime, waste)
- Safety
- Compliance risk

2. For each area, list **one process** that meets all three criteria:

- People feel the pain daily.
- Results can be achieved in two to five days.
- The team can implement changes within guardrails.

Part 3: Charter Your First Two Events

Using the **Kaizen Event Charter Template** in this chapter, complete two charters:

Event #1 (Credibility Builder)
Pick the most "winnable" event.

Event #2 (High-Impact Follow-Up)
Pick the next event that reinforces momentum and expands capability.

Your goal is to create belief first and scale second.

Part 4: Define Roles (Non-negotiable)

For each of your two events, assign the following roles by name:

- Sponsor
- Facilitator
- Process Owner (Post-event)
- Team Members
- Quality/Compliance Partner
- Finance Partner (If savings will be claimed)

Now answer this question:

If the sponsor cannot show up daily, should the event proceed?

Write your answer and explain why.

Part 5: Define Metrics (No Fake Wins Allowed)

For each event, define three to five metrics.

Mandatory rule: at least **one metric must be daily**, and at least **one must be quality or error related**.

Examples of strong kaizen metrics:

- Defects per day
- First-pass yield
- Lead time
- Changeover time
- Throughput per hour
- Walking distance
- Queue time
- On-time completion rate
- Number of handoffs
- Rework hours

Then answer:

How will you prevent "fake savings" in your kaizen system?

Part 6: Build Your Follow-Up System (30/60/90)

Pick one kaizen event you've already completed in the past.

Now apply the 30/60/90 method from this chapter:

- At thirty days, what should you verify?
- At sixty days, what should you verify?
- At ninety days, what should you verify?

Then answer:

What leadership habit must exist so kaizen doesn't die on Monday after the celebration?

Part 7: If You Are in a Regulated Industry

Choose one improvement opportunity that has been delayed due to validation or change control.

Now classify it:

- Lane A: Immediate Improvement (Do Now)
  or
- Lane B: Controlled Change (Requires Change Control)

Then answer:

What guardrails must exist so your teams can improve quickly without creating compliance risk?

Your Output for This Chapter

By the end of this chapter, you should have:

1. Two completed kaizen charters
2. A short kaizen backlog (ten ideas)
3. A ninety-day kaizen calendar
4. A defined sponsor and process owner for each event
5. A follow-up cadence (30/60/90) that will be enforced

If you don't have these outputs, you do not yet have a kaizen system.

You only have good intentions.

Chapter 8 Reflection and Action Answers

CHAPTER 9

Lean Thinking in the Office: *Simplifying Administrative Processes*

The Factory Was Fixed, but Nothing Got Better

In my first week at a new company, the plant manager was excited. He walked me through the production floor with the pride of someone showing off a renovated home.

The lines were clean, the boards were updated, the supervisors were engaged, material flow had improved, and even the changeovers were faster. It was a good operation. Better than most.

Then he said something that caught me off guard: "We're doing everything right in manufacturing… and yet, the business still feels stuck."

He wasn't wrong. Orders were late, customers were angry, Engineering was overwhelmed, Quality was buried in CAPAs, Purchasing was always "waiting on approvals." Customer Service was stuck in email loops. And Finance… Finance was somehow always the bottleneck.

So, I asked him a simple question: "Where do you think the real lead time lives?"

He pointed to the production line. "Right here."

I nodded, but I already knew the answer. So, I asked him to show me the **order-to-cash** process. Not the manufacturing routing. The real process, from the moment a customer placed an order… to the moment the product shipped… to the moment the company actually got paid. He hesitated, then called for a meeting with the office leaders: Customer Service, Finance, Quality, Planning, Purchasing, IT, Engineering.

Later that day, we went into a conference room and started mapping the process on a wall. At first, it looked reasonable. Then it got ugly.

The same order information was entered three different times in three different systems. Customer Service entered it once, Planning retyped it into their tool, and Finance reentered it again for invoicing.

Engineering had a separate spreadsheet for "special requests," which no one else could see. Quality had its own tracker, and Purchasing had an email folder with four hundred unread messages titled *"Urgent."*

At one point, the team argued for ten minutes about a single question: "Who owns the order once it's placed?"

No one had a clear answer. That was the moment the room went quiet. Not because people were embarrassed.

But because the truth hit them all at once: **the factory had improved, but the business hadn't.**

Because the biggest waste in the company wasn't on the shop floor; it was in the office.

The plant had flow, but the information didn't. The factory was disciplined, but the decision-making wasn't. The supervisors were aligned, but the departments weren't.

The value stream didn't end at the shipping dock. It ended at the customer, and the office was quietly adding weeks of lead time, thousands of dollars of rework, and an invisible layer of frustration that everyone had learned to tolerate.

That's when I told them: "Lean doesn't belong in manufacturing. Lean belongs wherever work happens."

And for most companies, **the office is where the biggest waste hides**.

In many companies, Lean starts in Manufacturing because that's where the product is made.

But after the early wins, leaders often hit a frustrating wall: the shop floor improves, yet customers still wait, mistakes still happen, and the business still feels slow. That's usually because the real bottleneck is no longer the factory. It's the office.

This chapter will show you how to apply Lean thinking to administrative and support processes, not by "making people work faster" but by removing friction from information flow, decisions, approvals, and handoffs.

I. Introduction: Why Lean in the Office?

Lean principles are most often associated with factory floors, yet a significant impact may lie within administrative office settings. In many organizations, the office is where critical decision-making, information flows, and customer interactions take place. Inefficiencies in the administrative areas, whether in process, information flow, or communication, create visible waste that permeates throughout the organization, slowing down every part of the business.

As you saw in the opening story, the shop floor can improve dramatically while the business remains stuck, simply because the office processes are still operating with hidden waste. Here is a reality most leaders discover too late: in many modern organizations, manufacturing is not the bottleneck. Information flow is.

To give you a sense of magnitude, through experience, we found out that Lean office transformations often achieve 30 to 50 percent reductions in processing time and error rates. These gains directly translate into faster billing cycles, fewer invoice errors, and more agile customer service.

If you are skeptical, that's normal. Most leaders assume office work is too variable to improve or that Lean is only for repetitive tasks. But office work has value streams, just like production does. The "product" is simply different: decisions, approvals, accurate data, and timely responses.

Here are some reasons the office processes can, and should, be simplified:

1. **Direct Impact on Customer Value and Experience**
   Just like it is in Production, the administrative side of the business often touches customers. Whether it is order processing, invoicing, customer support, research and development, or quality and regulatory, office

functions shape the customer's perception of your company. Applying Lean principles to streamline processes improves responsiveness while reducing errors.

2. **Identification and Removal of Hidden Waste**
   In offices, waste hides in plain sight. You can find evidence of that in unnecessary approvals, duplicate data entries, unclear responsibilities, email loops, and wait times. When you apply Lean principles in the office, you can remove steps from processes, eliminate redundant steps, assign clear responsibilities, and put systems in place to reduce batch sizes and eliminate errors and wait times.

3. **Cost Reduction and Resource Clarity**
   Administrative waste may not always be obvious on the balance sheet or in the profit and loss statement, but it drains labor hours, generates errors, and slows down the response times, translating into hard as well as soft costs. Fixing the administrative issues will allow you to free up resources and improve performance.

4. **Improved Flow and Fewer Bottlenecks**
   Think of the administrative areas in terms of processes, not departments. Many processes go through several departments, and if you only focus on one department at a time, you run the risk of missing huge opportunities. By focusing on the entire process flow, you will find redundancies, overlaps, delays, miscommunications, and other issues that you may not find when focusing on a single department. Let me illustrate this important point.

   Many years back, early in my career, I was leading a kaizen event in the administrative area of an automotive tier-one supplier in Northern Italy, a part of the world that is near and dear to my heart. The team mapped out the payroll process, from Production to Human Resources, Information Technology, and Accounting. We found that, at different steps of the process, each area kept track of the hours worked. Those hours were used to generate payroll, calculate vacation times, monitor attendance, etc. The departments reporting hours had their logs, IT compiled the time clock punches, HR also had a source of hours worked that includes corrections, and at the end, Accounting had a methodology to calculate hours worked to generate payroll.

In case you are wondering, yes, the figures were all different! When we mapped the entire process, this situation became evident, and at the end, we came up with a single, reliable method that satisfied everyone's requirements without the need for everyone to keep track of hours. If we had approached the process of streamlining by department, we would not have seen the redundancy of capturing hours in multiple departments.

5. **Empowering and Engaging Knowledgeable People**
   Administrative staff are often the first to notice breakdowns, delays, or data issues. They are usually the ones to face the customers when issues arise. By giving the staff the knowledge and tools to identify and solve these problems, you build engagement, morale, and a continuous improvement mindset. As you see on the shop floor, this process turns office workers into proactive problem solvers rather than task executors.

II. Unique Challenges and Opportunities in the Lean Office

The application of the Lean principles we have been discussing thrives in both production and administrative contexts, but the office presents some distinct challenges, as well as equally compelling opportunities, when compared to the structured world of the shop floor.

Unpredictable Workload, Non-standard Tasks
On the factory floor, work is repeatable and measurable. Each part follows a defined path, and task durations are consistent. In contrast, administrative work often varies dramatically. One email may be resolved in minutes, while another spins into a complex issue, taking hours or days to close. This irregularity makes the workload difficult to standardize and plan around.

Invisible Flow and Hidden Waste
Manufacturing lines have visible flow. All steps are in the open: raw materials enter, finished goods exit. In offices, however, work-in-progress, like reports, approvals, or data updates, flows invisibly through emails, shared drives, or systems. It can be challenging to "see" the process, spot bottlenecks, or identify waste without physical presence or visual tools like kanban boards or value stream maps. You may meet resistance as people feel their time is being diverted from urgent tasks. Counter this with visible, quick wins that free up time.

Difficulty Establishing Standard Work

Standardizing tasks at workstations is straightforward on the floor. In offices, setting standards is tougher. For instance, filling customer forms online may allow bypassing fields, and people might enter sloppy or incomplete data, yet the system still moves forward. Often, standards exist in manuals that no one follows, making them ineffective. Other processes, like CAPAs and nonconformance reporting and resolution, may vary wildly in magnitude from one to another.

Measurement Is Complex

Manufacturing yields clear metrics: units per hour, defect rates, cycle time. Administrative processes require creativity to define meaningful KPIs, like invoice processing time, response time to emails, customer complaint resolution time, forecast, or report accuracy. These metrics are often intangible and harder to track in real time. Here are some examples:

- **Invoice processing lead time:** Track the days between receiving and invoice and issuing payment to spot bottlenecks in approvals.
- **Cycle time for customer service requests:** Measure the average duration from a request being logged to its resolution and uncover hidden inefficiencies.
- **Error rate in administrative outputs:** Monitor the percentage of documents or entries that require correction or rework, highlighting defects in office work.
- **First contact resolution rate:** The share of customer inquiries or internal requests resolved on the first interaction.

However, these challenges lead to opportunities:

High Leverage from Quick Wins

Because administrative processes are often lengthy, manual, or erratic, even simple Lean interventions like streamlining a form, establishing a standard email template, or visualizing workloads can quickly deliver noticeable improvements. These "low-hanging fruits" often generate enthusiasm and buy-in.

Value of Visual Management

Introducing visual tools like digital Kanban boards, swim-lane diagrams, or simple progress dashboards brings immediate clarity: everyone sees what's in progress, who's overloaded, and where delays exist. This transparency not only improves flow but builds accountability and trust.

Cross-functional Collaboration
Administrative work often cuts across teams, e.g., Finance initiating a purchase order, Procurement executing it, IT providing approval, and Receiving managing delivery. Applying Lean here and focusing on processes that cut across departments, as mentioned earlier, naturally fosters collaboration and reduces redundancies, hand-off failures, and delays. This allows people to learn more about the entire flow and how their work affects the downstream areas.

Aligning Office Processes with Manufacturing
Once manufacturing processes are simplified and stabilized, administrative systems must support those changes. If production lead times drop but the order approval or finance processes remain slow, the full benefit is not realized. This alignment ensures the entire value stream, from customer order to delivery, is optimized end to end.

When leading or facilitating the Lean transformation of a business, we typically start with the manufacturing processes, pulling in the administrative processes as needed to ensure the most effective manufacturing process possible. Then, when all manufacturing processes are streamlined, we address the administrative areas to ensure the processes in the office support, rather than hinder, the value creation.

III. Applying the Seven Wastes to Office Work

Understanding how waste manifests in administrative processes is essential. Though the framework originates in manufacturing, each form of waste applies just as commonly among spreadsheets, approvals, emails, and meetings. In an office context, waste doesn't involve physical goods, but it drains time, attention, and resources without adding value. Let's explore each one deeply, with examples and solutions.

In office work, waste is any activity that consumes effort, money, or time without creating value for the customer or the organization. As with manufacturing, these non-value-added activities hide in plain sight. Once you know what to look for, inefficiency becomes obvious and unavoidable.

Let's take a look at the seven kinds of waste and talk about some examples of them. My intent is to help you easily identify them and correlate them to the kinds of waste we discussed in earlier chapters, where I used manufacturing operations processes to illustrate them. We will review the seven kinds of waste in the same "TIMWOOD" order.

Transportation

In the office, this waste typically refers to transfer of information between people, systems, or locations. Examples include handling paperwork, such as purchase orders or batch records, from one department to another or from one person to another. The same applies to emails being sent back and forth. As with every kind of waste, the team needs to understand well the causes of the waste before addressing them. Often, the solution to transportation lies in creating centralized data platforms or simply reducing the number of handoffs required.

Inventory

Just take a look at people's inboxes, either physical or virtual, where backlogs of documents, emails, printouts, or forms sit unused and block progress. Of course, items such as office supplies also count as inventory. Just think of how many contracts and important communications are left unread in email inboxes or huge piles of outdated print in binders. Now imagine if people only had relevant, clear, and actionable emails in their inboxes. Through policy, education, and effective spam filters, it is possible. Standardizing office supplies and applying kanban is also easy to do.

Motion

As in a manufacturing environment, motion relates to unnecessary movement of people. But this concept can be expanded, including such things as eyes and clicks. Think of the wasted time walking to deliver binders or digging through folders. How about inefficient software spreadsheets that require too many clicks? Think about optimizing office layout, bringing people closer together, implementing ergonomic desk setups, standardizing digital folders, and reducing clicks.

Waiting

Take a quick walk around the office. I imagine it won't take long for you to start seeing people waiting outside an office for an answer, waiting for a meeting to start, waiting by the printer, waiting for the coffee machine to finish a cycle, waiting for approvals and responses. Of course, I could go on and on, but I believe you see where I am going with this. Waiting is a prevalent waste in the office space.

Like many other wastes, you can work on the "quick-hitters" and address the easy causes of waiting first or quantify the different causes of waste and address the largest ones first. Some of the solutions will be simple, like implementing policies where meetings start on time so an entire group of people don't have to wait for that one late person. Other solutions may take time and investment, such as upgrading slow computer systems.

Overproduction

This happens when we generate documents, reports, or updates before anyone needs or asks for them. Some examples that come to mind include a team producing a twenty-page report to management when all they required was three indicators. Or printing the forms to be filled for the entire year when it is likely the forms may be damaged or lost, or become obsolete. The overproduction can be physical as well, like ordering too many supplies. A lot of these issues can be addressed with automated displays and dashboards, eliminating paperwork by moving to electronic systems.

Overprocessing

This involves taking extra steps that do not add value to the information flow, including duplicate entries or redundant approvals. Examples include entering the same data in multiple systems and adding layers of approval for small expenses. Imagine a buyer placing an order over the phone, then following up with an email and faxing the purchase order. Again, automating, standardizing, and linking processes usually help a lot. Like we do on the shop floor, first simplify the process and only then automate it.

Defects

Errors in reports, data, or procedures. They not only cause dissatisfaction and frustration, but they may also add rework. Some errors can be costly, especially if they involve product design, compliance, and wrong information. Examples include wrong prices on the price list or website, errors in payroll, wrong design, or acceptance criteria leading to recalls or even customer harm.

Personally, I am a fan of poka-yoke (error-proofing devices). They have to be properly designed and validated. For example, electronic batch records that do not allow the users to proceed if all fields are not adequately filled or if measurements fall outside the range.

IV. Mapping the Office Processes

When you mapped the value stream for the various product families, it should have included the material as well as the information flow. The information flow already touches on a few "office-related" processes, but not all of them. For those processes that were not addressed in the original VSM, I recommend you consider weighing the advantages versus the disadvantages of mapping them using a simple process flow diagram or the VSM methodology. In my experience, I find that a full VSM for each administrative process requires a significant number of resources, and the gains may not be that much more significant when compared to a simple process flow mapping.

VSM

If you decide to employ the VSM methodology, the "material flow" follows the document around the office, including how long it stays in people's inboxes, how much time and effort it takes at each step, etc. You can also map the information flow along with it, detailing how the information flows from person to person or from one department to another.

I recommend the following steps for your office VSM:

1. Select the process. If you have quantitative data to help you prioritize which processes you need to map first, you may want to start with it. Or you can go with the process that is causing you headaches, hindering progress, adding lead time, etc.
2. Put together a team of people familiar with the process and train them.
3. Identify the customer. In the administrative VSM, typically, the customer is the "internal customer" instead of the "external customer."
4. Understand what the customer, internal or external, considers "value" in the process you are mapping. This will allow you to define the value-added (VA) activities, or the steps necessary to deliver value to the customer, and the non-value-added (NVA) steps.

5. Define what is important to the customer. What do they expect from the process? Speed? Accuracy? Transparency?
6. Map the current state. Walk through and document each step, durations, wait times, rework cycles, hand-offs, system interactions, approvals, and error rates. Include the information flow, indicating the source of the information and how it moves through the system.
7. Draw the future state. Use your current map to brainstorm and collaborate on a future vision that minimizes wait and hand-offs, eliminates steps, reduces batching, and supports better flow.

When you perform the office VSM, consider process time as the time actually spent working on the process, like filling out the form, approving, etc. The lead time is the total time from initiation to completion and hand-off to the customer. You can calculate the value-add ratio as a percentage of time spent on customer-valued steps versus total flow time.

Process Map

The process map is simpler and process-specific. It is less formal than the VSM and usually quicker. You can also make it very visual and easy to communicate. People who are not trained in VSM may struggle to understand it, whereas most people understand process maps at a glance.

This is how I recommend you conduct your office process mapping:

1. As you do for the VSM, select the process you want to map. Use the same criteria recommended above.
2. Again, put together a team of knowledgeable folks.
3. Identify the customer.
4. What is considered "value" in the eyes of the customer of this process?
5. Define what is important to the customer. All these steps are the same as above.
6. When mapping the process, use flow diagram symbols. Start from the beginning of the process and map it out. As you do in the VSM, walk the process! You may find out steps no one knew existed. These steps may include phone calls, informal logs, and notes.
7. As you walk through the process, collect copies of all the paperwork generated. Include screenshots of items put in the computer. If you take pictures of some items you were unable to copy, print them out.

8. When the team is back in the conference room, physically map out the process. I like to use rolls of brown paper. Another option is to use easel pad sheets. Make it big and post it on the wall. I like to attach the copies of the documents generated on the process map itself. Some of these flow charts wrap around the entire conference room.
9. At each step, in addition to attaching the documents and screenshots, note relevant data as well, such as the time it takes to get the task done, waiting times, distances walked, etc.
10. The next step is to brainstorm ways to improve the flow, eliminate redundant or unnecessary steps, make the necessary steps quicker, etc. Keep asking questions to challenge the team: "Do we need physical forms? Does this step add value? What would happen if we stopped doing this?"
11. Finally, design the new-and-improved process and calculate the benefits.
12. Just as you do in the VSM process, note the activities necessary to move from the current state to the future state. Many of these activities can be implemented via kaizen events. Several Lean tools can be adapted to the office as well. We will discuss them next.

Before we move on to discussing the application of Lean tools in the office, I want to drop a final thought regarding mapping the office flow. I want to make sure you understand that either VSM or process flow mapping will work. The purpose of this section is not to confuse you but to give you options. You cannot go wrong either way you choose!

But how do you choose? I like to use VSM when the focus is on improving overall flow or tackling a major process. It offers guidance where deeper work is needed. Then apply a process map in specific areas, digging into the details to refine the solution.

Here's a table to help you select the most appropriate tool:

Feature	Value Stream Map	Process Map
Scope	Broad, cross-functional	Narrow, process-specific
Detail level	Includes lead-time, queue time, information flow	Step-by-step tasks, decisions, roles
Primary value	Exposes system-wide waste and delays	Optimizes individual process steps
Best used for	Streamline product or service from start to customer	Boost performance within a single process
Symbols	Uses VSM symbols (data/time boxes, inventory, info icons)	Flowchart shapes like ovals, rectangles, decisions

V. Core Lean Tools in an Office Context

Introduction

Lean tools are not limited to factory floors. When thoughtfully applied to administrative processes, they can convert cluttered workflows into smooth, efficient systems. In an office setting, you're dealing with information, decisions, approvals, and collaboration instead of materials and machines, but the foundational principles hold true. The tools you learned about in manufacturing chapters, like 5S, value stream mapping, visual management, kanban, and standard work can be adapted to streamline paperwork, email chains, meeting flow, data hand-offs, and more.

This section shows you how to Lean up office processes using the same logic: expose waste, simplify flow, systematize clarity, and engage people in ongoing improvement. As you become more familiar with each Lean technique or tool, applying them in any environment becomes second nature. This is a blessing and a curse. Not only will you continually see ways to improve things on the factory floor, but you will also see how they apply in the office.

To be honest, you will find yourself noticing how much better the market or restaurant in your neighborhood could run. And don't even get me started on airports. Once, my wife was making stuffed mushrooms, and yes, she was batch processing them, which was driving me crazy. So, I convinced her to make half of the mushrooms her way and the other half my way: one-piece flow.

If you are wondering, I can confirm she did roll her eyes when I suggested this and got my stopwatch. As you may expect, the one-piece-flow version, although counterintuitive, was a lot faster. But of course, she still batch processes them. The point is that the more you employ the techniques, the quicker they will become second nature.

Now let's take a look at some of the better-known Lean techniques and tools and see how they can be applied in the administrative world.

5S Bringing Order to Information and Space

5S in the office starts with sorting digital and physical files, shelving only items actually in use. Then comes "set in order," ensuring documents, folders, or shared drives are organized in a logical, labeled structure. "Shine" becomes keeping inboxes clean and systems error-free. "Standardize" means agreeing on naming conventions or retention schedules. Finally, "sustain" is regular audits, like a weekly cleanup of downloads or shared folders.

This is one example that can also be extrapolated to electronic files for your own computer or for shared drives within the company. Can you envision how the concept of 5S applies to the cafeteria, conference rooms, supplies area, and your desk?

Imagine getting a team together to sort, set in order, shine, standardize, and sustain a subset of the office area, let's say the office supplier area. The team goes in there and gets rid of anything that does not belong, including broken and obsolete items. These items can be old letterhead paper with obsolete logos or addresses and that stapler everyone knows does not work.

Once all the things that do not belong in the area are removed, the team agrees on what goes back in and where they should be located. Then it is time to shine. Clean the place up, replace old furniture, paint the walls, and do whatever is needed and within budget.

Now create a standard. Where does the paper go? What happens to the waste? Will the team recycle? How will the team make it obvious where things go? Can a visual kanban be implemented to replenish the copier toner cartridge, pens, or notepads? How will the team ensure the gains are sustained? I like assigning someone responsible for the area with the authority to train employees and address the issues that may arise, such as talking to people who do not comply.

Here's a best practice I would like to share. At some of the businesses I managed, we implemented a color-coded layout. I would basically get together with management and leaders of the various areas, along with other key people, and together, we would agree on who would be responsible for maintaining the standards for each area. Of course, some departments would fall under the responsibility of that area's leader. Other areas, such as public areas, were assigned to people who really cared about them, and they usually volunteered. As an example, I had my assistant volunteer to be responsible for the supplies area, and the customer service representative volunteered to sustain the cafeteria.

Where does the color-coded layout fit into this? Well, I like to bring a layout of the entire facility, along with markers or even crayons. As we assign the responsibility of an area to someone, we let that person pick a color, and we shade the area in the layout corresponding to the area assigned. Then we move on to the next person until every inch of the facility is assigned to someone.

Now the magic happens. When you see something out of place, go talk to the owner of the area, who is not only responsible for it but has the authority to address the issue.

Standard Work and Playbooks for Administrative Activities

After you map a process, fix it, and streamline it, turn repetitive tasks, such as expense approval, report generation, and onboarding, into standard work procedures. Document each step clearly, with guidance on who owns what and when it's due. Create "playbook" scenarios: for example, if someone is out sick, the backup steps ensure the task continues seamlessly. These aren't rigid rules, but they give stability to change and allow adaptation as workflows evolve.

Kanban

Use simple visual boards, physical or digital, to manage work in process. A kanban-inspired board with columns like *"To Do," "In Progress," "Waiting Approval,"* and *"Complete"* brings clarity and coordination. Color-coded markers or shared dashboards show status at a glance, making meetings shorter and decisions more informed.

As we mentioned under 5S, kanban can be used to replenish supplies, ensuring there is no excess inventory and that you never run out. As far as visual management goes, I like green and red colors to show status of projects and even to display the cafeteria's dishwasher status, where a magnetic red dot shows the dishes are dirty and green means clean.

Kaizen in the office

You can run kaizen events in the office as well, generating quick wins that build momentum. In some businesses, we have implemented what GE calls "fast breaks," or "point kaizens," which are mini, four-hour-long kaizen events.

The principles of the office kaizen events are like the factory ones. You basically select a process or an area to improve, put a team together, and focus on fixing the issue. Kaizen is also a great tool to implement the improvements that came up when you did the process mapping or VSM.

This list is not exhaustive, but it serves as a sample to help you understand how to shift out of the paradigm that Lean only works in manufacturing. Basically, all tools and techniques can be adapted to the office. Think about it. Do you see any applications in your office for error-proofing (poka-yoke)? How about creating flow? Visual management? Daily management? Inbox FIFO?

VI. Leadership and Cultural Foundations

Introduction

To embed Lean securely within an administrative context, your organization needs genuine leadership involvement and a supportive culture. This is not optional, either on the factory floor or in the office. Transforming your office processes isn't simply a matter of mapping workflows or changing software; it hinges on leadership behavior and culture.

A strong foundation of leadership and culture is essential when carrying Lean thinking from the factory floor into administrative functions. In manufacturing, we've already seen how leaders model by going to the gemba, coaching problem-solving, and reinforcing continuous improvement. In the office, these behaviors are just as important, but they must be adapted to fit different workflows, communication structures, and daily rhythms.

Leadership commitment is vital. Senior leaders must visibly champion Lean thinking, attend improvement huddles, review office KPIs, and walk through administrative areas to ask questions and offer support. They need to shift from commanding and controlling to mentoring and enabling, guiding teams to see waste and supporting experiments that test and improve processes.

Office culture often builds on hierarchy, email chains, and siloed decision-making. Lean leadership shifts toward trust, transparency, and cross-functional collaboration. That starts with respect for the people doing the work: listening to frustrations, asking for ideas, and empowering employees to solve their own problems. When leaders hold kaizen events in the office, they send a signal that administrative work has the same strategic value as production work.

Setting up cultural foundations in the office means creating habits: regular visual huddles to surface issues; shared problem-solving sessions where everyone contributes; visible metrics on shared boards; and educational routines like Lean training, coaching, and peer reviews. It takes leaders who not only approve the work but also prioritize it by setting time aside and protecting it from interruptions.

Finally, leading culture means architecting structures that reinforce new behaviors. Office environments benefit from techniques like "obeya" rooms, dedicated spaces for strategy deployment, cross-functional reviews, and quick problem-solving. Paired with standard work for key administrative routines (e.g., procurement approvals, reporting cycles), these spaces host shared accountability and continuous improvement. That transforms Lean from a one-time project into how things are done every day.

As we shift from manufacturing value streams to office processes, the same leadership and cultural mindsets must travel with us. Without them, Lean becomes a set of tools rather than a transformative system. In the next section, we'll explore how to extend these principles to structure, governance, and rituals in administrative areas so that Lean transformation is real, not just in the plant but throughout the organization.

Extending Lean Leadership and Culture into Administrative Areas

In office settings, Lean leadership still needs the same core qualities: respect for people, coaching, gemba awareness, and problem-solving. What shifts is how you structure daily rhythms, decision-making forums, visual signals, and governance across less visible, more knowledge-centric processes.

Rather than interacting around machines and conveyors, leaders in administrative areas navigate workflows through spreadsheets, emails, approvals, and digital handoffs. To embed Lean thinking there, leaders must adapt gemba visits into a context-sensitive "value stream awareness" rhythm and daily huddles into tightly run coordination rituals.

Lean-Aligned Governance Structure

In manufacturing, decision-making often happens at the point of work through visual boards, constant communication, quick reaction to out-of-control conditions, and continuous drive to improve. Why can't the same be done in an office setting? Let's tie back to one of our earlier discussions in Chapter 6, where we covered policy deployment (PD). At this point, every department should have metrics in support of the strategic goals of the company. Both the PD and daily management (DM) metrics should be displayed around the office.

Daily Coordination Rituals

Daily five-to-ten-minute huddles can be transformative. They can replace scattered status emails and long meetings, allowing teams to coordinate efforts, review yesterday's progress, highlight potential roadblocks, and coordinate the day's priorities.

Here's a recommended meeting cadence. Since production usually starts earlier and that's where the value is added to the product, production should meet first thing in the morning at the beginning of their shift, say at 7:30 a.m. This is just a quick stand-up huddle to ensure everyone starts the day with a mission. In this huddle, the production supervisors and their teams will be aligned when it comes to what needs to be accomplished and what support is needed.

Then a daily, cross-functional, stand-up huddle takes place, let's say at 9:00 a.m. I like to have this meeting at a central location, usually where all the facility metrics are. Some organizations create an **obeya**, or war room, for office initiatives. In this huddle, all departments become aware of the production priorities, and they determine the support they will need to get things done for the day. The office huddles should happen immediately after the cross-functional huddle, where actions are distributed, ensuring the entire plant is aligned and that production will get what they need to get the job done.

Although it may seem like a lot of meetings, each take less than ten minutes, and they happen early in the day. As a consequence, the entire organization is now in alignment with the priorities. These quick huddles also eliminate the need for many other unnecessary meetings.

I like it when each huddle takes place by their metrics boards. The boards should have the department's PD metrics, along with the corresponding countermeasures, the daily management metrics, and a list of actions and any announcements. The person leading each meeting should highlight relevant metrics and go over actions and announcements as needed.

Once this communication cascade is in place, there should be no more issues due to miscommunication. It is magical to see the various departments supporting each other, since they all have the same priorities. This collaboration results in better teamwork, and the end product of this teamwork is better results and a much more rewarding work experience.

Leadership

In a Lean transformation environment, it is imperative that the leader make him or herself visible: manage by walking around, ask open-ended questions, challenge the status quo. Managers should have a structured "leadership standard work" detailing their daily, weekly, and monthly routines, including time for gemba administrative processes, participation in the huddles, reviewing queue lengths, auditing standard procedures, validating metrics and countermeasures.

As the leaders walk around, they should ask questions like "Can you explain to me how you do this?" "Why do you do it this way?" "How can this be done better?" and "How could you do this in less steps or less time?"

When they combine the gemba walk with the right questions and coaching, leaders can uncover many opportunities, as they can pinpoint waste in the various processes.

Allow me to share one more tool that applies to the office as it does to manufacturing: **improvement boards**, or **process improvement boards**. They are a tool to capture and drive improvement opportunities. When left unchallenged, teams have a tendency of focusing solely on daily, repetitive tasks and not on improvements. These boards serve as a tool to capture the ideas that will drive improvements rather than routine tasks.

I'm always amazed by how many great ideas the teams have once they are inspired. Do this. Put up a board in each department. It can look something like this:

Process Improvement Board

IMPROVEMENT	TEAM	PLAN	KPI	ACTIONS	IMPACT/COMMENTS

Parking Lot	KPI's

Have the leaders hold an ideation meeting where their teams are encouraged to brainstorm ways to make things better. You can help the leaders by facilitating it. Encourage the teams to focus on improving processes. Usually, each department comes up with dozens of ideas. They can then rank the top ones, say, two to four improvement initiatives. These go on the board, with each initiative on a separate line. The remaining initiatives go in the *"Parking Lot."* Don't pick three super-hard initiatives. I recommend getting a couple of simple ones, even if they have low impact, and one or two with higher impact and harder to implement.

As initiatives are completed, erase them from the board, replacing them with initiatives from the Parking Lot. On a monthly basis, the leadership team should walk around and review each board. Then, at the boards, the teams responsible for each initiative should present their status. Management's role is to cheer them on, challenge them, and provide resources. When improvement ideas are implemented, they should be celebrated as well.

The figure below explains each section of the board. Notice that under *"Impact,"* we often choose to measure it in currency, like USD (or U.S. dollars). That's because currency is a common denominator. It is hard to add the overall impact of the initiatives when one is measured in number of complaints, another in reduction of hours, and yet another in reduction of safety issues. But just about everything can be converted to currency. Then you can log all initiatives in a single spreadsheet, keeping track of progress using a common measuring unit, like USD.

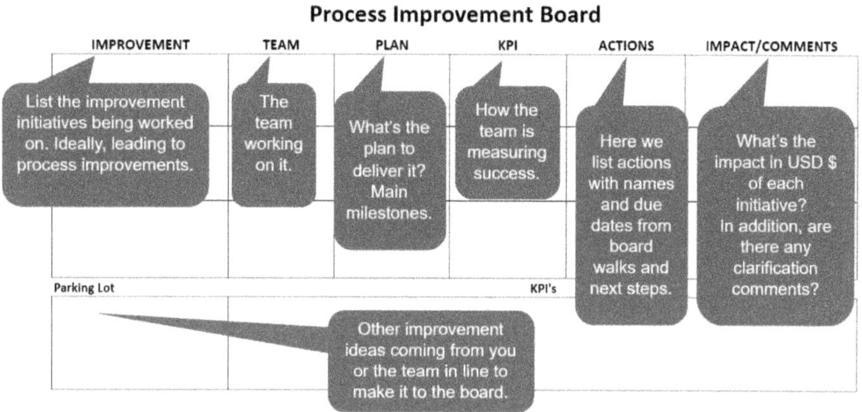

Leadership Standard Work

I mentioned the leadership standard work above. If you are not familiar with it, here's an example:

DAILY LEADER STANDARD WORK:

Time	**Activity**	**Purpose**
8:00 AM	Review KPI dashboards (e.g., email response time, order processing delays)	Monitor critical metrics; identify out of control
8:30 AM	Conduct gemba walk through workstations or team's office space	Observe firsthand how work is done; spot waste; build rapport
9–9:15 AM	Daily stand-up with team	Discuss previous day's wins/challenges; plan today's focus

10:30 AM	Check standard work compliance (shadow boards, process flow)	Ensure adherence; deviations trigger quick "catch and correct" coaching
Noon	Lunch break + informal check-ins	Encourage spontaneous feedback and capture "aha" insights
2:00 PM	Review action item tracker	Confirm ownership; track overdue items created in last kaizen events
3:30 PM	Gemba 2.0 walk/spot-check visual controls	Revisit morning observations; gauge impact of improvements
4:30 PM	End-of-day review/log update	Note deviations; prepare for next day; flag issues for escalation
5:00 PM	Quick email or huddle to align next day	Close loop; reinforce expected priorities

WEEKLY LEADER STANDARD WORK:

- **Weekly Review Meeting (Monday, 9 a.m.):** Deep dive into last week's KPI trends, identify patterns, and update team standard work as needed.
- **One-on-One Meetings with Team Members (Planned Throughout the Week):** Coach, build skills, and understand challenges.
- **Cross-functional Huddle (Mid-week):** Sync with upstream/ downstream teams to address handoff issues.
- **Audit Standard Work:** Ensure new best practices are reflected in documents and visuals.

MONTHLY LEADER STANDARD WORK:

- **Monthly Process Improvement Board Walkthrough:** Review progress against plan, remove roadblocks, provide support, ask questions, be a cheerleader.
- **Monthly PD Review:** Review bowlers; focus on the misses and review the countermeasures, challenge the problem-solving methodology, ensuring the root causes are addressed; challenge the team to bring the metric back to green; follow up on action plans.
- **Skills Gap and Training Review:** Identify development needs based on recent findings.

Again, these are generic examples of daily, weekly, and monthly leadership standard work. They should be changed to adapt to your company's reality and the stage they are in their Lean transformation. They can, and in many cases should, be specific for each position. For example, the quality and compliance VP may follow a different standard of work than that of the CFO. You may also want to have sections that are identical for all leaders, while other parts are specific for each position.

What is true is that standardizing how leaders work ensures consistency in management practices and reinforces the Lean habits of the gemba walks, standard compliance, and data-driven coaching. The leadership standard work embeds accountability, creating a routine layer to identify, analyze, fix, and standardize improvements aligned with the PDCA methodology.

Note that this standard work should not account for 100 percent of the leaders' time. Instead, aim for 70 to 80 percent, allowing time for problem-solving and development.

VII. Office Automation and Technology

Introduction

In office environments, technology should not be implemented too early. You should first streamline the underlying process so it operates smoothly and efficiently. Automating a convoluted process only enshrines inefficiency, increases complexity, and drives up cost. Once you've simplified the workflow by removing waste, stabilizing steps, and defining clear roles, you're ready to choose automation solutions that truly enhance performance rather than mask problems.

A key trend transforming office automation today is the rapid rise of intelligent automation that blends classic robotic process automation (RPA) with powerful AI capabilities. This convergence unlocks new levels of efficiency and effectiveness. Gone are the days of mere click-and-copy bots. Now office systems can extract information from unstructured documents, make decisions, and even learn from exceptions, handling extended workflows with minimal human input.

Beyond speed and accuracy, automation can improve quality, reduce errors, and empower your team to concentrate on strategic, customer-facing work. Yet we must proceed thoughtfully: automation is not a plug-and-play fix but a product of disciplined process improvement.

Robotic Process Automation (RPA)

Once your office processes are simplified and standardized, employing automation tools becomes powerful. RPA is a leading solution in this space, designed to handle high-volume, rule-based office tasks. Instead of automating first and simplifying later, which risks embedding inefficiency, Lean recommends "simplify, then automate." Your streamlined process acts as a firm foundation for deploying RPA to magnify productivity without transferring complexity into a bot.

In essence, RPA uses software "bots" that mimic human actions by clicking through menus, entering data, moving files, and more across existing applications without changing those systems. This low-code approach makes it fast to deploy; you simply teach the bot the steps instead of building new integrations.

RPA can significantly cut repetitive manual work, such as invoice processing, expense reporting, data reconciliation, order entry, and approvals. RPA bots can mimic keystrokes as well as clicks. In addition, they can do data uploads, downloads, and transfers. When freed from such activities, people can spend their time actually adding value in customer interaction, problem-solving, and innovation.

The field of artificial intelligence (AI) is growing fast. Already, combining RPA and AI enables bots to tackle more complex tasks and even understand documents, images, and natural language. Companies are using bots to perform invoice audits, staff scheduling, IT support tickets, payroll, etc. I am far from being an expert on the subject, but even I was able to develop a simple bot to populate a metrics spreadsheet with data scattered around in a company I work for.

In the immediate future, I can see that RPA is evolving into intelligent and autonomous systems. New approaches called **intelligent process automation** (IPA) incorporate machine learning, natural language processing, and predictive analytics, enabling bots to make nuanced decisions instead of executing fixed rules. I am not creative or knowledgeable enough to predict what office automation will look like in the long run, but I am certain that the technology will be there to automate a lot more than what I have described so far.

VIII. Reflection and Action

Turn Lean Office Thinking into a Thirty-Day Plan

Lean in the office is one of the highest-leverage opportunities in most organizations. The waste is real, the bottlenecks are often hidden, and the improvements can be dramatic. But just like in manufacturing, the only way to gain control is to move from opinions to facts and from frustration to structured action.

Use the questions below to build your first Lean office improvement plan.

A. Identify Your Highest-Impact Administrative Value Streams

1. List the top-five administrative processes that most directly impact the customer experience.
   Examples: order entry, quote-to-order, complaint handling, CAPA closure, invoicing, shipping documentation, regulatory submissions.

2. Which **one** of those processes causes the most pain today? Describe the pain using symptoms, not assumptions.
   Examples: "Customers complain about delays," "We miss shipments," "We have rework," "We constantly escalate," "We need heroics to get things done."

3. If you could improve only one office process this quarter, which one would you pick and why?

B. Define "Value" and the True Customer of the Process

1. Who is the customer of the process you selected?

- External customer
- Internal customer
- Both

2. What does "value" mean in this process? Pick the top two:

- Speed
- Accuracy
- Completeness
- Compliance
- Transparency
- Predictability

3. What is the most common defect in this process?
Be specific (missing information, wrong data, rework loops, unclear ownership, etc.).

C. Measure the Process Like a Lean Leader

1. What is the total lead time from start to finish today?
   If you do not know, estimate it and write down what you would need to measure it.
2. What is the actual process time (hands-on work time) inside that lead time?
3. What is the value-added ratio?
   (Value-added time ÷ total lead time)
4. Pick three metrics you will track weekly for this process.
   Here are examples you can choose from:
   - Total lead time
   - Queue size/work in process
   - Percent complete and accurate (first-pass yield)
   - Error rate/rework rate
   - Number of handoffs

  - Percent on-time completion
  - SLA adherence
  - Escalation count

D. See the Waste in Real Office Terms

1. Walk through the process and identify one example of each waste you observe:

- Transportation (handoffs, system transfers)
- Inventory (emails, backlogs, unread approvals)
- Motion (searching, clicks, unnecessary movement)
- Waiting (approvals, responses, system delays)
- Overproduction (reports no one uses)
- Overprocessing (duplicate entries, redundant approvals)
- Defects (wrong or incomplete information)

2. Which two wastes are the biggest drivers of lead time in your process?

E. Choose the Right Mapping Tool and Build a Team

1. Will you use a full VSM or a simple process map for this first effort? Explain your choice.
2. List the roles that must be represented on the mapping team. (Include upstream and downstream stakeholders, not just the department that "owns" the work.)
3. Who will sponsor the effort? What will you ask the sponsor to do to protect the time and remove obstacles?

F. Design the Future State (Simple, Not Perfect)

1. What is the biggest opportunity to simplify the process immediately? Examples:

- Eliminate a step.
- Reduce approvals.
- Combine two steps.
- Create one source of truth.
- Remove duplicate entries.
- Standardize inputs.
- Reduce batching.
- Define clear ownership.

2. What would the process look like if it had:

- One clear owner?
- One source of truth?
- Clear entry criteria ("complete and accurate")?
- A visible queue?
- A defined escalation path?
- A measurable SLA?

3. What is your target lead time for the future state?

G. Build Your First Thirty-Day Lean Office Plan

1. Identify three improvements you will implement in the next thirty days:

- One quick win (easy, visible, fast)
- One medium improvement (requires coordination)
- One structural improvement (removes a recurring root cause)

2. For each improvement, define:

- Owner
- Due date
- Expected impact
- Metric to prove the impact

H. Decide Where Automation Actually Belongs

1. Which part of the process is repetitive and rule-based enough to automate?
2. Before automation, what must be simplified or standardized first?
3. What is one "error-proofing" improvement you can implement without technology?
   Examples:
   - Mandatory fields
   - Checklists
   - Standardized templates
   - Simple forms
   - Clear entry criteria
   - Clear definitions

I. Sustainment: Make It Stick

1. What daily or weekly ritual will keep the process under control?
Examples:

- Ten-minute daily huddle
- Weekly KPI review
- Queue review
- Escalation review
- Improvement board walkthrough

2. What will leaders do differently starting next week to demonstrate commitment?
Be specific: what will they review, where will they go, and what questions will they ask?

Final Action Challenge (Highly Recommended)

Before you move to the next chapter, complete this:

Pick one office process. Map it within two weeks.

Then implement at least **one measurable improvement** within the following two weeks.

If you do that, you will have proven something critical:

Lean is not a manufacturing system. It is a management system.

Chapter 9 Reflection and Action Answers

CHAPTER 10

Measuring Your Progress: *The Key Performance Indicators for Your Lean Transformation*

The Company That Was Busy and Still Dying

On my first day with a new client, the CEO greeted me with a confident smile and a thick binder. He handed it to me like it was a trophy. "We've got a strategy," he said.

The binder was impressive: the cover was glossy, the slides were clean, and the language was bold. There were charts about market expansion, customer experience, innovation, and operational excellence. It was the kind of strategy that sounds great in a boardroom.

Then he said something I hear more often than people realize: "We just need help executing."

That afternoon, we walked the facility, and I could see that the shop floor was busy. The office was busy, too. Everyone looked overloaded, yet the business was bleeding.

They had late orders, quality escapes, too much expediting, tons of customer complaints. Their margins were shrinking and their employee turnover was rising.

The CEO kept talking as we walked. He pointed to a whiteboard filled with projects. "See? We've got initiatives everywhere."

The board was full of dozens of initiatives. Some were written in bright colors, some had check marks, and some had deadlines. It looked like progress, but the truth was obvious:

A company can be full of initiatives and still be completely directionless.

So, I asked him a question that made him stop walking: "Which one of these initiatives supports your strategy?" I frequently ask versions of this same question.

He looked back at the board, then at me, then back at the board again. "Most of them… I think."

I didn't say anything, just nodded. Then I asked the next question: "Okay. How do you know they're working?"

He smiled again, a little less confidently this time: "Well… we review them in meetings."

I kept going: "How do you measure success?"

He hesitated, and then he said the most honest sentence I've heard from a CEO in a long time: "We don't really. We just… try to get things done."

That's the moment I knew the real problem wasn't execution. It was their system. This company wasn't failing because people were lazy; it was because the organization had no way to answer three basic questions:

1. Are we working on the right things?
2. Are we winning?
3. If we're not winning, what are we going to do differently tomorrow?

The next morning, I sat in on their weekly leadership meeting. It was three hours long, with a room that was packed. Every department had slides, and every slide had numbers, including revenue, scrap, overtime, inventory, complaints, safety, and efficiency.

There were charts everywhere, but the meeting felt strange. No one challenged anything, and no one asked "why." They did not talk about countermeasures. The numbers were read aloud like a weather report. Then, at the end of the meeting, the CEO asked, "Any other topics?"

Someone brought up a new initiative, and everyone nodded. Just like that, the company added one more project to a system that was already drowning.

When we walked out, I asked the CEO, "Do you know what's happening here?"

He sighed and said, "Yeah, we're working hard."

I nodded. "You're not working hard. You're working blind."

He stared at me for a second. Then he said quietly, "So, what do we do?" He was clearly frustrated, and I had a feeling he was getting mad at me.

"We pick the vital few metrics that represent your strategy," I told him, "and we make them visible. We review them with discipline and connect initiatives to them. Then we kill everything else."

That was the day the company stopped "doing Lean" and started running a transformation. Not because they worked harder. **But because, for the first time, they could see**.

If policy deployment is the system that turns strategy into aligned work, KPIs are the system that tells you whether your strategy is working. Without them, you don't have a transformation. You have activity.

In this chapter, we will simplify KPIs down to what they were always meant to be: a practical leadership tool that makes reality visible, drives action, and keeps the organization aligned with its aspirations.

I. Introduction to KPIs

Here's a thought-provoking question: **how do you know your Lean journey is actually working and not just creating busy work?** What if I told you the answer lies in choosing just a few measures that truly matter? That's where **KPIs**, or key performance indicators, come in.

While KPIs are often seen as technical tools for measuring output and efficiency, their true value goes beyond numbers. They're a leadership tool that shapes behavior, builds trust, and engages people in the mission. When KPIs are introduced with the right context and purpose, they become part of the culture, helping everyone see how their contributions matter, fostering collaboration, and creating pride in improvement.

KPIs are not just metrics, and they're definitely not supposed to be bureaucratic burdens. They are the **"vital few"** measures that directly reveal whether your transformation is creating real value, whether you're reducing waste, improving flow, and delighting customers. The rest, those nice-to-know statistics, may be fun to track and may satisfy some corporate mandates, but they rarely drive behavior or change.

KPIs come in two forms: **lagging indicators**, which reflect results that have already happened, and **leading indicators**, which help you steer before problems surface. In a Lean transformation, these are not luxuries; they're essentials. Daily lead-time trends, quality ratios, and request-response delays—each KPI gives you a compass reading, a way to know if the ship is veering off course before you hit the rocks. Over time, those lagging indicators, like completed orders, revenue, and customer satisfaction, tell you if your course correction is working.

However, KPIs must meet four criteria to be effective: they must be **strategic**, pointing straight to your vision; **measurable**, based on data you can trust; **focused**, no more than a handful per team; and **actionable**, so that someone can, and will, do something if the numbers aren't trending toward green.

Numbers on a screen don't motivate change. The real power of KPIs comes when you're able to weave them into a story that captures what happened, why it matters, and what action should come next. The most effective KPI scoreboards combine three elements: context (why this metric matters today), trend (showing performance over time), and insight (highlighting an anomaly or success and defining the next step). A well-crafted dashboard or visual board becomes a storyline that focuses daily attention, sparks questions like "What caused the dip?" or "What actions pushed this up?" and propels teams into action rather than passive observation.

In this chapter, we begin with a clear definition grounded in Lean thinking: KPIs are the **guiding stars** of your transformation, reflecting what matters most and giving every person in your organization a simple question to ask each day: **"Are we heading in the right direction?"** Then we'll explore how to select KPIs, both leading and lagging, that fit your goals, structure them into daily visual management, and use them to review performance, troubleshoot problems, align resources, and celebrate success.

By the end, you'll clearly understand the difference between a useful KPI and a distracting data point. You'll know how to turn raw data streams into powerful storyboards. And you'll be able to speak and lead with metrics that guide your Lean transformation from day one.

II. The KPI Trap

Why Most KPI Systems Fail Even in Well-Intentioned Companies

If KPIs are so powerful, why do so many companies struggle with them, and why do KPI dashboards often feel like a burden instead of a leadership tool? Why do teams update numbers every week, yet performance doesn't improve?

The answer is simple: Most organizations don't have a KPI system. They have KPI noise.

They have metrics, charts, dashboards, and reports but not a disciplined way of using them to drive behavior, alignment, and improvement. In fact, I have seen KPI systems do more harm than good when they are poorly designed. They can create confusion, mistrust, defensive behavior, and a false sense of control.

Let's walk through the most common KPI traps. If you recognize your company in these examples, don't feel bad. These traps are extremely common. The good news is: once you see them, you can fix them.

Trap #1: "Metric Obesity" (Too Many KPIs)

This is the most common failure mode. A company starts with a few metrics. Then someone asks for more.

- Finance wants additional cost breakdowns.
- Quality wants more compliance indicators.
- Operations wants more productivity measures.
- Sales wants pipeline and conversion ratios.
- HR wants engagement scores.
- Corporate wants standardized global reporting.

Before long, the company is tracking forty, sixty, or 120 metrics. The problem is not that those metrics are wrong. It's that the human brain cannot manage that many priorities.

When everything is important, nothing is important, and when everything is measured, nothing is truly managed.

The predictable result:

- Teams stop paying attention.
- Metrics get updated late.
- People don't trust the numbers.
- Review meetings become long and boring.
- KPI discussions become superficial.
- The organization loses focus.

This is why, in Lean, we focus on the vital few. Not because we dislike data, but because focus drives behavior.

Trap #2: "Vanity KPIs" (Metrics That Look Good but Don't Matter)

Some KPIs exist because they are easy to measure, not because they drive value. They often fall into two categories:

Activity metrics
Examples: number of meetings, number of kaizens, number of trainings, number of audits, number of projects launched

Comfort metrics
Examples: metrics that are always green, or metrics that make a department look good but don't reflect customer impact

Vanity KPIs are seductive. They give people the feeling that they are in control. But they don't answer the only question that matters: is the business getting better in ways the customer can feel and the financials can prove?

Trap #3: KPIs That Are Not Connected to Strategy

This trap is subtle because the company believes it has alignment. The leadership team has strategic goals, each department creates its own dashboard, and each dashboard contains metrics that are logical only inside that department. But when you step back, the dashboards don't connect.

The organization ends up with:

- Local optimization
- Departmental wins that don't translate into business results
- Conflicting priorities
- Teams pulling in different directions

This is where policy deployment matters. PD forces you to ask:

- What is the strategy?
- What are the breakthrough priorities?
- What must improve for the strategy to succeed?
- What KPIs prove it is working?

Without PD, KPI systems become fragmented. With PD, KPIs become aligned.

Trap #4: KPIs Without Clear Definitions (Garbage In, Garbage Out)

A KPI is only useful if everyone measures it the same way, but in many organizations, KPI definitions are vague or inconsistent.

For example:

- What exactly counts as "on-time delivery"?
- Is it on the customer request date or promise date?
- Does partial shipment count?
- Do we measure on-time at shipping or at customer receipt?
- Do we exclude orders we didn't ship because we didn't have material?

If the definition is unclear, two things happen:

1. People argue about the metric instead of solving the problem.
2. People stop trusting the metric entirely.

When trust is lost, the KPI culture collapses.

Trap #5: KPIs Without Ownership (Everyone Sees It; No One Owns It)

This is another classic. The metric is on a dashboard, and everyone sees it and discusses it, but no one owns it. When the KPI turns red, people ask, "Why is this happening?"

And the room goes silent.

Because the KPI is not connected to a person who is accountable for:

- The definition
- Data accuracy
- Update cadence
- The analysis
- The countermeasure process

A KPI without an owner is a decoration, not a KPI.

Trap #6: KPIs That Don't Trigger Action

This trap creates what I call **"Red is normal."**

The dashboard shows red, and the team notices it and discusses it. Then they move on. Next week, it's still red. The same discussion happens again. Eventually, people stop reacting. The KPI becomes background noise. This is one of the most dangerous moments in a transformation.

Because it teaches the organization that *numbers don't matter.*

A KPI must trigger action, or it has no purpose.

That action might be:

- Investigation
- A quick countermeasure
- Escalation
- A kaizen event
- A structured problem-solving effort

Trap #7: KPI Reviews That Become "Meeting Theater"

This is where KPI systems go to die. You know what I'm talking about. The meeting is long, each department presents slides, they read numbers aloud, and the explanations are defensive.

No one asks, "Why?" in a structured way, no one owns countermeasures, and no one follows up.

The meeting feels productive because it consumes time and produces PowerPoint slides, but performance does not improve. This is what we call "theater," and this is not management.

Lean KPI reviews should be problem-solving sessions instead of simply reporting sessions.

Trap #8: Automating Too Early (Dashboards That Scale Confusion)

Automation is not the enemy, but automating too early is a mistake. I've seen companies spend significant money building dashboards, integrating systems, and installing digital KPI screens only to discover:

- The metrics were poorly defined.
- The data was wrong.
- The teams didn't know what actions to take.
- Leaders didn't use the system consistently.

In those cases, automation doesn't save time. It scales confusion. This is why Lean teaches that we should stabilize first, then automate. Build the habits and discipline manually, and only then use technology to accelerate. Later in this chapter, I'll show you a practical "manual first" path that prevents expensive dashboard regret.

The takeaway: KPIs fail when they become "measurement" instead of "management."

If you want KPIs to transform your business, you must treat them as a management system.

A real KPI system must:

- Simplify focus.
- Connect strategy to daily work.
- Create ownership.
- Make abnormalities visible.
- Trigger action.
- Reinforce learning.

In the next section, we will shift from theory to control.

We will show how great leaders use KPIs as a weapon against chaos and how to build a KPI operating system that makes your strategy real every day.

III. KPIs as a Leadership Weapon

How Great Leaders Use KPIs to Stop Chaos and Take Control

Most companies suffer from a lack of alignment, not a lack of effort.

People are busy, and meetings are full. Projects multiply, and dashboards glow red, yellow, and green. Yet, year after year, the organization feels like it is pushing hard without moving forward.

That happens when the business cannot answer a few basic questions with clarity:

- Are we working on the right things?
- Are we winning?
- If we're not winning, what are we going to do differently next?

That's why KPIs are not "measurement tools." Done right, KPIs are leadership tools. They are how you turn strategy into daily reality. They are how you stop initiative chaos. They are how you prevent the organization from confusing motion with progress.

The real enemy is the initiative soup.

When a business starts to struggle, the most common reaction is to add initiatives. When something goes wrong, we add an initiative. A new customer complaint? We add an initiative. How about when margins drop? We add an initiative. How about when a VP wants to prove they are doing something? Yeah, they add an initiative.

Before long, you get what I call "initiative soup":

- Ten projects per department
- No clear priorities
- Too many owners
- Weak follow-up
- Superficial reporting

- No clear definition of success
- No one willing to kill anything because it might offend someone

This is one of the reasons good companies stall. Not because they lack ideas, but because they lack focus and proof. The purpose of KPIs is to force focus.

A KPI is a number you use to make decisions. Don't just use it for show. It is not there for people to admire. It tells you whether something matters, whether something is working, and, maybe most importantly, whether something should stop.

KPIs stop random work by forcing one uncomfortable question.

Here's the question that changes everything:

"Which KPI will this initiative move, by how much, and by when?"

If a team cannot answer that question clearly, one of three things is true:

1. The initiative is not tied to strategy.
2. The team doesn't understand the root problem.
3. The initiative is more about activity than impact.

This is where KPIs become a weapon. They stop "random work" without you needing to argue about opinions. They also stop politics.

Because KPIs shift the discussion from:

- "I think this matters"
  to
- "Show me the trend."

KPIs eliminate executive disagreement the right way.

In many struggling companies, executives are not aligned. They don't say it out loud, but you can feel it. People tend to live within their silos, and they look at problems from their own perspectives. So, Marketing thinks the problem is brand awareness. Sales thinks the problem is pricing. Operations thinks the problem is delivery. Quality thinks the problem is discipline. Finance thinks the problem is cost. What happens then?

Everyone fights for their own initiatives, and the CEO tries to keep the peace by saying yes to everyone. And that's how initiative soup becomes initiative flood.

KPIs solve this, but not by forcing consensus. They solve it by forcing clarity.

A leadership team does not need to agree on everything, but they must agree on a small set of outcomes that define success. Those outcomes become the breakthrough KPIs.

Once the breakthrough KPIs are clear, executive disagreement becomes productive instead of chaotic because everyone can ask:

- Are we improving the outcome?
- If not, what is blocking us?
- What is the smallest countermeasure we can test?

KPIs turn executive discussions into problem-solving, not debates.

KPIs destroy vanity metrics without hurting morale.

Vanity metrics feel good. They look impressive in presentations. They give a false sense of control. Some common vanity metrics are:

- Number of meetings held
- Number of projects launched
- Number of training hours delivered
- Number of emails answered
- Number of reports generated
- Number of kaizens completed
- Number of ideas submitted

These are not useless, but they do not indicate success. They show activity. Lean leadership does not celebrate activity. Lean leadership celebrates results and learning.

So, how do you handle vanity metrics without making people feel attacked?

You classify them properly:

- **Outcome KPIs:** The results that matter (delivery, lead time, quality, cash, safety, retention)

- **Driver KPIs:** The behaviors that cause results (first-pass yield, WIP levels, adherence to standard work, response time, schedule attainment)
- **Activity Measures:** Things you do, which may or may not help (training hours, projects started)

Then you make one rule:

Activity measures only matter if they move driver KPIs, which move outcome KPIs.

Now you're not insulting anyone. You are simply clarifying what wins and what doesn't.

KPIs stop "meeting theater."

Meeting theater is when people spend hours talking about performance without changing performance.

You've seen it:

- Slides full of numbers
- Long explanations
- Defensive tone
- No root cause
- No countermeasure
- No owner
- No due date
- No follow-up
- Same problems next week

The KPI system is designed to prevent this because KPI reviews are not "presentations." They are a management routine with one purpose:

Identify abnormal conditions and trigger action.

The best KPI review meetings are short and intense. Not because people rush, but because the meeting is built around decisions, not reporting.

A KPI review should always produce one of three outcomes:

1. "We are on track, and here's what we learned."

2. "We are off track, and here is the root cause we are working."
3. "We are off track, and here is the countermeasure we are executing."

If your KPI review produces none of those outcomes, you are not reviewing KPIs. You are watching numbers.

IV. The KPI Operating System

A Simple Blueprint That Makes Strategy Real Every Day

As we've been doing in previous chapters, let's make this one practical as well. If you want KPIs to drive a Lean transformation, you need more than metrics. You need a system.

Think of it like this:

- Policy deployment defines direction.
- Daily management defines control.
- KPIs connect them and keep them honest.

Clearing up PD, DM, KPIs, and TTIs (So They Stay Simple)

Before we go further, let's clear up a common and important confusion. We use three terms that sound like separate systems: **policy deployment (PD), daily management (DM), and KPIs.** In reality, KPIs are not an "extra" layer you add on top. KPIs are the **measurement language** used inside both PD and DM.

Here is the simplest way to think about it:

- **PD is the strategy execution system.** It chooses the few breakthrough priorities that must change the future of the business.
- **DM is the process control system.** It keeps today's operations stable, safe, predictable, and improving.
- **KPIs are the measures inside both systems.** KPIs tell you whether PD is working and whether DM is in control.

So, yes, **TTIs** (targets to improve) **are KPIs.** They are simply a specific type of KPI used inside PD.

What's the difference between a PD metric and a DM metric?

The difference is not whether it's a KPI. The difference is **purpose, scope, and cadence.**

Policy Deployment KPIs (Often TTIs)

- Purpose: move the business toward its **strategy**
- Scope: cross-functional, "breakthrough" outcomes
- Cadence: typically weekly and monthly (sometimes daily if the work is intense)
- Examples: end-to-end lead time, on-time delivery, customer complaints rate, inventory turns, COPQ, cash conversion cycle

Daily Management KPIs

- Purpose: **keep processes stable** and highlight abnormalities early
- Scope: team-level, process-level performance, and compliance
- Cadence: hourly, daily, and weekly
- Examples: schedule attainment, first-pass yield, downtime, backlog size, response time, queue age, WIP levels, safety observations, CAPA cycle time

In plain terms:

PD tells you what must change.
DM tells you whether you are in control today.
KPIs exist in both because you can't manage what you don't measure.

So, how many metrics should a company have?

This is where simplification matters. The answer is:

A company can have many metrics in total, but only a few that truly matter at each level.

Think of it like a map:

- At the top, you need only a few landmarks.
- At the street level, you need detailed directions, but only for the streets you're actually driving on.

Here is a practical rule that prevents metric overload:

1. **Enterprise level (PD/Breakthrough):**
    - Three to five breakthrough KPIs total for the whole business.
    - These are your vital few that define whether the strategy is succeeding.
2. **Function or value-stream level:**
    - Three to five KPIs per major function/value stream (Quality, Ops, Supply Chain, etc.).
    - These connect directly to the breakthrough KPIs.
3. **Team level (DM):**
    - Three to five daily KPIs per team.
    - These are the ones people can influence today and respond to quickly.

If a team has twelve KPIs, what happens is predictable: people stop caring. They update numbers, not behavior. So, the goal is not *more measurement*. The goal is **the smallest set of measures that drives the right actions.**

The Simplification Rule: One KPI Must Earn Its Place

To keep your Lean transformation simple and effective, every KPI must pass this test:

- Does it support a PD priority or a DM control need?
- Will someone take action when it changes?
- Does it replace a weaker metric instead of adding clutter?

If the answer to any of these is no, it isn't a KPI. It's noise.

The Final Picture

So, the KPI operating system is not "PD + DM + KPIs" as three separate layers. It's really this:

- **PD uses KPIs (TTIs) to drive strategic change.**
- **DM uses KPIs to maintain control and expose abnormalities.**

- **Both systems stay simple by limiting KPIs to the vital few at each level.**

Once you see it this way, confusion disappears. and the design becomes clean: one strategy system (PD), one control system (DM), and one measurement language (KPIs) used by both.

Here is the KPI operating system I recommend. It is simple enough to run manually and strong enough to scale.

Step 1: Define the "North Star" Outcomes

Start with a small set of outcomes that define success for your business.

For most organizations, the core outcomes sit in five buckets:

- Safety
- Quality
- Delivery/Lead time
- Cost/Productivity
- Cash/Inventory (and sometimes, People metrics, like Retention)

These outcomes are not negotiable. They represent how a business survives and grows. You do not need forty outcomes. You only need the vital few.

Ask the leadership team:

"If we improved only three outcomes this year, which three would most change the future of the company?"

Those become your breakthrough outcomes.

Step 2: Translate Outcomes into Breakthrough KPIs

A breakthrough KPI is a metric that captures a strategic outcome clearly and forces focus.

Examples:

- On-time delivery to request date
- End-to-end lead time
- Customer complaints (rate + severity)

- First-pass yield
- COPQ (cost of poor quality)
- Inventory turns
- Cash-conversion cycle
- Employee turnover in critical roles

Breakthrough KPIs must be:

- Clearly defined
- Owned
- Visible
- Reviewed with discipline
- Tied to action

Step 3: Build the KPI Tree (Strategy to Work)

Now connect the breakthrough KPIs to what teams can influence daily.

This is where most companies fail.

They pick "big" metrics (revenue, margin, EBITDA), but those don't tell teams what to do tomorrow morning.

So, you create a KPI tree:

Breakthrough KPI → Driver KPIs → Team-level daily KPIs → Standard work

Example (Delivery):

- **Breakthrough KPI:** on-time delivery (OTD)
- **Driver KPIs:** schedule attainment, supplier OTIF, rework hours, queue time
- **Team KPIs:** pick accuracy, changeover adherence, planning stability
- **Standard work:** daily schedule review, escalation rules, WIP limits

This is how you go from aspiration to behavior.

The Vital Few KPI Tree

How to Translate Strategy into Daily Work Without Metric Overload

This is one of the most important concepts in the entire book. Most KPI systems fail because the metrics do not connect.

At the top of the organization, leaders track strategic outcomes.
At the bottom of the organization, teams track daily work.
But the middle is missing.

So, the company ends up with two disconnected realities:

- Leadership sees lagging results.
- Teams see local activity.
- Nobody can clearly explain how today's work drives tomorrow's success.

The tool that solves this is the **KPI tree.**

A KPI tree is a structured way of translating strategy into daily work without creating metric obesity. It ensures every KPI has a clear purpose and every team can answer a critical question: "What do we do today that moves the strategy forward?"

The KPI Tree in One Picture (Conceptually)

Think of it like a cascade:

1. Strategic Aspiration (Policy Deployment)
2. Breakthrough KPIs (TTIs)
3. Driver KPIs
4. Daily Management KPIs
5. Standard Work

Each level exists for a different purpose.

And most importantly: each level should only contain the vital few.

Level 1: Strategic Aspiration (PD)

This is the "why."

Examples:

- Become the most reliable supplier in our market.
- Reduce lead time by 50 percent.
- Double output without adding headcount.
- Achieve best-in-class quality.
- Become the easiest company to do business with.

These aspirations are not KPIs. They are direction.

Level 2: Breakthrough KPIs (TTIs)

This is the "what."

Breakthrough KPIs are the vital few measures that prove whether the strategy is succeeding.

Examples:

- On-time delivery to request date
- End-to-end lead time (order to shipment)
- Customer complaints rate (and severity)
- First-pass yield
- Inventory turns
- Cash-conversion cycle
- COPQ (cost of poor quality)

These are often TTIs in policy deployment.

They are the scoreboard for the strategy.

Level 3: Driver KPIs

This is the "what causes the outcome."

Driver KPIs are the few metrics that directly influence the breakthrough KPI and can be improved through targeted actions.

Example: if your breakthrough KPI is **on-time delivery**, driver KPIs might include:

- Schedule attainment
- Supplier on-time delivery
- Downtime hours
- Changeover adherence
- Rework hours
- Queue time in key bottleneck processes
- Engineering release cycle time

Driver KPIs are powerful because they allow leadership to steer before results collapse.

Level 4: Daily Management KPIs (Team Level)

This is the "What do we control today?"

Daily management KPIs are the metrics teams can influence within their daily work.

Examples:

- Hourly output vs. target
- Defect count vs. target
- Backlog size
- Queue age
- Response time
- WIP levels
- CAPA cycle time
- Training compliance
- Adherence to standard work

This is where the organization develops reflexes.

Daily management KPIs expose abnormalities early and trigger action while problems are still small.

Level 5: Standard Work (The Hidden Engine)

This is the "how."

Standard work is not a KPI, but it is what makes KPIs move.

For every KPI that matters, there must be standard work that explains:

- Who checks it
- When they check it
- What they do if it's green
- What they do if it's red
- What gets escalated
- How countermeasures are documented

This is where most KPI systems collapse.

Companies measure, but they don't build the habits.

They install dashboards, but they don't install behavior.

A Complete KPI Tree Example (Highly Practical)

Let's make it real.

Strategic Aspiration (PD)

"Become the most reliable supplier in our market."

Breakthrough KPI (TTI)

On-time delivery to request date (OTD)

Driver KPIs

- Schedule attainment
- Supplier OTIF
- Rework hours
- Unplanned downtime
- Planning stability (schedule changes per week)

Daily Management KPIs (Team Level)

- Hourly output vs. target
- Top-three downtime reasons
- First-pass yield per line
- WIP in front of bottleneck
- Open quality holds

Standard Work

- Hourly board update
- Escalation rule when behind
- Daily cross-functional huddle
- Structured downtime log + countermeasure
- Weekly trend review + problem-solving

Now you have a system instead of just numbers.

The Simplification Rule (This Keeps the Book Consistent)

The KPI tree is not an excuse to create hundreds of metrics.

It is a method to keep metrics few and meaningful.

Here is a practical guideline that works well:

- Three to five breakthrough KPIs for the whole business
- Three to five driver KPIs per major breakthrough KPI
- Three to five daily KPIs per team

This means a company can have many metrics in total, but each person only has to focus on a few. That is simplification.

Step 4: Assign KPI Ownership (No Owner = No KPI)

Every KPI must have an owner, and ownership is not symbolic. The owner must:

- Ensure the definition is correct.
- Ensure the data is trusted.
- Ensure the metric is updated on schedule.
- Lead problem-solving when it goes off track.
- Report actions and results in the review cadence.

If you cannot name the owner, the KPI does not exist.

KPI Ownership Rules

The Difference Between a KPI That Works and One That Dies

At this point, you may be thinking, *This sounds great, but how do we keep it from turning into another dashboard nobody trusts?* That question is exactly right because KPIs don't fail due to bad intentions. They fail because no one truly owns them.

Most companies can name who updates the KPI, but far fewer can name who owns it. And there is a huge difference because **updating is not ownership!** Updating a KPI is clerical. It is simply recording a number.

Ownership means:

- The KPI is clearly defined.
- The KPI is measured the same way every time.
- The KPI is trusted.
- The KPI is reviewed with discipline.
- When it goes off track, someone drives action.

This is why, in a Lean transformation, every KPI must have a named owner, and that owner must have both accountability and authority.

What a KPI Owner Must Do (Non-negotiable)

A KPI owner is responsible for six things:

1) Own the Definition

The owner must ensure the KPI has a written definition that answers:

- What exactly are we measuring?
- What counts, and what does not?
- What is the unit of measure?
- What is the formula?
- What is the data source?
- What is the timing rule?

If definitions are unclear, the organization will argue about numbers instead of improving performance.

2) Own the Data Integrity

If people don't trust the KPI, the system collapses.

The owner must ensure:

- Data is accurate.
- Data is collected consistently.
- Data is not manipulated.
- Changes to definitions are controlled.

A KPI must represent reality, not politics.

3) Own the Update Rhythm

KPIs are only powerful when they are current enough to drive action.

The owner must ensure:

- The KPI is updated on time.
- The trend is visible.
- The refresh cadence matches the need of the process.

4) Own the Review Process

KPIs do not manage themselves.

The owner must ensure the KPI is reviewed in the correct forum:

- Hourly board
- Daily huddle
- Weekly review
- Monthly PD review
- Quarterly strategy review

If a KPI is not reviewed, it is not a KPI.

It is a statistic.

5) Own the Countermeasure Trigger

The KPI owner must define what happens when performance is off track. This is one of the most important parts of the entire system because, if "red" does not trigger action, the organization learns that KPIs do not matter.

The owner must ensure every KPI has:

- A trigger condition
- An escalation rule
- A standard countermeasure process

6) Own the Learning-and-Improvement Loop

The purpose of KPIs is learning. Don't see them as punishment.

The owner must be able to answer:

- What happened?
- Why did it happen?
- What did we learn?
- What are we trying next?
- What will we standardize?

This is how KPIs become a driver of continuous improvement rather than a reporting tool.

The KPI Contract (A Tool That Prevents Confusion)

To make KPI ownership real, I recommend one simple discipline: every KPI must have a one-page KPI contract. I know, I know. This book is about simplification, and it feels like I am adding more bureaucracy. This is not bureaucracy. This is simplification. It prevents the endless confusion that destroys KPI systems.

Check out the KPI contract template in the Templates section at the end of the book.

Why the KPI Contract Matters

Most KPI confusion comes from the following:

- People use the same name but different definitions.
- They measure different scopes.
- They pull data from different sources.
- They review at different cadences.
- They don't know who owns it.
- They don't know what to do when it's red.

The KPI contract solves all of that by turning a metric into a controlled system.

The Simplification Payoff

This discipline creates an unexpected benefit: once every KPI has a contract, many KPIs get eliminated automatically. Because teams suddenly realize: "We don't know why we measure this."

The team will eliminate those KPIs no one uses. The same will happen to those that do not drive action, those that are always green, or those that are duplicates.

That is a win. Lean KPI systems should become **simpler** over time.

Not heavier.

Step 5: Set Targets That Force Learning (Not Fantasy)

Targets should not be wishful thinking. Targets are commitments tied to a plan.

The best targets are:

- Grounded in baseline capability
- Ambitious enough to require improvement
- Realistic enough to avoid cynicism
- Supported by resources and time
- Reviewed and adjusted when you learn more

One important rule: if you set a target but you don't change the system, you are not managing; you are hoping.

Step 6: Build Visual Management That Tells a Story

A KPI board is not a poster. It is a decision-making tool.

Every KPI display should answer, in ten seconds:

- Are we on track?
- What changed?
- What are we doing next?

The simplest and best visual format includes:

- KPI name + definition (short)
- Target line
- Trend chart (not a single number)
- Current status (green/red)
- Top abnormality or cause
- Current countermeasure + owner + due date

This turns KPIs into a living story.

Step 7: Create a Review Cadence That Triggers Action

Cadence is where KPI systems live or die.

Here's the rhythm that works:

- **Daily (ten minutes):** team huddle, yesterday's results, today's risks, quick countermeasures
- **Weekly (thirty to sixty minutes):** trend review, problem-solving, remove blockers, adjust plans
- **Monthly (sixty to ninety minutes):** strategy alignment, breakthrough KPI progress, resource decisions
- **Quarterly:** recalibrate targets, confirm strategy, retire or refresh KPIs

The purpose is not to meet. The purpose is to learn and act.

Step 8: Add Initiative Governance so Projects Stop Multiplying

This step is where you truly weaponize KPIs. Create one rule for every initiative:

No initiative lives without a KPI.

For each initiative, force a one-page **initiative contract**:

- Which breakthrough KPI does it support?
- Which driver KPI will it move?
- What is the baseline?
- What is the target improvement?
- What is the due date?
- Who owns it?
- How will we measure success weekly?

Then add the final rule that makes the system real:

If an initiative does not move a KPI trend within an agreed timeframe, it gets redesigned or killed.

This is how you stop project soup. And yes, killing initiatives is leadership.

Step 9: Build the Countermeasure Habit (KPIs Must Create Behavior)

A KPI that does not trigger action is decoration.

Every KPI must have an escalation rule, like:

- If it's red once, investigate.
- If it's red twice, launch a countermeasure.
- If it's red three times, escalate support and run structured problem-solving.

This prevents red numbers from becoming normal.

Step 10: Retire KPIs to Prevent Metric Obesity

Most companies never delete metrics.

That's why dashboards become useless over time.

Set KPI retirement rules:

- If it no longer supports strategy, remove it.
- If it is always green and no longer drives learning, replace it.
- If it duplicates another metric, consolidate.
- If no one uses it to make decisions, kill it.

Your KPI system should get simpler over time, not heavier.

If you implement this KPI operating system, three things will happen:

1. People will stop working on random initiatives.
2. Meetings will shift from reporting to problem-solving.
3. Strategy will start showing up in daily work.

That is what a KPI expert does.

Not track numbers.

Create a system where the right work gets done and results become unavoidable.

V. Choosing the Right KPIs

How to Select the Vital Few Without Creating Metric Obesity

At this point, you already understand that KPIs are not about measurement. They are about control. They help you take a strategy and turn it into daily reality. They stop initiative soup, prevent meeting theater, make problems visible, and force action.

Now we get to the practical question: **which KPIs should you choose?**

This is where many companies get it wrong, even with good intentions. They either pick too many metrics and drown in noise, or they pick a few big "executive" metrics that teams cannot influence. In both cases, people stop trusting the system, and KPIs become decoration. Let's make this simple and practical.

Step 1: Start with the Decision, Not the Number

Most KPI lists start like this:

- "What should we measure?"
- "What do other companies track?"
- "What does corporate require?"
- "What do we have data for?"

That is the wrong starting point. Instead, start with this: "What decisions do we need to make consistently, and what signals should trigger those decisions?"

A KPI is only valuable if it changes behavior. If a metric does not trigger a decision or an action, it is not a KPI; it is a statistic.

Step 2: Use the Three KPI Tests (The Filter That Prevents Chaos)

This is the simplest and strongest KPI filter I know. Every metric must pass all three tests:

1) The Decision Test

Would we make a different decision if this KPI moved?

If not, don't measure it.

2) The Action Test

If this KPI turns red, do we know exactly who acts and what the first action is? If not, the KPI will create frustration and blame, not improvement.

3) The Line-of-Sight Test

Can the team that owns this KPI influence it within the review cycle?

If the answer is no, the KPI will feel unfair and demotivating.

Step 3: Keep KPIs Few at Every Level (Simplification)

A company can have many metrics in total, but no person should have to focus on many. This is where many KPI systems collapse.

Someone says, "We only have five KPIs." Then you look closer and discover that every department has fifteen, every team has ten, and the executive team has twenty-five. That is not five KPIs. That is metric obesity.

Here is a simple rule that works well in practice:

- **Enterprise level:** three to five breakthrough KPIs
- **Function/value stream level:** three to five KPIs
- **Team level (Daily Management):** three to five KPIs

If you follow this rule, you will notice something interesting: the KPI system becomes easier to manage as the organization improves, not harder.

Step 4: Choose Outcome KPIs First, Then Driver KPIs

One of the biggest mistakes companies make is tracking drivers without tracking outcomes, or tracking outcomes without tracking drivers. You need both.

Outcome KPIs (What Success Looks Like)

These are the scoreboard metrics that prove whether performance is improving.

Examples:

- On-time delivery
- Lead time
- Customer complaints
- First-pass yield
- COPQ
- Inventory turns
- Cash-conversion cycle
- Employee turnover in key roles

Driver KPIs (What Causes the Outcome)

These are the few metrics that tell you what to fix.

Examples:

- Schedule attainment
- Downtime
- Queue time

- Backlog age
- Rework hours
- Supplier OTIF
- CAPA cycle time
- Response time for approvals
- WIP levels at bottlenecks

A Lean KPI system should feel like steering a car:

- Outcomes tell you where you are going.
- Drivers tell you what controls to adjust.

Step 5: Avoid the Two Classic KPI Mistakes

Two KPI mistakes show up constantly.

Mistake #1: Executive KPIs only

These are KPIs like:

- Revenue
- EBITDA
- Gross margin
- Cash on hand

These are important, but they are too far downstream to drive daily action. They are like weighing yourself once a month and hoping your diet improves. You need more direct drivers.

Mistake #2: Local KPIs Only

These are KPIs that make a department look good but don't help the business.

Examples:

- Purchasing measures "price reduction" while delivery collapses.
- Production measures "output" while quality deteriorates.
- Finance measures "inventory reduction" while customer service suffers.
- Engineering measures "projects completed" while lead time grows.

That is why balanced metrics matter.

Step 6: Use Balanced Metrics to Prevent Self-Inflicted Damage

Lean transformations fail when the company improves one thing by destroying another. Balanced metrics prevent that. Here's a simple example: If you only measure inventory reduction, the easiest way to hit the target is to stop buying materials. Inventory drops, and the KPI turns green. The problem is that deliveries collapse, and customers leave, and that is not improvement. That is self-inflicted damage.

Balanced metrics force the organization to improve in a healthy way, where one KPI cannot "win" by harming another.

This is why the SQDCP structure is so powerful:

- Safety
- Quality
- Delivery
- Cost
- People

Even if you don't use SQDCP exactly, the principle is the same: always balance speed, quality, cost, and people.

Step 7: Match the KPI Review Cadence to the Point of Impact

KPIs only work if they are measured and reviewed at the right frequency. This is another simplification principle: review KPIs only as fast as you can act.

If you measure something hourly but cannot react until next week, you are creating noise. If you measure something monthly but it requires daily attention, you are blind.

Here is a practical cadence guide:

Hourly or shift level

Use for KPIs that require immediate action.

Examples:

- Output vs. target
- Defects

- Downtime
- Safety incidents
- Bottleneck queue levels

Daily

Use for KPIs that affect daily performance and require daily coordination.

Examples:

- Schedule attainment
- Backlog size
- Response time
- Shipments vs. plan
- Daily quality escapes

Weekly

Use for KPIs that reveal patterns and require trend-based decisions.

Examples:

- Lead-time trend
- Weekly OTD trend
- Supplier performance
- CAPA aging
- Rework hours

Monthly or quarterly

Use for strategic outcomes that change slowly.

Examples:

- Inventory turns
- Financial margins
- Customer satisfaction
- Employee turnover
- Cash conversion cycle

Step 8: Retire KPIs Aggressively (This Is How Systems Stay Clean)

Most companies never delete metrics. That is why dashboards become useless. A Lean KPI system must have a "metric diet." Every quarter, ask:

- Which KPIs are no longer tied to strategy?
- Which KPIs are always green and no longer drive learning?
- Which KPIs duplicate others?
- Which KPIs are never used to make decisions?

Then remove them. This is not a loss; this is a sign that the organization is maturing.

Final Thought: Choosing KPIs Is an Act of Leadership

Choosing KPIs is not a technical task or an Excel task. It is not an IT task, either. It is a leadership decision about what matters. Your KPIs tell the organization what you truly care about, not what you *say* you care about. If you choose wisely, KPIs become a compass, a steering system, and a discipline that keeps strategy alive every day. If you choose poorly, KPIs become noise, confusion, and meeting theater.

In the next section, we'll take the KPIs you selected and do the next critical step: setting targets and benchmarks that create learning, focus, and momentum without demoralizing your teams.

VI. Setting Targets and Benchmarks: Defining "Good Enough" and Beyond

Once you've selected your vital few KPIs, the next question becomes: how do we define "good enough"? Targets and benchmarks are the bridge between measurement and meaningful action. A **benchmark** shows where you currently stand, internally or relative to industry standards, while a **target** is your stretch goal, setting the bar that challenges your team to improve.

Understanding Targets vs. Benchmarks

A benchmark gives you context, where you are right now versus where others stand. It is a reference point, based either on your historical performance, industry best practices, or peer-group data. It might be your historical performance ("Last year, our invoice cycle averaged three days"), industry best practices ("Top performers get that down to two days"), or internal peer comparisons ("Our sister plant in Ohio achieves 1.5-day invoices"). Benchmarks show what's possible.

A target is your commitment. It is a SMART goal you aim to hit. It reflects the level of performance that pushes towards, or beyond, the benchmark. For example, the average invoice processing time in your company is three days, while the industry leader does it in two days. You may set the target at 1.2 days, which is ambitious yet grounded.

Applying the SMART Criteria

Just as KPIs need to be effective, so do their targets. The SMART framework is an invaluable tool for ensuring your targets are clear, actionable, and motivational. This is the SMART model:

Specific: Clearly define what you are measuring. Instead of "Improve quality," state "Reduce customer defects per million opportunities (DPMO) by 15 percent."

Measurable: Quantify progress in meaningful units. This ties directly back to your selected KPIs.

Achievable (Yet Challenging): Or ambitious yet within reach. This is where the balance between "stretch" and "realistic" comes in. The target should be attainable given your resources and capabilities, but it should also require effort and perhaps some process innovation. It shouldn't be so easy that it requires no change, nor so impossible that it demoralizes the team.

Relevant: The target must directly align with your strategic objectives and the waste-reduction goals. Is achieving this target genuinely going to reduce waste, improve flow, or deliver more value to the customer?

Time bound: Bound by a clear deadline. "Reduce inventory by 20 percent" is incomplete; "Reduce inventory by 20 percent by the end of Q4" provides the necessary urgency and framework for planning.

Finding the Right Balance: Stretch vs. Realistic Goals

When setting targets, you'll constantly navigate the dynamic tension between stretch goals and realistic goals:

Stretch Goals: These are ambitious targets that push beyond current capabilities, often requiring innovative solutions, fundamental process redesign, or breakthrough thinking. They can be powerful motivators for radical improvement and can prevent complacency. However, if poorly managed or if resources are insufficient, they risk causing burnout, frustration, and a sense of failure. Basically, you can turn a powerful motivator into a demotivator. Mistakes usually come when the goals are too aggressive and the team is not given the time or resources to achieve them.

Another scenario that leads to demotivation is making every goal a stretch goal. The stretch goals are best used for critical, high-impact areas where significant gains are required. Then it is management's job to provide the incentives and resources, do adequate follow-up, and reward victories along the way, especially when the team develops breakthrough initiatives.

Realistic Goals: These targets focus on steady, incremental improvements, aligning with the philosophy of kaizen (continuous improvement). They foster consistent progress, build confidence within teams, and are typically less resource-intensive. Realistic goals are excellent for sustaining momentum and embedding a culture of ongoing refinement. These are goals you want to keep in check as the organization drives aggressive improvement in the "vital few" areas where the stretch goals were assigned.

The art of effective target setting lies in knowing when to apply each. For foundational Lean initiatives, such as establishing visual management or standardizing basic processes, realistic, achievable targets build early wins and confidence. For breakthrough objectives or when facing significant competitive pressure, well-defined stretch goals can unlock entirely new levels of performance. Always ensure that even stretch goals have a clear path (even if challenging) and that teams have the support and resources to pursue them. In summary, use stretch targets to spark transformational thinking, coupled with realistic targets to preserve team confidence and momentum.

Step-by-Step Target Setting

Setting effective targets should be a collaborative, data-driven process that involves those closest to the work. It should not be a top-down mandate. Here's the approach to selecting and committing to targets:

Establish Data-Driven Baseline Performance
Begin by thoroughly understanding your current performance. This means collecting reliable data on your chosen KPIs, analyzing historical trends, and understanding the inherent variation within your processes. This baseline forms the foundation for any target. What is your current capability?

Benchmark Intelligently
Compare your baseline performance against relevant internal or external benchmarks. Where are the gaps? What are others achieving? This step informs what's possible and helps calibrate ambition.

Co-create Targets with the Team
Engage the teams responsible for the process in setting the targets. Their frontline knowledge is invaluable for assessing feasibility, identifying potential obstacles, and fostering buy-in. When people are involved in setting their own goals, they are far more likely to be committed to achieving them.

Question the Status Quo
Facilitate discussions that challenge current assumptions. Use "What if?" scenarios. Are there wastes that can be eliminated? Can the process be redesigned? This Lean mindset helps push targets beyond mere incremental improvements.

Refine Targets Iteratively
Targets may not be perfect on the first pass. Be prepared to refine them based on further analysis, team input, or the unfolding reality of the process. It's an iterative process, much like kaizen itself.

Visualize Commitment
Once targets are set, they should be clearly communicated and visually displayed (e.g., on team boards, in "obeya" rooms, or on digital dashboards). This transparency creates shared understanding and accountability.

Making Subjective Goals Measurable

This is a challenge we often come across. We often hear, "We don't have metrics; what we do cannot be measured," or some other version of the same argument. Some meaningful improvements, like collaboration or problem-solving capability, aren't inherently numeric. That doesn't mean they can't be tracked. Here are some tricks of the trade to address subjective metrics:

Define specific behaviors. Clearly articulate what "improved collaboration" looks like in concrete terms. Does it mean more cross-departmental projects? Faster resolution of inter-departmental issues?

Use proxy metrics. Find indirect measures that correlate with the subjective goal.

Examples for "Improved Team Collaboration":

- Number of cross-functional improvement projects initiated and completed
- Frequency of joint problem-solving sessions
- Results from anonymous team surveys on perceived collaboration scores
- Reduction in interdepartmental-conflict resolution time

Examples for "Enhanced Problem-Solving Capability":

- Percentage of problems solved using structured methodology
- Reduction of recurring incidents or "repeat" failures (which indicates that root causes are being identified and neutralized rather than just patched)
- Mean Time to Resolution (MTTR) for complex problems, showing increased efficiency in the diagnostic process
- Ratio of proactive vs. reactive problem-solving tickets (measuring the shift from "firefighting" to preventive capability)

Apply rating scales. Conduct surveys with a one-to-five effectiveness rating for huddle meetings. Note: Make sure you define exactly what each point on the scale means; otherwise, you run the risk everyone will always give a "3" rating.

Measure activity frequency or duration. Examples include problem-solving training hours logged per team member or number of effective problems resolved.

Gather structured feedback. Anonymous engagement surveys reveal trends.

Focus on leading indicators. For example, increased participation in root-cause analysis may predict improved quality.

VII. From Measurement to Improvement

In this section, we will explore how KPIs evolve from simple measurements into powerful levers for continuous improvement. We will cover how to integrate KPIs into your Plan-Do-Check-Act (PDCA) cycles, turning raw data into decisions and actions. We will discuss automating the data collection and the steps to get there. We will also discuss how to present the information and, finally, how to sustain the system.

Integrating KPIs into the PDCA Cycle

In this section, our goal is to help you connect KPIs with the actual cycles of improvement so that the measurement becomes a launchpad for change, not just reporting.

Let me first explain the PDCA cycle. If you are already familiar with it, consider this a refresher. I want to make sure every reader is on the same page with me. This will ensure we are all starting from the same baseline.

The PDCA Cycle

Also known as the Deming cycle, it is a four-step iterative management method used for the control and continuous improvement of processes and products. It was popularized by W. Edwards Deming, who is considered by many to be the father of modern quality control. As you read the explanation of each cycle below, try to imagine what role KPIs can play, a subject we will cover later.

The four stages of the PDCA Cycle are:

PLAN (P)

The objective is to identify the problem or opportunity for improvement, define the desired outcome, and plan the changes needed to achieve it. In this phase, the team analyzes the current situation to understand the root causes of problems. They set clear, **s**pecific, **m**easurable, **a**chievable, **r**elevant, and **t**ime-bound (SMART) goals. Then they develop a detailed plan outlining the specific changes, who will be responsible, the resources needed, and how success will be measured, predicting the results of the changes.

DO (D)

At this step, the team implements the planned changes on a small scale or in a controlled environment, if possible. This is often referred to as a "pilot" or "test" phase. The main activities of the Do phase include the execution of the plan as defined in the Plan stage, collecting data on the implementation process and its effects, and documenting any observations, issues, user feedback, or unexpected outcomes.

CHECK (C)

Now it is time to analyze the results of the Do phase and compare them against the predictions made in the Plan phase. To complete the Check phase, the team must review the collected data and information, evaluate whether the changes achieved the desired results, identify what worked well and what didn't, look for deviations from the plan, and understand why they occurred. It is also a good idea to summarize the lessons learned.

ACT (A)

Finally, **Act** on what you have learned. If results meet or exceed the target, standardize the new process, expanding its scope from pilot to full deployment, documenting it, training everyone necessary, and revising relevant materials or dashboards. If the results did not meet expectations, go back to planning with new insights, tweak the approach, and iterate again. This ensures that improvements become lasting.

The PDCA cycle applies to large-scale changes just as it does to simpler, everyday situations. When you reflect upon the phases, you see that they are a structured view of our natural approach to improvement. Let's say you want to install some shelving in your house. When you **plan**, you must identify where the shelving will go, how big you want it, its color, placement, height, where to buy it, etc. Then, once you have the plan, even if it's all in your mind, you **do** by building and installing it. Afterwards, you **check** it to ensure it turned out as planned. You may find, for example, it is not as sturdy as you thought, or it needs to move further to the right. Then you **act** by reinforcing it and moving it further to the right.

Now let's tie it back to the KPIs. In the planning phase, where you set up the desired outcome, you need a way to measure that the outcome was achieved. This step demands converting vague objectives into precise statements, which will lead to the metric selection, along with the goal for each metric selected. As you move to the next phase and implement changes, you are usually taking measurements, either using your stopwatch, assessing output, gathering torque data, counting invoices, or even measuring the distance between that shelf and the door to ensure proper clearance.

Now, with the changes implemented, you run your process and check your metric(s). The amount of time you need to collect data and verify your metric will depend on your situation, plan, and protocol. But this is where you ensure the established goals are being met. When you act upon your findings, you make decisions based on the metrics. If you need to start the process over, assess if the metrics and goals selected are still relevant. Do you need to add additional metrics? If you were successful and decided to standardize the process, would you keep the metric? What do you need to measure to ensure the changes are sustainable?

VIII. Building Habits Before Automation

Before we talk about servers, dashboards, sensors, and integrations, let's slow down for a second and remember that technology amplifies whatever process you already have. If the process is messy, unclear, or misunderstood, automation will only make that mess happen faster and more consistently.

I've seen companies invest tens of thousands of dollars in slick KPI dashboards, only to discover six months later that the numbers flashing in red and green were wrong because the original data definitions were vague, the collection method was inconsistent, or the metric itself wasn't even tied to a business goal. When that happens, automation doesn't save time; it wastes it at scale.

That's why I always recommend a simple but powerful principle: walk before you run. Start with a manual system. Learn how the KPI should be measured, how the data should be used, and how it will drive action. It's easier to fix and adapt a manual process than to reconfigure an automated one that's hardwired into your IT systems.

The Day the Numbers Came to Life

I'll never forget the first time we introduced hourly production KPIs in a business. As you might expect, the idea didn't exactly get a standing ovation from the line staff. Resistance came fast and loud: fears about the data being used for punishment, complaints about "wasting time" writing numbers down, and doubts about whether any of it would make a real difference.

Before we even put a single number on a board, we set up a focused factory team. This meant moving key people from Engineering, Quality, Maintenance, Planning, and other support functions into the same space. More importantly, we gave them shared goals: safety, quality, delivery, cost, and inventory. If the production lines missed their targets, these departments would miss theirs, too. Suddenly, the support staff and the operators were in the same boat, rowing toward the same outcomes.

When the hourly boards finally went up, operators were asked to record output, note any quality issues, and log downtime reasons, all compared against an hourly target. But the real turning point wasn't the boards themselves. It was how we showed up.

That first day, the focused factory members spent as much time as possible on the shop floor. I was right there with them. Every hour, when it came time to record results, we didn't bark orders or check boxes. Instead, we gave gentle reminders, offered help, and stayed visible. For days, we kept this up until the habit took root.

And when a target was missed? We didn't wait for the end of the shift or the end of the day. We jumped on it immediately, working alongside the operators to fix problems and recover. The change was electric. Operators quickly realized this wasn't about catching mistakes; it was about making their problems visible so they could get solved quickly.

By the end of that first week, the results spoke for themselves. Performance improved overnight. The operators felt heard, supported, and motivated. And perhaps most importantly, the artificial gap between "support" and "production" had closed. We were one team, looking at the same numbers, working toward the same wins. That's the power of KPIs done right.

Let's Build the Right Habits

Step 1: Define the Metrics and the Process

Begin by agreeing on exactly what you're measuring and why. Clarify the calculation method, the unit of measure, and how often you'll collect it. Keep it simple. A basic spreadsheet, a whiteboard at the production line, or a printed form on a clipboard will do just fine. Assign someone to own the data collection and someone else to review it. At this early stage, you should not yet be concerned about making it pretty. Your goal should be to make it clear.

Step 2: Run and Refine Manually

Track the KPI manually for a few weeks. As the team collects and reviews the data, you'll quickly notice if something feels off:

- Maybe the number is hard to get because the definition is fuzzy.
- Maybe you're collecting it too often or not often enough.
- Maybe it's not telling you anything useful.

When teams track KPIs by hand, jotting down hourly outputs, defect counts, or lead times, something powerful happens. They learn the meaning behind the numbers. They start to connect the dots between cause and effect. They notice that production slows after lunch or that one supplier's shipments always arrive with more defects. Those observations are gold, and you don't get them if the first time you see the data is on a glowing screen at the end of the week.

Manual systems also make it much easier to tweak and improve your process. Adjusting a whiteboard column, changing a calculation on a paper form, or adding a new column to a spreadsheet takes minutes. Compare that to modifying an automated system: you'll need IT involvement, system downtime, maybe even vendor support. That's why starting with manual processes isn't old-fashioned; it's Lean. You stabilize first, then accelerate.

Step 3: Standardize the Manual Process

Once the metric makes sense, the collection and reporting are easy, and the data is accurate, lock in the process. Document the workflow, define the roles, and agree on the review cadence. By this stage, everyone should know what the metric means, where it comes from, and what to do if it's off target.

Step 4: Identify Automation Needs

Now you can ask:

- Which steps are repetitive and time-consuming?
- Where do errors creep in?
- What could be captured automatically without losing context?

Automation should remove friction, not replace thinking. Don't automate waste; fix the process first.

Step 5: Select the Right Technology

When the process is stable and the KPI is meaningful, look for tools that fit your maturity level. Maybe it's as simple as adding a barcode scanner to capture production counts or an API link between your ERP system and your dashboard. Choose tools that are flexible enough to adapt as your processes evolve. Select the simplest technology that delivers the accuracy and timeliness you need:

- Machine sensors and PLC integration for live production data
- Barcodes or RFID for tracking inventory and WIP
- ERP/MES integration to pull directly from existing systems
- APIs to link separate platforms

Design the data pipeline. Think of your data like a product moving through a value stream: collect, clean, store, visualize. Remove bottlenecks, eliminate duplicate work, and ensure the *flow* is smooth from source to dashboard.

Step 6: Pilot the Automation

Test your solution in one area or with one KPI. Compare the automated results to your manual logs. If they don't match, find out why. Don't assume the system is always right. Use this pilot to iron out bugs and train the team on interpreting and acting on the data. Data should trigger action, not just fill a dashboard. Use visuals that make trends obvious and highlight variances. At a glance, anyone should know if you're on or off target.

Step 7: Scale and Sustain

Train people to interpret the new system's outputs and act on them. Keep them engaged in the process so they trust the numbers. Once it's proven accurate and useful, roll it out more widely. But remember that automation doesn't replace discipline. Keep your review meetings. Keep asking questions. The goal isn't just to have the data faster; it's to use it better.

Pitfalls to Avoid

- Automating too early and locking in bad processes
- Mistaking a colorful dashboard for actual improvement
- Choosing tools so complex they become their own problem

The Bottom Line

Lean success doesn't come from technology. It comes from people who understand the work, see the numbers, and know how to act on them. Manual first. Automation second. The habits of reviewing, discussing, and acting on KPIs are the engine of continuous improvement. Automation is the turbocharger. It makes a good engine perform even better, but it won't fix a broken one.

IX. Sustaining a KPI Culture

Once your KPIs are defined, understood, and supported by a reliable system, whether manual, automated, or both, the real challenge begins: sustaining them. Technology can give you speed and accuracy, but it's the people who keep the data alive, relevant, and powerful. Without a culture that values measurement and acts on it, even the most advanced dashboards will turn into background noise.

A sustainable KPI culture isn't about management "owning" the numbers but creating an environment where every employee understands what the numbers mean, sees their connection to daily work, and feels responsible for influencing them. When that happens, KPIs shift from being a management scorecard to becoming a shared compass.

People First, Numbers Second

KPI culture starts with trust and involvement. If people feel metrics are just a tool to catch mistakes or assign blame, they'll hide problems, not solve them. Instead, make KPIs a way to guide improvement:

- Involve teams in defining the measures so they know why they matter.

- Connect each KPI to the work people actually do so they see their impact.
- Celebrate improvements publicly, whether the win is small or game-changing.

When employees can answer, "What's my role in moving this number?" they stop seeing KPIs as "management's problem" and start owning the outcomes.

Making the Data Visible

What you choose to measure is important. How you show it is just as critical. Data hidden in a spreadsheet on someone's laptop is dead data. Data made visual, on walls, boards, or screens, becomes a constant reminder and motivator.

A few proven display methods:

- **Team boards or whiteboards** near the work area, updated daily. Use simple graphs, color codes, and notes for context.
- **Digital dashboards** in high-traffic areas, like break rooms, entrance lobbies, or production floors, updated in real time or at set intervals.
- **Obeya rooms** (big, visual project rooms) for cross-functional KPI tracking and problem-solving.
- **Before-and-after visuals** to reinforce the progress made.

Rule of thumb: if someone can't glance at a board for ten seconds and know if things are on track, it's too complicated.

What a Great KPI Board Looks Like

The Layout That Makes Problems Visible and Triggers Action

At this point, you understand what KPIs are, how to select them, and how to connect them to strategy through policy deployment and daily management. Now comes the most practical question in the entire chapter:

What should the KPI board actually look like?

This is where many companies overcomplicate things. They build dashboards with too many colors, too many metrics, and too many charts. They create PowerPoint slides that look polished but don't drive behavior. Or they build beautiful boards that no one uses because they are not connected to daily routines.

The goal of a KPI board is not to display data. It's to make reality visible and trigger action. A great KPI board should allow any person in the company, even a visitor, to stand in front of it for thirty seconds and answer:

- Are we winning today?
- If not, what's the problem?
- Who is working it?
- What is the next action?

If the board cannot answer those questions, it's not a KPI board. Just call it a poster.

The Golden Rule of KPI Boards

A KPI board must show:

1. The vital few metrics
2. Trends (not just current numbers)
3. Abnormalities
4. Actions
5. Ownership

That's it.

Everything else is optional.

The Standard Lean KPI Board Layout (SQDCP)

The most effective structure I've seen across industries is a simple one:

SQDCP

- Safety
- Quality
- Delivery
- Cost
- People

This format works because it forces balance and prevents the organization from chasing cost while sacrificing quality, chasing output while sacrificing safety, or chasing delivery while burning out the workforce. Even in an office environment, this structure works well. You simply adjust the definitions.

Example 1: A Department Daily KPI Board (The Best "Starter Board")

Here is a simple, high-impact, daily board format that works for both production and office teams.

Section 1: Safety (Top Left)

- Days without recordable injury
- Safety observation count (optional)
- Top safety concern this week (one line)

Important:
Safety metrics should never become a scoreboard that punishes reporting. The purpose is visibility and prevention.

Section 2: Quality

Pick one or two metrics that matter most.

Examples in manufacturing:

- First-pass yield
- Defects per unit
- Customer complaints (weekly)

Examples in the office:

- Percent complete and accurate (first-pass)
- Rework rate
- Error rate in invoices, orders, CAPAs, or reports

Section 3: Delivery/Flow

This is where Lean transformations often live or die.

Examples in manufacturing:

- Schedule attainment
- On-time delivery
- Lead time
- Queue time at bottleneck

Examples in the office:

- Request response time
- Backlog size
- Queue age (how long requests sit untouched)
- Cycle time for approvals or closure

Section 4: Cost/Productivity

Keep it simple. If cost is too complex, use a driver metric.

Examples:

- Labor hours vs. plan
- Standard vs. actual hours
- Overtime hours
- Scrap cost
- Rework hours
- Expediting events

Section 5: People

This is often neglected, but it shouldn't be.

Examples:

- Absenteeism
- Turnover
- Training completion
- Cross-training coverage
- Improvement ideas implemented

A Lean transformation requires people. If the people system is unhealthy, performance will not sustain.

Section 6: Top Abnormalities

This is where the board becomes alive.

Every day, teams should capture:

- What went wrong

- What is unusual
- What is blocking flow

This section should be written in plain language, not corporate speak.

Examples:

- *"Line 2 down 45 minutes: sensor fault"*
- *"Three orders held: missing COA from supplier"*
- *"CAPA delayed: waiting on R&D input"*
- *"Invoice backlog: approver out sick, no backup"*

Section 7: Countermeasures and Actions

This is where KPI systems become management systems.

Every action must include:

- What we will do
- Who owns it
- When it is due
- Status (open/closed)

A KPI board without actions is a scoreboard, while a KPI board with actions is a control system.

Example 2: The Executive KPI Board (PD/TTIs)

Executive KPI boards should be even simpler. At the top of the organization, the job is not to track dozens of details.

The job is to confirm:

- Is the strategy working?
- Are we on track with the breakthrough priorities?
- Are the resources aligned to the problems?
- Are leaders holding the system?

The executive board should include:

- Three to five breakthrough KPIs (TTIs).
- Trend charts (rolling twelve-month, if applicable).

- Top-three risks to hitting the target.
- Top-three countermeasures.
- Key decisions needed this month.

The executive board should not become a "status meeting."

It should be a decision forum.

Example 3: A Lean Office KPI Board (The Simplest and Most Powerful)

Here is an office board that works extremely well, especially in Customer Service, Purchasing, Finance, Quality, Regulatory, and Engineering.

The Office Board should show:

- Backlog size (how many items are waiting)
- Backlog age (how old the oldest item is)
- Response/cycle time
- Percent complete and accurate (first-pass yield)
- Top blockers (waiting on approvals, missing info, system issues)
- Actions

This board often creates a shocking moment for leaders: They realize the "real WIP" in the company is not on the shop floor. It is in inboxes.

A Simple Rule That Prevents Board Clutter

If the KPI board contains more than:

- Ten total metrics
- Ten total action items
- Ten lines of abnormalities

... it becomes unreadable and ineffective. Don't let the board turn into a museum. It should be a cockpit.

How to Use the Board (This Is the Part That Matters)

A board is only as powerful as the ritual around it.

The daily board meeting should be:

- Five to ten minutes
- Standing
- Focused on abnormalities
- Focused on actions
- Not a long discussion

The goal is not to solve everything at the board.

The goal is to:

- Expose problems
- Assign ownership
- Trigger action
- Escalate as needed

Then problem-solving happens outside the huddle with the right people. This is critical; otherwise, your meetings will drag for a lot longer than needed.

In the beginning, I always get requests to cancel the board meetings. People ask to be excused because they have other priorities. I do not give in. The board review *is* the priority. When there are scheduling conflicts, I tell them to prioritize the board meetings. In time, the organization will learn not to schedule other meetings that conflict with the board review meetings. On the other hand, if you allow people not to participate early on, the discipline will die. When you stick with your guns, it creates a new habit.

Note: A KPI Board Is a Trust System

If leaders use boards to punish people, the boards die. If leaders use boards to solve problems, the boards become addictive, and people will look forward to the meetings. Teams start wanting the board because it becomes the fastest way to get support.

That is when KPI culture becomes real.

Reading, Not Just Looking

Visibility is only valuable if people know what they're looking at. Make sure displays are:

- **Readable:** large fonts, clear labels, color-coded status (green = on track, red = needs attention). No yellow, amber, or different tones of green or red. You are either on target or not.
- **Relevant:** show only the KPIs that matter to the audience viewing them.
- **Action-Oriented:** highlight variances and call out the next step. Don't just show raw data.

Train your teams to "read the story" the data tells: What's happening? Why? What do we do about it?

Management's Role in Sustaining the Culture

Leaders set the tone. They must:

- Visit KPI boards regularly and discuss results with the teams.
- Ask questions, not just for explanations but to encourage problem-solving.
- Recognize and reward teams for hitting targets and openly addressing misses.
- Keep the system alive by reviewing, updating, and retiring KPIs when they're no longer relevant.

If management ignores the boards, so will the teams.

Continuous Engagement

Over time, even the best KPI systems can fade into background noise if they aren't refreshed. Keep engagement high by:

- Rotating in new improvement-focused KPIs while keeping the strategic core steady.
- Running regular "KPI kaizen" events to review and improve how metrics are tracked and displayed.
- Sharing success stories company-wide, showing how data-driven decisions made a difference.

Final Thoughts

KPIs are more than just performance metrics; they are the foundation of your improvement journey. When chosen well, they do two essential things: they make reality visible, and they give you a fixed point from which to measure progress. Think of each KPI target as planting a stake in the ground. That stake marks your current capability, a clear, unambiguous point in time that says, "This is where we are."

From there, every improvement effort has a reference point. You can see exactly how far you've come, what worked, and where you still need to go. And once that original target is consistently achieved, you move the stake forward. That new position becomes the next standard, the new "normal," and the cycle repeats. This rhythm of measuring, improving, resetting, and pushing forward is the engine of continuous improvement. Each improvement cycle resets the benchmark and keeps the CI engine running.

This is why KPIs are so powerful. They turn vague aspirations into tangible, trackable commitments. They make progress visible not just to leaders but to everyone in the organization. And when you involve people in both setting and achieving those targets, you transform KPIs from a management tool into a shared language of success.

Ultimately, a KPI culture isn't about dashboards, charts, or reports. It is about building a workplace where people take pride in moving the stake forward, again and again, together. Over time, this becomes self-reinforcing: the more wins the team experiences, the more they believe in their ability to improve, and the more momentum you build. That's how KPIs, when used with purpose and integrity, stop being just numbers and start becoming the fuel for lasting transformation.

X. Reflection and Action

Measuring Progress: Build Your KPI Operating System (Thirty-Day Plan)

Build a KPI System That Drives Results, Not Meetings

KPIs are not the ultimate goal. They are the steering wheel, or simply, your dashboard. If your organization is busy but not improving, it is rarely because people don't care. More often, the company has no simple way to answer three questions:

1. Are we working on the right things?
2. Are we winning?
3. If not, what will we do differently next?

Use the exercises below to build a KPI operating system that aligns strategy, daily work, and continuous improvement. Keep it simple. The goal is not to measure everything. It's to measure what matters and act on it with discipline.

A. Define the Vital Few (Strategy Level)

1. Write your company's strategy in one sentence. Refer back to Chapter 6, if needed.
   If you cannot, write what you believe leadership *intends* the strategy to be.
2. List the top-three breakthrough priorities (policy deployment). These should be outcomes, not projects.
3. Define the three to five breakthrough KPIs (TTIs) that prove whether the strategy is working. Examples: lead time, on-time delivery, customer complaints, inventory turns, COPQ, cash conversion cycle.
4. For each breakthrough KPI, write:
   - The baseline
   - The target
   - The time horizon (six months, twelve months, etc.)

B. Build Your KPI Tree (Connection to Daily Work)

5. Choose **one** breakthrough KPI and build its KPI tree.
6. List three to five driver KPIs that strongly influence that breakthrough KPI.
7. List the three to five daily management KPIs that the frontline teams can influence.
8. For each daily management KPI, define:
   - Who owns it
   - Where it is displayed
   - How often it is updated
   - What happens when it is off target

C. Kill Initiative Soup (The KPI Discipline)

9. List your top-ten current initiatives. (If you have more than ten, that is already a signal.)
10. For each initiative, answer this question:

Which KPI will this initiative move, by how much, and by when?

11. Circle any initiative that cannot answer that question clearly.
12. Choose what you will do with those initiatives:
    - Kill them
    - Redesign them
    - Pause them until a KPI link is established

This is one of the strongest leadership moves you can make.

D. Write KPI Contracts (So the System Doesn't Collapse)

13. Select your top-five KPIs and write a one-page KPI contract for each. At minimum, define:
    - KPI
    - Formula
    - Data source
    - Owner
    - Review cadence
    - Trigger condition
    - Expected countermeasure process

14. Ask two people in different departments to explain the KPI definition back to you.

If they describe it differently, your KPI system is not stable yet.

E. Build Your KPI Boards (Make Reality Visible)

15. Design one board for one team using the SQDCP structure:
    - Safety
    - Quality
    - Delivery/Flow
    - Cost
    - People

- Abnormalities
- Actions

16. Make sure the board answers these questions in ten seconds:
    - Are we winning today?
    - If not, what's wrong?
    - Who owns the action?
    - When will it be resolved?

17. Decide where the board will live:
    - At the gemba
    - Near the work
    - In a shared digital workspace if the team is remote

F. Create the Review Cadence (The Rhythm That Makes KPIs Work)

18. Write your KPI review cadence for the next thirty days:
    - Daily huddle (five to ten minutes)
    - Weekly KPI review (thirty to sixty minutes)
    - Monthly PD review (sixty to ninety minutes)

19. For each meeting, define:
    - Who attends
    - What KPIs are reviewed
    - What decisions must be made
    - How actions are captured and followed up

20. Apply this rule: if a KPI review meeting does not create actions, it is not a KPI review.

G. Build Habits Before Automation

21. Choose one KPI and track it manually for two weeks.
22. During that period, document:
    - How easy it is to collect
    - Whether people trust it
    - What problems it reveals
    - What behaviors it triggers

23. Only after that, decide whether automation is needed.

Remember: automation should accelerate clarity, not confusion.

H. Simplify and Sustain (Prevent KPI Obesity)

24. List the KPIs you currently track.
25. For each KPI, ask:
    - Does it support PD or DM?
    - Does it trigger action?
    - Is it trusted?
    - Is it redundant?

26. Eliminate or retire at least 20 percent of your KPIs.

Don't see this as a loss. Instead, see it as Lean victory.

The Thirty-Day KPI Challenge (Highly Recommended)

If you want to bring your strategy to life, do this:

Week 1: Define

- Choose three to five breakthrough KPIs.
- Write KPI contracts.
- Align leadership on definitions and targets.

Week 2: Connect

- Build one KPI tree.
- Define driver and DM KPIs.
- Assign ownership.

Week 3: Visualize

- Build one KPI board.
- Launch daily huddles.
- Start capturing abnormalities and actions.

Week 4: Act

- Run countermeasures.
- Remove or redesign initiatives that don't move KPIs.
- Stabilize the rhythm.
- Celebrate the first measurable win.

Final Reflection (the question that matters most)

If you had to answer this question in front of your board tomorrow, could you?

"Are we winning, and how do we know?"

If you can, you are leading a transformation. If you can't, you are still hoping.

Chapter 10 Reflection and Action Answers

CHAPTER 11

The Continuous Improvement Operating System

"We Already Tried Lean"

The CEO's email was short:

"We need help. We're stuck. We've tried Lean before, and it didn't work. Can you come?"

When I arrived, the parking lot was full. The building looked busy. The lobby had framed posters on the wall. One of them was a faded Lean "house" diagram. Another one said:

"CONTINUOUS IMPROVEMENT IS EVERYONE'S JOB."

The posters looked like they had been there for years, untouched, like artifacts from another era. The CEO met me at the door. He was a good leader: smart, direct, and tired. We walked into a conference room where his leadership team was already waiting.

I started with my usual opening question: "What do you want to be true about this company twelve months from now?"

The answers came quickly.

- "Better delivery."
- "Less chaos."
- "More-predictable performance."
- "Higher margins."
- "A culture where people solve problems instead of escalating everything."

It was a good list, honest and reasonable. Then I asked my second question: "What are you doing today that directly supports those goals?" The room went quiet. Not defensive quiet, not angry quiet. More like the quiet you get when people know the truth but they're tired of talking about it.

The VP of operations finally said, "We're working hard."

The quality director added, "We're firefighting."

The supply chain manager shrugged. "We're expediting."

And the HR director said something that told me everything I needed to know: "We have a lot of fatigue. People don't believe initiatives matter anymore."

Then the CEO leaned back and said the sentence I hear all the time, but rarely on day one: "We already tried Lean."

He didn't say it with anger. He said it the way someone talks about a diet they failed. Like it was a phase. Like it was something they did for a while, then moved on from. Then he smiled, almost apologetically, and said:

"We did 5S. We did kaizens. We had boards. Heck, we still have many boards around the building. We even had a Lean leader. For a while, things looked better." He paused. "Then it all faded."

I asked him: "Why?"

He exhaled and looked down at the table. "I don't know. People stopped doing it. Managers got busy. Meetings got canceled. The Lean leader left. The boards stopped getting updated. And then we were back to normal."

He looked up at me. "That's why I'm cautious. I can't sell Lean to this team again."

I nodded. Because at that moment, I wasn't thinking about Lean tools. I was thinking about trust. When Lean fades, it leaves behind something worse than wasted effort: the belief that improvement is temporary. That "programs" don't last. That leadership will eventually lose interest. That the safest move is to wait it out. So, before we talked about strategy, KPIs, kaizen, or anything else, I asked a different question: "When Lean was working here, what exactly was happening weekly? Not in theory. In reality."

The operations VP answered immediately. "We had daily huddles."

"Okay," I said. "Then what?"

He thought. "We had weekly reviews. We tracked actions. We escalated issues."

"Then what happened?"

He didn't even hesitate. "Leadership stopped showing up."

That was the moment the room shifted. Because now it wasn't about Lean. It was about the system. Lean didn't fail because people didn't care. Lean failed because the company never built a management operating system strong enough to survive real life. They had tools, they had events, and they had enthusiasm. But they didn't have a structure that made Lean unavoidable. They didn't have a system that made improvement part of the work instead of something extra. They didn't have a system that could survive:

- A busy week
- A staffing shortage
- A leadership change
- A customer crisis
- A quarter-end push
- A plant emergency
- A new initiative from corporate

And that's when I told the CEO something that surprised him: "This is actually good news."

He looked at me like I was crazy. So, I explained: "If Lean failed here once, it means the company was willing to try. It means the people have seen improvement before. It means they know what 'better' feels like. The problem is not motivation. The problem is sustainment."

He nodded slowly, then said, "So, what do we do differently?"

"We stop treating Lean like a program," I replied. "We stop relying on energy and enthusiasm. And we build a continuous improvement operating system that survives real life."

Most companies don't fail at Lean because they chose the wrong tools. They fail because they never built the system that keeps Lean alive. A Lean transformation must be designed to survive reality:

- People get busy.
- Leaders get distracted.
- Emergencies happen.
- Priorities shift.
- Turnover occurs.
- Old habits pull the organization back to the familiar.

In this chapter, we will build the missing piece: a simple continuous improvement operating system (CI) that connects daily management, KPIs, problem-solving, kaizen, and strategy deployment into one sustainable rhythm.

Not a program. A system.

I. The Fade: Why Lean Dies After the First Wins

Most failed Lean transformations don't fail loudly. They don't collapse in a dramatic moment where everyone admits defeat. They fade. They start with energy, optimism, and early wins. People participate in kaizen events. Leaders walk the floor. Boards go up. Metrics become visible. The organization feels different for a while, and that difference creates hope.

Then, slowly, reality returns. Meetings get canceled. Leaders stop showing up. Visual boards stop being updated. Standard work becomes optional. Firefighting returns. And within months, the company is back to where it started, except now it carries something worse than poor performance: cynicism.

That cynicism is what makes your second attempt so much harder. When Lean fades, employees don't just lose faith in the tools. They lose faith in leadership. They conclude that improvement is temporary and every new initiative is just another program that will eventually be replaced by the next one. Even good people start protecting themselves. They stop investing emotionally. They stop raising problems. They stop offering ideas. They keep their heads down, do what they must, and wait for the next wave to pass. The organization becomes quieter but not healthier. The silence is not agreement. *It is resignation.*

This is why Lean must never be positioned as a project, program, or phase. Lean is a management system. It only works when it becomes part of the operating rhythm of the business, reinforced through consistent routines, leadership behaviors, and clear expectations. In other words, Lean survives when it is designed to survive. It cannot rely on motivation, charisma, or a single Lean champion. It must be built as a system that continues functioning even when leaders are busy, even when the business is under pressure, and even when key people leave.

In my experience, Lean fades for the same reasons almost every time. The first is that **the organization confuses activity with progress.** Early Lean efforts often focus on visible tools: 5S, kaizen events, value stream mapping, and visual boards. These tools can create quick improvements, but they are not the sustainment system. If leadership treats those tools as the transformation itself, the company gets stuck in what I call "Lean theater," where Lean exists in isolated events rather than in daily management. People see improvement during the event, but nothing in the organization's structure forces the improvement to remain.

The second reason Lean fades is that **daily management is weak or inconsistent**. A Lean organization must have a simple way to see whether processes are in control and whether performance is improving. If KPIs are not reviewed consistently, if abnormalities are not escalated, and if countermeasures are not tracked, then problems become normal again. Teams learn quickly what matters and what does not. If leaders do not respond to abnormalities, people stop surfacing them. Over time, the organization stops seeing the truth. It becomes blind, and once a company has that happen, the only remaining management style is firefighting.

The third reason Lean fades is that the organization does not have a **clear improvement funnel**. In a healthy Lean system, daily issues do not disappear into inboxes or meeting notes. They flow into a structured pipeline. Small problems are handled immediately by the team. Recurring issues trigger problem-solving. Bigger issues trigger kaizen events. Strategic issues become part of policy deployment. Without that funnel, improvement becomes random. People work on whatever is loudest, whatever is newest, or whatever the most powerful person in the room cares about. That is how initiative soup returns.

The fourth reason Lean fades is that **ownership becomes unclear** after the event. During a kaizen, roles are obvious. The facilitator leads. The team is engaged. The sponsor is visible. The energy is high. But after the event, the organization often fails to define who owns the new standard, who audits it, who trains new employees, and who responds when the process drifts. When ownership is unclear, drift is inevitable. Standards do not disappear because people are bad. They disappear because the system does not protect them.

The fifth reason Lean fades is that **leadership behavior quietly returns to old patterns**. This is the hardest one to admit, and it is also the most common. Leaders start by supporting Lean, but under pressure, they revert to what feels familiar. They jump into problem-solving without going to gemba. They demand results without asking what is preventing the team from achieving them. They reward heroics instead of stability. They accept late updates instead of insisting on discipline. They tolerate missed commitments because they want to be "reasonable." Over time, the organization learns the real standard. It is not what is written on the wall. It is what leadership tolerates.

The final reason Lean fades is that **the company never builds a sustainment cadence** that is strong enough to survive real life. Most organizations treat Lean activities as extra work. They schedule kaizens when they have time. They review metrics when they have time. They do gemba walks when they have time. But in a turnaround, there is never extra time. If Lean is optional, it will always lose to urgency. Sustainment requires the opposite approach: Lean must become the method by which urgency is handled. The company must build a rhythm where daily control, weekly improvement, and monthly strategic alignment are part of the job, not something added on top of it.

The good news is that none of these failure modes are mysterious. They are predictable. And because they are predictable, they can be designed out of the system. That is exactly what we will do in the rest of this chapter. We will build **a continuous improvement operating system** that is simple enough to implement in any organization yet strong enough to survive pressure, distractions, and turnover. If you build it correctly, Lean will stop fading. It will become how the business runs, how problems are surfaced, and how performance improves year after year.

As I've worked through this pattern over the years, I've come to see something interesting: the reasons Lean fades are often the same reasons quality management systems fail in practice. In many organizations, the QMS is technically compliant but culturally ignored. People treat it as something they must do in addition to their real work rather than the system that defines how the work should be done. Documents get updated right before audits. Deviations are written in a hurry. CAPAs become paperwork exercises. Training becomes a checkbox. And the moment pressure increases, the QMS becomes "something we'll catch up on later."

That is not because people do not care about quality. It is because the system was not designed to be lived daily. When a management system feels separate from the job, it will always lose to urgency. But when the system is designed to be the job, it becomes the organization's default behavior. The same is true for Lean. If Lean is treated as extra work, it will fade. If Lean is designed as the operating system of the business, it becomes the way the company thinks, works, and improves, even under pressure.

II. Tools Don't Sustain Transformations. Systems Do.

If Lean has been attempted in your organization before and faded, it is tempting to conclude that the tools did not work. People say, "5S didn't stick," "Kaizen didn't change anything," or "Visual management became a joke." Those statements may be true in the literal sense, but they are usually wrong in the deeper sense.

In most cases, the tools did work. The early wins were real. The energy was real. The improvements were real. What failed was not Lean itself. What failed was the organization's ability to sustain Lean after the first wave of momentum.

This is a critical distinction because it changes what you do next. If you believe Lean failed because the tools were ineffective, you will look for new tools. You will search for a different methodology. You will change terminology. You might rename Lean into something more "modern." You might rebrand the effort as "Operational Excellence," "Business System," "Continuous Improvement," or "Transformation Office." But if the underlying system is missing, the outcome will be the same. The new name will fade just like the old one.

To sustain Lean, you must stop thinking like a *tool user* and start thinking like a *system designer*.

A Lean tool is something you apply. A Lean system is something you operate. Tools can create improvement. Systems create consistency. Tools can generate wins. Systems keep the wins from disappearing. Tools are often visible. Systems are often invisible, but they are always more powerful.

This is why so many organizations experience the same frustrating cycle. They run a few kaizen events, get results, and feel optimistic. They implement boards, track metrics, and see better performance. Then the first crisis hits. A key person leaves. A major customer escalates. A new product launch creates instability. The plant has a bad month. Leadership gets distracted. The organization shifts into survival mode. And because Lean was never built into the company's default operating rhythm, it gets pushed aside.

When Lean is treated as a program, it competes with daily work. It is something you do when you have time. When Lean is built as an operating system, it becomes how you do the work, especially when you do not have time. That is the point. A sustainment system is not designed for calm weeks. It is designed for pressure.

This is also where many companies misunderstand what "culture" really means. Culture is not a poster, a slogan, or a set of values on the wall. Culture is the collection of behaviors that repeat themselves when nobody is watching. Those behaviors are not created by speeches. They are created by systems. They are created by what is reinforced, what is measured, what is reviewed, what is escalated, what is ignored, and what is tolerated. If the system rewards heroics and firefighting, you will get a culture of heroics and firefighting. If the system rewards stability, problem-solving, and follow-through, you will get a culture of stability, problem-solving, and follow-through.

This is why Lean sustainment is not primarily a training problem. Most organizations do not fail because people "don't understand Lean." They fail because the organization does not have a consistent structure that forces Lean behaviors to happen daily. Training matters, but training without system reinforcement is temporary. People will revert to what the system rewards. They will also revert to what the system allows.

A sustainable Lean transformation requires three things working together: a control system, an improvement system, and a strategy system. You have already learned the strategy system in policy deployment. You have already learned the control system through daily management and KPIs. Now we add the missing third piece: the improvement system that converts daily problems into structured learning and permanent gains.

When these three systems operate together, Lean becomes self-sustaining. When one is missing, Lean becomes fragile. It may work for a while, but it will not survive reality.

You can think of it like a three-legged stool. Policy deployment sets direction and focus. Daily management stabilizes processes and makes abnormalities visible. Continuous improvement is what turns those abnormalities into lasting improvements. If you remove any leg, the stool falls. If you strengthen all three, the system becomes stable enough to support the business through growth, crises, turnover, and change.

The rest of this chapter is designed to help you build that operating system in a simple, practical way. We will not create bureaucracy. We will not create an "improvement department" that owns the transformation. Instead, we will build a structure that makes continuous improvement part of the work, owned by leadership, supported by a small enablement function, and reinforced through a rhythm that is strong enough to survive real life.

In the next section, we will start with the core mechanism that most organizations are missing: a clear improvement funnel that ensures problems and ideas flow into the right level of action instead of disappearing into meetings, email threads, or personal frustration.

III. The Continuous Improvement Funnel

The Missing Mechanism in Most Organizations

If I had to pick the single most common reason Lean fades after early wins, it would be this: the organization never builds a reliable way to convert daily problems into lasting improvement. Teams surface issues, leaders nod, actions get written down, and then the week moves on. Some problems get solved through heroics. Others get escalated and bounced between departments. Many simply disappear. The same issues return again and again, and people eventually stop bringing them up. Not because they don't care, but because they've learned the pattern: nothing really changes.

A sustainable Lean organization does not rely on memory, motivation, or individual initiative to drive improvement. It uses a funnel. That funnel is the mechanism that sorts problems and opportunities into the right level of response. It prevents everything from becoming a project. It prevents everything from becoming a kaizen. It prevents everything from being escalated to leadership. It also prevents the opposite failure mode: a company where people keep problems to themselves because escalation feels pointless.

The purpose of the funnel is simple. It ensures that work enters the system in an organized way and that the organization responds at the right level, with the right speed, and with the right amount of structure. Without it, improvement becomes random. With it, improvement becomes a predictable habit.

A good funnel is designed around a reality that many leaders underestimate: most problems are small at the moment they first appear. They become large because they are ignored, repeated, or normalized. Lean organizations build the habit of addressing problems early, while they are still manageable. This is not about perfection. It is about preventing drift.

The funnel has four levels. Each level has a different purpose, time horizon, and response method.

The **first level** is immediate containment and correction. These are the issues a team can address right away in daily management: a missing tool, a label printer that keeps failing, an unclear handoff, a safety concern, a recurring data entry error, a backlog that is starting to grow. These issues should be visible on a team board, discussed in the daily huddle, and acted on quickly.

Many organizations mistakenly ignore these problems because they seem too small to matter. In reality, these small issues are often the early warning signs of deeper system weaknesses. When teams learn that they can solve small problems quickly, trust builds, and people start believing that improvement is real.

The **second level** is structured problem-solving. These are the issues that repeat, cross a boundary, or create meaningful performance loss. They are too complex for a quick fix but not large enough to justify a major project. This is where PDCA discipline matters. The team must define the problem clearly, collect enough data to understand what is happening, identify root causes, test countermeasures, and verify results.

In many companies, this level is missing. Problems either remain stuck in daily huddles with no resolution or get escalated too quickly into leadership meetings. A healthy funnel creates a middle layer where recurring issues are solved systematically and learning is captured and standardized.

The **third level** is kaizen. Kaizen is the right response when the problem is cross-functional, requires redesign of a process, or has enough impact to justify focused time with a dedicated team. This is where you stop squeezing improvement out of the margins and instead step back and redesign the work. Kaizen events are powerful because they compress time. They bring the right people together. They create momentum. They also create visible wins that rebuild belief.

But kaizen should not be the default response to every issue. If a company constantly runs kaizen events without a funnel, kaizen becomes a replacement for daily management. Teams start waiting for an event instead of fixing what they can today. The funnel prevents that by making kaizen the right tool for the right level of problem.

The **fourth level** is breakthrough improvement through policy deployment. These are the issues and opportunities that require strategic focus, investment, and leadership alignment. They are not solved by a single team, department, or event. They may require capital, system redesign, supply chain changes, product design changes, organizational restructuring, or multi-month cross-functional execution.

This is where TTIs, breakthrough KPIs, and the policy deployment system come in. The funnel ensures that the biggest problems and opportunities are not lost in the noise of daily operations. It gives leadership a structured way to select what truly matters, fund it, and execute it with discipline.

When you look at these four levels together, you start to see the funnel for what it really is: a control mechanism for improvement. It prevents initiative soup by giving every problem a home. It prevents overreaction by ensuring that small problems don't become large projects. It prevents underreaction by ensuring that recurring problems do not remain stuck in daily huddles forever. It also prevents the leadership team from becoming a dumping ground for everything that the organization doesn't know how to solve.

This is where continuous improvement becomes a system rather than a slogan. Instead of asking people to "bring ideas," you give them a structure that answers the most important questions in a Lean organization: Where do problems go? Who owns them? How fast do we respond? How do we decide what deserves escalation? How do we make sure improvements stick?

If you want the funnel to work, it must be visible, and it must be used consistently. That does not mean complex software. It can be as simple as a physical board, a shared digital tracker, or a structured tier meeting rhythm. What matters is not the tool. What matters is the flow. When a problem is identified, it must move forward. When it moves forward, it must not disappear. When it is solved, it must be standardized. When it is standardized, it must be sustained.

In Section V, we will turn this funnel into a practical operating rhythm. You will see exactly how daily huddles, weekly reviews, monthly kaizens, and quarterly PD reviews fit together. This is where Lean stops fading, because the organization no longer depends on enthusiasm. It depends on a cadence that keeps improvement alive.

IV. How Work Enters the Funnel (Without Initiative Soup)

A continuous improvement funnel is only as good as what you allow into it. If everything becomes an "initiative," the funnel collapses under its own weight. If nothing is allowed in unless it is perfect, improvement stalls, and people disengage. The goal is not to capture every idea. The goal is to create a simple system that captures the right problems, routes them to the right level, and produces results consistently.

Most organizations don't struggle with a lack of opportunities. They struggle with too many. Every department has a list. Every manager has a list. Every employee has frustrations. Every leader has opinions. And once the organization decides it wants to "improve," the natural impulse is to start collecting ideas and launching projects. This is where initiative soup is born. Leaders feel productive because activity increases, but the organization loses focus, follow-through becomes weak, and people start seeing continuous improvement as just another layer of work.

A healthy CI system needs a **gate**. Not a bureaucracy gate but a clarity gate. A simple way to answer: What qualifies as improvement work, and what does not? What stays in daily management, and what needs escalation? What becomes a kaizen, and what becomes a policy deployment priority?

To keep this simple, I recommend you classify work entering the funnel into four categories. Each category has a different response and, most importantly, a different expectation for speed.

The first category is abnormalities. These are problems that interrupt flow or performance today. They include safety issues, quality defects, missing information, equipment failures, backlog spikes, late shipments, or anything else that causes the team to fall off plan. Abnormalities are not "projects." They are signals. They must be captured visibly and responded to quickly through daily management. The purpose of daily management is not to discuss abnormalities. It is to expose them and trigger action. If a team cannot respond to abnormalities quickly, they are not managing the process. They are simply observing it.

The second category is recurring problems. These are issues that show up repeatedly and consume time, money, or attention. They are the problems people complain about constantly. They are also the problems that create the feeling that the company is stuck. Recurring problems require structured problem-solving. They should not live forever in the daily huddle, and they should not be escalated to leadership prematurely. This is where a disciplined PDCA cycle, root-cause thinking, and countermeasures become the default response. The goal is not to assign blame. The goal is to break recurrence.

The third category is improvement opportunities. These are changes that would simplify work, reduce waste, reduce lead time, improve quality, or reduce cost, but they are not necessarily tied to a crisis. Many of these opportunities come from employees who are closest to the work. They may also come from leaders during gemba walks, from customer feedback, or from analysis of KPI trends. These opportunities are valuable, but they must be prioritized. Not every opportunity should be acted on immediately. This is where the funnel protects the organization. It allows you to capture ideas without turning the entire company into a project factory.

The fourth category is strategic breakthroughs. These are the big moves that require leadership alignment, cross-functional effort, and often investment. They typically connect directly to your breakthrough KPIs and your policy deployment priorities. These are not nice-to-have improvements. These are the few changes that will most affect the future of the business. The funnel ensures that strategic breakthroughs do not get lost in the noise of daily problems. It also ensures that the organization does not label every improvement as "strategic" just to gain attention.

Once you classify work this way, you need a routing rule. This is where simplification becomes real. Without routing rules, the organization defaults to politics. The loudest problem wins. The most senior person wins. The newest idea wins. The team that complains the most wins. That is not management. That is survival.

A good routing rule answers three questions: How urgent is it? How big is it? How cross-functional is it?

If the issue is urgent and local, it belongs in daily management. The team should contain it and restore control. If it repeats or crosses boundaries, it becomes structured problem-solving. If it requires redesign of a process and concentrated time, it becomes kaizen. If it changes the company's trajectory, it becomes policy deployment.

This is not complicated, but it requires discipline. Leaders must resist the temptation to treat every issue as a fire drill. They must also resist the temptation to treat every issue as a kaizen. Kaizen is powerful, but it is not the operating system. Daily management is the operating system. Kaizen is one of the engines inside it.

The next gate is the most important one: the KPI gate. Every improvement effort that goes beyond daily management must connect to a KPI. If the organization allows projects to exist without a measurable outcome, initiative soup returns immediately. People will work on what feels good, what is politically safe, or what looks impressive in presentations. Over time, the company becomes full of activity and empty of results.

The KPI gate is simple. For any improvement effort that requires time, resources, or cross-functional support, ask: which KPI will this move, by how much, and by when? If the team cannot answer that question, the effort is not ready. It may still be a good idea, but it must be clarified before it enters the system. This is one of the most powerful simplification tools in Lean leadership. It forces clarity and focus, and it prevents random work.

Another essential gate is the ownership gate. If the company cannot name a single owner, the work should not enter the funnel. Many organizations assign improvement work to groups, committees, or departments. That feels inclusive, but it is deadly. A group can contribute. A group can support. A group can review. But a group cannot own. Improvement work requires a single accountable owner with a deadline, even if many people support the effort. Without ownership, follow-through collapses and cynicism grows.

The final gate is the capacity gate. This is where leadership must be honest. Most companies dramatically overestimate how many improvement efforts they can execute well. They launch ten initiatives and finish two. They start five kaizens and sustain one. They assign improvement work on top of already overloaded managers and then act surprised when nothing sticks. A sustainable CI system requires a different mindset. Instead of asking, "What else should we start?" leaders must ask, "What should we stop so we can finish what matters?"

This is where simplification becomes a leadership act. If the organization has too many improvement efforts, the solution is not better tracking. The solution is subtraction. Leaders must be willing to kill projects, pause work, and protect capacity. This is not a nice-to-have discipline. It is the only way a CI system stays healthy.

When these gates are in place, improvement becomes calmer. The organization stops thrashing. People stop feeling like everything is urgent. The work becomes more focused. Follow-through improves. Wins accumulate. And most importantly, trust begins to return, even in organizations where Lean has faded before.

In the next section, we will turn the funnel into a rhythm. You will see exactly how to connect daily huddles, weekly tier meetings, monthly kaizens, and quarterly policy deployment reviews into a simple operating cadence. This cadence is the heart of sustainment. It is what makes continuous improvement survive in real life.

V. The Meeting Rhythm That Keeps Lean Alive

Daily, Weekly, Monthly, and Quarterly Cadence Without Bureaucracy

Lean does not sustain itself through inspiration. It sustains itself through rhythm. When Lean fades, it is rarely because people stopped believing in improvement. It is because the organization stopped practicing the routines that make improvement inevitable. Meetings got canceled. Leaders got busy. KPIs stopped being reviewed. Action lists stopped being followed up. Escalations stopped being resolved. Over time, the system lost its heartbeat, and the organization returned to old habits.

That is why a continuous improvement operating system must be built around a simple cadence. This cadence does not exist to create more meetings. It exists to create clarity, stability, and learning. It ensures that problems surface early, countermeasures are tracked, initiatives remain aligned, and improvement does not depend on heroic effort.

A good cadence has four levels: daily, weekly, monthly, and quarterly. Each level has a different purpose. Each level should be short, and each level must connect to the others. When the cadence is designed correctly, it prevents initiative soup, reduces firefighting, and keeps strategy alive in daily work.

The daily cadence is the foundation. This is where teams maintain control of their processes and surface abnormalities before they grow. Daily huddles should be short, standing, and focused. The purpose is not discussion. The purpose is visibility and action. A good daily huddle answers three questions:

- How did we perform yesterday?
- What risks do we see today?
- What actions are we taking immediately?

If a team spends twenty minutes in a daily huddle, they are usually compensating for a lack of clarity. Either the board is too complex, the metrics are too many, or the team is trying to solve problems in the meeting instead of triggering problem-solving outside the huddle. Daily huddles should feel like a cockpit check: fast, focused, and disciplined.

The daily cadence also serves another critical purpose: it trains the organization to respond to abnormalities without panic. In most struggling companies, abnormalities trigger escalation and emotional reactions. People scramble, blame, and expedite. In a Lean operating system, abnormalities trigger a calm response. The team identifies the issue, contains it, assigns ownership, and escalates only when necessary. Over time, this changes the emotional tone of the organization. Work becomes more stable. People become less reactive. And performance improves without exhausting the workforce.

The weekly cadence is where the organization learns. Daily huddles are about control. Weekly reviews are about trends, patterns, and problem-solving. This is where you ask: "Are we improving, or are we simply surviving?" A weekly review should not be a longer version of the daily huddle. It should be a different type of meeting. It should focus on KPI trends, recurring abnormalities, and the status of countermeasures. It is also the correct place to review the improvement funnel: what problems were escalated from daily management, which ones require structured problem-solving, which ones qualify for kaizen, and which ones are becoming strategic risks?

This weekly rhythm is also where many organizations succeed or fail. If weekly reviews become slide presentations, the system turns into a meeting theater. If weekly reviews become blame sessions, people hide problems. If weekly reviews become vague conversations with no action tracking, the organization loses discipline. But when weekly reviews are run properly, they become the organization's learning loop. They create a predictable structure for problem-solving. They ensure actions are followed up. And they prevent recurring issues from becoming permanent.

The monthly cadence is where alignment happens. Monthly reviews should connect performance and improvement work back to policy deployment. This is where leadership confirms that the organization is still focused on the breakthrough priorities, resources are aligned, and the right cross-functional efforts are being supported. Monthly reviews are also where leadership should actively remove barriers that teams cannot remove themselves.

In a Lean organization, escalation is not a complaint. It is a signal that the system needs leadership support. If leadership ignores escalations, the organization learns that the system is not real. If leadership responds consistently, the organization learns that problems will be addressed and that improvement is worth the effort.

Monthly reviews are also where initiative soup is prevented at the leadership level. This is where the leadership team should ask a disciplined question: "Are we working on the right things?" If the answer is unclear, the leadership team should not add more initiatives. They should clarify the strategy, simplify priorities, and remove work that does not support the breakthrough KPIs. This is one of the most important leadership disciplines in a turnaround. You cannot improve everything at once. You must choose. And the monthly cadence is where those choices are protected.

The quarterly cadence is where the system is renewed. This is where the organization reviews progress against the breakthrough KPIs, reassesses priorities, and makes adjustments based on what has been learned. Quarterly reviews are also the correct time to evaluate whether the CI system is working. Are daily huddles happening consistently? Are weekly problem-solving routines producing real countermeasures? Are kaizen events being sustained? Are KPIs trusted? Are leaders showing up? Is the improvement funnel flowing, or is it clogged? Without a quarterly renewal rhythm, Lean systems slowly decay. Not because anyone chooses decay, but because drift is natural. Quarterly reviews are how you catch drift before it becomes a failure.

This cadence is often described as a "tier meeting system." Some companies formalize it into Tier 1, Tier 2, Tier 3, and Tier 4 meetings. That structure can work well, but the terminology is not important. What matters is that the cadence creates flow. Problems should be solved at the lowest possible level and escalated quickly when they exceed that level's authority. The cadence ensures that escalation is not emotional or political. It is systematic.

To keep this cadence simple, I recommend one guiding rule: Every meeting must produce one of three outcomes. It must create an *action*, create a *decision*, or create *learning*. If a meeting produces none of those, it is not a Lean meeting. It is wasted time. This rule sounds harsh, but it is essential in a turnaround. The goal is not to meet more. The goal is to manage better.

Another rule is equally important: never confuse cadence with bureaucracy. A Lean operating system should feel lighter than the old way, not heavier. If your cadence creates more work than it removes, you have built the wrong system. The purpose of daily huddles is to reduce expediting. The purpose of weekly reviews is to reduce recurring problems. The purpose of monthly reviews is to reduce misalignment and initiative soup. The purpose of quarterly reviews is to reduce drift. If those outcomes are not happening, the cadence must be simplified.

Finally, a cadence only becomes real when leaders treat it as non-negotiable. This is where most companies fail. Leaders cancel meetings when they get busy. They delegate the routines to others. They skip gemba. They allow boards to go stale. They stop asking for countermeasures. Then they act surprised when Lean fades.

If you want a CI operating system that survives real life, leadership must treat the rhythm as the job. Not something in addition to the job. This is the same principle we discussed with Quality Management Systems. When the system is designed as extra work, it dies under pressure. When it is designed as work, it survives pressure.

In the next section, we will define governance. We will clarify who owns the system, what roles are required, and how continuous improvement can be supported without creating a CI bureaucracy. This is where many organizations make a costly mistake: they build a "Lean department" and unintentionally remove ownership from line leadership. We will avoid that trap and keep the system simple, scalable, and leader-owned.

VI. Governance and Ownership

Who Owns Continuous Improvement (And Who Should Not)

A continuous improvement operating system cannot survive without clear ownership. This is often misunderstood. Many companies assume that if they hire a Lean leader, create a CI department, or assign an OpEx manager, they have solved the ownership problem. In reality, they often create a new problem: the organization begins to believe continuous improvement is someone else's job.

This is just another way to kill all that work you put into Lean.

Lean is sustained by line leadership, not by a department. The people who own the value stream must own the improvement of the value stream. The people who manage the work must manage the improvement of the work. If that responsibility is outsourced, even unintentionally, the organization will revert to old habits the moment the CI person is busy, leaves, or loses influence. Make it part of their jobs.

At the same time, line leadership cannot sustain Lean alone. They need support. They need coaching. They need facilitation. They need training. They need someone who protects the method. They need someone who helps the organization learn. That is where governance comes in. Governance is not bureaucracy. Governance is simply the structure that ensures continuous improvement has ownership, clarity, and follow-through.

A strong CI governance model answers three questions clearly:

- Who owns the system?
- Who supports the system?
- Who holds the system accountable?

The owner of continuous improvement must be the leadership team, led by the CEO or site leader. That statement may sound obvious, but in practice, it is rare. Many leadership teams treat Lean as an operations project. They support it verbally, but they do not own it. They delegate it to a Lean leader or an operations director. The result is predictable: Lean becomes optional. It becomes something that can be postponed. And once Lean becomes postponable, it fades.

Ownership does not mean the CEO runs kaizen events. It means leadership owns the operating rhythm. Leadership owns the breakthrough priorities. Leadership owns the KPI system. Leadership owns the escalation path. Leadership owns the expectation that improvement is part of the job. Without that ownership, the system has no authority.

The second component is support. This is where a CI leader or team plays an important role. The support function exists to build capability and protect the method. They *train* teams, and they *facilitate* Kaizen events. They *coach* leaders on gemba behaviors, and they *help* teams build KPI boards. They *teach* problem-solving, help *standardize* best practices, and help the organization *avoid* common failure modes, but they do not own performance. They do not own the value stream, and they do not become the "improvement police."

If the CI team becomes the police, the organization will resist them. If the CI team becomes the owner, the organization will outsource improvement to them. In both cases, Lean becomes fragile, and I see this happen way too often.

The third component is accountability. This is the mechanism that ensures the system is held consistently, even when the organization is busy. Accountability is not punishment. It is not an audit designed to shame people. Accountability is the discipline of follow-up. Are huddles happening? Are KPIs updated? Are actions closed? Are standards being sustained? Are kaizens producing measurable results? Are leaders showing up? Are escalations being resolved? Without accountability, the system slowly decays. And because decay happens gradually, leaders often don't notice until performance drops again.

To keep governance simple, I recommend a structure with three levels:

- A steering level
- An operating level
- A team level

The steering level is where the leadership team owns the system. This group sets the expectations, confirms the breakthrough priorities, reviews progress against the breakthrough KPIs, and makes decisions that remove barriers. In many organizations, this is not a new meeting. It is a disciplined upgrade of an existing leadership meeting. The difference is that the agenda becomes focused on performance, improvement, and system health, not on reporting and updates.

The operating level is where the CI system is managed. This includes the CI leader, key functional leaders, and value stream owners. This group ensures the improvement funnel is flowing, kaizen events are scheduled and supported, problem-solving is happening at the right level, and the cadence is being maintained. This group also ensures that improvement work is aligned to the KPI tree and policy deployment priorities. The operating level is the bridge between strategy and daily work.

The team level is where daily management happens. This is where the system either becomes real or theater. Teams run huddles, update boards, surface abnormalities, and execute countermeasures. This is also where improvement ideas are generated and where people learn the habits of problem-solving. If the team level is weak, no number of steering meetings will sustain Lean.

Now let's make the roles clear because ambiguity here is yet another reason Lean fades.

The CEO or site leader is **the sponsor** of the operating system. Their role is not to "support Lean." Their role is to make the operating rhythm non-negotiable. They must show up consistently, reinforce expectations, remove barriers, and protect focus. They must also *model the behavior* that Lean requires: going to gemba, asking good questions, and treating problems as opportunities for learning rather than reasons for blame. When the CEO treats Lean as optional, the organization treats it as optional. When the CEO treats Lean as the job, the organization follows.

The functional leaders and value stream owners are **the system owners** at their level. They own performance and improvement. They are responsible for ensuring KPIs are meaningful, abnormalities are surfaced, and countermeasures are executed. They also own sustainment. If a kaizen improves a process, the functional leader must ensure the new standard is maintained, audited, and trained. Without this ownership, kaizen becomes temporary.

The CI leader is **the architect and coach**. Their job is to build capability, protect the method, and keep the system simple. They facilitate. They train. They coach. They standardize. They help leaders build strong routines. They help teams solve problems. They also help leadership see where the system is drifting. But they do not own the results. If they do, the organization will quietly outsource improvement to them, and Lean will collapse when they leave.

Process owners are a critical role, and they are often missing. A process owner is the person who owns the process after the kaizen. They own the standard, the documentation, the training, and the audit, and they own the response when the process drifts. This is the role that prevents the most common sustainment failure: a great event followed by slow decay.

Team leaders and supervisors are the daily heartbeat. They run the huddles. They update the boards. They respond to abnormalities. They capture actions. They escalate when needed. They also protect the time for improvement. In many organizations, supervisors are overloaded and undertrained. If you want Lean to sustain, you must develop supervisors. They are not just labor schedulers. They are the frontline leaders of the operating system.

Finally, there is a role that many organizations neglect: support functions. Quality, Finance, HR, IT, Engineering, and Supply Chain are not "gatekeepers." They are enablers and must support the operating system, not slow it down. This is where governance matters. A Lean organization must define how support functions participate, how quickly they respond to escalations, and how they contribute to problem-solving and sustainment. When support functions are disconnected, improvement stalls. When they are integrated, the system becomes powerful.

The governance model must also include one critical rule: *continuous improvement cannot become a parallel organization*. If you create a separate Lean hierarchy with separate priorities, meetings, and reporting, you will create friction and resistance. Lean must be embedded into the normal management structure. It must use the same leaders, the same accountability, and the same business priorities. The only thing Lean adds is a better method.

When governance is designed correctly, it creates a powerful effect. People stop asking, "Who owns this?" because ownership is clear. They stop asking, "Is Lean still important?" because the rhythm is consistent. They stop treating improvement as extra work because the system is integrated into daily management. And they stop relying on heroics because problems are surfaced and solved systematically.

In the next section, we will bring all of this together into the sustainment system itself. We will define what happens after kaizen, how standards are protected, how drift is detected early, and how improvement becomes permanent. This is where many organizations lose their gains, and it is also where the continuous improvement operating system proves its value.

VII. Leader Standard Work as Sustainment

What Leaders Must Do to Keep Lean Alive When Life Gets Busy

When Lean fades, the first thing most people blame is the workforce. Leaders say employees stopped caring, teams stopped updating boards, supervisors stopped running huddles, and the organization went back to old habits. That explanation is comforting because it points downward. It also happens to be wrong most of the time.

Lean fades from the top down, not from the bottom up.

The reason is simple: Lean is a management system, and management systems survive only when leaders hold them consistently. The frontline can carry a system for a while, especially when there is energy and momentum. But when pressure increases, the organization will always revert to what leadership reinforces. If leaders stop showing up, stop asking for countermeasures, stop following up on actions, and stop treating the cadence as non-negotiable, Lean becomes optional. Once Lean becomes optional, it fades quickly.

This is why leader standard work is not a "nice Lean concept." It is the sustainment mechanism that makes Lean survive the real world. It turns continuous improvement from something leaders support into something leaders do. It creates predictable leadership behavior, which is the foundation of predictable organizational behavior.

Leader standard work also solves another problem that is common in turnarounds: leadership overload. In a struggling organization, leaders are pulled into everything. They are constantly responding to escalations, solving problems personally, and making decisions under pressure. Their calendars become chaotic, their days are reactive, and because they are busy, they convince themselves they do not have time for Lean routines.

The irony is that those routines are exactly what would reduce the chaos. Leader standard work is the structure that protects leaders from being consumed by firefighting. It forces leaders to spend time on prevention, stability, and improvement, even when urgency is loud.

To keep this simple, think of leader standard work as three commitments: a weekly gemba commitment, a weekly KPI commitment, and a weekly coaching commitment. If leaders hold those three consistently, Lean will not fade.

The weekly gemba commitment is not about "walking around." It is about going to where the work happens and seeing reality. Leaders should not go to gemba to check compliance or catch mistakes. They should go to gemba to understand flow, see abnormalities, and remove barriers that teams cannot remove on their own.

The gemba walk should feel calm and structured, not random. It should include a standard route, a standard set of questions, and a standard follow-up method. If gemba walks become inconsistent or performative, teams will treat them as theater. But when leaders show up consistently and ask good questions, gemba becomes one of the most powerful sustainment tools in the organization.

The weekly KPI commitment is where leadership proves the system is real. KPIs only drive behavior when leaders treat them as triggers for action, not as numbers to admire, as mentioned in previous chapters. A leader's job is not to ask, "Why is this red?" in a way that makes people defensive. A leader's job is to ask, "What is the abnormality? What do we know? What are we doing about it? What support do you need?"

When leaders ask these questions consistently, the organization learns that problems will not be ignored and escalation is safe. This is one of the most important cultural outcomes of a KPI system: it creates psychological safety around surfacing reality. Without that safety, people hide problems, and the system collapses.

The weekly coaching commitment is where Lean becomes capability rather than dependency. If leaders solve every problem personally, they create a hero culture. The organization becomes dependent on a few strong individuals, and improvement stops when those people are absent. In a Lean operating system, leaders coach problem-solving rather than solving everything themselves. They ask teams to define the problem clearly, show data, test countermeasures, and reflect on what was learned. This is slower at first, but it is the only way to build an organization that can improve without constant leadership intervention. Coaching is how Lean becomes scalable.

Leader standard work must also include one discipline that most leaders avoid: follow-up. This is where Lean often dies. Leaders attend a huddle, nod at the board, and then move on. Actions are written down but not closed. Escalations are raised but not resolved. Problems are discussed but not solved. Over time, the organization learns the truth: the system is not real. People stop putting effort into it. The board becomes stale. Meetings become repetitive. And the company returns to firefighting. Sustainment requires leaders to treat follow-up as non-negotiable. If an action has an owner and a due date, leadership must insist it is closed or escalated. Not harshly, but consistently.

To make leader standard work practical, I recommend leaders operate on three time horizons: daily, weekly, and monthly. Daily leadership routines should be light. A leader does not need to attend every huddle. But they should have a daily touchpoint with the system. This might include reviewing the top abnormalities from the previous day, checking whether critical KPIs were updated, and confirming that escalations are being handled. Weekly routines are where leaders spend meaningful time at gemba, in KPI reviews, and in problem-solving coaching. Monthly routines are where leaders connect performance back to policy deployment, confirm priorities, and protect focus.

What leaders review matters as much as what leaders do. Leaders should not review everything. They should review the vital few. In a Lean sustainment system, leaders should review the breakthrough KPIs, the key driver KPIs, the health of daily management routines, the status of major countermeasures, or the sustainment of recent Kaizen events. If leaders review dozens of metrics, they will drown in noise and stop seeing what matters. If they review too few, they will miss drift. The right answer is not more dashboards. The right answer is disciplined focus.

Leaders must also ask the right questions at gemba. The purpose of gemba questions is not to test employees. It is to reveal system weaknesses. The most effective gemba questions are simple: What is the target? What is the actual? What is preventing you from hitting the target? What is your current abnormality? What countermeasures are you trying? What help do you need? These questions reinforce the idea that performance is managed through facts and countermeasures, not through blame. Over time, teams start thinking in this way automatically. That is sustainment.

Equally important is what leaders must stop doing. This is the hardest part, and it is also the part that determines whether Lean survives. Leaders must stop rewarding heroics. In many organizations, the most celebrated people are the ones who fix emergencies at the last minute. They are praised for expediting, staying late, and saving the day. That feels good in the moment, but it teaches the organization the wrong lesson: instability is normal, and firefighting is success. A Lean leader must instead reward stability, prevention, and follow-through. That is a cultural shift, and it is not easy, especially in turnarounds where leaders have lived in crisis mode for years.

Leaders must also stop changing priorities constantly. Nothing kills continuous improvement faster than a leadership team that adds new initiatives every week. Teams learn that the safest move is to wait because priorities will shift again. This is where Chapter 10's KPI discipline becomes essential. Leaders must protect focus, kill initiative soup, and insist that improvement work connects to the vital few KPIs. Sustainment requires leaders to become ruthless about what the organization will not do.

Finally, leaders must stop tolerating drift. Drift is the natural tendency of systems to degrade over time. It is not a moral failure. It is a predictable outcome. Standards decay, boards become stale, meetings lose discipline, definitions get fuzzy, and actions get delayed. The role of leadership is not to punish drift. It is to detect it early and correct it quickly. Leader standard work is the mechanism that makes that possible. When leaders hold the system consistently, drift is caught before it collapses.

If you want Lean to survive, you must treat leader standard work as part of the operating system, not as a Lean add-on. It should be written down, scheduled, and expected. It should be reviewed like any other standard. It should also be improved over time. Leaders should experiment with what works, simplify what does not, and refine the rhythm until it becomes natural.

In the next section, we will go deeper into the sustainment system itself. We will cover what happens after a kaizen event, how standards are protected, how audits should work, and how to build a sustainment calendar that prevents backsliding without creating bureaucracy. This is the section where most organizations fail, and it is also where the continuous improvement operating system becomes real.

VIII. The Sustainment System

What Happens After Kaizen: How Audits Should Work and How to Prevent Backsliding

If you want to know whether a company has a mature Lean system, don't look at their kaizen schedule. Look at what happens two weeks after a kaizen event. That is where the truth lives.

During a kaizen, everything is easy. The team is focused. Leaders are paying attention. The facilitator is present. The process is being observed closely. Problems are visible. Decisions happen quickly. People feel momentum. In many organizations, a kaizen week is the only time the company feels calm, aligned, and productive. The improvements are real, and the energy is contagious. Then the event ends.

People go back to their normal jobs. Urgency returns. Emails pile up. Production pressure rises. Customer issues escalate. Leaders get pulled into other priorities. And slowly, the process begins to drift.

A step is skipped because "we don't have time today." A visual control is not updated because "the board isn't that important." A checklist is ignored because "I already know what to do."
A new operator is trained informally because "the supervisor is too busy." A problem returns and gets solved through heroics instead of fixing the system.

None of this happens because people are bad. It happens because drift is natural. A process will always revert toward disorder unless the organization has a sustainment system that protects the new standard.

This is why sustainment must be designed intentionally. It cannot be left to hope. It cannot rely on good intentions. It must be built into the operating rhythm, with clear ownership, visible follow-up, and simple accountability.

A Big Sustainment Mistake Is Confusing Implementation with Adoption

Many companies believe a kaizen is complete when the new process is implemented. They measure success by whether the new layout was installed, the standard work document was created, or the board was updated. Those are implementation tasks, and they are not what we mean when we say "adoption."

Adoption means the new way of working is happening consistently when no one is watching. It means the process will survive the next busy week. It means the new standard is being used by new employees. It means abnormalities are handled through the new system, not through old habits. Adoption is the real goal, and it is what sustainment is designed to protect.

This is why a kaizen event should never end with "we're done." It should end with "we are now entering the sustainment phase." That phase is where Lean becomes permanent.

What Should Happen Immediately After a Kaizen (The First Forty-Eight Hours)

The sustainment system begins the moment the kaizen ends. Within the first forty-eight hours, four things must be true.

First, the process owner must be clearly named, and that ownership must be visible. This is the person who owns the process after the event. They are responsible for the standard, the training, the audit, and the response when drift occurs. Without a named process owner, sustainment becomes everyone's responsibility, which means it becomes nobody's responsibility.

Second, the new standard must be simple enough to use. Many companies unintentionally sabotage sustainment by creating overly detailed standard work documents that no one will ever read. Standard work must be usable, not perfect. It should be visual, practical, and close to the work. If the standard is too complex, the organization will revert to tribal knowledge.

Third, the training plan must be defined. This does not mean everyone must attend a formal training session immediately. It means the organization must know who needs to be trained, how training will happen, and how competency will be verified. Sustainment collapses quickly when new employees are trained informally and inconsistently.

Fourth, the performance measures must be defined. The team must know how success will be measured and how frequently it will be reviewed. If a kaizen produces improvement but no one measures it, the improvement becomes invisible. Invisible improvements do not survive.

What Happens Two Weeks After Kaizen

Two weeks after a kaizen, the company must perform a structured sustainment check. This is not an audit in the traditional sense. It is a simple reality check designed to answer one question: is the new process being used consistently?

This is where many organizations avoid the truth. They assume that because the process was implemented, it is being followed. Or they assume that because the team was enthusiastic, the change will stick. But enthusiasm fades quickly when urgency returns. Sustainment requires verification.

The two-week sustainment check should focus on three things: First, compliance with the critical steps of the new standard. Second, the presence and health of the visual controls that support the process. Third, the KPI trend associated with the improvement. If the process is being followed and the KPI is improving, the kaizen is on track. If the process is drifting or the KPI is not improving, the organization must respond immediately. Waiting a month is too late. Drift becomes a habit quickly.

This is also the moment when leadership behavior matters. If leaders treat the sustainment check as policing, the system will be resisted. If leaders treat it as learning and support, the system will be strengthened. Sustainment is not about catching people doing things wrong. It is about catching the system drifting and correcting it early.

The Sustainment Calendar

To make sustainment reliable, you need a calendar. Not a complicated one but a simple rhythm that makes sustainment unavoidable.

I recommend a standard sustainment calendar for every kaizen:

- **Forty-eight hours:** Confirm ownership, training plan, KPI definition, and visual controls.
- **Two weeks:** Conduct sustainment check (compliance + KPI trend + abnormalities).
- **Thirty days:** Confirm adoption and close open actions.
- **Sixty days:** Verify performance stability and standardize further if needed.
- **Ninety days:** Confirm the improvement is permanent and remove the kaizen from active tracking.

This calendar is powerful because it prevents the most common sustainment failure: the organization moves on too quickly. In many companies, kaizen events happen back to back, and leadership celebrates the next event before the previous one is stable. That creates the illusion of progress while results remain fragile. A sustainment calendar forces discipline. It ensures improvements become permanent before attention shifts elsewhere.

Why Most Audits Fail and How to Fix Them

Many organizations attempt to sustain improvements through audits. Unfortunately, most audit systems are designed in a way that guarantees failure. They are either too bureaucratic, too punitive, or too disconnected from daily work.

When audits feel like inspections, people resist them. They hide problems. They fill out paperwork. They perform for the auditor. The audit becomes another theater, and the process drifts anyway.

When audits are too complex, they stop happening. Leaders get busy, and the audit is postponed. After that, it becomes easy to postpone again. Soon, the audit system disappears.

When audits are disconnected from KPIs, they feel pointless. People ask, "Why are we checking this?" They don't see the connection to performance, so they treat the audit as compliance work rather than improvement work.

A Lean sustainment audit must be different. It must be short, practical, and directly connected to process performance.

The simplest audit that works is a layered audit system. This means different levels of leadership check the process at different frequencies. The frontline checks daily, the supervisor checks weekly, the manager checks biweekly, and the site leader checks monthly. The checks are short and focus on critical process steps and visual controls. Each check includes one essential question: if we are not following the standard, what is preventing us?

This last part matters. A sustainment audit should never end with "people are not following the process." That is not the root cause. The audit should reveal why. Is the standard unrealistic? Is training incomplete? Is the process missing a tool? Is the workload too high? Is the layout wrong? Does the system encourage shortcuts? The aim of sustainment audits is not enforcing behavior. They aim at strengthening the system so the right behavior becomes the easiest one.

Standard Work Ownership Rules

If you want sustainment, you must treat standard work like a controlled system, not a document. This is where many organizations unintentionally sabotage themselves. They create standard work, but they do not assign ownership, they do not version control it, they do not train consistently, they do not verify adherence, and they do not update it when reality changes. Over time, the standard becomes outdated, and people stop using it. Then leadership blames the workforce for "not following the standard," when, in reality, the standard is no longer relevant.

To prevent this, every standard must have an owner, and that owner must have a clear responsibility: keep the standard alive. That means ensuring it reflects reality, that training is consistent, that drift is detected early, and that improvements are captured and standardized. Standards should not be static. They should evolve. But they should evolve in a controlled way.

This is where your quality management system experience becomes relevant. In regulated environments, we understand that uncontrolled changes create risk. Lean sustainment requires the same thinking. The goal is not to freeze the process. The goal is to ensure changes are intentional, tested, and standardized.

The Sustainment Mindset

Improvement is not finished when it is implemented. It is finished when it survives pressure.

A kaizen that works only when the facilitator is present is not a success. A standard that works only when leadership is watching is not a standard. A KPI that improves only during the event is not improvement. The goal is not temporary performance. The goal is a stronger operating system.

When the sustainment system is designed correctly, the organization begins to trust itself again. Employees stop associating Lean with temporary programs, while leaders stop fearing that improvements will fade. The company begins to accumulate gains, not just generate them. And once gains accumulate, the transformation becomes self-reinforcing.

In the next section, we will address the final major challenge: scaling continuous improvement across the organization without creating bureaucracy. Remember, this book is about simplicity. This is where many companies overcorrect. They build a large CI infrastructure, create complex tracking systems, and slow improvement. We will take the opposite approach by focusing on building a CI habit that spreads naturally, stays simple, and accelerates over time.

IX. Scaling Continuous Improvement Without Bureaucracy

Don't Build a CI Empire; Build a CI Habit

Once a company begins to see real benefits from Lean, a predictable risk appears. Leaders start thinking, *This is working. We need more of it.* They want to scale quickly. They want more kaizen events, more training, more projects, more dashboards, and more structure. They want to roll Lean into every department, site, and function.

The intention is good. The outcome is often disastrous. Instead of scaling improvement, the company ends up scaling complexity. Please don't do that.

This is one of the great ironies of Lean transformations. Lean begins as a simplification effort, but if leaders are not careful, the Lean system itself becomes complicated. New meetings and templates appear. New reporting requirements appear. A large CI infrastructure forms, and people spend more time managing improvement than doing improvement. The organization becomes full of activity again, except now the activity is labeled "Lean." This is how Lean becomes bureaucracy.

If you want continuous improvement to scale, you must scale the **habit**, not the machinery.

The habit is simple: see abnormalities, respond quickly, solve recurring problems, run focused kaizens, and align the big work through Policy Deployment. That is the operating system. Scaling means spreading those behaviors and routines across the organization. It does not mean building a parallel structure that sits on top of the business.

The first principle of scaling without bureaucracy is to keep the system embedded in line leadership. As I mentioned in previous chapters, if Lean becomes something managed by a CI department, the organization will treat it as separate. If Lean is owned by line leaders, it becomes part of how the business runs. This is why the CI function must remain small and focused. Their job is to teach, coach, facilitate, and protect the method. Their job is not to own performance. Their job is not to become the "Lean police." And their job is not to create a complex reporting machine.

A useful way to think about this is to treat the CI team as an enablement function, not an execution function. They are there to make leaders stronger, not to replace leaders. If the CI team is doing all the kaizens, updating all the boards, writing all the standards, and managing all the action lists, the organization is outsourcing instead of learning. That model is fragile, and it collapses the moment the CI team is overloaded or changes.

The second principle is to scale one area at a time but standardize the method. Many companies attempt to roll Lean out everywhere simultaneously. They train everyone, run dozens of events, and launch multiple systems at once. This creates overload and confusion. It also makes it difficult to sustain. The better approach is to scale through a deliberate sequence. Choose one value stream, department, or business unit as a "pilot area." Build a strong operating system there. Prove the rhythm, prove sustainment, and build belief. Then expand to the next area.

This approach is slower at the start but faster in the long run. It prevents the organization from building a fragile Lean system that collapses under pressure. It also creates internal credibility. People learn best when they see success in a peer area. They trust what they can observe. A single strong model area is more powerful than ten weak rollouts.

The third principle is to standardize the cadence, not the tools. This is important because different functions will require different visual boards, KPIs, and workflows. If you force every area to use the same board format, you will create resistance and lose relevance. But if you standardize the cadence, the organization stays aligned.

The cadence is the universal structure. Daily huddles. Weekly reviews. Monthly alignment. Quarterly renewal. That rhythm can exist in manufacturing, the office, quality, supply chain, and engineering. The tools will vary. The rhythm should not.

The fourth principle is to keep the number of metrics small. Scaling Lean often triggers metric inflation. Every department wants their own dashboards. Every leader wants more visibility. Every team adds measures. Soon, the organization is drowning in data, and no one is actually managing performance. Metrics become reporting again. The system slows.

This is where what we covered in Chapter 10 must be protected. A Lean organization does not win by measuring everything. It wins by measuring what matters and acting on it consistently. When scaling, the temptation to add metrics is strong, especially in support functions. Leaders want proof. They want control. But too many metrics create noise and reduce action. If you want Lean to scale, you must keep the KPI tree disciplined and the vital few protected.

The fifth principle is to scale improvement through leaders, not training. Many companies attempt to scale Lean by training more people. They send supervisors to Lean training. They send managers to workshops. They run belt programs. They certify people. Training is useful, but it is not the scaling mechanism. Leadership routines are the scaling mechanism.

If leaders do not run daily management, training will not matter. If leaders do not review KPIs consistently, training will not matter. If leaders do not hold sustainment, training will not matter. Training can accelerate learning, but it cannot replace system reinforcement. This is why the most effective way to scale Lean is to scale leader standard work and the meeting cadence. When leaders adopt the rhythm, the organization follows.

The sixth principle is to avoid overengineering the improvement funnel. Once companies start tracking improvement work, they often create complex project management systems. They build software platforms. They create scoring models. They require detailed business cases for every idea. They add governance layers. The funnel becomes slow, and improvement becomes frustrating.

This is the opposite of what Lean is meant to do.

A good improvement funnel should feel lightweight. It should capture problems and opportunities clearly. It should route them quickly. It should prioritize based on impact and capacity. It should track actions visibly. It should close loops. That's it. The funnel is not a bureaucracy. It is a flow mechanism.

The seventh principle is to protect speed. Speed is one of the most underestimated sustainment factors. When improvement moves slowly, people lose faith. They stop bringing problems. They stop participating. They assume nothing will happen. But when improvement moves quickly, belief grows. People feel momentum. They invest emotionally. They engage. This is why the

CI operating system must be designed to move issues forward fast. Not recklessly but consistently.

This is also where leadership must make a deliberate choice. Scaling Lean requires leaders to remove obstacles quickly. If escalations sit unresolved for weeks, the system slows down. If resources are not available, kaizens get postponed. If IT requests take months, office improvements stall. If quality approvals take too long, standardization becomes painful. Leaders must treat response speed as part of the system. Continuous improvement cannot be "everyone's job" if it is constantly blocked by slow decision-making.

The final principle is to keep the system human. When Lean scales, leaders often start focusing on compliance. They want every board updated perfectly. They want every meeting to run exactly the same. They want every department to use the same templates. They want perfect consistency. That impulse is understandable, especially in regulated environments. But Lean is not sustained through perfection. It is sustained through usefulness.

If the system helps people do their jobs, it will be used. If it feels like extra work, it will be resisted. This is the ultimate test. Lean must make work easier, clearer, calmer, and more predictable. If it does not, it is not Lean. It is bureaucracy wearing a Lean label.

Scaling without bureaucracy is ultimately about discipline. Leaders must resist the temptation to build a large CI infrastructure. They must resist the temptation to measure everything. They must resist the temptation to add more meetings. They must resist the temptation to create complex governance. Instead, they must protect the simple operating rhythm and spread it gradually, one area at a time, with strong sustainment.

If you do this well, continuous improvement becomes a habit. It becomes normal. It becomes part of how the company thinks and works. And most importantly, it becomes durable. It survives leadership changes, staffing turnover, growth, and crisis. That is the real definition of sustainment.

In the final section of this chapter, we will bring everything together into a practical implementation plan. You will build your own continuous improvement operating system using a set of templates and checklists: a thirty-day plan, a CI funnel template, a meeting rhythm plan, a governance RACI, and a drift detection checklist. This is where the chapter becomes actionable. You will not just understand the system. You will be able to implement it.

X. Reflection and Action: Build Your Continuous Improvement Operating System

If you take one idea from this chapter, let it be this: continuous improvement is not sustained by enthusiasm. It is sustained by design. You do not need a larger CI department, more training, or more meetings. You need a simple operating system that makes improvement unavoidable and makes drift visible early. When that system exists, Lean stops fading. It becomes how the business runs.

This Reflection and Action section is designed to help you build that operating system. You do not need to implement everything at once. In fact, trying to do so is one of the fastest ways to recreate initiative soup. The goal is to start small, build belief through results, and then expand.

A. Your Thirty-Day CI Operating System Launch Plan

A Lean operating system becomes real only when it shows up on calendars, boards, and behaviors. The next thirty days should not be spent designing the perfect system. They should be spent launching a simple version, learning from reality, and improving it.

Week 1: Establish the Foundation (Visibility and Ownership)
Start by selecting one pilot area. Ideally, this should be an area where the work is visible, leadership has influence, and there is enough pain that people will engage. Define the process owner for that area and make the ownership visible. Confirm the three to five KPIs that matter most.

Build a simple board that shows the KPIs, abnormalities, actions, and the improvement funnel. Keep it practical. If the board looks impressive but no one uses it, it is not a Lean board. Don't design this in the vacuum. Pull the team in and let them shape it with you.

By the end of Week 1, your pilot area should have a daily huddle, a visible board, and a named owner.

Week 2: Activate the Funnel (From Abnormalities to Action)
Now focus on the improvement funnel. Create a simple abnormality log. Capture the top recurring problems. Decide which issues stay in daily management and which move into structured problem-solving. Assign owners and due dates. Begin tracking countermeasures visibly. In Week 2, your goal is not to solve everything. Your goal is to make problems flow into the system instead of disappearing.

By the end of Week 2, your pilot area should have at least three recurring problems actively being solved through PDCA.

Week 3: Launch Sustainment (Stop Drift Before It Starts)
Week 3 is where most companies fail. They run meetings and track actions, but they do not build sustainment. Choose one improvement from the pilot area and apply the sustainment calendar: forty-eight hours, two weeks, thirty days. Confirm the standard work is usable. Confirm training is happening. Confirm a layered audit is in place. Keep audits short and supportive. Your goal is not compliance. Your goal is early detection of drift.

By the end of Week 3, your pilot area should have one improvement that has survived a busy week without collapsing.

Week 4: Scale the Rhythm (Not the Bureaucracy)
Now stabilize the cadence. Confirm the daily huddle is happening consistently. Add a weekly KPI review. Connect the weekly review to escalation rules. Confirm that leadership follow-up is consistent. Identify one kaizen opportunity and schedule it, but do not rush into it. The goal is to prove the operating rhythm first. Once the rhythm is stable, kaizen becomes more powerful and easier to sustain.

By the end of Week 4, your pilot area should feel calmer, more visible, and more under control than it did thirty days ago.

At the end of thirty days, do not declare victory. Instead, ask a better question: is the system functioning without heroic effort? If the answer is yes, you are ready to expand to the next area.

B. Your CI Funnel Template (Simple, Practical, and Fast)

A funnel only works if it routes work quickly and prevents initiative overload. Use this template to classify every problem or improvement idea:

Level 1: Daily Management (Abnormalities and Immediate Corrections)
Use this level when the issue can be contained quickly by the team and does not require cross-functional coordination.

Level 2: Structured Problem-Solving (Recurring Issues)
Use this level when the issue repeats, causes measurable loss, or cannot be solved with a quick fix.

Level 3: Kaizen (Cross-Functional Process Redesign)
Use this level when the issue requires redesign of a process, coordination across roles, or dedicated focused time.

Level 4: Policy Deployment (Breakthrough Priorities)
Use this level when the issue impacts the company's strategic direction, requires investment, or needs leadership alignment across functions.

For every item entering the funnel, apply four gates before work begins:

1. **KPI Gate:** Which KPI will this improve, by how much, and by when?
2. **Ownership Gate:** Who owns it (one name, not a committee)?
3. **Capacity Gate:** What are we stopping to make room for this?
4. **Routing Gate:** What level does it belong to, and why?

If an item cannot pass these gates, it is not ready. Capture it, but do not launch it.

C. Your Meeting Rhythm Plan (The Cadence That Prevents Drift)

Lean does not require more meetings. It requires better meetings with clear purpose.

Use this rhythm as your baseline:

Daily (Team Level):
Short huddle focused on KPIs, abnormalities, and immediate actions.

Weekly (Department Level):
KPI trend review, recurring problems, countermeasure tracking, escalation decisions.

Monthly (Leadership Level):
Review progress on breakthrough KPIs, confirm priorities, remove barriers, prevent initiative soup.

Quarterly (Business Level):
Review policy deployment, adjust priorities, renew the CI system, detect drift early.

For each meeting, enforce one rule: every meeting must create an action, a decision, or learning. If it does not, redesign it.

D. Governance RACI (Keep Ownership Clear)

The most common governance failure is unclear ownership. Use this RACI as a starting point and simplify it as needed.

CEO/Site Leader

- Accountable for the operating rhythm
- Accountable for protecting priorities
- Responsible for leadership follow-up
- Responsible for removing barriers

Functional Leaders/Value Stream Owners

- Accountable for KPI performance
- Accountable for sustainment in their areas
- Responsible for escalation resolution
- Responsible for supporting kaizen and problem-solving

CI Leader/CI Team

- Responsible for facilitation and training
- Responsible for coaching leaders
- Responsible for protecting the method
- Responsible for system health visibility
- Not accountable for business results

Process Owners

- Accountable for process standards
- Accountable for training and audit
- Responsible for keeping standard work alive
- Responsible for responding to drift

Supervisors/Team Leaders

- Responsible for daily huddles
- Responsible for abnormality response
- Responsible for action tracking
- Responsible for escalation

Support Functions (Quality, Finance, HR, IT, Engineering)

- Responsible for enabling improvement
- Responsible for responding to escalations
- Responsible for participating in problem-solving
- Not gatekeepers, but partners

Your governance system should feel clear, not heavy. If your RACI requires a meeting to interpret, it is too complex.

E. The Drift Detection Checklist (Your Early Warning System)

Drift is inevitable. Collapse is optional.

Use this checklist monthly to detect drift early:

1. Are daily huddles happening consistently, or are they being skipped?
2. Are boards current, or are they stale?
3. Are abnormalities being surfaced, or are teams staying quiet?
4. Are actions closing on time, or are due dates meaningless?
5. Are leaders following up, or are they delegating the system away?
6. Are KPIs trusted, or are people arguing about the data?
7. Are recurring problems being solved, or are they being tolerated?
8. Are kaizen improvements being sustained, or are they fading after two weeks?
9. Is initiative soup returning, or is the organization still focused?
10. Is improvement still connected to strategy, or has it become random work?

If you answer "no" to more than three of these questions, your operating system is drifting. The solution is not more tools. The solution is to restore the cadence, restore ownership, and simplify.

F. Reflection Questions (For You as the Leader)

1. If Lean has faded before in your organization, what specifically faded first: cadence, ownership, follow-up, or leadership behavior?
2. What does your organization currently reward: stability and prevention or heroics and firefighting?
3. Which part of your improvement funnel is weakest today: daily management, problem-solving, kaizen, or policy deployment?
4. Do your leaders treat the operating rhythm as the job or as something extra?
5. If you hired a CI leader tomorrow, would your organization outsource improvement to them? How would you prevent that?
6. What is the one behavior you must stop tolerating if you want sustainment?
7. What is the one routine you must protect if you want the system to survive real life?

G. Your Action Commitment (Do This Now)

Before you move on to the next chapter, make one commitment in writing:

In the next thirty days, you will launch a CI operating system in one pilot area with:

- A daily huddle
- Three to five KPIs
- A visible abnormality and action system
- A working improvement funnel
- A sustainment calendar
- Leadership follow-up

Then you will expand only after the system is stable.

This is how Lean becomes permanent.

Chapter 11 Reflection and Action Answers

CHAPTER 12

The Future of Lean: *Adapting to a Changing World*

Two Plants, Two Futures

Several years ago, I visited two manufacturing sites within the same industry. They produced similar products, and they had similar headcounts, similar automation levels, the same ERP systems, and even similar age profiles in their workforce. On paper, they looked nearly identical.

In reality, they were living in two completely different futures.

The first plant felt tense. Schedules changed daily, and expedites were common. Quality problems were discovered late, often by customers. Supervisors were constantly reacting. The leadership team spent most of its time reviewing dashboards and arguing about what the numbers meant. When demand spiked, overtime exploded, and when demand dropped, morale dropped with it.

The second plant was not perfect by any means. Machines failed, suppliers slipped, and orders fluctuated, but it behaved differently. Issues were detected early, and abnormalities were visible within hours, not weeks. Escalation happened naturally through structured routines, while leaders spoke less about numbers and more about systems. When demand increased, the plant absorbed it with calm adjustments. When supply was disrupted, cross-trained teams flexed without panic.

Both plants had technology, but only one had an operating system. The difference was not robotics, software, or budget. The difference was discipline, visibility, standard work, and structured learning. It was Lean.

The future does not belong to the most automated organization. It belongs to the organization that learns and acts the fastest.

And Lean, when properly understood, is a learning system.

Three months after that visit, both plants were tested.

A critical electronic component, used in one of their highest-volume products, was sourced from the same supplier. That supplier experienced an unexpected shutdown due to regulatory issues in its home country. Within days, both plants received the same message: shipments would be delayed indefinitely.

There was no alternate source immediately available. The component was unique, qualified, and embedded in multiple assemblies. The disruption did not affect one plant more than the other. It affected them equally.

The difference lay in what happened next.

At the first plant, the news triggered a series of reactive decisions. Planners manually reshuffled production schedules. Purchasing began calling brokers. Engineering explored emergency substitutions without a structured impact assessment. Supervisors were instructed to "build what we can." Meetings multiplied. Emails multiplied even faster. Each department tried to optimize its own piece of the problem, but no one had a clear, shared view of the system-wide impact.

Within a week, partially built products began accumulating. Inventory grew in the wrong places. Overtime increased in some areas, while other lines sat idle, waiting for parts. Customer service teams provided inconsistent delivery dates because the production plan changed daily. The organization was working harder, but its effort was fragmented. The supplier disruption became an internal coordination crisis. Sound familiar?

At the second plant, the response began differently.

The first action was not rescheduling. It was visibility.

The leadership team pulled the most current value stream data and mapped the exposure. They identified exactly which finished goods depended on the component, how much on-hand inventory existed at each stage, and how many days of demand that inventory covered under different scenarios. Using a simple simulation model built from their standard cycle times and takt assumptions, they tested three possible paths: allocate remaining components to the highest-margin products, prioritize strategic customers, or reduce production across all affected lines proportionally. The discussion was structured, the constraint was clear, and the trade-offs were explicit.

Within forty-eight hours, a deliberate plan was in place. Cross-trained operators were reassigned to unaffected lines. Preventive maintenance work that had been scheduled for later in the quarter was advanced to use idle capacity productively. Engineering evaluated a potential alternate component, not in isolation but through a documented change-control process tied to risk assessment. Daily tier meetings included a specific supplier disruption review, with clear ownership for each countermeasure.

There was still pressure, and there were still difficult conversations with customers, but the system held. The first plant experienced volatility as chaos. The second experienced volatility as a problem to be solved.

When supply resumed six weeks later, the contrast became measurable. The first plant had built significant excess work-in-progress inventory tied to incomplete assemblies. It took weeks to unwind the imbalance. Expedites created downstream quality escapes that required containment actions. Customer confidence had eroded, and several accounts demanded pricing concessions. The financial hit extended well beyond the original disruption window.

The second plant also experienced lost volume. It could not ship what it did not have. But it had deliberately allocated available components to its highest-priority customers, communicated realistic delivery windows early, and avoided building unfinished inventory. When supply resumed, production restarted cleanly. Within two weeks, the backlog was stabilized. Margin erosion was limited, and customer trust remained intact.

Neither plant avoided pain, but only one avoided self-inflicted damage. Neither avoided disruption, but only one absorbed it.

What separated them was not luck, capital, or heroics. It was the presence of stable standard work, clear escalation routines, cross-training discipline, accessible process data, and leadership that managed the system rather than chasing symptoms.

In other words, it was Lean. When volatility is low, the difference between organizations can be subtle. When volatility rises, the operating system is exposed. Technology existed in both plants: ERP systems, dashboards, planning tools. But in the first plant, the tools amplified confusion, while in the second, they amplified clarity.

This is where the conversation about the future of Lean must begin. Not with robotics or with artificial intelligence. Not with digital twins or predictive algorithms. It begins with a simple question: when the unexpected happens, does your organization fragment or align?

Because the future will not reward those who avoid disruption. It will reward those who detect it early, evaluate it intelligently, and respond to it in a coordinated way.

That capability is not accidental. It is designed.

And it is built on the foundations we have discussed throughout this book.

Why Lean Matters Now More Than Ever

If that supplier disruption had occurred twenty years ago, the impact would still have been serious, but the surrounding conditions would have been different. Product portfolios were simpler, supply chains were shorter, and customer expectations were less immediate. Information moved more slowly, and the operating environment tolerated more lag. Today, that same disruption travels at digital speed.

Customers expect updates in real time. Supply chains span continents. Product variants multiply year after year. Regulatory scrutiny increases. Talent turnover is higher. Demand volatility is sharper. At the same time, organizations have access to more data than ever before, yet clarity often decreases as dashboards multiply and meetings expand.

The external environment has become faster and more complex, and the internal operating systems of many companies have not kept pace. That is why Lean is not becoming less relevant. It is becoming more critical.

Cost reduction has not been the only goal. Cost reduction was the outcome of better system design. The deeper purpose of Lean has always been to create visibility, shorten feedback loops, and build disciplined problem-solving capability across the organization. In a stable world, that produces efficiency, while in a volatile world, it produces adaptability.

Adaptability is the defining capability of modern operation. It is the ability to detect change early, assess impact realistically, and respond without destabilizing the entire system. It is structured response under pressure.

Consider what happened in the two plants during the supplier disruption. Both experienced the same constraint. The difference lay in how quickly each organization could see the system-wide impact, align around a decision, and consistently execute countermeasures. The second plant did not have better luck. It had shorter feedback loops, clearer standards, and leaders accustomed to managing the system rather than chasing symptoms. That distinction becomes more important every year.

Volatility is no longer an exception. It is the norm. Demand patterns shift quickly, customers change ordering behavior with little notice, geopolitical events interrupt supply chains, energy prices fluctuate, transportation networks experience bottlenecks, and talent shortages strain capacity planning. Even internal dynamics, such as the introduction of new digital tools, can destabilize workflows if not integrated properly.

In such an environment, the goal of operations cannot be limited to maximizing efficiency under stable conditions. The goal must be reducing the cost of instability. Lean, when properly understood, reduces that cost in several ways.

First, it builds process clarity. When work is defined, visual, and standardized, deviations are easier to detect. Ambiguity is reduced. The organization spends less time debating what is happening and more time deciding what to do.

Second, it institutionalizes escalation. Abnormalities are not hidden or absorbed silently. They move upward through structured routines. That creates speed without panic.

Third, it develops people who can solve problems methodically rather than emotionally. When teams are accustomed to identifying root causes and testing countermeasures, disruption becomes a technical challenge rather than a psychological threat.

Fourth, it aligns daily work with strategic intent. Policy deployment ensures that when trade-offs are required, decisions reflect agreed priorities rather than local convenience.

These capabilities are not glamorous. They do not appear in marketing brochures. But under stress, they determine whether an organization fragments or coheres.

There is another important reason Lean matters more now. Technology has lowered the barrier to complexity. It is easier than ever to introduce new systems, automate tasks, integrate platforms, and generate reports. Every improvement initiative can add another layer of process, another dashboard, another interface. Over time, complexity accumulates quietly.

Lean acts as a counterbalance. It forces the question: Does this add value? Does this simplify or complicate the flow? Does this reduce cognitive load or increase it? In an era where digital tools can proliferate rapidly, that discipline becomes essential. Without Lean, digital transformation often produces sophisticated disorder. With Lean, digital tools can reinforce clarity.

The future will not reward organizations that accumulate the most technology. It will reward those that integrate technology into a coherent operating system. That integration requires a shift in how we define success.

For decades, operational excellence was measured by efficiency metrics under steady-state conditions. Today, we must also ask: How quickly can we reconfigure? How much margin do we lose during disruption? How long does recovery take? How accurately can we simulate impact before committing resources? How consistently do we communicate under pressure? These are not abstract questions. They determine survival.

The organizations that thrive in the coming decade will not necessarily be those with the largest automation budgets. They will be those with the clearest standards, the shortest learning cycles, and the most disciplined leadership routines. Lean provides the foundation for that clarity, and technology, applied intelligently, amplifies it.

From Efficiency to Adaptability

For a long time, operational excellence was treated as a steady-state problem. You designed a process, optimized it, eliminated waste, reduced cost, improved productivity, and then tried to keep everything stable. That model worked when markets were predictable and product portfolios changed slowly. That is not the world most leaders operate in today.

In a turnaround, the pressure is even sharper. You do not have the luxury of optimizing for one narrow plan and hoping reality cooperates. You are trying to stabilize performance while the ground is moving. Demand shifts, suppliers slip, and staffing changes. Product mix changes, customers change priorities, regulatory needs change, and corporate strategies change, sometimes all in the same quarter. This is where efficiency, by itself, becomes an incomplete goal. Efficiency matters, but it cannot be the only design target.

The more important question becomes: how well can your operation adapt without falling apart?

Adaptability is the ability to absorb change while preserving control. It is the ability to make adjustments quickly without introducing chaos, quality escapes, or uncontrolled cost. It is the difference between a system that bends and one that breaks.

When most people hear "adaptability," they think of improvisation. They picture leaders making quick decisions, teams working late, and the organization "being agile." In the short term, that may feel like adaptability, but it is usually just heroics. True adaptability is the opposite of heroics. It is *planned flexibility*.

It is built into the design of your processes, equipment choices, standard work, training strategy, meeting cadence, and decision rules. In other words, adaptability is engineered.

Adaptability Includes Flexibility

Flexibility is one element of adaptability, and many companies overlook it because it requires thinking ahead. When you design a new production line, for example, it is tempting to optimize it around today's highest-volume product. The line runs fast, cycle time is excellent, and everything looks efficient. Then the mix changes.

A new product grows faster than expected, a major customer shifts demand, a new product is introduced, a supplier disruption forces substitution, or a margin pressure pushes volume into a different SKU. Suddenly, the highly optimized line becomes a trap with painful changeovers. The team avoids switching because it costs too much time. Schedules become rigid, and the operation becomes fragile.

A turnaround leader cannot afford fragile.

If you learned anything from SMED, it is this: Changeover time is not just an inconvenience. It is a strategic constraint. When changeovers are long and difficult, the business is forced into larger batches, higher inventory, longer lead times, and slower reaction. When changeovers are short and repeatable, you can run smaller batches, adjust quickly, and serve a shifting mix without panic. So, when you build or redesign a line, you should not only ask, "How fast can this line run?" You should also ask, "How easily can this line change?"

Can it run a range of products with minimal adjustment? Can it handle different bottle sizes, label placements, pack configurations, or parameter settings without hours of downtime? Are the adjustments built into a defined, teachable changeover sequence, or do they live only in one technician's head?

Flexibility is what allows you to keep flow as the mix changes. Adaptability is what allows you to keep stability as the world changes.

A Clear Definition You Can Use

To make this practical, let us define adaptability in operational terms.

Adaptability is your organization's ability to do five things reliably:

1. Detect change early.
2. Understand its impact quickly.
3. Decide on a response with clear trade-offs.
4. Execute that response without destabilizing the system.
5. Learn and improve so the next response is faster and less costly.

That is a closed loop. It is not a motivational idea. It is a system requirement.

In a turnaround, you are not trying to become "adaptive" someday. You are trying to reduce the cost of disruption now, while performance is under pressure. That means you need a practical model you can implement step by step, even if the organization is not mature yet.

The Evolution to Full Adaptability

Most companies do not go from chaos to full adaptability in one leap. They evolve. The mistake leaders make is expecting the organization to behave like a mature Lean system before the foundations exist. When that happens, leaders conclude that "Lean doesn't work here," when the truth is that the system was never staged correctly. Adaptability evolves in stages. Each stage builds capability that enables the next.

Think of it like this: you earn adaptability by building stability, then visibility, then disciplined response, then flexibility, and finally predictive capability. You do not get to skip steps without paying for it later.

Below is a step-by-step model you can apply during a turnaround. It is written as an operating sequence, not as theory.

The Adaptability Model: A Step-by-Step Path You Can Implement

Step 1: Stabilize the Basics so Reality Becomes Visible

If everything is chaotic, nothing is measurable. If nothing is measurable, improvement becomes opinion. And if improvement becomes opinion, the organization will argue instead of learning.

The first step is stabilizing the work enough that you can see what is actually happening.

This means defining and reinforcing standard work in the areas that matter most. Not perfect standard work. Not a binder. Just clear, teachable methods for the critical processes that drive output, quality, and safety.

It also means defining what "abnormal" looks like. In unstable organizations, abnormal becomes normal. People stop noticing it. They survive it. They build workarounds around it. You want the opposite. You want abnormalities to stand out. Your objective at this stage is simple: make problems visible without blame. If you cannot stabilize, you cannot adapt. You can only react.

Step 2: Shorten the Feedback Loop so You Learn Faster Than the Disturbance

Adaptability is impossible with long feedback loops. If you discover defects two weeks later, your response will always be slow. If you discover schedule misses at the end of the month, your countermeasures will always lag. If you review supplier performance quarterly, you will always be late.

So, the second step is building a short learning cycle. This is where daily huddles, coaching, visual boards, and tier escalation routines become essential. Don't just see them as meetings; they are sensors. A daily tier meeting is how the organization detects drift while it is still small. It is how leaders see reality early enough to respond calmly.

At this stage, do not expand the system across the whole company. Build it where it matters most. Choose the value stream that is hurting you the most and install the rhythm there. Make it work, make it real, then expand. The objective of Step 2 is not motivation. It is speed of learning.

Step 3: Build Decision Rules and Trade-Off Logic so Responses Are Aligned

In a disruption, the biggest danger is usually not the disruption itself but the uncoordinated decisions. One department tries to protect utilization. Another tries to protect customer service. Another tries to protect cost. Another tries to protect quality. Everyone is acting rationally inside their silo, but the organization behaves irrationally as a system.

Adaptability requires shared trade-off logic. This is where policy deployment becomes a practical tool, not a strategy exercise. See Chapter 6 to learn more about policy deployment.

Leaders must define the priorities clearly enough that when disruption occurs, the response is consistent. If a supplier disruption happens, do you protect your highest-margin product first? Your strategic customer first? Your regulatory commitments first? Do you maintain service level for a few key accounts at the expense of others? These are hard decisions, but they are easier when you have agreed on the logic and priorities before pressure hits. Your objective at Step 3 is to prevent improvisation. You want the organization to respond predictably, even under stress.

Step 4: Engineer Flexibility into Flow

Once you have basic stability, fast feedback loops, and aligned decision rules, you can start building true flexibility. This is where adaptability becomes a design feature.

Flexibility comes from several sources. It comes from SMED and changeover discipline. It comes from equipment choices that reduce setup complexity. It comes from modular fixtures. It comes from quick-connect utilities. It comes from standard parameter sets. It comes from shared tooling strategies. It comes from designing lines to run families of products instead of one product.

Flexibility also comes from people. Cross-training is not a nice-to-have; it is a resilience strategy. In volatile environments, capacity is not only machines. Capacity is capability. At this stage, your work becomes more proactive. Instead of reacting to mix changes, you prepare for them. Instead of building rigid lines, you build adaptable lines.

Your objective at Step 4 is to reduce the time and cost of switching.

Step 5: Use Data and Technology to Detect Drift Early and Act Sooner

Only after the first four steps are functioning does technology begin to accelerate adaptability instead of complicating it. At that point the organization already understands its processes, has defined what normal looks like, and has routines for responding when something is abnormal. Technology then becomes a layer that strengthens those capabilities rather than replacing them.

Many companies invest in digital tools hoping they will provide answers automatically. In reality, the greatest value of technologies such as IoT sensors, vision systems, advanced analytics, and AI is not prediction in the abstract. Their real power lies in revealing small signals much earlier than human observation alone typically would.

Consider equipment reliability. In many operations, a machine seems to fail "suddenly." In truth, small warning signs often exist long before the failure occurs. A bearing may begin vibrating slightly differently. Motor temperatures may rise gradually. Electrical load may shift. Without continuous monitoring, those signals are easy to miss.

When sensors track these indicators continuously, patterns emerge. Over time, the system can recognize that a certain vibration profile often appears several days before a breakdown. Maintenance teams can then intervene earlier, during a controlled window, instead of reacting to an unexpected stoppage. The system did not predict the future in a magical way. It detected drift early enough to allow a planned response.

Vision systems create a similar advantage in quality control. A camera inspecting products may initially serve a simple purpose: identifying defects before they reach the customer. As data accumulates, however, patterns can appear. Perhaps defects increase slightly when a particular parameter shifts. Perhaps one supplier lot shows a different visual signature. With proper analysis, those patterns allow teams to investigate the source and correct the process sooner.

Environmental monitoring provides another example. Sensors measuring humidity, temperature, or particulate levels can reveal gradual movement toward an out-of-spec condition. Instead of discovering the problem hours later during a manual check, the system signals that the process is drifting. That earlier visibility allows the team to stabilize the situation before product quality is affected.

In each of these cases, the technology does not replace Lean thinking. It strengthens it. Lean defines what normal should look like and establishes how teams respond to abnormalities. The digital layer simply makes those abnormalities visible sooner and with greater precision.

This is why sequencing matters so much. If processes are unstable, sensors will generate constant alarms. If decision rules are unclear, teams will argue about what the data means. If the culture discourages transparency, signals will be ignored or hidden. Technology cannot solve those problems. In fact, it often amplifies them.

But when stability, clear standards, and disciplined routines are already in place, technology becomes a powerful extension of the system. Leaders can see trends earlier. Teams can analyze causes faster. Countermeasures can be tested sooner. Over time, the organization begins to anticipate issues instead of merely reacting to them.

Your objective at this stage is not simply to collect more data. It is to shorten the time between the first signal of change and the moment the organization takes intelligent action. That is what makes adaptability real.

Designing Flexibility into the System

Up to this point, we have discussed stability, visibility, and the ability to detect change early. Those capabilities allow an organization to respond intelligently, but there is another dimension of adaptability that must be engineered deliberately: flexibility. Flexibility determines how painful change will be.

Many operations appear efficient when everything goes according to plan. Equipment runs fast. Labor utilization looks high. Schedules are tightly packed. The system works well as long as demand, supply, and product mix remain exactly as expected. Then reality changes.

Unexpected changes, such as a customer shifting volume to a different product, a new SKU growing faster than expected, a supplier forcing a substitution, or a regulatory requirement introducing a modification, and suddenly the highly optimized process reveals a hidden weakness. It was efficient, but it was not flexible.

In a turnaround environment, that weakness becomes expensive very quickly. Long changeovers force larger batches. Larger batches increase inventory. Inventory hides problems and slows response. Lead times stretch. Customers become frustrated. Internally, the organization becomes reluctant to switch because each change disrupts the plan. This is why flexibility must be considered a *design objective*, not an afterthought.

One of the most practical lessons from SMED is that changeover time is not just an operational inconvenience. It is a strategic constraint. The longer it takes to switch a process, the more rigid the entire business becomes. Conversely, when changeovers are fast and repeatable, the organization gains the ability to adapt its mix without destabilizing flow. This principle applies not only to machines but to the entire system.

When designing or redesigning a production line, leaders should ask a broader set of questions than simply how fast the line can run a single product. Can the line run a family of products with minimal adjustment? Are tooling changes simple and visible? Are settings standardized and documented? Are utilities designed with quick connections? Can operators perform adjustments without waiting for a specialist every time?

A line that runs slightly slower but changes quickly is often far more valuable to the business than a line that runs extremely fast but resists change. Flexibility also exists in people, not just equipment.

Organizations that rely on narrow specialization become fragile under pressure. If one person is absent or reassigned, capacity disappears. Work slows not because the machines are unavailable but because the knowledge is concentrated.

Cross-training spreads capability across the team. When done thoughtfully, it increases resilience without sacrificing quality. Operators begin to understand the upstream and downstream effects of their work. Scheduling becomes easier. Temporary disruptions are absorbed more naturally.

One of the most practical ways to manage cross-training is through a **skills matrix**. A skills matrix is simply a visual map of who on the team can perform each critical task and at what level of proficiency. At first glance, it looks almost too simple to matter, but it quickly reveals the hidden fragility in many operations.

When leaders see the matrix for the first time, patterns often appear immediately. Some processes are supported by only one experienced person. Others depend heavily on a small group, while the rest of the team has little exposure. Training priorities that once felt abstract suddenly become clear. Instead of saying, "We should cross-train more," the team can see exactly where capability gaps exist.

In a stable environment, those gaps may not cause daily problems. During disruption, however, they become constraints. If demand shifts to a different product line, if someone is absent, or if a new process must ramp up quickly, the organization's ability to respond depends on how broadly those skills are distributed.

A well-maintained skills matrix allows leaders to strengthen the system deliberately. Training can be scheduled with a clear objective rather than assigned randomly. Progress becomes visible as more people gain proficiency in critical tasks. Over time, flexibility increases not because the organization is working harder, but because knowledge is no longer concentrated in a few individuals.

At the end of this book, in the Templates section, you will find a simple skills matrix template that you can use with your own team. The goal is not to create a complicated training database. It is to make capability visible, identify the most important gaps, and build a practical plan to close them. Like many Lean tools, its power lies in clarity rather than complexity.

During a disruption, cross-trained teams can shift to where they are needed most instead of waiting for perfect conditions.

Flexibility also applies to planning systems. When schedules are constructed in ways that assume nothing will change, every deviation becomes a crisis. When planning incorporates realistic buffers, clear priorities, and well-understood changeover capabilities, adjustments become manageable.

The goal is not to create unlimited flexibility. That would be inefficient. The goal is to design enough flexibility that the system can respond to predictable forms of change without collapsing.

One way to think about this is to ask a simple question during system design: "If our product mix shifted significantly next quarter, how difficult would it be for this operation to respond?"

If the honest answer is "very difficult," the system may be efficient today but vulnerable tomorrow.

Adaptability is not built in the moment of disruption. It is built months or years earlier, when leaders choose how processes, equipment, skills, and information flows are structured. Organizations that recognize this early have a major advantage. Instead of constantly reacting to change, they gradually reduce the cost of responding to it. That is one of the quiet strengths of a mature Lean system.

Step 6: Institutionalize Learning so the Next Disruption Costs Less

This last step is where adaptability becomes durable. After every major disruption, most organizations move on quickly. They do not want to relive it. They do not want to assign blame. They do not want to revisit painful weeks. Mature organizations do the opposite. They learn deliberately.

Mature organizations conduct structured reflection. They document lessons, update standard work, improve escalation rules, adjust buffers, revise supplier strategies, and strengthen cross-training. They turn disruption into capability. The goal is not to avoid disruption. The goal is to reduce its cost the next time.

That is what a resilient operating system does.

A Practical Staging Tool: The Adaptability Ladder

If you want a simple way to assess where you are, use this ladder. You do not need to be at the top to succeed. But you need to know where you are and what the next step is.

You can place your organization on one of these levels:

- Level 1: Reactive and fragmented
- Level 2: Stable enough to see problems
- Level 3: Short feedback loops and escalation
- Level 4: Aligned decisions and trade-off logic
- Level 5: Engineered flexibility in flow
- Level 6: Predictive capability and institutional learning

A turnaround leader's job is to move the organization up the ladder, not by slogans but by installing the system, step by step.

At this point many leaders focus their attention on improving the processes that already exist inside the factory. That work is important, and it often produces meaningful gains. But there is another lever that is frequently overlooked because it sits upstream from day-to-day operations.

Some of the biggest improvements in stability, flexibility, and cost do not come from refining how a product is built. They come from reconsidering how the product itself is designed. When design decisions support manufacturing instead of complicating it, the entire operating system becomes easier to manage.

Designing Products for Manufacturability

Another important dimension of adaptability sits upstream from the factory floor. Many operational difficulties are not created in manufacturing at all. They originate in product design.

When engineers develop products without considering how those products will be built, the consequences appear later in the form of excessive part counts, complicated assemblies, fragile processes, long changeovers, and inventory that grows quietly in the background. None of those outcomes are intentional, yet they are remarkably common.

Designing for manufacturability is the discipline of preventing those problems before they appear.

At its core, the concept is straightforward. Products should be designed so they are easy to build correctly, easy to build consistently, and easy to adapt as demand changes. When that philosophy guides development, the entire operating system becomes simpler.

One of the most powerful ways to achieve this is through thoughtful part commonality. When different products share components wherever possible, the number of unique parts decreases. Fewer unique parts means fewer suppliers to manage, fewer changeovers, simpler planning, and lower inventory exposure. It also reduces the likelihood that a disruption in one small component will halt multiple product lines simultaneously.

Many organizations accumulate SKUs over time without questioning whether those differences truly add value. Designers may make small variations to solve a short-term issue, and those variations remain in the system for years. Eventually, the factory is supporting dozens of slightly different parts that could have been standardized.

Leaders who encourage product families built around shared components create a much more resilient supply chain and a far more manageable operation.

Design simplicity is equally important. A well-designed product should guide the assembler toward the correct outcome almost naturally. Components should fit together in only one orientation when possible. Fasteners should be minimized. Adjustments should be limited. The sequence of assembly should be logical and visible.

This is where the concept of poka-yoke becomes powerful at the design stage rather than only on the shop floor. When error-proofing is built into the product itself, the manufacturing process becomes more reliable before any fixtures or sensors are introduced. Products that are easy to assemble require less labor effort, less training time, and fewer workarounds. They are also easier to automate later if volumes justify it.

Another advantage often overlooked is the effect on adaptability. When products share components, assemblies are simple, and error-proofing is inherent in the design, production lines can switch between variants with far less disruption. New products can be introduced faster. Capacity can be rebalanced more easily. In other words, good product design increases operational flexibility long before the first unit is built.

This is why strong organizations encourage close collaboration between engineering, manufacturing, quality, and supply chain during development. Manufacturing teams bring practical knowledge about what creates friction in the real world. Engineers bring creativity and technical expertise. When those perspectives combine early, the result is a product that performs well in the market and behaves well in production.

During a turnaround, this collaboration is especially valuable. Simplifying product structures, reducing unnecessary variation, and introducing built-in error proofing can remove significant complexity from the system. The impact often exceeds what can be achieved through process improvements alone. In many cases, the easiest process to improve is the one that was designed well in the first place.

As organizations begin to simplify their processes and product designs, another question naturally appears: how do modern technologies fit into this picture? Artificial intelligence, connected equipment, automated inspection, advanced analytics, and digital planning tools are now part of everyday conversations about the future of manufacturing. Some leaders see these developments as a replacement for traditional operational disciplines. Others are unsure how they fit into the systems they have spent years building.

The reality is simpler. Technology does not replace Lean. It extends it. To understand how, we need to separate what should remain constant from what can evolve.

Lean and the Digital Layer: What Changes, What Does Not

As conversations about the future of operations unfold, technology inevitably enters the discussion. Artificial intelligence, connected equipment, predictive analytics, advanced automation, and digital twins are transforming how companies gather information and make decisions. Many organizations now speak of Industry 4.0 or smart manufacturing as if a new operating model has replaced the old one. It has not.

What has changed is the power of the tools available to support a well-designed system. The underlying principles of good operations management remain remarkably consistent. Work still needs to be clearly defined. Problems still need to be visible. Decisions still need to be made close to reality. Teams still need a structured way to escalate issues and learn from them. Leaders still need to spend time where value is created rather than relying exclusively on reports. Technology does not remove these requirements. In many ways, it makes them more important.

When organizations adopt advanced tools without a stable operating system, the result is often confusion disguised as sophistication. Dashboards multiply, alerts fire continuously, and large volumes of data circulate through the company without improving the quality of decisions. Teams begin to spend more time explaining numbers than solving problems. Leaders are pulled further away from the gemba because they believe the system is "visible" through screens, even when the reality on the floor remains unclear. Lean acts as the stabilizing framework that prevents this outcome.

In a Lean environment, technology has a clear role. It strengthens visibility, shortens feedback loops, and supports better decisions. Instead of overwhelming people with information, it amplifies signals that the organization has already agreed are important. To understand this relationship, it helps to separate what should never change from what can evolve.

Certain elements of effective operations are timeless. Processes must be understandable, standards must exist and be followed, abnormal conditions must be easy to recognize, people must know how to respond when something goes wrong, and leaders must coach and remove barriers rather than simply monitor results. These behaviors formed the backbone of operational excellence long before modern analytics existed, and they remain essential today.

What technology changes is the **speed and depth** at which these principles can operate. Sensors can reveal equipment conditions earlier than human observation alone. Analytical tools can highlight patterns in quality data that would be difficult to detect manually. Simulation models can test different planning scenarios before the organization commits resources. Automated verification systems can catch defects at the moment they occur rather than at the end of the line. Used properly, these tools do not replace Lean thinking. They accelerate it.

A useful way to think about the relationship is this: Lean defines the questions, and technology helps answer them faster. If your system already asks, "Is this process drifting from standard?" sensors and analytics can surface the answer quickly. If your planning process already examines trade-offs between capacity and demand, simulation tools can evaluate those trade-offs with more precision. If your teams already investigate root causes carefully, data analysis can reveal patterns that strengthen the investigation. But if those questions are not part of the system, technology cannot invent them.

This is why sequencing matters so much during a transformation. Organizations are often tempted to introduce advanced tools early, believing that technology will force discipline. In reality, the opposite tends to happen. Without clear processes and decision rules, digital systems amplify inconsistency. Teams interpret the same data differently. Leaders request additional reports to resolve disagreements. Complexity increases rather than decreases.

When Lean foundations are in place first, technology becomes far more powerful. The organization knows what matters, how work should flow, and how problems should be addressed. Digital tools then provide earlier signals, richer insights, and faster response capability.

Another important shift occurs when technology is integrated correctly: leaders spend less time chasing information and more time improving systems. Instead of asking people to assemble reports, they can focus on understanding causes. Instead of reacting to surprises at the end of the month, they can intervene earlier. Instead of debating whose numbers are correct, they can concentrate on what action is required. In this way, the digital layer does not change the purpose of leadership. It strengthens the leader's ability to fulfill it.

For organizations working through a turnaround, this perspective is particularly important. Technology investments can be attractive during difficult periods because they promise rapid improvement. But technology applied to unstable processes often produces expensive disappointment. Stabilizing the operating system first ensures that any digital tools introduced later will accelerate progress rather than complicate recovery.

As we look at specific technologies in the following sections, keep this relationship in mind. The goal is not to replace Lean with digital tools. It's to extend Lean's reach. When the two work together, the organization gains something powerful: the ability to see problems earlier, understand them faster, and respond with greater confidence. That, ultimately, is what adaptability requires.

AI, Simulation, and Data-Driven Decision Making

One of the most promising developments in modern operations is the ability to evaluate complex situations much faster than in the past. For many years, leaders relied primarily on experience, spreadsheets, and a limited set of reports when deciding how to respond to changes in demand, supply, or capacity. Those tools are still valuable, but the scale of data now available allows organizations to see patterns and evaluate options with far greater clarity.

Artificial intelligence and advanced analytics are especially powerful in this area. Their role is not to replace leadership judgment or operational expertise. It's to help process large amounts of information quickly and highlight relationships that might otherwise remain hidden.

In practical terms, this means organizations can move beyond simply reporting what happened yesterday. They can begin exploring what is likely to happen next and what different choices might produce.

Consider the supplier disruption example earlier in this chapter. When a critical component becomes unavailable, leaders immediately face a series of difficult questions: Which customers should receive the limited supply that remains? Should production prioritize high-margin products or long-term relationships? How will different allocation decisions affect inventory, lead times, and future demand?

In the past, answering these questions required significant manual analysis. Teams would build several spreadsheets, estimate outcomes, and debate assumptions. Valuable time was often lost while the organization tried to understand the implications of each option.

Modern analytical tools can dramatically accelerate this process. By combining historical data, current orders, capacity information, and supplier constraints, simulation models can quickly evaluate multiple scenarios. Leaders can explore the consequences of different decisions before committing to them. Instead of arguing about what might happen, the team can examine likely outcomes and choose a path with greater confidence.

This ability to run "what if" scenarios is particularly valuable in volatile environments. Demand shifts, supply disruptions, and capacity changes rarely occur in isolation. Each decision affects multiple parts of the system. Simulation allows leaders to see those connections more clearly.

Another powerful use of advanced analytics is identifying patterns that human observation might miss. Quality data, machine performance records, supplier variability, and customer demand signals all contain insights that are difficult to detect manually when volumes become large. Analytical tools can scan those data sets quickly, highlighting correlations or anomalies that deserve attention.

This does not eliminate the need for investigation. In fact, it often strengthens it. Instead of spending time searching for a problem, teams can focus their energy on understanding causes and implementing countermeasures.

It is important, however, to approach these capabilities with the same discipline applied to Lean tools. Data alone does not improve performance. The organization must still ask the right questions, verify conditions at the gemba, and test solutions carefully. When analytics are treated as a shortcut to thinking, they often create confusion instead of clarity. But when they are integrated into a strong operating system, they extend the organization's ability to learn.

Leaders gain faster insight into emerging risks. Teams can evaluate improvement ideas more effectively. Planning becomes less reactive and more deliberate. Over time the company develops a deeper understanding of how its system actually behaves.

This is where the combination of Lean thinking and modern analytics becomes especially powerful. Lean provides the structure for identifying problems and improving processes. Advanced analytics accelerates the feedback loop. Together, they help the organization make better decisions sooner.

Real-Time Operations: IoT, Vision Systems, and Immediate Feedback

For most of industrial history, managers learned about problems after the fact. A quality report arrived at the end of the shift. A machine failure appeared in yesterday's maintenance log. Production numbers were reviewed the following morning. By the time leaders understood what had happened, the opportunity to prevent it had already passed. Lean changed that by emphasizing visual management, standard work, and rapid escalation. Problems were no longer hidden in reports. They became visible in the process.

Today, modern sensing technologies extend that principle even further. Connected equipment, often referred to as the **Internet of Things**, or **IoT**, allows machines to communicate their condition continuously. Sensors track vibration, temperature, cycle times, energy usage, and other indicators that reveal how a process is behaving. Instead of waiting for a breakdown, the system can signal that performance is drifting away from normal.

The goal is not to replace human observation but to strengthen it. Operators and technicians still understand the process best. Sensors simply help ensure that small signals are not missed when production becomes busy.

Vision systems are another powerful extension of this idea. Cameras trained to recognize correct and incorrect conditions can instantly verify assemblies, labels, fill levels, or packaging details. In the past, many of these checks relied on sampling or manual inspection. With modern systems, verification can occur on every unit without slowing the process. This does not mean defects disappear. What changes is the timing of discovery.

When problems are detected immediately, the organization can react while the situation is still small, such as a tool that may need adjustment, a supplier lot that may require inspection, or a training gap that may have become visible. Instead of discovering hundreds of defects later, the team stops, understands the cause, and stabilizes the process. That shift alone can dramatically reduce waste.

Real-time visibility also changes the role of leadership. Instead of spending hours compiling status reports, leaders can focus on understanding abnormalities and improving systems. Conversations become grounded in what is actually happening rather than what someone believes might be happening. However, just as with analytics, these tools must be introduced carefully.

If processes are poorly defined, sensors will produce constant alarms. If standards are unclear, teams will debate whether a signal matters. If leadership reacts punitively, people will find ways to silence the system. **Technology does not create discipline. It amplifies whatever discipline already exists**.

When Lean foundations are present, the effect can be remarkable. Abnormal conditions surface quickly. Teams respond with practiced routines. Data collected over time reveals opportunities for deeper improvement. The factory becomes not only more visible but also more understandable. In that environment, technology stops being a novelty and becomes part of the operating system. The result is an organization that learns faster because it sees reality sooner.

Automation That Strengthens the System

By the time organizations reach this point in their journey, the question of automation inevitably surfaces. Advances in robotics, machine vision, and intelligent equipment have made automation more accessible than ever before. Vendors promise speed, consistency, and lower labor costs. For leaders under pressure to improve performance, the appeal is obvious. But automation is often misunderstood.

Earlier in this book, we discussed the danger of automating unstable processes. When waste is built into a system, machines simply produce that waste faster. That lesson still holds, but once a process is stable and well understood, automation can play an important and valuable role.

The purpose of automation in a Lean system is not to replace people indiscriminately. It's to strengthen flow, reduce variation, and free human capability for higher-value problem-solving.

Some tasks are naturally suited for automation. Repetitive motions that add little cognitive value, heavy or unsafe operations, and extremely high-volume processes can often be performed more consistently by machines. When automation is applied in those areas, it can improve quality and protect employees from unnecessary strain.

However, the most successful automation efforts usually share another characteristic: they support a process that already works well manually.

When a team has built a stable process by hand, they understand the sequence, risks, and critical variables. They know where mistakes occur and how the product behaves in reality. That knowledge becomes invaluable when designing automation. Instead of guessing what the machine should do, the organization already understands what good looks like.

In contrast, companies that automate too early often discover that the machine has simply locked in the complexity that existed before. Adjustments become difficult. Small product changes require expensive engineering work. The system becomes rigid just when the market demands flexibility.

Lean organizations approach automation with a slightly different mindset. Rather than asking, "How quickly can we automate this?" they ask, "What problem are we solving, and is automation the best solution?"

Sometimes, the answer is yes. A vision system might eliminate a recurring inspection issue. A collaborative robot might stabilize a precise assembly step. An automated material handling system might improve flow in a high-volume environment. Other times, the answer is surprisingly simple. A better fixture, a clearer standard, or a small process change may solve the problem at a fraction of the cost.

Automation should therefore be treated as one tool among many, not as the default destination. When used thoughtfully, it can elevate an already-strong system. When used prematurely, it often introduces new layers of complexity.

Another important consideration is adaptability. Highly specialized automation can deliver impressive efficiency under stable conditions, but it may struggle when product mix changes or volumes fluctuate. Flexible automation, modular equipment, and configurable tooling often provide better long-term value, even if the initial cycle time is slightly slower.

In a world where change is constant, the ability to adjust may matter more than the ability to run at maximum speed. Ultimately, the goal is not to build the most automated factory. It's to build the most capable one.

Automation earns its place when it improves safety, stability, quality, or flow without sacrificing the organization's ability to adapt. When those conditions are met, machines and people form a powerful partnership.

Lean and Six Sigma: Speed and Precision Working Together

As organizations modernize their operations, another familiar question often returns: is Lean still relevant in a world where Six Sigma, advanced analytics, and data science are becoming more prominent? The honest answer is that the two approaches were never meant to compete.

Lean and Six Sigma solve different types of problems. When used together, they strengthen the operating system far more than either one can alone.

Lean focuses primarily on flow. It asks how work moves through a system, where delays occur, and how unnecessary complexity can be removed. Its goal is to make problems visible quickly and improve the speed and stability of processes.

Six Sigma approaches problems from a different angle. It concentrates on variation. Instead of asking only how fast work moves, it asks how consistently a process produces the desired result. Statistical tools help teams understand patterns, identify root causes, and confirm that improvements truly solve the issue.

In practical terms, Lean helps organizations move faster, while Six Sigma helps them move with greater precision. Many companies unknowingly need both.

Imagine a production line that struggles to meet customer demand because changeovers are long and scheduling is rigid. Lean tools such as value stream mapping, SMED, and visual management can dramatically improve flow and reduce waiting. But once the process moves more smoothly, another issue may appear. The product still fails quality checks intermittently.

That is where Six Sigma thinking becomes valuable. Statistical analysis can reveal subtle sources of variation that were difficult to see before the process was stabilized. Teams can test hypotheses, validate improvements, and confirm that results hold over time.

The sequence matters. When processes are chaotic, statistical analysis becomes difficult because the noise overwhelms the signal. Lean's focus on stability and visibility creates the conditions where deeper analytical tools can be effective. In many ways, Lean prepares the ground, and Six Sigma refines the result.

Modern technology strengthens this partnership. The same sensors, data platforms, and analytical tools discussed earlier in this chapter provide richer information for both approaches. Lean benefits from faster feedback loops, while Six Sigma gains access to larger and more detailed data sets. This combination allows organizations to move quickly while maintaining confidence in their results.

However, the goal should never be to create separate improvement empires inside the company. When Lean teams and Six Sigma specialists operate in isolation, confusion often follows. Projects compete for attention, terminology becomes fragmented, and employees struggle to understand which system matters most.

Strong organizations integrate the principles into one coherent approach. Leaders focus on improving flow, reducing variation, and solving problems methodically. Teams use whichever tools help achieve those outcomes.

In a turnaround situation, this integration becomes especially valuable. Lean methods can quickly expose bottlenecks, eliminate obvious waste, and restore momentum. Once the system stabilizes, Six Sigma tools can help address deeper technical issues that affect yield, reliability, or compliance. Together, they create a balanced improvement capability. Lean ensures the organization moves forward. Six Sigma ensures it moves in the right direction.

As the pace of technological change accelerates, this balance becomes even more important. Companies that combine operational simplicity with analytical rigor are far better equipped to adapt without losing control of quality or cost.

In the end, the future of operational excellence will not belong to one methodology. It will belong to organizations that understand how to combine them intelligently.

Improving When Things Are Going Well

One of the unintended consequences of writing a book about fixing troubled operations is that it can create the impression that improvement begins when things start going wrong. Many of the examples in this book come from difficult situations. Plants losing money, systems breaking down, customers escalating, and leadership under pressure are some of the examples we brought up. Those situations are real, and they reveal weaknesses quickly, but the best leaders do not wait for crises.

Visionary managers understand that the most effective time to improve a system is often when the system is already working reasonably well. When a business is stable, people have the mental space to think clearly. Resources are available, and decisions can be made deliberately instead of defensively. Changes can be tested without the stress of an immediate financial threat.

In a crisis, improvement becomes urgent, but the environment is rarely ideal. Teams are tired, emotions run high, short-term survival competes with long-term design, and leaders are forced to fix problems while the system is still moving.

During good times, the opposite is true. You can step back and redesign with intention.

You can reduce changeover times before product mix shifts dramatically. You can simplify workflows before complexity accumulates. You can standardize processes before tribal knowledge spreads too far. You can build cross-training before staffing becomes tight. You can strengthen supplier relationships before a disruption forces the conversation. Most importantly, you can remove cost from the system while margins are still healthy. That matters more than many leaders realize.

When organizations become more efficient during periods of growth, they are not simply increasing profitability in the moment. They are building shock absorbers. Lower structural costs, faster changeovers, clearer processes, and stronger teams create room to maneuver when the inevitable disruption arrives.

And disruption always arrives.

Markets shift. Technology changes. Supply chains tighten. Regulations evolve. Competitors innovate. Even well-run companies encounter moments where yesterday's assumptions stop working.

Organizations that waited until that moment to improve will find themselves trying to redesign the airplane while flying through turbulence. Organizations that improved during the good years face the same turbulence with a much stronger aircraft.

This is one of the reasons Lean organizations tend to age well. Continuous improvement is not activated only during emergencies. It becomes the normal way of working. Small improvements accumulate quietly. Waste disappears gradually. Skills deepen over time. When pressure arrives, the organization already knows how to respond.

A crisis can reveal the need for Lean. But stability is often the best time to build it.

Looking Forward Without Losing the Fundamentals

Every few years, a new wave of terminology appears in the world of operations. Smart factories. Digital transformation. Industry 4.0. Artificial intelligence. Predictive systems. Autonomous supply chains. The language evolves quickly, and the technologies behind it continue to advance.

Yet, when you walk into organizations that consistently perform well, the foundations often look familiar. People understand the process they are responsible for, problems are visible, standards exist and are followed, leaders spend time where value is created, teams know how to surface issues and solve them methodically, and improvements are made steadily rather than in occasional bursts of enthusiasm. In other words, *the fundamentals still matter*.

Technology will continue to change how information is gathered and how decisions are supported. Machines will become more capable, data will become richer, and some tasks that once required significant human effort will be automated or assisted by intelligent systems. But none of these developments eliminate the need for clarity, discipline, and learning inside an organization.

If anything, they make those qualities more important. The more tools are available to a company, the more important it becomes to understand what problem those tools are meant to solve.

Lean, when understood properly, is not a collection of techniques frozen in time. It is a way of thinking about systems, people, and improvement. That mindset adapts naturally as new technologies appear because it focuses on principles rather than trends.

Organizations that build this capability do not chase every new idea; they evaluate it. They test it, and they integrate what strengthens their system and discard what does not.

The future of operations will certainly look different from the past. Factories will be more connected. Decisions will be informed by deeper data. Automation will handle tasks that once required intense manual effort.

But the organizations that thrive will not be the ones with the most impressive technology. They will be the ones that understand their systems best and improve them continuously.

And that, ultimately, is what this book has been about.

Reflection and Action

This final chapter looks toward the future, but the goal of this book has always been practical: helping leaders stabilize, improve, and transform real organizations. The ideas discussed here become meaningful only when they influence how you think and act inside your own operation.

Use the questions below as a way to translate these concepts into a starting point for your next steps.

1. How adaptable is your operation today?

If demand changed significantly next quarter, how easily could your system respond?

Consider:

- Changeover times
- Cross-training across teams
- Supplier flexibility
- Product design complexity
- Scheduling rigidity

Where would the system struggle first?

2. Are your processes designed for stability or only for efficiency?

Many operations optimize for speed under ideal conditions. Reflect on whether your processes remain stable when reality becomes messy.

Ask yourself:

- Are abnormalities visible quickly?
- Do teams know how to escalate problems?
- Are decision rules clear during disruptions?
- Can leaders understand what is happening without waiting for reports?

3. Where could better design eliminate future problems?

Think beyond the factory floor.

- Are product designs creating unnecessary complexity?
- Are too many unique parts being introduced?
- Could assemblies be simplified or error-proofed?
- Are engineering and manufacturing collaborating early enough?

Sometimes, the most powerful improvement is preventing the problem from existing.

4. Is technology strengthening your system or distracting from it?

Evaluate the tools currently in place.

- Do your dashboards help teams act or only observe?
- Are sensors highlighting real issues or generating noise?
- Are analytics supporting decisions or creating debates?
- Are new tools integrated into daily routines?

Technology should shorten the time between signal and action.

5. Are you improving only when pressure forces it?

Reflect honestly on the rhythm of improvement inside your organization.

- Do major changes occur only during crises?
- Are teams encouraged to improve when things are stable?
- Are leaders allocating time for system design, not just firefighting?

The strongest organizations build capability before they need it.

6. What is one constraint you could reduce in the next ninety days?

Large transformations often begin with a small, focused improvement.

Identify a constraint that, if improved, would increase flexibility or stability. It might be:

- A long changeover
- A fragile supplier dependency

- A training gap
- A product design complication
- An unclear process

Start there.

Progress builds momentum.

Final Thoughts

Turning around a struggling operation is challenging work. Building an organization that continues to improve long after the crisis has passed is even more demanding.

But the path is rarely mysterious.

Make problems visible.
Simplify processes.
Develop people.
Design systems thoughtfully.
Improve continuously.

Do this consistently, and the results compound over time. That is the real power of Lean.

If there is one idea I hope stays with you after reading this chapter, it is this: strong operations are not built by reacting faster than everyone else. They are built by designing systems that make the right actions easier to take in the first place.

Technology will evolve, and markets will shift. New tools will appear, and new terminology will replace the language we use today. But organizations that understand their processes, develop their people, and improve steadily will continue to adapt no matter how the environment changes.

The future will always favor companies that learn faster than their problems grow.

Lean, at its heart, is simply a structured way to make learning part of everyday work.

In the next and final chapter, we will step back from the individual tools and ideas discussed throughout this book and look at how they fit together into a complete turnaround journey.

Chapter 12 Reflection and Action Answers

CONCLUSION

Bringing It All Together

1. Why So Many Transformations Fail

Over the years, I have walked into many companies trying to improve their operations. Such companies usually have good intentions. The leadership team knows something has to change. Costs are too high, lead times are too long, quality problems keep coming back, or customers are beginning to lose patience. The decision is made to "do Lean," launch a transformation, or bring in new methods that promise better performance.

For a short period, the organization feels energized. Workshops are scheduled, and training sessions take place. New terminology enters everyday conversations, and people start talking about waste, flow, root causes, and continuous improvement. There is movement, and for a moment, it looks like the company has finally turned a corner.

But after the initial enthusiasm fades, many of these efforts stall.

Daily pressures return and start pushing improvement work to the side. Production targets dominate the agenda again. Managers spend most of their time in meetings or reacting to problems instead of preventing them. Teams that were excited during the early workshops slowly return to the habits they know best. The language of improvement remains, but the behavior beneath it starts to look very familiar.

In many cases, the problem is not resistance or lack of intelligence. It's that the transformation never becomes the way the business actually runs. It remains something extra. Something added on top of the real work instead of shaping how the work is done.

When that happens, complexity quietly returns.

Processes that were simplified begin to accumulate exceptions. Visual boards stop reflecting reality. Standard work becomes outdated but continues to hang on the wall. Metrics are still reported, yet fewer people truly believe them. Problems are discussed repeatedly, but the system that created them remains unchanged.

Eventually, the improvement effort fades into the background, becoming another initiative the company once tried. People remember parts of it, maybe even some useful tools, but the organization itself has not fundamentally changed.

This pattern is incredibly common. It explains why so many leaders become skeptical of operational transformations. Many of them have already seen programs come and go. Each one started with optimism. Few actually changed how the business performed over the long term.

The organizations that succeed approach things differently.

They do not treat improvement as a program that runs alongside the business. They build a way of operating where problems are expected, processes are continuously refined, and leaders stay connected to the work itself. Over time, improvement stops being an event and becomes part of everyday management.

That shift is what turns a struggling operation into a continuously improving one. And it is the journey this book has been preparing you to lead.

2. The Real Turnaround Sequence

When people look at successful operational transformations from the outside, they often assume the improvements came from a collection of tools. Someone introduced Lean. A few kaizen events were run. Visual boards appeared on the walls. New metrics were introduced. From a distance, it can look like progress happened because the organization applied the right techniques. People see the tools in place and assume that those tools alone are what's required to fix a business.

In reality, companies that truly change their performance tend to follow a much more predictable path. The steps are not always labeled the same way, and the pace can vary, but the sequence shows up again and again. It usually begins with something simple but uncomfortable. Someone decides to face reality.

Leaders go to the floor and look carefully at how the work is actually being done. They follow the product, listen to operators, and ask questions that have not been asked in a long time. At this stage, involving the people doing the work is essential. They often understand the problems better than anyone else, and when they see leaders paying attention, the tone of the organization begins to shift. Once reality is clear, the next step becomes obvious: **the system needs to be simplified**.

Most struggling operations are not failing because people are careless or unmotivated. They are struggling because the process itself has become unnecessarily complicated. Too many handoffs, too many exceptions, too many layers of workarounds built over the years. Simplifying the system removes barriers that make good performance difficult in the first place. After simplification comes stabilization.

At this stage, the goal is not dramatic improvement. It's consistency. Processes are defined clearly, responsibilities become easier to understand, and standard work begins to take shape. When an organization can produce the same result repeatedly, it finally has a reliable starting point for improvement.

Once stability improves, problems begin to stand out in ways they never did before. This is where visibility becomes powerful.

Simple visual controls, clear metrics, and regular reviews allow teams to see issues while the work is happening instead of weeks later in a report. Rather than arguing about opinions, people can focus on what the process is actually telling them. Only then does the organization fully unlock the potential of its people.

Employees have been involved from the beginning, but now they are working within a system that makes improvement possible. Problems are visible, processes are understandable, experiments can be tested without creating chaos, and operators, supervisors, engineers, and managers start solving issues together and building confidence in their ability to improve the operation.

From that point forward, continuous improvement stops being an event and starts becoming a habit.

Small changes accumulate. Teams begin fixing issues before they grow into major disruptions. Ideas come from the people closest to the work instead of being pushed from conference rooms. Over time, the organization develops the capability to solve harder and more complex problems.

Eventually, the improvements spread. What started in one area moves into others. The company develops a shared way of operating, and the gains reinforce one another.

Looking back, the journey may appear impressive. While living through it, it rarely feels dramatic. It is simply a series of practical steps, taken in the right order, with people engaged throughout the process.

That is the real turnaround sequence. And if you have read this far in the book, you already have the map.

3. What Leaders Must Do Differently

By the time an organization decides it needs a real operational turnaround, the problems are rarely a mystery. The costs are too high, lead times are unpredictable, quality issues keep returning, customers are starting to notice, and inside the company, people feel the pressure every day. Usually, there is a combination of factors, and they lead to morale issues. Eventually, the best people start to leave, the workload increases on those remaining, morale sinks lower, and then more people leave. This is the "death spiral."

What is often missing is not intelligence or effort. What is missing is a different kind of leadership behavior.

Many organizations try to improve operations without changing how leaders operate. The same meetings continue, the same reports circulate, the same distance remains between decision makers and the actual work. All they do is create a new slogan, followed by some posters and slide presentations. No real changes. When that happens, even the best improvement tools struggle to gain traction.

Real transformations begin when *leaders start behaving differently*.

One of the most important shifts is returning to the place where the work happens. Processes do not improve from conference rooms. They improve when leaders regularly go see the work, understand how it flows, and talk to the people responsible for it. This does not mean occasional tours or symbolic visits. It means developing a habit of staying connected to reality.

When leaders spend time at the gemba, several things start to change. Problems that once sounded abstract become specific. Small frustrations that slow people down become visible. Opportunities for simplification reveal themselves in ways that reports never show. Just as important, employees notice the attention. They realize the work they do every day actually matters to the people running the company.

Another change involves *the kinds of questions leaders ask.*

In struggling organizations, managers often feel pressure to provide answers quickly. When something goes wrong, the instinct is to jump in, give direction, and move on to the next issue. While this may solve a few short-term problems, it does very little to strengthen the organization.

Leaders who build strong operations spend more time asking thoughtful questions: What is the process supposed to be? What actually happened? What do the facts show? What is preventing the team from solving this permanently? These questions slow the conversation just enough to move people away from blame and toward understanding.

A third shift may be the most uncomfortable of all. Leaders must become willing to *let problems be seen.*

In many companies, issues are hidden because people fear the reaction they might trigger. Numbers are softened. Explanations are offered quickly. The goal becomes avoiding attention rather than improving performance. Over time, this creates an organization where leaders receive a filtered version of reality.

Turning this around requires a clear signal from leadership: problems are not something to hide; they are something to learn from. When teams see that issues can be raised without punishment, the flow of information improves dramatically. The organization becomes faster and smarter simply because it is no longer protecting itself from the truth.

Finally, leaders must *focus on building systems* instead of relying on individual heroics.

Most struggling operations have a few talented people who somehow keep things moving. They stay late, solve crises, and carry knowledge that the rest of the organization does not have. While their dedication is admirable, it is not a sustainable way to run a business.

Strong operations depend on clear processes, shared understanding, and consistent management routines. When the system works, performance does not depend on who happens to be present that day. The organization becomes more stable, and improvement becomes easier to sustain.

None of these leadership shifts require dramatic speeches or complicated programs. They require consistency. Leaders show up where the work happens. They ask better questions. They make it safe to surface problems. And they invest their time building processes that help people succeed.

When those behaviors become normal, the rest of the transformation accelerates.

4. What the First Ninety Days Should Look Like

A typical error leaders make when starting an operational transformation is trying to fix everything at once. The list of problems is long, the pressure is high, and the instinct is to launch multiple initiatives immediately. New metrics, new meetings, new projects, new expectations. Everyone becomes busy very quickly. Unfortunately, this approach usually creates more confusion than progress, and very quickly people will be asking for more resources you probably cannot afford.

When organizations attempt too many changes at the same time, priorities become unclear. Teams spend more time coordinating initiatives than improving the work itself. Energy spreads thin, and before long, the transformation begins to feel like another management program competing with daily operations. This is not simplification. The most effective turnarounds begin in a much simpler way.

During the first ninety days, the goal is not to solve every problem. The goal is to understand the operation deeply, stabilize the most critical processes, and establish a rhythm of improvement that people can trust.

The first priority is *presence*.

Leaders must spend time where the work happens. Not as visitors but as students of the process, watching carefully, asking questions, and learning how the operation actually functions. This is where trust begins to build and where the real opportunities for improvement start to reveal themselves. Just think of the respect, trust, and collaboration leaders will get when they step off their pedestals and humbly enlist people's help to learn.

The second priority is *clarity*.

Many struggling organizations operate without a shared understanding of what good performance looks like. Different departments measure success differently, and expectations vary depending on who is asking. Within the first few months, leaders should work with their teams to define a **small number** of meaningful performance indicators and make them visible to everyone. When people can see the same information and talk about the same goals, alignment improves almost immediately.

The third priority is *simplification*.

Instead of launching dozens of improvement projects, focus on a few areas where the process is clearly broken or unnecessarily complex. Work with the people involved to remove obstacles, shorten the flow, and eliminate steps that add no value. Early improvements do not need to be dramatic, but they should be real and visible. This will help you gather momentum while teaching the methodology to those involved. These early wins are priceless and matter more than most leaders realize. They show the organization that change is possible.

The fourth priority is building a *basic management system*.

Daily conversations around performance, simple visual boards, and regular problem-solving routines create structure. Without this foundation, improvement depends on individual effort and fades quickly when attention shifts elsewhere. With it, the organization begins developing a habit of noticing and addressing issues every day.

By the end of the first ninety days, the goal is not perfection. It is **momentum**.

People should see that leadership is serious about improving the operation. They should feel invited to participate rather than judged from a distance. Most importantly, the organization should begin moving away from reacting to problems and toward understanding them.

Once that shift happens, the transformation truly begins.

5. The Long Game

One of the most damaging misconceptions about operational excellence is the idea that it has a finish line. Companies often launch improvement efforts with the hope that after enough projects, workshops, and investments, the operation will finally be "fixed." Once that point is reached, they assume they can return their attention to other priorities. In practice, organizations that think this way rarely sustain their gains for very long.

Processes begin to drift, small inefficiencies return, and new products, new people, and new pressures slowly introduce complexity back into the system. Because the improvement discipline is no longer active, these changes accumulate quietly until performance begins slipping again. This cycle is so common that many leaders begin to see it as inevitable.

But the companies that consistently perform at a high level operate with a different mindset. They do not treat improvement as a phase. They treat it as part of how the organization runs every day. In these environments, the question is not whether improvement work should happen. The question is what the next opportunity for improvement is.

Supervisors regularly review how the process performed during the day. Operators suggest small adjustments that make the work easier or more reliable. Engineers spend time understanding recurring issues instead of only reacting to emergencies. Leaders remain curious about how the system can function better tomorrow than it did today. Over time, this creates something powerful. Improvement stops feeling like extra work and starts feeling like normal work.

Another important shift also takes place. Success does not slow the organization down. In fact, it often increases the pace of learning.

When operations become more stable and predictable, people have more capacity to think ahead. Instead of constantly reacting to problems, they begin preventing them. Instead of accepting limitations in the process, they start challenging them.

This is why some companies seem to pull further ahead of their competitors year after year. Their advantage is not a single breakthrough or technology. Their advantage is the habit of continuously refining how the business operates. That habit compounds.

A small improvement today makes tomorrow's improvement easier. Knowledge spreads. Confidence grows. The organization becomes more capable of solving difficult problems because it has practiced solving smaller ones consistently.

From the outside, the results can look impressive. Inside the company, it simply feels like the normal way of working.

And that is the point where operational excellence stops being an initiative and becomes part of the culture.

6. Final Reflection

If there is one lesson that repeats itself in every struggling operation, it is this: Most organizations are not failing because people do not care or because they lack talent. They are struggling because the system around them has slowly become too complicated to manage effectively.

Over time, small decisions accumulate. Extra steps are added. Exceptions become normal. Workarounds become permanent. Reports multiply. Meetings increase. Before anyone realizes it, the organization is spending more energy navigating the system than improving it. At that point, performance begins to feel difficult and unpredictable.

The encouraging news is that the path back is rarely mysterious. When leaders choose to face reality, simplify the work, stabilize the process, and involve the people closest to it, progress begins to appear. Not always dramatically and not always immediately, but steadily enough that the organization starts to regain confidence.

That confidence matters.

When people see problems being addressed instead of explained away, they begin speaking more openly. When processes become clearer, teams begin improving them. When leaders show genuine curiosity about the work, the distance between management and operations begins to shrink.

Little by little, the organization changes its habits.

What once felt chaotic becomes understandable. What once felt frustrating becomes solvable. Improvements that once required major effort start happening as part of normal work.

This is how real transformations unfold. Not through slogans or isolated projects but through consistent attention to how the business actually operates.

If you decide to begin this journey in your own organization, resist the urge to do everything at once. Start by observing and asking questions. Simplify what you can. Help people see problems and solve them together. Build momentum step by step.

You do not need a perfect plan to begin. You only need the willingness to improve the next process, the next conversation, and the next decision.

Over time, those small actions accumulate into something meaningful.

Operations become clearer. Teams become stronger. Results become more predictable. The organization spends less time fighting complexity and more time creating value. In the end, that is what this entire book has been about.

Not adding more management techniques or layers of activity but removing what gets in the way of good work.

Making things understandable again.

Making improvement possible again.

And ultimately, teaching you how to manufacture simplicity.

Glossary

5S. Workplace organization method (Sort, Set in Order, Shine, Standardize, Sustain).
Strategic Impact: Operational Discipline: A proxy for leadership consistency and the ability to follow standards. (Ch. 2, 3, 7, 8, 9)

Abnormality. Any condition that deviates from the standard or plan.
Strategic Impact: Early Warning System: Identifies drift early enough to allow for a planned response rather than a crisis. (Ch. 7, 10, 11)

Andon. Visual signals that alert leaders to breakdowns, quality issues, or safety concerns.
Strategic Impact: Response Speed: Shortens the interval between a system failure and leadership intervention. (Ch. 7)

Annual Breakthrough Objective. A high-level, measurable goal for the current year that moves the organization toward its long-term vision.
Strategic Impact: Strategic Focus: Prevents "initiative soup" by centering resources on the vital few annual priorities. (Ch. 6, 10)

Bowler (Bowling Chart). A visual tool that tracks monthly KPI performance against targets.
Strategic Impact: Execution Visibility: Provides an objective scoreboard to determine if strategic initiatives are actually working. (Ch. 6, 8, 10)

Catchball. A collaborative process of sharing goals and ideas up and down the hierarchy to ensure alignment and buy-in.
Strategic Impact: Organizational Alignment: Transitions strategy from "top-down mandate" to "shared mission." (Ch. 5, 6)

Countermeasure. An action taken to address the root cause of a problem and prevent it from recurring. *Strategic Impact:* Permanent Resolution: Shifts leadership from "firefighting" to "fire prevention." (Ch. 7, 10, 11)

Daily Management System (DMS). A set of routines (huddles, boards, checks) used to manage the day-to-day business. *Strategic Impact:*
Stability: Creates a predictable foundation so that breakthrough improvements can actually "stick." (Ch. 8, 9, 10)

Gemba. "The real place," where value is created or the work actually happens.
Strategic Impact: Data Integrity: Ensures decisions are based on "facts on the ground" rather than "reports in the boardroom." (Ch. 4, 8)

Hoshin Kanri (Policy Deployment). A strategic planning process that aligns an organization's goals with its resources and actions.
Strategic Impact: Strategic Linkage: Connects the CEO's 5-year vision directly to a frontline worker's daily task. (Ch. 5, 6, 10)

KPI (Key Performance Indicator). Metrics used to evaluate the success of an organization or a particular activity.
Strategic Impact: Accountability: Provides the "Ground Truth" needed to objectively assess health and progress. (Ch. 3, 8)

Leader Standard Work (LSW). A documented set of tasks and behaviors that leaders follow to ensure process stability and team support.
Strategic Impact: Cultural Continuity: Moves leadership from "reactive heroics" to "proactive coaching." (Ch. 4, 9)

Muda. Japanese term for "Waste"—any activity that consumes resources but creates no value for the customer.
Strategic Impact: Margin Expansion: Uncovering hidden waste is the fastest way to improve profitability without raising prices. (Ch. 2, 3)

North Star (True North). The long-term vision or ultimate goal that guides all of an organization's efforts. *Strategic Impact:* Purpose: Acts as a "Compass" to keep the organization on track during times of turbulence. (Ch. 5)

Pareto Principle (80/20 Rule). The concept that 80 percent of effects come from 20 percent of causes.

Strategic Impact: Resource Leverage: Helps leaders identify the "Vital Few" issues that will yield the biggest return on effort. (Ch. 3, 10)

PDCA (Plan-Do-Check-Act). A four-step iterative management method used for the control and continuous improvement of processes.
Strategic Impact: Scientific Thinking: Embeds a "learning loop" into the culture, reducing the cost of failure. (Ch. 1, 7, 11)

Root Cause Analysis (RCA). A method of problem-solving used for identifying the root causes of faults or problems.
Strategic Impact: Waste Elimination: Prevents "Band-Aid" solutions that hide underlying system weaknesses. (Ch. 10, 11)

Standard Work. The current best-known way to perform a task, documented and followed by all. *Strategic Impact:* Baseline for Growth: You cannot improve a process that is not first standardized. (Ch. 2, 7, 9)

Tactical Implementation. The specific actions and projects taken to achieve the Annual Breakthrough Objectives.
Strategic Impact: Velocity: Translates high-level "Theory" into bottom-line "Results." (Ch. 6, 10)

Takt Time. The pace at which a process must produce one finished unit in order to match customer demand.
Strategic Impact: Flow: Establishes the operating rhythm of the business, helping leaders balance work, expose problems, prevent overproduction, and align processes with real demand. (Ch. 5, 7, 10)

Value Stream Mapping (VSM). A visual tool used to analyze the flow of materials and information currently required to bring a product or service to a consumer.
Strategic Impact: Systems Thinking: Reveals the "Big Picture" to prevent improving one department at the expense of the whole. (Ch. 2, 10)

Special Section: The 8 Kinds of Waste (8KW)

- **T — Transportation.** *Example:* Moving paperwork between desks or sending excessive email chains. *Strategic Impact:* Lead-Time Erosion: Increases the risk of information loss and delays response cycles.

- **I — Inventory.** *Example:* Unread emails, unapproved invoices, or bloated digital backlogs. *Strategic Impact:* Working Capital Trap: Hides system instability and slows down "Order-to-Cash" cycles.
- **M — Motion.** *Example:* Unnecessary clicks in software or walking to a distant printer. *Strategic Impact:* Productivity Loss: Increases cognitive load and worker fatigue.
- **W — Waiting.** *Example:* Waiting for manager approvals or for a slow system to load. *Strategic Impact:* Customer Frustration: The most visible driver of missed delivery dates.
- **O — Overproduction.** *Example:* Generating long reports that no one reads or printing excess forms. *Strategic Impact:* Mother of All Wastes: Consumes capacity that should be used for value-adding work.
- **O — Over-processing.** *Example:* Requiring three signatures when one would suffice or re-entering data into multiple systems. *Strategic Impact:* Quality Risk: Creates more opportunities for human error and rework.
- **D — Defects.** *Example:* Data entry errors, missed requirements, or incorrect billing. *Strategic Impact:* Brand Damage: The most expensive waste; costs 10x more to fix a defect at the customer than at the source.
- **S — Skill (Unused).** *Example:* Failing to ask frontline staff for improvement ideas or assigning "busy work" to high-performers. *Strategic Impact:* Talent Turnover: The ultimate strategic failure; leads to a "brain drain" of your most capable people.

TEMPLATES

The Lean Transformation Communication Plan

(Chapter 4)

1) Communication Plan Overview

Transformation Name: ______________________________

Business Objective (12 months):
Example: *"Improve on-time delivery from 72 percent to 95 percent, reduce complaints by 50 percent, and restore profitability."*

Primary Message (The Sentence Everyone Should Remember):

____

Case for Change:

- ______________________________
- ______________________________
- ______________________________

What Will Be Different This Time:

- ______________________________
- ______________________________
- ______________________________

Leadership Commitments (Non-negotiables):

- Leaders will show up to daily/weekly routines.
- Problems will be discussed without blame.
- Improvement work will be protected time.
- Standards will be followed and improved (not ignored).

2) The Transformation Communication Arc (Staging to Sustainment)

This plan is built in phases. Each phase has a purpose, tone, and different "job."

Phase 1: Staging (Before Kickoff)

Purpose: readiness + alignment + trust-building
Tone: honest, direct, grounded in reality
Outcome: people understand why change is necessary and believe leadership is serious.

Phase 2: Kickoff

Purpose: clarity + energy + direction
Tone: confident, practical, no hype
Outcome: people understand the approach and what will happen next.

Phase 3: Execution

Purpose: credibility + momentum
Tone: visible progress, real wins, real learning
Outcome: Lean becomes believable.

Phase 4: Expansion

Purpose: scaling + stability
Tone: disciplined, consistent, structured
Outcome: Lean becomes the operating rhythm.

Phase 5: Sustainment

Purpose: ownership + independence
Tone: normal business management
Outcome: Lean survives without you.

3) Communication Cadence (The Non-negotiable Rhythm)

This cadence is your "minimum viable system."
If you do nothing else, do this.

Daily

Daily Tier Huddles (Frontline)

- Ten to fifteen minutes
- Performance + abnormalities + actions
- Escalate issues quickly
- Reinforce problem-solving culture

Weekly

Weekly KPI Review (Leadership)

- Review the vital few.
- Assign countermeasures.
- Remove blockers.
- Track actions.

Monthly

Monthly Transformation Update (All Hands)

- Show wins.
- Show learning.
- Show next priorities.
- Reinforce the case for change.
- Recognize teams.

Quarterly

Policy Deployment Review (Strategy Alignment)

- Refresh priorities.
- Adjust resources.
- Prevent drift.
- Connect Lean to business strategy.

4) The Communication Standard Worktable (Core Template)

Use this table to design your full plan. This is just a simple schedule. Feel free to modify and add content as needed.

Touchpoint	Frequency	Audience	Speaker	Message (What they must hear)	(What must happen)	Inputs	Output
Lean Staging Alignment Meeting	Once	Exec Team	CEO/COO	"Here's the truth. Here's what we must change."	Exec alignment + commitment	Assessment results	Transformation charter
Supervisor Pre-Kickoff Briefing	Once	Supervisors	Ops leader	"This is your role. This is what will change."	Supervisors ready + aligned	plan + cadence	supervisor playbook
Company Kickoff	Once	All employees	Site leader	"Why, what, how, what happens next."	shared understanding + energy	case for change	launch + Q&A
Daily Tier 1 Huddle	Daily	Operators	Supervisor	"Here's today's reality."	problems surfaced + actions	KPI board	action list
Tier Escalation Meeting	Daily	Leaders	Ops manager	"What is blocking flow today?"	decisions made quickly	escalations	countermeasures
Weekly KPI Review	Weekly	Leadership	Site leader	"Are we winning? If not, why?"	actions assigned	KPI trends	owner + due date
Monthly All Hands	Monthly	All	CEO/COO	"Progress, wins, lessons, next month."	belief reinforced	results + stories	alignment + energy
Kaizen Report-Out	Every event	Area teams	Sponsor	"Here's what changed."	credibility + recognition	before/after	updated standard
Sustainment Audit Review	Weekly	Leaders	CI leader	"Are standards holding?"	drift correction	audit results	corrective actions

5) Meeting Design Rules (So It Doesn't Become Bureaucracy)

A communication plan fails when meetings become:

- Long
- Vague
- Passive
- Presentation-heavy
- One-way
- Disconnected from action

So, apply these rules:

Rule 1: Every meeting must produce an output

Examples:

- Decisions
- Countermeasures
- Actions with owners
- Escalation
- Updated standards
- Recognition
- Learning

If the meeting produces no output, it becomes theater.

Rule 2: Communication must be two-way

Every key touchpoint must include a mechanism for:

- Questions
- Feedback
- Concerns
- Suggestions

Rule 3: Leaders speak less, ask more

Lean communication is not persuasion.

It is coaching.

Rule 4: Never communicate Lean as "extra work"

Lean is not extra work.

Lean is how you remove extra work.

6) The Messaging Framework (Keep It Consistent)

This is the simplest messaging framework I've ever used, and it works.

Use it in:

- Town halls
- Weekly updates
- Kaizen report-outs
- Leadership meetings
- Emails

The Five-Part Lean Message

1. **Reality:** What is happening?
2. **Impact:** Why does it matter?
3. **Learning:** What did we learn?
4. **Action:** What are we doing next?
5. **Support:** What do we need from you?

If you stick to this, communication stays clear, grounded, and useful.

7) The Case for Change Template (Simple and Powerful)

Your case for change should be clear enough that an employee can repeat it to their spouse.

The Case for Change (Fill In)

The problem we must solve is:

____

It is hurting us by:

- ______________________________________

- ____
- ____

If we do nothing, the likely future is:

____

If we succeed, the future we can create is:

____

What we are committing to as leaders is:

____

What we are asking from every employee is:

____

ASSESSMENT

(Chapter 3)

(The following pages show examples of assessment interview forms for the various levels within the organization.)

Senior Management Evaluation Questionnaire (Owner, CEO, Directors)

Date:

Interviewee:

Position:

Company time:

On vision and strategy

- How do you describe the general situation of the business today?
- What are the three most important strategic priorities for the next twelve months?
- How aligned is the team with those priorities?

About Lean

- What does Lean mean to you in practice?
- Where do you feel Lean has worked well here, and where has it gotten stuck?
- What has been the biggest cultural obstacle to advancing in Lean?

On culture and leadership

- How would you describe the current culture of the plant?
- What behaviors do you see every day that tell you, "Yes, we're making progress"?
- And what behaviors do you see that worry you or slow progress?

On staff engagement

- Do you feel that people are willing to change? Why or why not?
- What signals do you get about people's loyalty to the company?
- What motivates you to stay here? What would make them leave?

On organizational stability

- How do you describe the rotation? Are some areas more sensitive than others?
- What actions do you take to develop supervisors and frontline leaders?

MIDDLE MANAGEMENT EVALUATION QUESTIONNAIRE
(AREA HEADS, MANAGERS, SENIOR SUPERVISORS)

Date:

Interviewee:

Position:

Company time:

On operations and execution

- How has your area changed in the last twelve months?
- What are the three most important strategic priorities for the next twelve months?
- What operational issues keep popping up over and over again?
- How do you prioritize work when everything is urgent?
- What are the main problems of the company?
- If you had a choice, how would you improve or solve the company's problems?

About Lean

- Which Lean tools do you use most often?
- What standard Lean activities are done every day or every week?
- How comfortable are you leading improvement activities?

About culture

- How do you perceive your team's attitude towards change?
- What behaviors do they show when something new is implemented?

- Do people have an open opinion, or do they remain silent? Why do you think that happens?

On loyalty and commitment

- What signs tell people that their team is committed to the company?
- What makes people proud to work here?
- What things affect staff morale the most?

On leadership

- What support do you receive from management?
- What do they need to be able to do their job better?

OPERATOR EVALUATION QUESTIONNAIRE

(These are simple, straightforward, non-technical questions to make people feel comfortable.)

Date:

Interviewee:

Position:

Company time:

About your work

- What do you like most about your job?
- What is the most difficult or frustrating thing about it?
- If you could change one thing tomorrow, what would it be?

About the environment

- How do you get along with your supervisor?
- Can you give your opinion here without any problem?
- When something fails, what usually happens?

About the company

- Do you feel valued by the company?
- How confident do you feel about your future work here?
- If a friend asked you what it's like to work here, what would you say?

About Lean

- What continuous improvement changes have you seen lately?

- Have you been asked to participate in ideas for improvement? How did you do?

On loyalty/permanence

- What makes you stay in this company?
- What would make you think about going to another one

Administrative Staff Evaluation Questionnaire

Date:

Interviewee:

Position:

Company time:

About your work and processes

- What processes depend on you for production to work well?
- What administrative steps do you feel add little value?
- How clear is the relationship between your work and plant operation?

About culture

- How would you describe communication between areas?
- How quickly are problems resolved when they involve multiple areas?

On change and loyalty

- Do people here adopt changes quickly, or does it take a long time?
- What makes them proud to be in the company?
- What would make them look for another job opportunity?

HUMAN RESOURCES EVALUATION QUESTIONNAIRE

Date:

Interviewee:

Position:

Company time:

On talent and climate

- How do you describe the current work environment?
- What indicators of turnover and absenteeism are you concerned about?

About culture

- What positive and negative behaviors do you observe most often?
- What are the main reasons why people quit?

About development

- How do you select and prepare supervisors?
- How mature is the internal training structure?

About Lean

- How integrated is Lean into HR processes?
- What are the biggest cultural challenges from your point of view?

Front-Line Supervisors Evaluation Questionnaire

Date:

Interviewee:

Position:

Company time:

On operations and execution

- How has your area changed in the last twelve months?
- What are the three most important strategic priorities for the next twelve months?
- What operational issues keep popping up over and over again?
- How do you prioritize work when everything is urgent?

About Lean

- Which Lean tools do you use most often?
- What standard Lean activities are done every day or every week?
- How comfortable are you leading improvement activities?

About culture

- How do you perceive your team's attitude towards change?
- What behaviors do they show when something new is implemented?
- Do people have an open opinion or do they remain silent? Why do you think that happens?

On loyalty and commitment

- What signs tell people that their team is committed to the company?
- What makes people proud to work here?
- What things affect staff morale the most?

On leadership

- What support do you receive from management?
- What do they need to be able to do their job better?

KAIZEN

(Chapter 8)

Kaizen Event Charter Template

A Practical One-Page Setup Tool (Use This Before Every Event)

A kaizen event should never begin with a vague goal like "improve efficiency." That's how you end up with a week of sticky notes, opinions, and no measurable results.

This one-page charter forces clarity before the event starts.

You can print it, fill it out by hand, and post it in the kaizen war room (obeya).

1) Kaizen Event Title

Event Name: ____
Department/Area: ______________________________________
Event Dates: ____
Sponsor (Leader): _____________________________________
Facilitator: ____
Process Owner (Post-Event Owner): __________________________

2) Problem Statement (One Sentence)

Write this as a factual statement, not an opinion.

Problem Statement:

Examples:

- "This process produces an average of 8.5 percent rework per week."
- "This line misses hourly output targets three out of five days."
- "This workflow requires fourteen handoffs and causes an average lead time of nine days."

3) Why This Matters (Business Impact)

Check all that apply:

☐ Quality
☐ Delivery/Lead Time
☐ Cost
☐ Safety
☐ Compliance
☐ Customer Complaints
☐ Capacity/Output
☐ Morale/Retention

Explain briefly:

4) Scope (Make It Winnable)

A kaizen event must have boundaries.

In Scope

Out of Scope

5) Target Condition (Measurable Goal)

The goal must be measurable.

Current Performance: ____
Target Performance (by Day 5): ____________________________________

Examples:

- Reduce changeover time from ninety minutes to forty-five minutes.
- Reduce defects from 6 percent to 2 percent.
- Reduce lead time from four days to one day.
- Reduce walking distance by 50 percent.
- Increase throughput from forty-two/hour to fifty-five/hour.

6) Baseline Metrics (Pick 3–5 Only)

List the metrics you will measure before, during, and after.

Metric	Current Baseline	Target	How Measured
1			
2			
3			
4			
5			

7) Team Members (6–10 People Is Ideal)

Include the people who do the work and the people who support it.

Name	Role	Function
1		
2		
3		
4		
5		
6		
7		
8		
9		
10		

8) Kaizen Guardrails (Especially Important in Regulated Industries)

Changes the team CAN implement during the event:

☐ Layout changes inside the area
☐ 5S and point-of-use storage
☐ Visual management and signage
☐ Work sequence improvements
☐ Checklists/job aids
☐ Non-capital fixtures or minor tooling
☐ Training and onboarding improvements

Changes that REQUIRE escalation/change control:

☐ Product specs or acceptance criteria
☐ Validated parameters or equipment changes
☐ Label content changes
☐ Software/ERP changes
☐ Supplier or material changes
☐ Sampling plan or QC method changes
☐ Anything requiring regulatory or customer approval

Quality representative assigned: ____

9) Logistics (Remove Friction Before Day 1)

☐ Kaizen room reserved
☐ Calendars blocked
☐ Supplies ready (Post-its, markers, flip charts, tape, stopwatches)
☐ Baseline data collected
☐ Current standard work available (if it exists)
☐ Before photos planned
☐ Safety considerations reviewed

10) Expected Deliverables by Day 5

A kaizen is not complete unless it produces these outputs:

☐ Before/after metrics
☐ Before/after photos

☐ Updated standard work at the point of use
☐ Visual management improvements installed
☐ Training completed for impacted employees
☐ Open action plan with owners and due dates
☐ 30/60/90 follow-up schedule

11) Post-Event Follow-Up (Non-Negotiable)

30-day review date: ______________________________
60-day review date: ______________________________
90-day review date: ______________________________

Weekly owner check-in cadence (until all actions closed):

Final Question (The One That Predicts Success)

If the Kaizen team delivers the improvements…

Will leadership protect the new standard?
☐ Yes
☐ No

If "No," do not run the event yet. Fix leadership commitment first.

Kaizen Event Daily Tracker

Day-by-Day Execution Tool (Print and Use)

Event Name: ______________________________
Area: ______________________________
Dates: ______________________________
Sponsor: ______________________________
Facilitator: ______________________________

DAY 1 TRACKER

Understand the Current State (Reality, Not Opinions)

Day 1 Goals (check when complete)

☐ Team kickoff completed (purpose, targets, expectations)
☐ Safety briefing completed

☐ Gemba observation completed (end to end)
☐ Current state mapped (flow, steps, handoffs, WIP)
☐ Baseline metrics captured (3–5)
☐ Top wastes observed documented
☐ Before photos taken

Baseline Metrics (Record Actual)

Metric	Baseline
1	
2	
3	
4	
5	

Top-Ten Observations (Waste/Variation/Friction)

1. ______________________________
2. ______________________________
3. ______________________________
4. ______________________________
5. ______________________________
6. ______________________________
7. ______________________________
8. ______________________________

9. ______________________________

10. ______________________________

Day 1 Decisions Made (Not "To Do")

- ______________________________
- ______________________________

Sponsor Check-In Notes (Ten Minutes)

What barriers did leadership remove today?

DAY 2 TRACKER

Analyze, Identify Root Causes and Design the Future State

Day 2 Goals

☐ Root cause analysis completed (Five Whys/Fishbone)
☐ Waste prioritized (impact vs. effort)
☐ Future state designed (layout/flow/sequence)
☐ Improvement ideas selected for testing
☐ Implementation plan drafted (Days 3–4)
☐ Materials/tools needed identified

Root Causes (The Three That Matter Most)

1. ______________________________

2. ______________________________

3. ______________________________

Prioritized Improvements (Impact vs. Effort)

Improvement Idea	Impact (H/M/L)	Effort (H/M/L)	Test on Day 3?
1			
2			
3			
4			
5			
6			

Day 2 Decisions Made

- ____
- ____

Sponsor Check-In Notes

What approvals/resources were granted today?

DAY 3 TRACKER

Test and Implement (Where Kaizen Becomes Real)

Day 3 Goals

☐ Improvements tested in the process (not just discussed)
☐ Layout/flow changes implemented (as applicable)
☐ 5S improvements implemented
☐ Visual controls drafted/installed
☐ New work sequence tested
☐ Results measured and compared to baseline
☐ Adjustments made based on real outcomes

Experiments Run Today (PDCA in Action)

Experiment	What changed?	Result	Keep/Modify/Drop
1			
2			
3			
4			
5			

Metrics Check (Midweek Reality)

Metric	Baseline	Today	Trend
1			☐ Up ☐ Down ☐ Flat
2			☐ Up ☐ Down ☐ Flat
3			☐ Up ☐ Down ☐ Flat
4			☐ Up ☐ Down ☐ Flat
5			☐ Up ☐ Down ☐ Flat

What We Implemented Today (Visible Wins)

1. ____

2. ____

3. ____

4. ____

5. ____

Sponsor Check-In Notes

What got unblocked today?

DAY 4 TRACKER

Lock the Gains (Standardize, Train, Sustain)

Day 4 Goals

☐ Final layout/process confirmed
☐ Standard work updated (draft completed)
☐ Visual management finalized at point of use
☐ Training completed for impacted operators
☐ Audit method defined (simple and practical)
☐ Open actions assigned to owners with due dates
☐ Before/after photos organized

Standard Work Update Checklist

☐ New sequence documented
☐ Key quality checkpoints defined
☐ Safety points included
☐ Visuals posted at point of use
☐ "Normal vs. abnormal" made obvious
☐ Training method updated

Open Actions (Not Completed Yet)

Action Item	Owner	Due Date	Status
1			
2			
3			
4			
5			

Sustainment Plan (Simple)

Audit cadence: ☐ Daily ☐ Weekly ☐ Monthly
Audit owner: ______________________________

What gets checked?

Sponsor Check-In Notes

What must leadership protect after Friday?

DAY 5 TRACKER

Report Out, Celebrate, and Launch the Follow-Up System

Day 5 Goals

☐ Before/after metrics finalized
☐ Before/after photos ready
☐ Storyboard completed (problem → action → results)
☐ Report-out delivered to leadership
☐ Recognition/celebration completed
☐ 30/60/90 reviews scheduled
☐ Action plan ownership confirmed

Final Results Summary (The Headlines)

Metric	Baseline	Final	Improvement
1			
2			
3			
4			
5			

What Changed (In Plain Language)

- ______________________________
- ______________________________
- ______________________________

What We Learned (So the Next Kaizen Is Better)

1. ______________________________
2. ______________________________
3. ______________________________

Follow-Up Commitments (Non-Negotiable)

30-day review: ______________________________
60-day review: ______________________________
90-day review: ______________________________

Escalation rule (if actions slip):

Optional Add-On Page (Highly Recommended)

Kaizen Photo Log (Before/During/After)

Photo #	Description	Taken By	Date
1	Before		
2	Before		
3	During		
4	During		
5	After		
6	After		

Kaizen Storyboard Template

The One-Page Report-Out That Builds Credibility

A kaizen event should end with a clear story. Not a long PowerPoint. Not a technical report. A story that anyone can understand in five minutes.

A storyboard does that.

It shows:

- What was wrong
- What you changed
- What improved
- What the new standard is
- What remains open

Print this and post it in the area. It becomes a living reminder that improvement is real.

KAIZEN STORYBOARD (ONE PAGE)

1) Event Title and Dates

Kaizen Title: ____

Area: ____

Dates: ____

Sponsor: ____

Facilitator: ____

Process Owner (Post-Event): ______________________________

2) The Problem (One Sentence)

Problem Statement:

3) Why It Matters (Business Impact)

Check all that apply:

☐ Quality
☐ Delivery/Lead Time
☐ Cost
☐ Safety
☐ Compliance
☐ Customer Complaints
☐ Capacity/Output
☐ Morale/Retention

Short explanation:

4) Current State (What We Saw at the Gemba)

List the key facts, not opinions.

Top Observations (3–7)

1. ______________________________

2. ______________________________

3. ______________________________

4. ______________________________

5. ______________________________

6. ______________________________

7. ______________________________

5) Baseline Metrics (Before)

Use only the metrics that matter.

Metric	Baseline
1	
2	
3	
4	
5	

6) Root Causes (The Few That Drove the Pain)

Root cause is not "people." Root cause is the system.

1. ____

2. ____

3. ____

7) Improvements Implemented (What We Changed)

Countermeasures (List 5–10)

1. ____

2. ____

3. ____

4. ____

5. ____

6. ____

7. ____

8. ____

9. ____

10. ____

8) Visual Proof (Before/After)

Attach photos, sketches, or a simple layout.

☐ Before photos attached
☐ After photos attached
☐ Layout sketch included
☐ New visual controls included

9) Results (After)

Metric	Baseline	After	Improvement
1			
2			
3			
4			
5			

10) The New Standard (How We Will Prevent Backsliding)

Check all that apply:

☐ Standard work updated
☐ Visual work instructions posted at point of use
☐ Training completed for impacted employees
☐ Audit method created
☐ Owner assigned for sustainment
☐ Playbook updated (if applicable)

Where is the standard posted?

11) Open Actions (If Any)

If actions remain open, they must be owned.

Action	Owner	Due Date	Status
1			
2			
3			
4			

12) Follow-Up Cadence (Non-Negotiable)

30-day review: ______________________________
60-day review: ______________________________
90-day review: ______________________________

13) Team Recognition

Team Members:

One-Sentence Recognition:

The Rule of the Storyboard

If someone can't understand the kaizen in five minutes from this storyboard, the kaizen was not communicated clearly.

KPIs

(Chapter 10)

KPI CONTRACT

KPI Name: (Example: On-time delivery to request date)

Purpose: Why does this KPI matter? What strategic outcome does it support?

Type:
☐ Breakthrough KPI (PD/TTI)
☐ Driver KPI
☐ Daily Management KPI

Definition (plain language): Write the definition in one sentence.

Formula: (Example: # orders shipped on or before request date ÷ total orders shipped)

Unit of measure: %, days, $/month, defects per million, etc.

Scope: Which value stream, product family or department does it cover?

Data source: ERP, manual log, spreadsheet, CRM, etc.

Owner: Name + role.

Update frequency: Hourly/daily/weekly/monthly.

Review forum: Hourly board, daily huddle, weekly staff meeting, PD review, etc.

Target: Include baseline + target + time horizon.

Trigger condition (when it's "red"):
Define the rule clearly.
Example: below target for two days in a row, or downward trend for three weeks.

Expected action when off track:
Quick containment? Root cause? Kaizen? Escalation?

Escalation path:
Who gets involved when the KPI is off track?

Retirement rule:
When do we remove, replace, or revise this KPI?

THE SKILLS MATRIX

(Chapter 11)

MANUFACTURING SIMPLICITY

Lean transformation made simple.

Skills Matrix

Processes

Employee	Position	1	2	3	4	5	6	7	8	9	10

Department_______________

Revision_______________

Supervisor_______________

No competence ○	No knowledge of the process
Low Competence ◔	Able to perform under supervision
Some Competence ◑	Able to performe basic tasks with no supervision
High Competence ◕	Able to operate, setup and troubleshoot
Expert ●	Able to train others

MANUFACTURING SIMPLICITY

Lean transformation made simple.

Skills Matrix

Employee	Position	Processes									
		Chem	Press	Fill	Cap	Label	DHR	Seal	Lap	Grind	Insp
M. Smith	Op 1	○	◔	○	○	○	◔	◔	◑	○	○
L. Delgado	Op1	◕	◑	○	◕	○	◔	◕	●	◔	◑
W. Young	Op 2	○	○	◕	◔	○	●	◑	●	◑	◕
A. Torres	MC 1	○	●	○	◑	○	◔	○	●	◔	◑
G. Natale	MC 1	●	○	○	◕	◔	◕	○	●	◕	○
L. Ying	MC 2	●	◕	◑	◑	◔	○	◔	◑	●	◕
K. Collins	SU 3	◕	◕	◕	●	●	●	◕	●	●	●

Department ______________

Revision ______________

Supervisor ______________

No competence	○	No knowledge of the process
Low Competence	◔	Able to perform under supervision
Some Competence	◑	Able to performe basic tasks with no supervision
High Competence	◕	Able to operate, setup and troubleshoot
Expert	●	Able to train others

THANK YOU FOR READING MY BOOK!

Just to say thanks for buying and reading my book, I would like to give you a few free bonus gifts, no strings attached!

Scan the QR Code:

I appreciate your interest in my book and value your feedback, as it helps me improve future versions. I would appreciate it if you could leave your invaluable review on Amazon.com with your feedback. Thank you!

www.ingramcontent.com/pod-product-compliance
Lightning Source LLC
LaVergne TN
LVHW010222110826
845148LV00022B/1238

9798901582190